The Oxford Handbook of Tax System in India

The Oxford India Handbooks are an important initiative in academic publishing. Each volume offers a comprehensive survey of research in a critical subject area and provides facts, figures, and analyses for a well-grounded perspective. The series provides scholars, students, and policy planners with a balanced understanding of a wide range of issues in the social sciences.

Other Titles in the Series

HANDBOOK OF THE INDIAN ECONOMY IN THE 21ST CENTURY
Understanding the Inherent Dynamism
Ashima Goyal (Editor)

HANDBOOK OF POLITICS IN INDIAN STATES
Regions, Parties, and Economic Reforms
Sudha Pai (Editor)

HANDBOOK OF POPULATION AND DEVELOPMENT IN INDIA (OIP)
A.K. Shiva Kumar, Pradeep Panda, and Rajani R. Ved (Editors)

HANDBOOK OF URBAN INEQUALITIES
Darshini Mahadevia and Sandip Sarkar

HANDBOOK OF GENDER
Raka Ray (Editor)

HANDBOOK OF CLIMATE CHANGE AND INDIA
Development, Politics, and Governance
Navroz K. Dubash (Editor)

HANDBOOK OF MODERNITY IN SOUTH ASIA
Modern Makeovers
Saurabh Dube (Editor)

HANDBOOK OF PSYCHOLOGY IN INDIA
Girishwar Misra (Editor)

THE RIGHT TO INFORMATION ACT 2005
A Handbook
Sudhir Naib

GLOBALIZATION AND DEVELOPMENT
A Handbook of New Perspectives (OIP)
Ashwini Deshpande (Editor)

HANDBOOK OF MUSLIMS IN INDIA
Empirical and Policy Perspectives
Rakesh Basant and Abusaleh Shariff (Editors)

HANDBOOK OF ENVIRONMENTAL ECONOMICS IN INDIA
Kanchan Chopra and Vikram Dayal (Editors)

HANDBOOK OF AGRICULTURE IN INDIA (OIP)
Shovan Ray (Editor)

HANDBOOK OF ENVIRONMENTAL LAW
P.B. Sahasranaman

HANDBOOK OF LAW, WOMEN, AND EMPLOYMENT
Policies, Issues, Legislation, and Case Law
Surinder Mediratta

HANDBOOK OF HUMAN DEVELOPMENT
Concepts, Measures, and Policies
Sakiko Fukuda-Parr and A.K. Shiva Kumar (Editors)

HANDBOOK OF ENVIRONMENTAL DECISION MAKING IN INDIA
An EIA Model
O.V. Nandimath

HANDBOOK OF URBANIZATION IN INDIA (SECOND EDITION) (OIP)
K.C. Shivaramakrishnan, Amitabh Kundu, and B.N. Singh

MAKING NEWS
Handbook of the Media in Contemporary India (OIP)
Uday Sahay (Editor)

HANDBOOK OF INDIAN SOCIOLOGY (OIP)
Veena Das (Editor)

MANAGING BUSINESS IN THE 21ST CENTURY
A Handbook (OIP)
Anindya Sen and P.K. Sett (Editors)

The Oxford Handbook of Tax System in India
An Analysis of Tax Policy and Governance

MAHESH C. PUROHIT
VISHNU KANTA PUROHIT

Oxford University Press is a department of the University of Oxford.
It furthers the University's objective of excellence in research, scholarship,
and education by publishing worldwide. Oxford is a registered trademark of
Oxford University Press in the UK and in certain other countries

Published in India by
Oxford University Press
YMCA Library Building, 1 Jai Singh Road, New Delhi 110 001, India

© Mahesh C. Purohit and Vishnu Kanta Purohit 2014

The moral rights of the authors have been asserted

First Edition published in 2014

All rights reserved. No part of this publication may be reproduced, stored in
a retrieval system, or transmitted, in any form or by any means, without the
prior permission in writing of Oxford University Press, or as expressly permitted
by law, by licence, or under terms agreed with the appropriate reprographics
rights organization. Enquiries concerning reproduction outside the scope of the
above should be sent to the Rights Department, Oxford University Press, at the
address above

You must not circulate this work in any other form
and you must impose this same condition on any acquirer

ISBN-13: 978-0-19-809227-8
ISBN-10: 0-19-809227-X

Typeset in 10.5/13.2 Minion Pro
by Excellent Laser Typesetters, Pitampura, Delhi 110 034
Printed in India by Thomson Press (India) Ltd, New Delhi 110 020

Contents

List of Tables, Figures, and Boxes	vi
Preface	ix
List of Abbreviations	xiv
1. The Tax System of India: An Overview	1
2. Fiscal Significance of Taxes	28
3. Taxes on International Trade	49
4. Union Taxes on Income and Property	66
5. Central Domestic Trade Taxes	105
6. State Taxes on Income and Property	149
7. States' Domestic Trade Taxes	224
8. Local Taxes	319
9. Need for Further Reforms	329
References	381
Index	393
About the Authors	403

Tables, Figures, and Boxes

Tables

1.1	Deficit Indicators of the Centre and the Combined Deficits of Centre and State Governments	6
1.2	Combined Revenue and Capital Expenditure of the Centre and the States	12
1.3	Trends in Debt of Centre and State Governments	16
1.4	Savings–Investment in the Indian Economy as a Percentage of GDP	19
2.1	Tax–GDP Ratio in Select Countries of the World	30
2.2	Trends in Tax–GDP Ratios in India	32
2.3	Total Tax Revenue in India	34
2.4	Tax Revenue of the Central Government of India	40
2.5	Trends in Tax Revenue in Indian States	42
3.1	Trends in Revenue from Customs Duty	51
3.2	Changes in Peak Rate of Customs Duty	56
3.3	Tariff Rates of Customs Duty from 2003–4 to 2007–8	57
3.4	Effective Rates of Customs Duty from 2003–4 to 2007–8	59
4.1	Trends in Revenue from Union Taxes on Income and Property	68
4.2	Rates of Corporate Income Tax	71

4.3	Profile of Sample Companies Across the Range of Effective Tax Rate	74
4.4	Rate of MAT and DDT in India	77
4.5	Trends in the Maximum Marginal Rate of Personal Income Tax, Cesses, and Surcharges	86
5.1	Trends in Revenue from Union Excise Duty and Service Tax	107
6.1	Trends in Revenue from Taxes on Income and Property: All States	150
6.2	States' Tax Effort in Land Revenue	152
6.3	State-wise Trends in Land Revenue	153
6.4	State-wise Trends in Revenue from Agricultural Income Tax	163
6.5	Agricultural Income Tax Rates for Individuals in Different States	164
6.6	Agricultural Income Tax Rates for Companies in Different States	165
6.7	State-wise Trends in Stamp Duty and Registration Fee	171
6.8	States' Tax Effort in SD&RF	175
6.9	States' Tax Effort in Profession Tax	187
6.10	State-wise Trends in Revenue from Profession Tax	188
7.1	Yield from State Taxes on Commodities and Services	226
7.2	Fiscal Significance of Sales Tax in States	228
7.3	Tax Effort of States: Sales Tax	233
7.4	Yield from Motor Vehicles Tax in Different States	242
7.5	Tax Effort of States: Motor Vehicles Tax and P&GT	247
7.6	Rates of Motor Vehicles Tax	249
7.7	Yield from Passengers and Goods Tax in States	259
7.8	Rates of Passengers and Goods Tax	262
7.9	Revenue from State Excise Duty	267
7.10	Methods of Levying State Excise Duty in States	272
7.11	Rates of State Excise Duty in Select States	275
7.12	Licence Fee in Select States	277
7.13	Revenue from Electricity Duty	283
7.14	Rates of Electricity Duty	287
7.15	Revenue from Entertainment Tax	291

8.1	Methods of Property Valuation in Use in Sampled Cities in India	320
8.2	Statutory Property Tax Rates in Select Cities in India	322

Figures

2.1	Trends in Tax–GDP Ratio in India	33
2.2	Trends in Tax Revenue in India	35
3.1	Organizational Chart of the Central Board of Excise and Customs	63
4.1	Fiscal Significance of Personal and Corporate Income Tax	70
4.2	CBDT's Organizational Chart	102
5.1	Trends in Revenue from Domestic Trade Taxes of Union	108

Boxes

1.1	Assignment of Taxes—Union and State Governments	2
6.1	Rate of Stamp Duty on Conveyance in Major States	176
6.2	Revenue Implications of Concessions Given to Women on Account of Registered Documents in Madhya Pradesh	177
6.3	Torrens System of Registration	185
7.1	TIN Formats	239
A9.1.1	Recommendations of the First State Finance Ministers Committee of 1995	352
A9.1.2	Recommendations of the Second State Finance Ministers Committee of 1998	352
A9.1.3	Introduction of State VAT in Indian States	355

Preface

This study is an attempt to explain the twists and turns in the Indian fiscal system over the years, especially since the 1990s when reforms became a part of the government's agenda. In doing so it brings out all the changes in the overall tax system brought about by various tax reforms.

Since the beginning of the 1990s, India has adopted a structural adjustment programme with reforms undertaken through financial and fiscal policies in each major sector of the economy. Reforms were also attempted in government expenditure, followed by the disinvestment of public sector undertakings. The objective of these reforms was to increase operational efficiency through the transfer of ownership to private hands and thus improve the existing management practices.

The fiscal reforms undertaken in the early 1990s brought in a breath of fresh air and released clogged up economic energies. The country witnessed high growth rates and there was a major structural shift in the composition of output. It also brought about a compositional shift in the tax system. This helped in removing excessive dependence on regressive indirect taxes and increasing the dependence on direct taxes. It also paved the way for the industry to have enhanced competitiveness in a globalized economy.

Revenue from corporation tax witnessed a high growth rate which was a result of the expanding tax base due to higher industrial growth, globalization, and buoyant growth in the corporate sector. Personal income tax had also been buoyant due to an increase in per capita incomes, the growth of the economy, and better compliance. Keeping in view the economic slowdown and to revive consumer demand, the budget for 2010–11 declared an upward revision of tax slabs while keeping the marginal rate and exemption limit at the same level. Notwithstanding substantial changes in the structure of personal income tax, it still remains studded with a multitude of tax incentives and exemptions.

Union excise duty, known as CenVAT, has many variants; each one having its own objectives. These include additional duties of excise (ADE), additional duty on tea and tea waste, additional duty on motor spirit, high speed diesel oil, ADE on *pan masala* and certain tobacco products, ADE on textiles and textile articles, and cesses and surcharges.

The central government also levies a tax on services at the rate of 12 per cent. The coverage of the tax includes all services except those mentioned in the negative list or the ones specifically exempted. Input tax credit (ITC) is available for taxes paid on goods and services used as inputs in providing services.

States levy and collect some taxes related to income and property. These include taxes that can be better administered at the regional level such as land revenue, agricultural income tax, stamp duty and registration fee, and profession tax. Important domestic trade taxes assigned to the states include sales tax, state excise, motor vehicles tax, passengers and goods tax, electricity duty, and entertainment tax.

Due to the efforts of the central government and the Empowered Committee of States' Finance Ministers, sales tax has now been replaced by State VAT. This has been a paradigm shift in the states' tax system.

Although several reforms have been attempted, the Indian tax system still remains distorted and fragmented. Further reforms are needed to make the tax system compatible with the competitive open economy and to achieve a unified Indian market. Second generation reforms to make the tax system user friendly have yet to be implemented.

More importantly, while there are numerous research studies that have been published in various academic journals on different aspects of reforms in individual taxes, no single work has been attempted so far that analyses at length the reforms of all individual taxes. This study fills this gap and presents a treatise on the Indian tax system covering all the aspects from 1991–2 to 2012–13. The study would be useful for undergraduate honours and postgraduate students of Indian Public Finance. It would equally be a work of significance for all Indian and foreign scholars interested in the area of public finance, particularly in taxation at all three levels. It is a sort of gateway for each of the taxes and many of the fees and duties at central, state, and local levels. Also, this book would be quite useful to legal professionals and foreigners looking for information on taxation in India, government servants who need conveniently collated information, business persons, and financial analysts.

The effort in the book is to present a comprehensive review of contemporary issues in the Indian tax policy and administration with a long-term perspective, tracing its evolution since 1991. The general approach of the book is one of microeconomic partial equilibrium but enough care has been taken to consider macroeconomic implications whenever desirable. The book covers all taxes on income and property as also those on goods and services levied by the centre, states, and local bodies. It encompasses an evaluation of existing trends in revenue, structure, and administration of the overall tax system in India, including taxes at the sub-national level, and recommends reforms in their structure and administration. In addition, it also presents a brief review of all the important local taxes.

The volume is divided into nine chapters. Chapter 1 includes the evolution of the reform process in the Indian economy in general and tax reforms in particular. Chapter 2 analyses the fiscal significance of each and every tax at the central and at the state level. It also gives an analysis of the tax–GDP ratio. Chapter 3 presents the existing structure and administration of taxes on international trade—customs duties. It discusses the weaknesses of the existing system and suggests suitable reforms. Chapter 4 deals with the system of taxes on income and property levied by the union government. This includes corporation tax, personal income tax, wealth tax, and gift tax. Chapter 5 is an analysis of CenVAT and service tax levied by the union government. Chapter 6 examines all the taxes on income and property levied by the states. These include land revenue, agricultural income tax, stamp duty and registration fee, and profession tax. Chapter 7 looks into the details of the taxes on domestic trade levied by the states—State VAT, state excise duty, motor vehicles tax, passengers and goods tax, electricity duty, and entertainment tax. Chapter 8 analyses the existing system of local taxes. This includes property tax, octroi, and other taxes. In analysing the taxes in each of the chapters the scope of the study includes the base, the rates, exemptions, and a brief analysis of the administration of the tax. Finally, Chapter 9 presents the roadmap for transition to the Direct Taxes Code (DTC) and to Goods and Services Tax (GST) in India. These two major innovative measures would help India achieve a transparent, neutral, and efficient tax system. Each of the taxes is generally dealt with under the following heads: fiscal/revenue significance assessed in terms of its share in total tax revenues as well as its proportion to GDP or GSDP as the case may be; structure of tax/duty along with rate; rebates, concessions, and exemptions, as well as the details of variety in terms of basic, additional, or special; trend of revenue over the period of 1991–2 to 2012–13 with computation of growth rate(s) and buoyancy; administration and administrative structure of assessment, levy, collection; and recommendation on reforms along with justification on the grounds of better performance in terms of revenue and at times on those of enhancing efficiency of the economy. All in all, it is a useful compendium on taxes in India as well as a piece of analysis for suggesting reforms—both in policy and administrative aspects—to improve their performance as also to improve efficiency in the economy.

The study is a result of the collective effort of the project team under the guidance of Mahesh C. Purohit and Vishnu Kanta Purohit, who prepared the final draft. Special mention needs to be made of the research assistance received from our colleagues at the Foundation for Public Economics and Policy Research. We owe special gratitude to Madhulika, Surajita Rout, and Samarpita Sinha for their help in collecting information and writing down points for the first draft of a few chapters.

The study was attempted with the grant-in-aid provided by the Indian Council of Social Science Research (ICSSR), New Delhi. The authors wish to acknowledge ICSSR's financial support without which the study would not have taken its present shape. However, ICSSR is not in any way responsible for the findings of or opinions expressed in this work, the responsibility for which rests solely with the authors.

The study team received valuable help with regard to data on central and state taxes from the Central Board of Excise and Customs and state finance departments, respectively. Special thanks are due to Vivek Johri and Gautam Bhattacharya of the Tax Research Unit (TRU), and to all the persons who worked as Director-Generals of the Data Management Centre of CBEC during the period of the study. Very useful help was received from the finance secretaries and commissioners of commercial taxes in all the states who made the data available for the study. Without having the requisite information from them, the study could not have taken its present shape. The authors are indebted to all of them.

We are greatly indebted to R.K. Chakraborti, T.R. Rustagi, and S.B. Singh in helping us with the intimate knowledge of their respective areas, which was fruitfully interwoven into the chapters. Thanks are also due to G.L. Agarwal, D.N. Rao, and Brijesh C. Purohit for their valuable insight during the course of this study. We owe our special gratitude to Arbind Modi and Pawan Aggarwal who spared time in spite of their busy itinerary to give extremely useful comments on the draft of the book. P.K. Chaubey did a commendable job in meticulously going through the full draft of the book to suggest changes wherever required and offer suggestions to improve its presentation. We owe our sincere thanks to him. However, the responsibility of any remaining errors falls squarely on us.

Last but not least, the competent secretarial assistance provided by the administrative staff, especially Rakesh Kumar, is gratefully acknowledged.

The governing body of the foundation does not bear any responsibility for the contents or views expressed in this study. The responsibility rests with the authors.

New Delhi   Mahesh C. Purohit
21 March 2014   Vishnu Kanta Purohit

Abbreviations

%age	Percentage
A&C	Assessor and collector
ACCT	Assistant Commissioner of Commercial Taxes
ACP	Accredited Client Programme
AHT	Agricultural holding tax
AIT	Agricultural income tax
AL	Alcoholic litre
ARV	Annual rental value
ATF	Aviation turbine fuel
BE	Before estimate
BL	Bulk litre
c.c.	Cubic capacity
c.i.f.	Cost, insurance, and freight
CARD	Computer-aided administration of registration department
CBDT	Central Board of Direct Taxes
CBEC	Central Board of Excise and Customs
CCT	Commissioner of Commercial Taxes
CECA	Comprehensive Economic Cooperation Agreement
CenVAT	Central value added tax
CESTAT	Customs, Excise, and Service Tax Appellate Tribunal
CL	Country liquor
CSD	Canteen stores department
CST	Central sales tax
CTO	Commercial Tax Officer
CVD	Countervailing duty
DDT	Dividend distribution tax
DEPB	Duty entitlement pass book

DGFT	Director General of Foreign Trade
DP	Declared price
DRO	Dispute resolution organization
DTAA	Double Taxation Avoidance Agreement
DTC	Direct Taxes Code
EC	Empowered Committee
EDI	Electronic data interchange
ELSS	Equity linked savings scheme
EOU	Export-oriented units
ERC	Expenditure Reforms Commission
FOB	Free on board
FRBM Act	Fiscal Responsibility and Budget Management Act
FTA	Free trade agreement
GAAR	General Anti-Avoidance Rule
GDP	Gross domestic product
GSDP	Gross state domestic product
GST	Goods and services tax
GTR	Gross tax revenue
HSD	High speed diesel
HSN	Harmonized System of Nomenclature
HUF	Hindu undivided family
ICEGATE	Indian Customs and Excise Gateway
IGR	Inspector-General of Registration and Collector of Stamps
IMF	International Monetary Fund
IMFL	Indian made foreign liquor
ITC	Input tax credit
JCCT	Joint Commissioner of Commercial Taxes
JWGgst	Joint Working Group on GST
LCS	Land customs station
LPG	Liquefied petroleum gas
LPL	London proof litre
LTU	Large taxpayer unit
MAT	Minimum alternate tax
MAV	Multi-axle vehicle
MC	Manufacturing cost
MCD	Municipal Corporation of Delhi
MGQ	Minimum guaranteed quantity
MIS	Management information system
ModVAT	Modified value added tax

MRP	Maximum retail price
MVT	Motor vehicles tax
NCCD	National calamity contingent duty
NPO	Non-profit organization
NPS	National Pension Scheme
NSC	National Saving Certificate
P	Provisional estimate
P&GT	Passengers and goods tax
PAN	Permanent Account Number
PDS	Public distribution system
PL	Proof litre
PSU	Public sector undertaking
PTA	Preferential trade agreement
PTO	Profession tax officer
R&D	Research and development
RE	Revised estimate
RF	Registration fee
RTA	Regional trading agreement
SAD	Special additional duty
SAP	Simplified assessment procedure
SCD	Special customs duty
SCSS	Senior Citizens Savings Scheme
SD	Stamp duty
SDO	Sub-divisional officer
SD&RF	Stamp duty and registration fee
SEB	State Electricity Board
SEC	State Excise Commissioner
SED	State excise duty
SEZ	Special economic zone
SME	Small and medium enterprise
SOTR	States' own tax revenue
SRO	Self-regulatory organization
SSI	Small-scale industry
STT	Securities transaction tax
TAV	Two-axle vehicle
TDS	Tax deducted at source
TIN	Taxpayer Identification Number
TRC	Tax Reforms Committee
UAM	Unit area method
UAV	Unit area value

UED	Union excise duties
ULIP	Unit Linked Insurance Plan
ULW	Unladen weight
UT	Union territory
VAT	Value added tax

CHAPTER 1

THE TAX SYSTEM OF INDIA

an overview

The Indian Constitution has provided for three tiers of government—the union government, the state government,[1] and the local government.[2] However, the Seventh Schedule to the Constitution assigns fiscal powers to the union and state governments only. These powers have been enumerated in the union list and the state list of the Indian Constitution.[3] Some of the fiscal powers are mentioned in the concurrent list but none of the taxing powers are given in this list. The taxes assigned to the centre and to the states are given in Box 1.1.

With the above assignment of taxes between the centre and the states, India has followed the path of planned economic development since Independence. The basic objective of Indian fiscal policy was to ensure accelerating growth with social justice. Gradually, the emphasis has shifted to inclusive growth. Accordingly, the fiscal policy has adopted the following objectives:

1. To accelerate the rate of savings and investments in the economy;
2. To mobilize savings through budgetary surplus and surpluses of public enterprises;
3. To direct investment into the most desirable channels according to the Five Year Plan priorities;

---

[1] The Indian union comprises 29 states and seven centrally administered areas known as union territories. (For a complete list of names of states and union territories, see Annexure A1.1.)
[2] The local government has been given constitutional status by the Seventy-third and Seventy-fourth Constitutional Amendments carried out in 1992.
[3] See Annexure A1.2 for details.

Box 1.1 Assignment of Taxes—Union and State Governments

Union Taxes	State Taxes
1. Taxes on income other than agricultural income	1. Land revenue
2. Duties on customs including export duties	2. Agricultural income tax
3. Union excise duty	3. Sales tax/state VAT
4. Corporation tax	4. State excise
5. Stamp duty with respect to bills of exchange, cheques, promissory notes, bills of lading, letters of credit, policies of insurance, transfer of shares, debentures, proxies, and receipts*	5. Profession tax
6. Wealth tax	6. Electricity duty
7. Estate duty	7. Entertainment tax
8. Gift tax	8. Stamp duty and registration fee
9. Central sales tax*	9. Taxes on motor vehicles
10. Taxes on transactions in stock exchanges and futures markets	10. Passengers and goods tax
11. Service tax	11. Entry tax

Note: * These taxes are assigned to the centre but are collected by the states according to provisions in the Indian Constitution.

4. To decrease the consolidated fiscal deficit and to evolve a suitable public debt policy to reduce the interest burden;
5. To reduce economic inequalities; and
6. To contain inflationary tendencies.

To fulfil these objectives, the fiscal policy has been accorded top priority for providing social justice through equitable distribution and determining the structure, level, and pattern of fiscal operations. Accordingly, it has raised larger resources from the richer sections of society to direct massive investments into the public sector, especially in infrastructure development and areas that have large externalities.[4]

---

[4] During the First Five Year Plan, the main task of the fiscal policy was to 'raise, to the extent possible, through taxation, through loans and through surpluses earned on State enterprises, a considerable portion of the savings needed. The financing of investment through public savings would help to ensure a pattern of development in consonance with accepted social criteria.' See Government of India (1953: 39, para 31).

Fiscal Reforms

With these objectives, the Indian fiscal policy showed significant achievements during the period of planned economic development. India succeeded in its attempt to expand production of foodgrains through the Green Revolution, to evolve a broad base for industrial growth, and to improve various socioeconomic indicators. However, the overall growth rate of the economy was not up to the mark and the results on many fronts could not meet planned expectations. Some countries, in a similar situation, attained a very high rate of growth during the same period, leaving India way behind in many respects. Due to sluggish growth and the adverse balance of payments situation, financial stability was on the brink of collapse prior to the adoption of the structural adjustment programme. Growth performance across states was not satisfactory and it also varied among states (Ahluwalia 2000).

Under the new regime beginning with 1991–2, the main objective of the fiscal policy was to give a thrust to investments and provide for a system that did not have trade-barriers and quantitative restrictions. It received an added impetus in directing the flow of investments through the delicensing of industries.

Since 1991, growing fiscal deficit has been the major problem facing the Indian economy. To cope with the situation, India adopted the structural adjustment programme. It aimed at correcting the imbalances and achieving a higher rate of growth in the economy. It encompassed reforms in each major sector of the economy. Fiscal reforms were an important and integral part of the overall economic reforms.

The Indian economy was characterized by a strong fiscal deficit bias. This was due to the deficit of the centre as well as of the states, caused by a mounting wage bill, widespread subsidies, proliferation of tax concessions, and rising interest costs. This was further aggravated by lack of expenditure control. All these factors caused fundamental problems in the finances of the government. The need of the hour was to restore the macro-balance in the economy through a correction in the fiscal imbalance.

Revenue and Fiscal Deficit

Reducing revenue deficit has been the main concern of fiscal policy during the period. This was mainly due to higher revenue expenditure as compared to revenue receipts. Despite various efforts at reducing expenditure and mobilizing additional resources through taxation, the revenue deficit of the central government increased almost continuously up to 1993–4, when it reached 3.78 per cent of GDP (Table 1.1). The period 1994–7 witnessed a decline in revenue deficit. Following the Fifth Pay Commission award, revenue deficit again rose to 3.04 per cent of GDP during 1997–8. After reaching a peak of 4.40 per cent of GDP in 2001–2 and remaining at the same level in 2002–3, it declined by 0.83 per cent to reach 3.57 per cent of GDP in 2003–4. With the Fiscal Responsibility and Budget Management (FRBM) Act in place, revenue deficit has declined over the years and was merely 1.06 per cent of GDP in 2007–8. However, it again rose to 4.55 per cent of GDP in 2008–9 and 5.10 per cent of GDP in 2009–10 (RE).

Deterioration in the finances of state governments was sharper than that of the central government. All the major fiscal indicators reveal worsening of the fiscal situation as compared with the indices obtained in 1990–1. States' fiscal deficit as a proportion of GDP increased from 3.19 per cent in 1990–1 to 4.27 per cent in 2003–4. With the FRBM Act in place, the fiscal deficit declined over the years and was merely 1.50 per cent of GDP in 2007–8. However, it again rose to 3.21 per cent of GDP in 2009–10 (RE).

Revenue deficit of the states witnessed a sharper improvement, declining from 0.90 per cent of GDP in 1990–1 to 0.40 of GDP in 1993–4. But again the deficit increased to 2.75 per cent of GDP in 1999–2000. Thereafter the revenue deficit was under control and it turned into revenue surplus. The surplus in 2009–10 was 0.56 per cent of GDP. The factors responsible for such acceleration include growing burden of interest payments, pension liabilities, and administrative expenditure. Losses of state-owned public enterprises, inappropriate user charges, and deceleration in central transfers further compounded the problem. However, after 2003–4, the revenue deficit of states started falling and became negative from the year 2006–7 (Table 1.1).

The central government's fiscal deficit in 1990–1 was over 6.60 per cent of GDP (Table 1.1). Due to its determined efforts, this gradually came down to 4.08 per cent in 1996–7. Thereafter, the deficit again increased continuously till 2001–2 to reach a level of 6.19 per cent of GDP. In 2002–3 there was an improvement in the fiscal deficit to 5.91 per cent of the GDP due to a reduction in the primary deficit, although the revenue deficit continued almost at the same level as in 2001–2.

However, fiscal indicators showed a dramatic turnaround in 2005–6, with the level of fiscal deficit falling below the target of 3 per cent of GDP that had been mandated to be achieved three years later. The important factors that lowered the fiscal deficit included the award of the Twelfth Finance Commission in terms of grants and the incentive scheme of debt consolidation and waivers linked to fiscal consolidation under fiscal rules, improved revenue buoyancy of the centre, and the introduction of state-level value added tax (VAT), which proved to be a buoyant source of revenue for the states.

The combined fiscal deficit of the centre and the states, which showed a promising decline in the early 1990s from 9.29 per cent of GDP in 1990–1 to 6.21 per cent in 1996–7, worsened subsequently to rise again to 9.64 per cent in 2001–2 (Table 1.1). Thereafter, the combined deficit went down continuously till 2007–8 (4 per cent of GDP).

Further, with the adoption of the FRBM Act in 2003, the fiscal deficit declined until 2006–7 except in 2005–6 (Table 1.1). In 2005–6, the process of fiscal adjustment was affected on account of the higher devolution of resources arising out of the award of the Twelfth Finance Commission; this increased the centre's fiscal deficit to 4.08 per cent as compared to 3.99 per cent in 2004–5. The situation has improved in 2007–8 with the fiscal deficit declining to 2.56 per cent (Table 1.1). A similar kind of trend is observed in revenue deficit.

The worst part was the financing of more and more current expenditure (rather than capital expenditure) through fiscal deficit. A significant aspect of the reforms was, therefore, related to reducing fiscal deficit which had reached alarming levels. Revenue deficit is the basic reason for an increase in fiscal deficit. This issue came to the fore when the Government of India entered into an agreement with the International Monetary Fund (IMF) for borrowings to sort out international outstanding dues.[5] A similar trend was observed in primary deficit. This reduction was made possible through the harmonized fiscal policies followed by both the centre and state governments.

High fiscal deficit results in an adverse effect on economic growth but the magnitude of this depends on the way it is financed. For example, excessive monetization leads to an uncontrolled expansion of the money supply and an increase in inflationary pressure. Similarly, financing through borrowings from the domestic market could be unsustainable if the interest rate exceeds the growth rate of GDP, resulting in an increase

---

[5] These aspects have been analysed by many researchers, notable among them being Favaro and Lahiri (2004), Roy (1998), and Stern (2002).

Table 1.1 Deficit Indicators of the Centre and the Combined Deficits of Centre and State Governments

(Figures in Rs Crore)

Year	Fiscal Deficit			Revenue Deficit			Primary Deficit		
	Centre	States	Combined	Centre	States	Combined	Centre	States	Combined
	1	2	3	4	5	6	7	8	9
1990–1	37,606	18,151	52,913	18,561	5,107	23,668	16,108	9,470	27,907
	(6.60)	(3.19)	(9.29)	(3.26)	(0.90)	(4.16)	(2.83)	(1.66)	(4.90)
1991–2	30,844	18,421	45,328	16,261	5,652	21,913	4,248	7,457	14,334
	(4.71)	(2.81)	(6.92)	(2.48)	(0.86)	(3.35)	(0.65)	(1.14)	(2.19)
1992–3	35,909	20,000	50,726	18,574	5,059	23,634	4,834	7,369	14,862
	(4.77)	(2.66)	(6.74)	(2.47)	(0.67)	(3.14)	(0.64)	(0.98)	(1.97)
1993–4	55,257	19,610	69,794	32,716	3,475	36,191	18,516	4,239	27,241
	(6.38)	(2.26)	(8.06)	(3.78)	(0.40)	(4.18)	(2.14)	(0.49)	(3.15)
1994–5	48,030	26,673	70,062	31,029	5,575	36,604	3,970	7,617	18,129
	(4.73)	(2.63)	(6.90)	(3.05)	(0.55)	(3.60)	(0.39)	(0.75)	(1.78)
1995–6	50,253	32,021	77,428	29,731	8,734	38,465	208	10,120	18,484
	(4.22)	(2.69)	(6.50)	(2.49)	(0.73)	(3.23)	(0.02)	(0.85)	(1.55)
1996–7	56,242	36,430	85,590	32,654	16,065	48,719	(–)3,236	10,814	15,659
	(4.08)	(2.64)	(6.21)	(2.37)	(1.17)	(3.53)	(–0.23)	(0.78)	(1.14)

1997–8	73,204	43,388	1,08,989	46,449	16,702	63,151	7,567	13,001	30,438
	(4.79)	(2.84)	(7.14)	(3.04)	(1.09)	(4.14)	(0.50)	(0.85)	(1.99)
1998–9	89,560	72,660	1,55,760	66,975	43,580	1,10,555	11,678	36,708	63,168
	(5.11)	(4.15)	(8.89)	(3.82)	(2.49)	(6.31)	(0.67)	(2.10)	(3.61)
1999–2000	1,04,717	90,241	1,83,282	67,597	53,763	1,21,356	14,468	44,995	73,231
	(5.36)	(4.62)	(9.39)	(3.46)	(2.75)	(6.22)	(0.74)	(2.31)	(3.75)
2000–1	1,18,816	82,412	1,92,429	85,234	50,175	1,35,409	19,502	32,065	69,637
	(5.65)	(3.92)	(9.15)	(4.05)	(2.39)	(6.44)	(0.93)	(1.53)	(3.31)
2001–2	1,40,955	89,298	2,19,727	1,00,162	56,942	1,57,105	33,495	27,616	78,837
	(6.19)	(3.92)	(9.64)	(4.40)	(2.50)	(6.89)	(1.47)	(1.21)	(3.46)
2002–3	1,45,072	95,255	2,28,631	1,07,879	54,220	1,62,099	27,268	29,061	74,232
	(5.91)	(3.88)	(9.31)	(4.40)	(2.21)	(6.60)	(1.11)	(1.18)	(3.02)
2003–4	1,23,272	1,17,494	2,29,956	98,262	59,016	1,57,278	(–)816	36,569	53,583
	(4.48)	(4.27)	(8.35)	(3.57)	(2.14)	(5.71)	(–0.03)	(1.33)	(1.95)
2004–5	1,25,794	1,00,743	2,28,664	78,338	34,202	1,12,540	(–)1,140	12,322	36,297
	(3.99)	(3.20)	(7.26)	(2.49)	(1.09)	(3.57)	(–0.04)	(0.39)	(1.15)
2005–6	1,46,435	86,054	2,35,634	92,300	752	93,052	13,805	(–)508	29,244
	(4.08)	(2.40)	(6.57)	(2.57)	(0.02)	(2.59)	(0.38)	(0.01)	(0.82)
2006–7	1,42,573	78,219	2,18,857	80,222	(–)29,711	50,510	(–)7,699	17,241	14,163
	(3.45)	(1.89)	(5.30)	(1.94)	(–0.72)	(1.22)	(–0.19)	(0.42)	(0.34)

(*contd.*)

Table 1.1 (contd.)

(Figures in Rs Crore)

Year	Fiscal Deficit			Revenue Deficit			Primary Deficit		
	Centre	States	Combined	Centre	States	Combined	Centre	States	Combined
	1	2	3	4	5	6	7	8	9
2007–8	1,26,912	74,452	1,98,137	52,569	(–) 48,569	4,000	–42,267	20,467	–51,058
	(2.56)	(1.50)	(4)	(1.06)	(–0.98)	(0.08)	(–0.85)	(–0.41)	(–1.03)
2008–9	3,36,992	1,27,244	4,59,831	2,53,539	(–)15,701	2,37,838	1,44,788	29,607	1,82,193
	(6.05)	(2.28)	(8.25)	(4.55)	(–0.28)	(4.27)	(2.60)	(0.53)	(3.27)
2009–10 (RE)	4,14,041	2,07,374	6,16,317	3,29,061	(–)35,989	3,65,050	1,94,541	97,069	2,97,825
	(6.41)	(3.21)	(9.54)	(5.10)	(–0.56)	(5.65)	(3.01)	(1.5)	(4.61)
2010–11 (BE)	3,81,408	1,89,206	5,67,287	2,76,512	(–)12,098	2,88,610	1,32,744	67,327	2,07,299

Source: Ministry of Finance, *Indian Public Finance Statistics*, Government of India (various issues).
Note: Negative figures indicate surplus; Figures within parentheses are percentages to GDP.

in the real interest rate.[6] As stated in the Report of the Advisory Council, the government borrowed at a nominal rate of nearly 11 per cent when the inflation averaged around 5 per cent. That is, the government was borrowing at a 6 per cent real interest rate. Given this scenario, banks had no incentive for lending to creditworthy private investors resulting in the crowding out of private investment. Also, with the liberal interest rate regime, the government is adopting 'debt swapping' to reduce the interest burden.

India's high fiscal deficit has been sustained in recent years without an exploding debt to GDP ratio due to the liberal interest rate regime. However, it is important to note that this has had an adverse impact on private investments and on growth.[7] On the one hand, a substantial amount of private savings has been absorbed through internal debt to finance the fiscal deficit, while on the other hand, public investment is being crowded out by the mounting revenue expenditure on wages and salaries and loss making public sector undertakings (PSUs).

To control the fiscal crisis, the Government of India set up a committee to recommend draft legislation for fixing fiscal responsibility. Based on the recommendations of this committee, the government introduced a Bill in December 2000. After a multi-year process of debate and discussion, the FRBM Act 2003 was finally passed and its notification was issued in July 2004. The Act envisaged a set of permanent fiscal policy rules that required the government to eliminate revenue deficit by 2007–8. The government moved an amendment to this Act to suggest that the revenue deficit will be eliminated by 2008–9. Under the amended Act, 2008–9 onwards, the government will continue to issue bonds, within limits, but only to finance capital expenditure which creates assets. Increasing debt to finance revenue expenditure will not be permitted (Government of India 2004). Thus, the enactment of the FRBM Act marks a watershed in fiscal reforms and ensures intergenerational equity in fiscal management as well as long-term macroeconomic stability. In fact, there is large potential for fiscal adjustment through increase in public savings, fiscal measures, and an increase in public investment in agriculture, infrastructure, and poverty-related programmes.

---

[6] This phenomenon has been cogently explained by Rakshit (2002), and Joshi and Little (1996). This is also explained by Shome (2002), and Rangarajan and Srivastava (2005).

[7] Stern (2002).

Reforms in Expenditure

The central government's expenditure largely consists of plan expenditure, expenditure on defense and administration, subsidies, and payment of interest on borrowings. Planned development initially witnessed a phenomenal growth in the size of the public sector and this led to an increase in government expenditure since the 1980s—both in terms of the proportion of investments and in terms of ratio to GDP. Accordingly, the relative share of interest liabilities in government expenditure steadily increased while the share of plan expenditure declined or remained stagnant. Initially, the increased expenditure was met from available resources and there was no fiscal imbalance in revenue and expenditure.

The gap between revenue and expenditure started increasing in the 1970s and reached an alarming level in the late 1980s. During 1990–1 to 2008–9, revenue receipts have increased by 13.7 per cent and the revenue expenditure by 13.18 per cent per annum. Also, the growth rate in capital expenditure during 1990–1 to 2008–9 is only 12.06 per cent per annum, as compared to the growth rate of 13.28 per cent in revenue expenditure. The share of revenue expenditure in total expenditure was about 80 per cent in 1990–1, which increased to 88.86 per cent in 2002–3. Thereafter, it declined steadily until 2007–8 (81.20 per cent) but once again the share of revenue expenditure has shown an upward trend (Table 1.2). The faster growth of government expenditure as compared to revenue has been an important concern in the framing of the fiscal policy.

Efforts have been made to control the increasing expenditure. With a view to doing so, the government appointed an Expenditure Reforms Commission (ERC). Also, the FRBM Act was implemented. ERC suggested that there should be a mandatory 10 per cent cut in budgetary allocation for non-Plan and non-salary expenditure; a cut in the revenue and fiscal deficit (as suggested by the FRBM Act); and the downsizing of subsidies in food and fertilizers which should be targeted for the population living 'below the poverty line'. Recommendations of some other committees pointed out that: (a) the central government should withdraw from expenditures that are the primary responsibility of the state, which is agriculture; (b) administrative costs, especially the wage bill, must be reduced; (c) subsidies must be restructured and user charges be increased; (d) expenditure should be evaluated to see that expenditure incurred had yielded the expected results; and (e) departmental undertakings should run without any budgetary support by reducing costs and restructuring charges.[8]

In recognition of the suggestions of all these studies, some stern measures have been taken to curtail non-Plan expenditure, especially interest payments. Measures have also been taken to cut down expenditure on subsidies and public administration. These include suspension of transfers, economy in inventories, curtailing activities based on zero-based budgeting, and ban on government employment. In fact, this resulted in an increase in the share of interest payment from 20.34 per cent in 1990–1 to 27.47 per cent in 2004–5 which reduced thereafter. Also, the share of defence expenditure almost halved over the years from 8.84 per cent in 1990–1 to 5.23 per cent in 2010–11 (BE).

With the starting of the reform process in 1991–2, there has been a change in government's policy for PSUs. The new policy involves disinvestment of PSUs. The rationale for disinvestment is found in the changing role of the state from a provider of a wide range of goods and services to a selective provider of public goods and services (which the market fails to provide in desirable quantities) with a sharper focus on the provision of physical and social infrastructure.

While a Commission for Disinvestment is already working in this direction, the progress has remained slow. From 1999–2000, the emphasis has shifted in favour of strategic sales. The primary objective of disinvestment is that with the transfer of management into private hands, private capital and management practices will be effectively used to increase operational efficiency.

Interest payments, an important component of non-Plan expenditure, has become a matter of great concern due to the increasing quantum of borrowings in the recent past. This has resulted in the increasing indebtedness of the centre as well as the states. In fact, this increased from 20.34 per cent in 1990–1 to 21.57 per cent in 2010–11 (BE) of the combined revenue expenditure of the centre and the states (Table 1.2). The primary contributors to this escalation are the growing debt burden and the upward trend in interest rates.

---

[8] The broad areas for improving the quality of expenditure and reducing the scope of the government have been discussed in the Expenditure Committee Report (Government of India 1997) and by the Kelkar Committee on FRBM Act (Government of India 2004).

Table 1.2 Combined Revenue and Capital Expenditure of the Centre and the States

Year	Revenue Expenditure					Capital Expenditure					Total Non-dev. Exp. (3+8)	Total Dev. Exp. (4+9)	Total Expenditure (5+10)
	Non-dev. Exp.				Total Revenue Exp.	Non-dev. Exp.			Total Non-dev. Exp.	Total Dev. Exp.	Total Capital Exp.			
	Interest Payments	Defence Exp.	Total Non-dev. Exp.	Total Dev. Exp.		Defence Exp.	Fiscal Services						
	1	2	3	4	5	6	7	8	9	10	11	12	13
1990–1	25,006 (20.34)	10,874 (8.84)	64,368 (52.35)	57,498 (46.77)	1,22,950 (80.28)	4,552 (15.07)	725 (2.4)	5,378 (17.81)	16,502 (54.64)	30,202 (19.72)	69,746 (45.54)	74,000 (48.32)	1,53,152
1995–6	58,944 (24)	18,841 (7.67)	1,42,801 (58.14)	1,02,751 (41.83)	2,45,635 (85.12)	8,015 (18.67)	3,276 (7.63)	11,410 (26.58)	23,767 (55.37)	42,927 (14.88)	1,54,211 (53.44)	1,26,518 (43.84)	2,88,562
1999–2000	1,10,051 (24.54)	35,216 (7.85)	2,62,012 (58.43)	1,83,404 (40.90)	4,48,445 (87.06)	11,855 (17.79)	1,977 (2.97)	14,929 (22.4)	36,409 (54.63)	66,651 (12.94)	2,76,941 (53.77)	2,19,813 (42.67)	5,15,096
2000–1	1,22,792 (25.30)	37,238 (7.67)	2,85,893 (58.90)	1,94,956 (40.16)	4,85,388 (88.86)	12,384 (20.35)	1,117 (1.83)	14,471 (23.77)	41,140 (67.59)	60,870 (11.14)	3,00,364 (54.99)	2,36,096 (43.22)	5,46,258
2001–2	1,40,890 (26.26)	38,059 (7.09)	3,20,327 (59.71)	2,10,498 (39.24)	5,36,476 (88.44)	16,207 (23.12)	611 (0.87)	18,370 (26.2)	43,080 (61.45)	70,106 (11.56)	3,38,697 (55.84)	2,53,578 (41.80)	6,06,582
2002–3	1,54,399 (26.39)	40,709 (6.96)	3,51,860 (60.14)	2,26,329 (38.68)	5,85,107 (88.86)	14,953 (20.38)	1,310 (1.79)	18,397 (25.07)	45,629 (62.19)	73,374 (11.14)	3,70,257 (56.23)	2,71,958 (41.30)	6,58,481

2003–4	1,76,373	43,203	3,82,820	2,63,304	6,53,977	16,863	1,577	21,004	65,362	94,499	4,03,824	3,28,666	7,48,476
	(26.97)	(6.61)	(58.54)	(40.26)	(87.37)	(17.84)	(1.67)	(22.23)	(69.17)	(12.63)	(53.95)	(43.91)	
2004–5	1,92,367	43,862	4,24,724	2,65,932	7,00,307	31,994	870	36,298	76,860	1,25,380	4,61,022	3,42,792	8,25,687
	(27.47)	(6.26)	(60.65)	(37.97)	(84.82)	(25.52)	(0.69)	(28.95)	(61.30)	(15.18)	(55.83)	(41.52)	
2005–6	2,06,390	48,211	4,61,045	3,20,495	7,89,337	32,338	1,032	36,809	97,566	1,46,311	4,97,854	4,18,061	9,35,648
	(26.15)	(6.11)	(58.41)	(40.60)	(84.36)	(22.10)	(0.71)	(25.16)	(66.68)	(15.64)	(53.21)	(44.68)	
2006–7	2,33,020	51,681	5,14,349	3,98,129	9,21,053	33,828	404	38,507	1,20,981	1,70,680	5,52,856	5,19,110	10,91,733
	(25.30)	(5.61)	(55.84)	(43.23)	(84.37)	(19.82)	(0.24)	(22.56)	(70.88)	(15.63)	(50.64)	(47.55)	
2007–8	2,49,195	54,219	5,62,164	4,43,492	10,11,221	37,462	649	44,106	1,77,839	2,34,170	6,06,270	6,21,331	12,45,391
	(24.64)	(5.36)	(55.59)	(43.86)	(81.20)	(16.00)	(0.28)	(18.84)	(75.94)	(18.80)	(48.68)	(49.89)	
2008–9	2,77,638	73,305	6,78,301	6,07,289	12,90,509	40,919	2,409	49,360	1,63,320	2,22,855	7,27,661	7,70,609	15,13,364
	(21.51)	(5.68)	(52.56)	(47.06)	(85.27)	(18.36)	(1.08)	(22.15)	(73.28)	(14.73)	(48.08)	(50.92)	
2009–10 (RE)	3,18,492	88,440	8,26,915	7,14,216	15,48,767	47,824	14,212	71,224	1,98,667	2,90,592	8,98,139	9,12,883	18,39,359
	(20.56)	(5.71)	(53.39)	(46.12)	(84.2)	(16.46)	(4.89)	(24.51)	(68.37)	(15.80)	(48.83)	(49.63)	
2010–11 (BE)	3,59,988	87,344	8,86,819	7,73,156	16,69,255	60,000	1,315	76,648	2,17,699	3,19,116	9,63,467	9,90,855	19,88,371
	(21.57)	(5.23)	(53.13)	(46.32)	(83.95)	(18.8)	(0.41)	(24.02)	(68.22)	(16.05)	(48.46)	(49.83)	
Growth Rate (1990–1 to 2008–9)	14.20	10.71	13.65	12.80	13.28	13.43	–3.65	11.56	14.23	12.06	13.46	13.12	13.09

Source: Ministry of Finance, *Indian Public Finance Statistics*, Government of India (various years).

Note: Figures in parentheses in columns 1, 2, 3, and 4 are percentages of column 5; columns 6, 7, 8, and 9 are percentages of column 10; and columns 5, 10, 11, and 12 are percentages of column 13.

Though a liberal interest rate structure prevailed in the latter half of the 1990s, the shift in the Reserve Bank of India's (RBI's) policy towards market-oriented government borrowings instead of loans from RBI (at a concessional rate) increased the interest burden. Also, earlier borrowings from international agencies were at a subsidized rate as India was considered to be a 'developing' economy. With India attaining a higher level of growth, this status is no longer available now. Therefore, subsidized funds are not available to India.

Subsidies constitute negative taxation. They create positive externalities and augment social welfare by inducing a higher level of demand for subsidized commodities through lower relative prices. Subsidies are often justified on the ground that they serve distributional objectives. Subsidies are given for merit goods such as health, education, and the environment, and non-merit goods like agriculture, irrigation, industry, and power. It is another major item of the revenue expenditure of the central and the state governments.

Among the subsidies for inputs and for final production, the former are not justifiable since they are more easily dispersed to the non-target population. Hence, subsidies for fertilizers, electricity, diesel, and irrigation should be rationalized vigorously. Studies indicate that around one-third of the subsidies are provided by the centre and about two-thirds are given by the states. The share of non-merit subsidies is much higher as compared to merit subsidies on social services. The share of subsidies in social services is only 4.39 per cent while in economic services it is 61 per cent of the total subsidies of the centre and the states. Estimates by different studies suggest that central subsidies have increased over the years and this is attributed to the petroleum sector (which has become a part of the central budget). Further, the share of explicit subsidies has gone up without any substantive increase in recovery rates, increasing the burden on the exchequer.[9]

In general, subsidies are advocated when the social benefits of a particular commodity or service are greater than the sum of the private benefits of the consumers. Unduly low user prices, reflected in correspondingly low recovery rates, lead to an excessive demand for scarce resources.

---

[9] The first report on subsidy titled 'Committee on Controls and Subsidies' was given by Dagli (1979). Other studies on the subject were: Government of India (2004) and Mundle and Rao (1992); at the state level by Rao and Mundle (1992); and for both the tiers of government by Srivastava et al. (2003) and Srivastava and Sen (1997). The Expenditure Commission (Government of India 2000) also analyses subsidies and recommends those that could be curtailed.

Thus, while power and water may be over used, or even wasted in some sectors, other sectors remain starved of such vital resources leading to supply side bottlenecks and a reduction in the overall efficiency of the system. Subsidies also cause distortions in relative prices leading to the misallocation of resources.

Subsidies given directly to the final consumer or producer, on the other hand, are more desirable since they accrue directly to targeted beneficiaries. However, leakages as well as the poor designs of subsidy regimes make it difficult to ensure this equity objective. The pattern of inter-state distribution of subsidies on social and economic services indicates a high level of per capita subsidies for high income states which progressively falls as we move towards the middle and low income states.

Two politically sensitive subsidies relate to food and fertilizers. The food subsidy is meant to help the poorest in society. However, most of the studies suggest that the poor have not benefited from the public distribution system. It is, therefore, suggested that the subsidy should be transparent, well targeted, and suitably designed for practical implementation. Also, existing state subsidies are regressive in nature. The higher the per capita income of the state, the greater is the per capita subsidy, particularly non-merit subsidies. In India, although subsidies account for a significant share of the government's expenditure, only a small part of the subsidies is made explicit in budget documents. Since substantial subsidies remain implicit in the provision of social and economic services, these become unmanageable and exert further pressure on the fiscal deficit.

Sustainability of Public Debt

Borrowing being the softer option, it is important that some exogenous limit is fixed on it. Such limits can be exercised through the FRBM Act. Debt itself is not stressful for the economy but it should be sustainable for the economy. Sustainability is seen as the capacity to keep a balance between the cost of additional borrowings and the returns from them.

Increasing fiscal deficit results in the enlargement of public debt, that is, more funds are needed for the servicing of debt. This is a vicious cycle and puts the economy in a debt trap. Consequently, borrowings have increased considerably over time resulting in increasing indebtedness of the centre as well as the states. Since 1984–5, debt has been growing rapidly. In the last few years, it grew by Rs 4,000 crore a year. The combined domestic debt of the government (centre plus states) as a proportion of GDP also increased from 73.46 per cent in 1990–1 to 91.65 per cent in 2004–5. Since then it shows a downward trend (Table 1.3). The debt–GDP ratio went down to 71.2 per cent in 2010–11 (BE).

Table 1.3 Trends in Debt of Centre and State Governments

(Figures in Rs crore)

Year	Total Liabilities at the End of the Years			Debt as %age of GDP		
	Central Government	State Governments	Combined	Central Government	State Governments	Combined
1990–1	3,14,558	1,28,155	4,18,428	55.22	22.50	73.46
1991–2	3,54,662	1,47,030	3,68,824	54.17	22.46	56.33
1992–3	4,01,924	1,68,365	4,79,035	53.41	22.37	63.65
1993–4	4,77,968	1,87,922	5,64,806	55.21	21.70	65.23
1994–5	5,38,611	2,17,100	6,40,796	53.03	21.37	63.09
1995–6	6,06,232	2,50,889	7,28,208	50.87	21.05	61.10
1996–7	6,75,676	2,88,103	8,18,206	49.01	20.90	59.35
1997–8	7,78,294	3,33,897	9,44,228	50.96	21.86	61.83
1998–9	8,91,806	3,99,575	10,92,374	50.93	22.82	62.38
1999–2000	10,21,029	5,09,530	13,00,228	52.31	26.10	66.61
2000–1	11,68,541	5,94,147	15,24,033	55.58	28.26	72.49
2001–2	13,66,408	6,90,747	18,07,605	59.96	30.31	79.32
2002–3	15,59,201	7,86,427	20,96,449	63.52	32.04	85.41
2003–4	17,36,678	9,13,375	24,57,072	63.05	33.16	89.20
2004–5	19,94,421	10,52,178	28,86,554	63.33	33.41	91.65
2005–6	22,60,145	11,67,865	32,71,006	63.13	32.62	91.36
2006–7	25,38,596	12,50,818	36,41,888	61.23	30.17	87.85
2007–8	28,37,425	13,28,302	40,20,629	57.30	26.80	81.30
2008–9	31,59,178	14,70,196	44,85,504	56.60	26.30	80.30
2009–10 (RE)	35,15,906	16,38,475	50,05,652	53.70	25.00	76.40
2010–11 (BE)	39,44,598	18,20,156	56,09,056	50.10	23.10	71.20
Growth Rate 1990–1 to 2008–9	13.92	15.57	15.48			

Source: Ministry of Finance, *Indian Public Finance Statistics*, Government of India (various years).
Note: State governments' total liabilities include loans from the centre; GDP used is at current market prices.

The increase in debt, along with inadequate returns from the use of borrowed funds, increases the burden of interest payment. The fiscal crisis and the exponential growth of public debt arose not merely because revenue expenditure was more than current revenue, but also because the capital expenditure financed by borrowings did not yield adequate returns. In fact, a higher interest burden leads to a squeeze on budgetary capital outlays, thereby stifling economic growth.

The combined interest expenditure grew to approximately 20.43 per cent of the total expenditure in 1994–5 and subsequently increased to 23.56 per cent in 2003–4. In fact, the internal debt trap emerged some time ago forcing the government to mobilize fresh loans from the market to pay the interest obligations. RBI drew attention to this possibility in its annual report for 1999–2000, wherein it said, 'the debt growth has generally exceeded the nominal GDP growth since 1997–8 with an exception to 1998–9' (Reserve Bank of India 2000). It is, therefore, important that the fiscal policy should determine the degree of adjustment needed to restrict the growth of public debt.

Another important aspect has been the critical level of the debt–GDP ratio. In the early phases of planned development it was argued that a limited amount of deficit financing was useful to give a boost to the economy; it was given a place of pride in the Plan document. Hence, there was no check on the rising deficit that was often considered as a residual, after determining all the other aspects of the budget. It was argued that while private investments are squeezed out, the economy at least benefits from public investments especially if such investments took place in critical infrastructure. However, the centre and the states are presently running large revenue deficits which are financed through borrowings. Consequently, the deficit as a percentage of GDP has increased and public investment as a percentage of GDP has fallen steadily. The level of debt is now so high that funds have to be borrowed even to service the debt. A high and growing debt–GDP ratio makes public debt unsustainable as it tends to increase the interest rate, thereby increasing the debt–service component of the budget and reduces the flexibility of fiscal policy.

A high debt–GDP ratio is unsustainable because at some point of time the financial market will realize that the present policies are not creditable. The subsequent change in expectations will make it increasingly difficult for the government to sell its debt. It is important to emphasize that there is no absolute sustainable debt–GDP ratio which can be suggested as an optimum ratio.[10] The debt–GDP ratio is sustainable only if the rate of real interest is less than or equal to the rate of real economic growth.

An important aspect of the Indian economy has been its openness to the foreign investments. However, growth is still driven by the domestic savings. The trend of savings–investment in the Indian economy shows that savings and investment are directly proportional to the growth rate. The overall savings–investment gap for household, private, and public sectors indicates a widening of public sector balance. This gap is lowest in household sector. The sectorial saving–investment gap reflects the gap between gross domestic savings and gross capital formation of a sector. This gap declined significantly for the public sector as its savings increased (Table 1.4). The movements in public-sector savings and corporate investment explain the slowdown and subsequent recovery in the respective years. Thus the trends in savings–investment gap reflect the need to finance the investment requirement from foreign savings.

Tax Reforms

The worsening of the deficit and the mounting public debt created problems for the overall economy due to the low revenue base. Major tax reforms were needed to improve the efficiency of resources, to ensure smooth flow of business activities, to minimize costs, and to improve the equity. Therefore, since 1991, major reforms have been attempted in the Indian tax system. The Report of the Tax Reforms Committee (TRC) (Government of India 1991, 1991–3), headed by R.J. Chelliah, became the base for initiating reforms in the Indian tax system.

The tax reforms of the 1990s set the stage for achieving a higher tax–GDP ratio and this has helped the country to achieve a higher level of growth. It has focused mainly on simplifying and rationalizing the rate structure; reducing high marginal rates and rate categories; reducing dispersion in the tax rates; and lowering tax rates. Efforts have also been made to rationalize the structure and scope of tax incentives. The thrust has been on broadening the tax base; improving the tax administration; and promoting fairness in the tax system to check adverse effects on efficiency and neutrality. Based on TRC's recommendations, a wide range of reform measures were undertaken which led to a moderation of tax rates, the

[10] Bagchi (2001); Rakshit (2002); Rangarajan and Srivastava (2005).

Table 1.4 Savings–Investment in the Indian Economy as a Percentage of GDP

(at Current Market Prices)

Years	Household Sector Savings	Household Sector Inv	Household Sector Gap (S–I)	Private Corporation Sector Savings	Private Corporation Sector Inv	Private Corporation Sector Gap (S–I)	Public Sector Savings	Public Sector Inv	Public Sector Gap (S–I)	Total Savings	Total Inv	Gap (S–I)	%age of Public Savings in Total Savings
1990–1	18.40	9.68	8.71	2.66	4.49	–1.83	1.77	9.98	–8.22	22.82	24.16	–1.33	7.74
1991–2	15.81	6.32	9.48	3.10	6.18	–3.08	2.64	9.48	–6.84	21.55	21.98	–0.43	12.25
1992–3	16.39	7.70	8.69	2.65	6.97	–4.31	2.18	9.11	–6.93	21.22	23.77	–2.56	10.27
1993–4	17.27	6.33	10.94	3.45	6.12	–2.67	1.22	8.77	–7.55	21.94	21.22	0.72	5.55
1994–5	18.59	6.70	11.89	3.47	7.50	–4.02	2.30	9.33	–7.03	24.36	23.53	0.84	9.46
1995–6	16.87	8.00	8.87	4.96	10.40	–5.43	2.59	8.20	–5.61	24.42	26.59	–2.18	10.60
1996–7	16.03	5.75	10.28	4.51	8.89	–4.37	2.17	7.48	–5.31	22.71	22.12	0.59	9.55
1997–8	17.70	8.02	9.68	4.31	8.82	–4.51	1.80	7.06	–5.26	23.80	23.90	–0.10	7.55
1998–9	18.83	8.53	10.30	3.93	7.09	–3.16	–0.51	7.02	–7.52	22.26	22.64	–0.38	–2.28
1999–2000	21.13	10.55	10.58	4.47	7.35	–2.88	–0.79	7.41	–8.20	24.81	26.10	–1.29	–3.20
2000–1	21.64	11.40	10.24	3.86	5.19	–1.33	–1.75	6.88	–8.63	23.74	24.16	–0.43	–7.39
2001–2	22.12	11.26	10.86	3.37	5.42	–2.05	–2.03	6.87	–8.90	23.47	24.18	–0.71	–8.63
2002–3	22.95	12.63	10.32	4.04	5.93	–1.88	–0.65	6.09	–6.74	26.34	25.21	1.13	–2.46
2003–4	24.11	12.74	11.37	4.61	6.83	–2.22	1.07	6.34	–5.27	29.79	26.80	2.99	3.60
2004–5	22.76	12.68	10.08	6.73	10.76	–4.02	2.19	6.89	–4.70	31.68	31.63	0.06	6.91
2005–6	24.11	12.37	11.74	7.71	13.72	–6.01	2.42	7.58	–5.16	34.24	34.82	–0.58	7.07
2006–7	22.88	11.93	10.95	7.99	14.51	–6.52	3.56	8.40	–4.84	34.43	36.00	–1.57	10.34
2007–8 (P)	22.64	11.47	11.17	8.72	16.09	–7.36	5.05	8.94	–3.89	36.41	37.58	–1.17	13.86
2008–9 (Q)	22.63	12.20	10.43	8.44	12.71	–4.27	1.44	9.40	–7.97	32.50	35.59	–3.10	4.42

Source: Reserve Bank of India (various issues).
Notes: P = Provisional Estimates and Q = Quick Estimates; All data are from the New Series (Base: 1999–2000).

widening of the tax base, tax incentives for development of infrastructure and housing, and strengthening of tax enforcement. In the case of indirect taxes, steps were taken to reduce multiplicity of rates, rationalization of the rate structure, and adoption of the VAT procedure in union excise duty and sales tax.

In recent years, studies have been attempted to pinpoint the factors that are responsible for the prevailing low tax–GDP ratio. The Kelkar Task Force on Direct and Indirect Taxes, (Government of India 2002) and the Shome Committee on Tax Policy and Tax Administration for the Tenth Plan (Government of India 2001) have highlighted that the factors responsible for this relate to the structure as well as the administration of taxes. While it is recognized that the key to restoring fiscal health lies in attaining the correct tax–GDP ratio, efforts have not yet given the desired results.

Fiscal Reforms at the State Level

Though fiscal reforms at the central level started at the beginning of the 1990s, the states resorted to it in early twentieth century only. State-level fiscal reforms are, however, critical for accelerating growth in the country.[11] Major reforms are required in infrastructure. The most important area here is the power sector, which is dominated by State Electricity Boards (SEBs), which suffer from large losses, negative net worth, and lack of investible surpluses. In addition, most public sector enterprises have a low and irrational tariff structure. These inefficient public sector enterprises need to be substantially improved by overhauling tariffs, restructuring, and privatization. The problems in water supply and irrigation are similar to those in the power sector.

Reforms at the state level took place in various forms such as proposals relating to new tax and non-tax measures aimed at strengthening the revenue base, and in expenditure management measures to arrest the growth in the current expenditures of states. Expenditure on the states' non-developmental component has been growing over a period of time and therefore the objectives of state fiscal reforms are curtailing expenditure and augmenting revenue. Some states have also initiated measures

---

[11] The need for and the slow speed of such reforms are analysed in Guhan (1995) and Howes et al. (2003).

to reduce non-merit subsidies. A path-breaking reform in state taxes was replacing sales tax by the state VAT.

OBJECTIVES AND SCOPE OF THE STUDY

Notwithstanding a plethora of reforms attempted in the last decade and a half, there is a need to take these reforms further and make the tax system suited to a competitive open economy and to have a unified Indian market.

It is also important to note that while reforms have been attempted to rationalize the existing structure, some new taxes have also been levied and some existing taxes have been replaced by iniquitous and complicated structures that do not fulfil the criteria of equity, efficiency, etc. For example, surcharge has been removed and levied again. In addition, 'additional cess' has also been added to the base. This is levied for a variety of purposes, making the tax structure more complicated. The incidence of special additional duty (SAD) is meagre in comparison to the adverse effects of non-taxation of state VAT on imports for which no preparatory work has so far been done. In the case of union excise duties (now known as CenVAT), many exemption notifications have been curtailed; however, in reality, many of the former exemptions have been simply merged to reduce the counting of exemptions. In fact, there still exists the need to further rationalize these notifications.

At the state level, barring sales tax and stamp and registration fee, no reforms have been attempted. More importantly, the reformed structures do not go hand in hand with prescribed procedures inviting more interaction between the public and tax officials which results in corruption in the tax system.

It is, therefore, felt that the reforms already initiated are a halfway house. In addition, reforms initiated earlier at the central level have been undone and further vitiated in recent years. At the state level, much more needs to be done to reform the overall tax system. In fact, it is high time that the second generation reforms, both at the central and state levels, are implemented. In this context this study aims at:

1. analysing the reforms undertaken since 1991–2, both at the centre and in the states, in the context of the objectives of the tax policy;
2. evaluating the present tax system of the centre and the states;

3. reviewing the proposal of a comprehensive goods and services tax (GST), as proposed by the Kelkar Committee and announced by the present government to be implemented by 2012;
4. recommending second generation reforms in all the taxes levied by the centre and the states, keeping in view the principles of taxation; and
5. suggesting reforms in the structure and administration of GST, keeping in view the autonomy of the states and objectives of tax policy.

In the context of the objectives of the tax reforms presented earlier, this book includes all the central and state taxes. Attention is thus paid to all the taxes on income and property as also to all the taxes on commodities and services.

Presentation Scheme

Keeping these objectives in view the book follows the following plan:

Chapter 2 analyses the fiscal significance of each and every tax at the central and the state level. It also delves into an analysis of the tax–GDP ratio.

The next three chapters analyse the issues in policy and administration of taxes levied by the central government. Chapter 3 presents the existing structure and administration of taxes on international trade, that is, customs duties. It delves into the weaknesses of the existing system and suggests reformative measures. Chapter 4 deals with the system of taxes on income and property levied by the union government. This includes corporate income tax, personal income tax, wealth tax, and gift tax. Chapter 5 is an analysis of CenVAT and the service tax levied by the union government. This chapter discusses in detail the existing structure, administration, and fiscal significance of CenVAT and its components; tax on services, paying special attention to the issues involved and the reformative measures.

The following two chapters delve into issues related to state taxes. Chapter 6 examines all the taxes on income and property levied by the states. These include land revenue, agricultural income tax, stamp duty and registration fee, and profession tax. This chapter gives a detailed analysis of fiscal significance (including an analysis of trends, growth rate, buoyancy, and tax effort made by states), and the existing structure and administration of state taxes on income and property. Chapter 7 looks into the details of taxes on domestic trade levied by the states, which are State VAT, state excise duty, motor vehicles tax, passengers and goods tax, electricity duty, and entertainment tax. It covers all aspects of states' domestic trade taxes encompassing issues and further policy imperatives. Besides analysing the growth rate and buoyancy for individual taxes, this chapter also analyses the tax effort made by the states for some of the taxes.

Chapter 8 analyses the existing system of local taxes. This includes property tax, octroi and other taxes of third-tier of government.

Finally, Chapter 9 presents a summary and conclusions of all the chapters and puts forth possible further reforms in the policy and administration of the Indian tax system. It also presents a roadmap for transition to the Direct Taxes Code (DTC) and to GST in India. These two major innovative measures will help India achieve a transparent, neutral, and efficient tax system.

ANNEXURE A1.1

List of Indian States and Union Territories

States
1. Andhra Pradesh
2. Arunachal Pradesh
3. Assam
4. Bihar
5. Chhattisgarh
6. Goa
7. Gujarat
8. Haryana
9. Himachal Pradesh
10. Jammu and Kashmir
11. Jharkhand
12. Karnataka
13. Kerala
14. Madhya Pradesh

15. Maharashtra
16. Manipur
17. Meghalaya
18. Mizoram
10. Nagaland
20. Odisha
21. Punjab
22. Rajasthan
23. Sikkim
24. Tamil Nadu
25. Telangana
26. Tripura
27. Uttar Pradesh
28. Uttarakhand
29. West Bengal

Union Territories
1. Andaman and Nicobar Islands
2. Chandigarh
3. Dadra and Nagar Haveli
4. National Capital Territory of Delhi
5. Daman and Diu
6. Lakshadweep
7. Puducherry

Annexure A1.2

Division of Tax Powers between the Union and the States

List I—Union List

Relevant Clauses	Items
82	Taxes on income other than agricultural income.
83	Duties of customs including export duties.
84	Duties of excise on tobacco and other goods manufactured or produced in India except: (a) Alcoholic liquors for human consumption;

	(b) Opium, Indian hemp, and other narcotic drugs and narcotics, but including medicinal and toilet preparations containing alcohol or any substance included in sub-paragraph (b) of this entry.
85	Corporation Tax
86	Taxes on the capital value of the assets, exclusive of agricultural land, of individuals and companies; taxes on the capital of companies.
87	Estate duty in respect of property other than agricultural land.
88	Duties in respect of succession to property other than agricultural land.
89	Terminal taxes on goods or passengers, carried by railway, sea or air; taxes on railway fares and freights.
90	Taxes other than stamp duties on transactions in stock exchanges and future markets.
91	Rates of stamp duty in respect of bills of exchange, cheques, promissory notes, bills of lading, letters of credit, policies of insurance, transfer of shares, debentures, proxies and receipts.
92	Taxes on the sale or purchase of newspapers and on advertisements published therein.
92A[12]	Taxes on the sale or purchase of goods other than newspapers, where such sale or purchase takes place in the course of inter-state trade or commerce.
92B[13]	Taxes on consignment of the goods (whether the consignment is to the person making it or to any other person), where such consignment takes place in the course of inter-state trade or commerce.
92C[14]	Taxes on services.
97.	Any other matter not enumerated in list II or list III including any tax not mentioned in either of those lists.

[12] Inserted by the Constitution (Sixth Amendment) Act, 1956, Sec. 2 (w.e.f. 11 June 1956).

[13] Inserted by the Constitution (Forty-sixth Amendment) Act, 1982, Sec. 5 (w.e.f. 2 February 1983).

[14] Inserted by the Constitution (Ninety-fifth Amendment) Act, 2003.

List II—State List

Relevant Clauses	Items
45	Land revenue, including the assessment and collection of revenue, the maintenance of land records, survey, for revenue purposes and records of rights, and alienation of revenues.
46	Taxes on agricultural income.
47	Duties in respect of succession to agricultural land.
48	Estate duty in respect of agricultural land.
49	Taxes on lands and buildings.
50	Taxes on mineral rights subject to any limitations imposed by Parliament by law relating to mineral development.
51	Duties of excise on the following goods manufactured or produced in the State countervailing duties at the same or lower rates on similar goods manufactured or produced elsewhere in India: (a) Alcoholic liquors for human consumption; (b) Opium, Indian hemp, and other narcotic drugs and narcotics; but not including medicinal and toilet preparations containing alcohol or any substance included in sub-paragraph (b) of this entry.
52	Taxes on the entry of goods into a local area of consumption, use or sale therein.
53	Taxes on the consumption or sale of electricity.
54	Taxes on the sale or purchase of goods other than newspapers, subject to the provisions of entry 92A of list I.
55	Taxes on advertisements other than advertisements published in the newspapers and advertisements broadcast by radio or television.
56	Taxes on goods and passengers carried by road or on inland waterways.
57	Taxes on vehicles, whether mechanically propelled or not, suitable for use on roads, including tramcars subject to the provisions of entry 35 of list III.
58	Taxes on animals and boats.
59	Tolls.

60	Taxes on professions, trades, callings and employments.
61	Capitation taxes.
62	Taxes on luxuries, including taxes on entertainments, amusements, betting and gambling.
63	Rates of stamp duty in respect of documents other than those specified in the provisions of list I with regard to rates of stamp duty.

List III—Concurrent List

Relevant Clauses	**Items**
35	Mechanically propelled vehicles including the principles on which taxes on such vehicles are to be levied.
44	Stamp duties other than duties or fees collected by means of judicial stamps, but not including rates of stamp duty.

Source: Bakshi (2003), pp. 362–72.

Note: 1. Inserted by the Constitution (Fifteenth Amendment) Act, 1956, Sec. 2.

2. Inserted by the Constitution (Forty-sixth Amendment) Act, 1982, Sec. 5.

3. Submitted by the Constitution (Sixth Amendment) Act, 1956, Sec. 2.

4. Inserted by the Constitution (Sixth Amendment) Act, 1956, Sec. 57.

CHAPTER 2

FISCAL SIGNIFICANCE OF TAXES

In India, as in the other economies of the world, there has been an overwhelming dependence on indirect taxes during the initial stages of economic growth. The increase in revenue came mainly from the levy of taxes on commodities and services consisting principally of union excise duties and customs duties at the central level and sales tax at the states' level. Over a period of time, this difference kept on widening as the share of revenue from taxes on income and property fell.

During its initial phase of development, the economy mainly depended on primary activities; the industrial sector did not contribute significantly to the gross domestic product (GDP). As a result, the GDP and per capita income were not very high and the government depended heavily on taxes on commodities and services for mobilizing resources rather than on taxes on income and property. Such a situation prevails in almost all developing economies and, as an economy develops, the proportion of revenue generated from taxes on income and property rises.

In India, the tax reforms were initiated in the mid-1980s and this move towards restructuring the tax system intensified during the 1990s. There was a compositional shift in the structure of the tax system—from excessive dependence on regressive indirect taxes to progressive direct taxes.

The new tax structure ensured enhanced competitiveness of the Indian industry. The outlook of tax revenue changed and growth in revenue from indirect taxes, such as union excise duties, slowed down while revenue from direct taxes, like personal income tax and corporation tax, showed an accelerated growth rate during the period.

TAX–GDP RATIO

The tax–GDP ratio in India is very low in comparison to not only developed countries, but also as compared to many developing countries. While developed countries like New Zealand, Belgium, and the United Kingdom have tax–GDP ratios of more than 30 per cent, many of the developing countries too have a higher ratio—South Africa (30.58 per cent), Seychelles (35.93 per cent), and Belarus (33.99 per cent) (Table 2.1).

At the time that India launched its First Five Year Plan, the tax–GDP ratio (centre and states combined) was less than 10 per cent. This increased to 13.8 per cent in 1980–1 and to 15.8 per cent in 1991–2. Owing to structural adjustments and rationalization of the tax structure during the 1990s, the ratio declined to 13.4 per cent in 1998–9. Since then the ratio has shown mild improvement. It reached 17.94 per cent in 2006–7; however, it again went down to 17.59 per cent in 2007–8, 17 per cent in 2008–9, and continued to fall to 14.73 per cent in 2010–11 (Table 2.2 and Figure 2.1).

As is the case in other developing countries, indirect taxes contributed significantly to the tax–GDP ratio in India. The ratio of indirect taxes to GDP was 11.53 per cent in 1980–1, which increased to 13.25 per cent in 1991–2. It plummeted to 10.56 per cent in 1998–9 but then increased to 12.34 per cent in 2006–7. However it again went down to 10.52 per cent in 2008–9 and further to 9.15 per cent in 2009–10 (RE); showing a little increase in 2010–11 (BE) (Table 2.2).

Due to the implementation of some major tax reforms in the central government in the 1990s, its tax–GDP ratio has declined but the tax revenue collected by the states, as a percentage of GDP, has increased steadily. Since the 1990s, a low and stagnant tax–GDP ratio of 8–10 per cent has characterized the central government revenue for a considerable period of time. This was partly due to the fact that the reform of the tax structure through lower rates in indirect taxes and the size of the tax base were not fully compensated for by the rise in the rates of direct taxes.

However, in recent years, the direct tax to GDP ratio of the centre has seen an uptrend because of the reforms in personal income tax and corporation income tax. These reforms have simplified the tax system, reduced exemptions and tax rates, and provided incentives for better compliance. At the same time, the indirect tax–GDP ratio has fallen because of

Table 2.1 Tax–GDP Ratio in Select Countries of the World

Name of the Country	Year	Tax–GDP Ratio
Industrial Countries		
United States	2006	21.24p
Canada	2006	29.51p
Australia	2006	29.70
Japan	2005	17.64
New Zealand	2006	35.68p
Austria	2006	27.11
Belgium	2006	30.39p
France	2006	27.51
Germany	2006	23.02
Italy	2006	29.29
Luxembourg	2006	25.33
Switzerland	2005	22.20
United Kingdom	2006	30.27p
Developing Countries		
Rep. of Congo	2003	08.83
Mauritius	2006	17.62
South Africa	2006	30.58p
India	2008–9	16.40
Seychelles	2005	35.93
Swaziland	2003	27.75
Malaysia	2003	18.53p
Singapore	2005	12.68
Bhutan	2000	09.11
Thailand	2006	18.55p
China, PR: Hong Kong	2005	12.66
China, PR: Macao	2006	21.99
Maldives	2006	20.08p
Belarus	2006	33.99
Bulgaria	2006	25.03
Poland	2006	21.56
Armenia	2006	14.80
Russia Federation	2006	26.63
Kyrgyz Republic	2006	16.73

Israel	2006	30.70
Iran, IR	2004	07.53
Kuwait	2006	00.82
Chile	2006	21.97
Paraguay	2006	12.73p
Costa Rica	2006	14.74
Bolivia	2006	24.73
Peru	2005	13.80p

Source: Government of India (2011) for India, and the International Monetary Fund, (2010), for all other countries.

reduction in peak rates of custom duties and rationalization of rates and exemptions in union excise duties.

The direct tax–GDP ratio of the centre increased from 3.25 per cent in 2000–1 to 4.20 per cent in 2004–5, and further to 5.81 per cent in 2009–10 (RE) but declined to 5.36 in 2010–11 (BE) (Table 2.2).

In the states' own tax revenue, the tax–GDP ratio of the states increased from 4.64 per cent in 1980–1 to 5.49 per cent in 1991–2, and reached a high of 6.37 per cent in 2006–7. However, it went down to 5.56 per cent in 2008–9 and further fell to 5.25 per cent in 2010–11. Similarly, the states' indirect tax–GDP ratio moved from 4.45 per cent in 1980–1 to 5.29 per cent in 1991–2. It fell to 4.98 per cent in 1998–9 after which it again started rising till 2006–7 (6.22 per cent). However, it again fell 5.41 per cent in the year 2008–9 and further to 5.13 per cent in 2010–11 (BE).

Direct taxes in the case of states have contributed more than a half a percentage point, as there are no major taxes assigned to states (see Annexure A1.2). In the late 1990s and in the early part of the recent decade, even while revenue from central indirect taxes relative to GDP went down, the revenue of the states actually improved.

Trends in Total Taxes of the Union and State Governments

The total tax revenue collected by the union and the states (combined) increased from Rs 1,03,117 crore in 1991–2 to Rs 3,15,157 crore in 2001–2,

Table 2.2 Trends in Tax–GDP Ratios in India

Years	Central taxes (gross)			States taxes (SOTR)			Total tax revenue, India		
	Indirect Tax/GDP	Direct Tax/GDP	(Direct+Indirect)/GDP	Direct Tax/GDP	Indirect Tax/GDP	(Direct+Indirect)/GDP	Direct Tax/GDP	Indirect Tax/GDP	Total tax/GDP
	1	2	3 = (cols.1 + 2)	4	5	6 = (cols. 4 + 5)	7 = (cols. 2 + 4)	8 = (cols. 1 + 5)	9 = (cols. 7 + 8)
1980–1	7.08	2.08	9.16	0.19	4.45	4.64	2.27	11.53	13.80
1991–2	7.96	2.35	10.31	0.20	5.29	5.49	2.55	13.25	15.80
1994–5	6.45	2.66	9.11	0.19	5.30	5.49	2.85	11.75	14.60
1995–6	6.54	2.83	9.37	0.19	5.20	5.39	3.02	11.74	14.76
1996–7	6.64	2.84	9.48	0.16	5.05	5.21	3.00	11.69	14.69
1997–8	5.97	3.17	9.14	0.15	5.20	5.35	3.32	11.17	14.49
1998–9	5.58	2.68	8.26	0.14	4.98	5.12	2.82	10.56	13.38
1999–2000	5.83	2.97	8.80	0.15	5.12	5.27	3.12	10.95	14.07
2000–1	5.72	3.25	8.97	0.16	5.39	5.55	3.41	11.11	14.52
2001–2	5.17	3.04	8.21	0.17	5.42	5.59	3.21	10.59	13.80
2002–3	5.40	3.40	8.80	0.16	5.56	5.72	3.56	10.96	14.52
2003–4	5.42	3.82	9.24	0.16	5.64	5.80	3.98	11.06	15.04
2004–5	5.49	4.20	9.69	0.16	5.86	6.02	4.36	11.35	15.71
2005–6	5.69	4.53	10.22	0.15	6.04	6.19	4.68	11.73	16.41
2006–7	6.02	5.45	11.47	0.15	6.22	6.37	5.60	12.34	17.94
2007–8	5.68	6.31	11.99	0.13	5.47	5.60	6.44	11.15	17.59
2008–9	5.11	5.73	10.84	0.14	5.41	5.56	5.88	10.52	16.40
2009–10 (RE)	3.86	5.81	9.67	0.12	5.29	5.41	5.93	9.15	15.08
2010–11 (BE)	4.11	5.36	9.48	0.12	5.13	5.25	5.48	9.25	14.73

Source: Government of India, *Indian Public Finance Statistics*, (2010–11), New Delhi.
Note: SOTR: States' Own Tax Revenue; RE: Revised Estimates; BE: Budget Estimates.

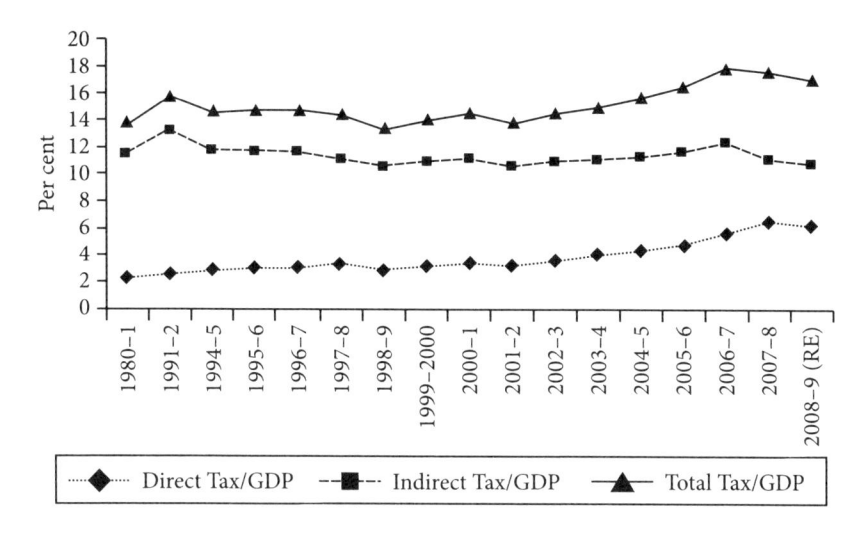

FIGURE 2.1 Trends in Tax–GDP Ratio in India
Source: Data taken from Table 2.2.

and further to Rs 1,441,249 crore in 2011–12. It recorded a growth rate[1] of 13.6 per cent per annum and a buoyancy[2] of 0.7 from 1991–2 to 2009–10.

The yield from taxes on income and property increased from Rs 19,166 crore in 1991–2 to Rs 85,239 crore in 2001–2, and further to Rs 5,70,575 crore in 2011–12. It recorded a growth rate 18.3 per cent and buoyancy 1.0 from 1991–2 to 2009–10. Consequently, the share of direct taxes in total tax revenue increased at a moderate rate from 18.6 per cent in 1991–2 to 27 per cent in 2001–2, and further to 40.14 per cent in 2010–11. However, it has shown a decline in 2011–12; the share of direct taxes has come down to 39.59 per cent (Table 2.3).

The overall yield from taxes on commodities and services increased but at a rather slow pace over the years. While the yield was Rs 82,165 crore in 1991–2, it increased to Rs 2,28,179 crore in 2001–2, and further to Rs 5,62,127 crore in 2009–10 (Figure 2.2). The increase in recent years has

---

[1] Growth rate refers to trend rate calculated by the relationship $Y = ab^t$; where b= (l+r) and Y is the growth rate of tax revenue and t varies from 1 to n.

[2] Buoyancy indicates percentage change in revenue with respect to change in GDP or any other base.

Symbolically, this is expressed as $\delta R/R \div \delta Y/Y$, where R and Y represent the tax revenue and GDP respectively.

If the coefficient is greater than unity, revenue is said to be buoyant.

Table 2.3 Total Tax Revenue in India

(Rs crore)

Year	Centre's Gross Tax Revenue	State's SOTR	Combined (Centre + States)	Combined Direct Tax	Combined Indirect Tax
	1	2	3 = cols. 1 + 2	4	5
1991–2	67,361	35,756	1,03,117	19,166	82,165
	(65.30)	(34.70)	(100)	(18.60)	(79.70)
1995–6	1,11,224	63,865	1,75,089	41,673	1,32,561
	(63.50)	(36.50)	(100)	(23.80)	(75.70)
1996–7	1,29,762	71,102	2,00,864	47,321	1,51,590
	(64.60)	(35.40)	(100)	(23.60)	(75.50)
1997–8	1,39,220	81,229	2,20,449	57,682	1,61,571
	(63.20)	(36.80)	(100)	(26.20)	(73.30)
1998–9	1,43,797	88,995	232792	56,550	1,74,916
	(61.80)	(38.20)	(100)	(24.30)	(75.10)
1999–2000	1,71,752	1,02,582	2,74,334	69,431	2,03,559
	(62.60)	(37.40)	(100)	(25.30)	(74.20)
2000–1	1,88,605	1,17,981	3,06,586	81,463	2,23,505
	(61.50)	(38.50)	(100)	(26.60)	(72.90)
2001–2	1,87,060	1,28,097	3,15,157	85,239	2,28,179
	(59.40)	(40.60)	(100)	(27.00)	(72.40)
2002–3	2,16,266	1,42,143	3,58,409	1,00,672	2,55,840
	(60.30)	(39.70)	(100)	(28.10)	(71.40)
2003–4	2,54,348	1,59,921	4,14,269	1,25,567	2,86,737
	(61.40)	(38.60)	(100)	(30.30)	(69.20)
2004–5	3,04,958	1,89,133	4,94,091	1,56,836	3,35,414
	(61.70)	(38.30)	(100)	(31.70)	(67.90)
2005–6	3,66,151	2,12,307	5,78,458	1,87,787	3,81,425
	(63.30)	(36.70)	(100)	(32.50)	(65.90)
2006–7	4,73,512	2,52,548	7,26,060	2,58,556	4,55,252
	(65.20)	(34.80)	(100)	(35.60)	(62.70)
2007–8	5,93,147	2,86,546	8,79,693	3,40,716	5,20,613
	(67.40)	(32.60)	(100)	(38.70)	(59.20)
2008–9	6,05,299	3,21,930	9,27,229	364796	546427
	(65.30)	(34.70)	(100)	(39.30)	(58.90)
2009–10	6,24,528	3,65,527	9,90,055	4,15,680	5,62,127
	(65.28)	(34.72)	(100)	(39.34)	(58.93)
2010–11 (p)	7,93,072	4,58,272	12,51,344	5,02,251	7,39,028
	(63.38)	(36.62)	(100)	(40.14)	(59.06)

2011–12 (RE)	9,01,664	5,39,585	14,41,249	5,70,575	8,62,536
	(62.56)	(37.44)	(100)	(39.59)	(59.85)
Gr. Rate	13.70	13.60	13.60	18.40	11.70
Buoyancy	0.70	0.70	0.70	1.00	0.60

Source: Government of India, Budget Documents, Various issues and RBI, *State Finances*, Various issues.

Note: P: Provisional; RE: Revised Estimate. SOTR: States' own tax revenue. Figures within parentheses indicate share of the respective taxes in the combined tax revenue. Growth rate and buoyancy are calculated for 1991–2 to 2009–10.

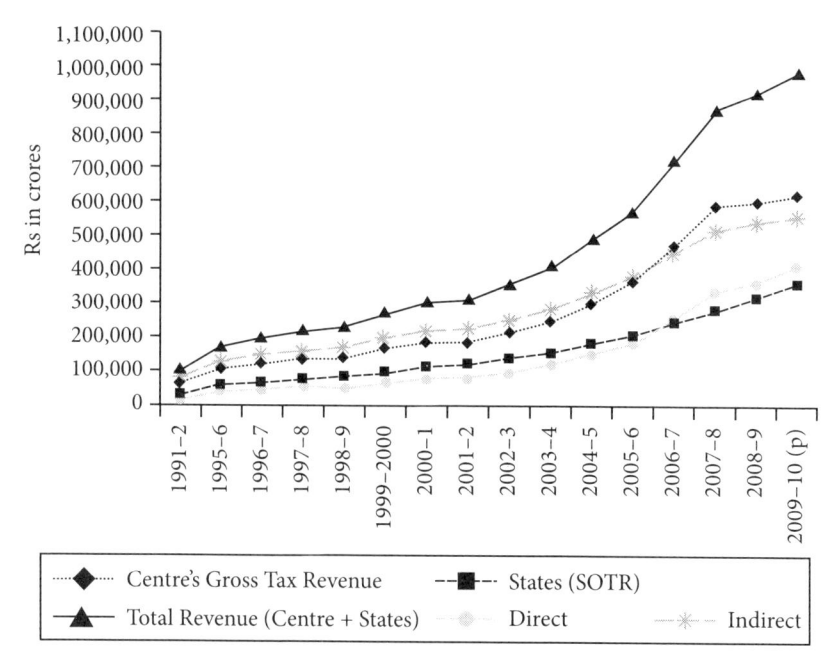

FIGURE 2.2 Trends in Tax Revenue in India
Source: Data taken from Table 2.3.

been remarkable; it has increased to Rs 8,62,536 crore in 2011–12 (RE). Consequently, the growth rate and buoyancy during the period 1991–2 to 2009–10 was 11.7 per cent and 0.6, respectively. The share of taxes on commodities and services in total tax revenue has exhibited variations. While the share was 79.7 per cent in 1991–2, it fell to 73.3 per cent in 1997–8 but again rose to 75.1 per cent in 1998–9. However the share has shown an increasing trend in recent years, being 58.9 per cent in 2008–9 and 59.85 per cent in 2011–12.

Trends in Union Taxes on Income and Property

The central government collected a total tax revenue of Rs 67,361 crore in 1991–2; this increased to Rs 1,88,605 crore in 2000–1 and further to Rs 9,01,664 crore in 2011–12 (RE) (Table 2.4), recording a growth rate of 13.7 per cent per annum and 0.7 buoyancy from 1991–2 to 2009–10.

Taxes on income and property at the central level comprise corporation tax, personal income tax, estate duty, wealth tax, gift tax, etc. The share of these taxes in the total tax revenue remained less significant although their share has increased over the years. The share of taxes on income and property at the central level showed an increasing trend from 22.58 per cent in 1991–2 to 36.22 per cent in 2000–1, and further to 54.95 per cent in 2011–12 (RE). Direct tax revenue exceeded indirect tax collections in 2008–9 and, within direct tax revenue, the major contribution came from corporate income tax.

Corporation Tax

Corporation tax has proved to be the greatest source of direct tax revenue for the government. The revenue increased rapidly from Rs 7,853 crore in 1991–2 to Rs 35,696 crore in 2000–1, and to an impressive magnitude of Rs 3,27,680 crore in 2011–12 (RE) (Table 2.4). This is due to high growth rate and buoyancy of the tax. During the period 1991–2 to 2009–10 the revenue from corporation tax has increased at the rate of about 21.5 per cent (the maximum growth rate among the direct taxes collected by the centre). The buoyancy coefficient of the corporation tax during the same period was 1.6, indicating high responsiveness of the growth in tax revenue to the changes in GDP during the above period.

The share of corporation tax in the gross tax revenue of the centre has also increased from 11.66 per cent in 1991–2 to 18.93 per cent in 2000–1 and further to a whopping 39.19 per cent in 2009–10. However, due to higher growth of indirect taxes in recent years, the share of corporation tax has declined slightly; it has come down to 36.84 per cent in 2011–12 (RE).

Since the mid-1980s, tax reforms have resulted in a compositional shift in the tax system, away from excessive dependence on regressive indirect taxes to direct taxes. This has helped the Indian industry to be more competitive in the open economy.

Personal Income Tax

Personal income tax is a significant source of direct tax revenue in India. It contributed almost one-third of the central tax collections in 1950–1. However, its relative contribution declined over the years due to gaining of momentum by the corporation tax.

The share of personal income tax in the centre's gross tax revenue showed fluctuations in the 1990s. It increased from 10 per cent in 1991–2 to 14.2 per cent in 1996–7, and then fell to 12.3 per cent in 1997–8. It increased steadily from 16.8 per cent in 2000–1 to 17 per cent in 2002–3. It reduced to 15.9 per cent in 2006–7 but again rose to 19.61 per cent in 2009–10. Thereafter, it has shown fluctuation in the trend; it declined to 17.54 per cent in 2010–11 and increased to 18.49 per cent in 2011–12 (RE). The sharp decline in the relative revenue significance of personal income tax indicates adjustments in the tax rates and base resulting in a lower tax burden on household incomes.

However, the centre's efforts in mobilizing further resources and also in improving the governance of the taxes, have meant that it has been able to mobilize further resources from this tax. Consequently, the tax recorded a growth rate of 17 per cent during 1991–2 to 2009–10 and showed a buoyancy of 1.3 during the same period.

TRENDS IN UNION TAXES ON COMMODITIES AND SERVICES

Owing to adoption of reforms in the overall tax system there was a decline in the share of indirect taxes during the period 1991–2 to 2009–10. While the share of indirect taxes in 1991–2 was 74.77 per cent it decelerated to 39.19 per cent in 2009–10. The share started picking up since then, which increased to 44.15 per cent in 2011–12 (RE).

However, the revenue has increased in absolute terms over time. While the overall indirect tax revenue collection in 1991–2 by the central government was Rs 50,367 crore, this increased to Rs 118,681 crore in 2000–1 and further to Rs 2,44,737 crore in 2009–10, recording a growth rate of 10.3 per cent per annum and 0.6 buoyancy over the period (Table 2.4). The yield has further increased to Rs 3,98,075 crore in 2011–12 (RE).

Customs Duty

Customs duty is one of the important sources of indirect tax revenue for the central kitty. It is mainly composed of import duties levied on a wide range of commodities. In absolute terms, it contributed Rs 22,257 crore in 1991–2, which increased to Rs 47,542 crore in 2000–1; its share in the union government's total tax revenue, however, declined over the period. This was primarily due to the adoption of the policy of liberalization and adjustments in the structure of the customs duties from 1990–1 onwards. The rates of customs duties had to be lowered to be at par with the international level. While its share in 1994–5 was 29 per cent, it consistently declined up to 2008–9 to reach 16.5 per cent, except for 1995–6 and 1996–7 which recorded shares of 32.1 and 33.3 per cent respectively. With minor fluctuations, the yield from customs duties was recorded at Rs 1,04,119 crore—a share of 17.6 per cent of the total tax revenue of the union government in 2007–8 (Table 2.4). The growth in this tax during 1991–2 to 2009–10 has been 8.40 per cent with a buoyancy of 0.67. The yield from this tax has further increased in recent years; it was Rs 1,53,000 crore in 2011–12 (RE).

Union Excise Duty

In the 1970s, union excise duties (UED) were one of the major sources of indirect tax revenue at the central level in India. These duties became the star performers by contributing more than 50 per cent to the union government's total tax revenue. Although its share has started falling in recent years, it is still the highest contributor among indirect taxes to the union government's gross tax revenue.

The yield from UED was Rs 28,110 crore in 1991–2, contributing 41.73 per cent to the total central tax revenue during this year (Table 2.4). The revenue increased to Rs 68,526 crore in 2000–1 and further to Rs 1,02,991 crore in 2009–10. The overall rate of growth over 18 years was 9.05 per cent with a buoyancy of 0.71.

However, there was a declining trend in the share of UEDs in the central government's total tax revenue in the early 1990s till 1997–8; thereafter, this share has shown a fluctuating trend. While it was 40.5 per cent in 1994–5, it came down to 34.5 per cent in 1997–8. In 1998–9 it increased to 37 per cent but again decelerated to 36 per cent in 1999–2000. It reached 16.64 per cent in 2011–12 (RE) (Table 2.4).

Service Tax

With structural reforms and significant changes in the institutional framework in India, the services sector has grown at a rapid rate. Since a significant portion of GDP is obtained from the services sector, efforts have been made to incorporate this in the tax net. This helped redressing the asymmetric and distortionary treatment of goods and services in the tax framework and widening the tax net but its yield has increased considerably over time.

This tax was levied for the first time in 1994–5 by the union government on three services. Gradually the coverage was expanded and, by 2011–12, the central government was levying tax on 116 services. Presently, the tax is levied on all services except those in the Negative List and which are specifically exempted from the tax. Initially, the government was able to mobilize revenue worth Rs 407 crore only but its yield has increased considerably over time. The yield from this tax, which was Rs 3,302 crore in 2001–2 contributing 1.8 per cent of the total central tax revenue, increased to Rs 9,50,000 crore in 2011–12 (Table 2.4). With an increase in the coverage of the tax, the share of service tax revenue in the central government's gross tax revenue also increased from 0.78 per cent in 1995–6 to 1.39 per cent in 2000–1 and to 10.54 per cent of gross tax revenue of the centre in 2011–12.

Trends in Taxes on Income and Property of State Governments

Tax revenue is vital for planned economic development. Own tax revenue at the level of all state governments increased from Rs 35,756 crore in

Table 2.4 Tax Revenue of the Central Government of India

(Rs Crore)

	1991–2	1995–6	2000–1	2005–6	2006–7	2007–8	2008–9	2009–10	2010–11 (p)	2011–12 (RE)	GR	B
Gross Tax Revenue#	67,361	1,11,224	1,88,605	3,66,151	4,73,512	5,93,147	6,05,299	6,24,528	7,93,072	9,01,664	13.70	0.70
(a) Direct Taxes	15,207	33,563	68,306	1,57,557	2,19,722	2,95,938	3,19,859	3,67,648	4,38,477	4,95,451	19.00	1.00
	(22.58)	(30.18)	(36.22)	(43.03)	(46.4)	(49.89)	(52.84)	(58.87)	(55.29)	(54.95)		
Corporation Tax	7,853	16,487	35,696	1,01,277	1,44,318	1,92,911	2,13,395	2,44,725	2,98,688	3,27,680	21.50	1.60
	(11.66)	(14.82)	(18.93)	(27.66)	(30.48)	(32.52)	(35.25)	(39.19)	(37.66)	(36.84)		
Personal Income Tax	6,731	15,592	31,764	55,985	75,093	1,02,644	1,06,046	1,22,475	1,39,069	1,66,679	17.00	1.30
	(9.99)	(14.02)	(16.84)	(15.29)	(15.86)	(17.3)	(17.52)	(19.61)	(17.54)	(18.49)		
(b) Indirect Taxes	50,367	76,806	1,18,681	1,99,348	2,41,538	2,78,845	2,69,433	2,44,737	3,44,530	3,98,075	10.30	0.60
	(74.77)	(69.06)	(62.93)	(54.44)	(51.01)	(47.01)	(44.51)	(39.19)	(43.44)	(44.15)		
Customs Duty	22,257	35,757	47,542	65,067	86,327	1,04,119	99,879	83,324	1,35,813	1,53,000	8.40	0.67
	(33.04)	(32.15)	(25.21)	(17.77)	(18.23)	(17.55)	(16.5)	(13.34)	(17.12)	(16.97)		
Union Excise Duty	28,110	40,187	68,526	1,11,226	1,17,613	1,23,425	1,08,613	1,02,991	1,37,701	1,50,075	9.05	0.71
	(41.73)	(36.13)	(36.33)	(30.38)	(24.84)	(20.81)	(17.94)	(16.49)	(17.36)	(16.64)		
Service Tax		862	2,613	23,055	37,598	51,301	60,941	58,422	71,016	9,50,000	40.52	2.90
		(0.78)	(1.39)	(6.30)	(7.94)	(8.65)	(10.07)	(9.35)	(8.95)	(10.54)		

Source: Government of India, Budget Documents, Various years.

Note: # Gross tax revenue includes taxes referred to in (a) and (b) and taxes of Union Territories; and 'other' taxes; P = Provisional; RE = Revised Estimate; GR = Growth Rate; B = Buoyancy.

The figures within parentheses indicate percentage share of the respective taxes in the gross tax revenue. Growth rate and buoyancy of tax revenue is calculated for the period 1991–2 to 2009–10.

1991–2 to Rs 1,28,097 crore in 2001–2, and further to Rs 3,65,527 crore in 2009–10, showing a growth rate of 13.6 per cent per annum (Table 2.5). Consequently, the states' share in the total combined revenue of the states and the centre went up from 34.7 per cent in 1991–2 to 40.6 per cent in 2001–2, and fell to 34.72 per cent in 2009–10 (Table 2.3).

Among the taxes on income and property, taxes such as land revenue, agricultural income tax, and profession tax have been insignificant sources of revenue in state finances. Major taxes on property at the states' level are stamp duty and registration fee. However, the share of these taxes in states' own tax revenue is much less than the share of the taxes levied on commodities and services.

Land Revenue

Land revenue, which used to form the mainstay of states' tax revenue in the early post-independence period, has become an insignificant tax over the years. In some states, land revenue has been abolished altogether. The revenue from this tax (for all states) was Rs 635.9 crore in 1991–2; it went up to Rs 1,717.5 crore in 2001–2, and further to Rs 5,149 crore in 2009–10, recording a growth rate of 11.91 per cent and buoyancy of 0.90 (Table 2.5). The importance of land revenue can be seen in the light of its contribution to the states' own tax revenue. A look at all states' receipts from land revenue indicates that the trend of revenue receipts from this tax has not been steady and therefore, these receipts as a percentage of states' own tax revenue show a ups and downs.[3]

Agricultural Income Tax

Agricultural income tax (AIT) is a source of direct tax revenue for Indian states. But in comparison to other direct taxes the proceeds from this are relatively insignificant. Although agriculture contributes a lot in terms of providing livelihood and employment to a large section of the people, in terms of its revenue contribution it has always occupied an insignificant position in all the states levying it. Except for Assam, the percentage share of revenue realized from AIT in all the other states' own tax revenues is

---

[3] Some states like Gujarat, Kerala, Madhya Pradesh, Maharashtra, and Odisha show a rising trend in land revenue with minor fluctuations.

Table 2.5 Trends in Tax Revenue in Indian States

(Rs Crore)

	1991–2	1995–6	2000–1	2005–6	2006–7	2007–8	2008–9	2009–10	2010–1 (RE)	2011–2 (BE)	GR	Buoyancy
Total Revenue	80536	1,36,803	2,37,953	4,31,021	5,30,556	6,23,747	6,94,657	7,68,136	9,68,070	11,21,844	13.10	0.98
Total Tax Revenue	52604	92,913	1,68,715	3,06,331	3,72,841	4,37,948	482983	5,28,075	6,73,419	7,90,479	13.50	1.01
	(65.32)	(67.92)	(70.90)	(71.07)	(70.27)	(70.21)	(69.53)	(68.75)	(69.56)	(70.46)		
Own Tax Revenue	35,756	63,865	1,17,981	2,12,307	2,52,548	2,86,546	3,21,930	3,63,061	4,58,272	5,39,585	13.60	1.01
	(67.97)	(68.74)	(69.93)	(69.31)	(67.74)	(65.43)	(66.65)	(68.75)	(68.05)	(68.26)		
1. Direct Taxes	3958.53	8,110	13,157	30,230	38,834	44,778	44,937	48,994	63,774	75,124	15.42	1.14
	(11.15)	(12.70)	(11.15)	(14.24)	(15.38)	(15.63)	(13.96)	(13.49)	(13.92)	(13.92)		
(a) Agricultural Income Tax	202	154	107	17	15	26	43.13	123.65	134.36	142.77	−10.06	−0.78
	(0.57)	(0.24)	(0.09)	(0.01)	(0.01)	(0.01)	(0.01)	(0.03)	(0.03)	(0.03)		
(b) Land Revenue	636	1,326	1,415	2,716	3,298	3,969	4,834.35	5,149	6,863	7,633	11.91	0.90
	(1.78)	(2.08)	(1.20)	(1.28)	(1.31)	(1.39)	(1.50)	(1.42)	(1.50)	(1.41)		
(c) Profession Tax	443	681	1864	2547	2847	3292	3,510.98	3,749	4,044	4,507	13.38	0.99
	(1.24)	(1.07)	(1.58)	(1.20)	(1.13)	(1.15)	(1.09)	(1.03)	(0.88)	(0.84)		
(d) Stamp and Registration	2,654	5,897	9,675	24,868	32,452	37,162	36,066.35	39,576	52,189	62,201	16.59	1.22
	(7.42)	(9.23)	(8.20)	(11.71)	(12.85)	(12.97)	(11.20)	(10.90)	(11.39)	(11.53)		
2. Indirect Taxes	31798	55,755	1,04,824	1,82,077	2,13,714	2,41,768	2,76,994	3,14,067	3,94,498	4,64,461	13.29	0.99
	(88.93)	(87.3)	(88.85)	(85.76)	(84.62)	(84.37)	(86.04)	(86.51)	(86.08)	(86.08)		
(a) Sales Tax	21,064	35,477	73,364	1,28,769	1,53,573	1,73,422	1,98,327	2,20,644	2,81,928	3,34,025	13.85	1.03
	(58.91)	(55.55)	(62.18)	(60.65)	(60.81)	(60.52)	(61.61)	(60.77)	(61.52)	(61.90)		

(i) State VAT	16588	28,520	58,500	1,04,737	1,28,776	1,53,007	1,78,715.10	20,039	2,46,613	2,96,230	10.48	0.78
	(46.39)	(44.66)	(49.58)	(49.33)	(50.99)	(53.40)	(55.51)	(5.52)	(53.81)	(54.90)		
(ii) CST	3417	4,890	10,221	15,611	17,889	16,545	15,996	1,802	23,434	24,041	6.43	0.46
	(9.56)	(7.66)	(8.66)	(7.35)	(7.08)	(5.77)	(4.97)	(0.50)	(5.11)	(4.46)		
(b) State Excise	5,439	8,516	16,036	25,036	29,316	34,127	40,989.70	48,375	57,649	69,767	12.12	0.92
	(15.21)	(13.33)	(13.59)	(11.79)	(11.61)	(11.91)	(12.73)	(13.32)	(12.58)	(12.93)		
(c) Motor Vehicle Tax	1,837.10	3,658.80	6,534.50	11,835.60	13,294.20	14,226.10	16,446.40	19,140	22,802	28,007	13.23	0.99
	(5.14)	(5.7)	(5.5)	(5.60)	(5.30)	(5)	(5.10)	(5.30)	(4.98)	(5.20)		
(d) Passenger & Goods Tax	1,135.60	1,508	2,075	6,450	6,808	6,808	8,540.90	9,857	11,296	11,663	13.12	0.97
	(3.18)	(2.36)	(1.76)	(3.04)	(2.70)	(2.38)	(2.70)	(2.70)	(2.50)	(2.20)		
(e) Motor Vehicles & P&G Tax	2,972.70	5,166.50	8,609.30	18,285	20,102	21,034	24,987.30	28,997	34,098	39,670	13.25	0.99
	(8.30)	(8.10)	(7.30)	(8.60)	(8.00)	(7.30)	(7.80)	(7.99)	(7.40)	(7.40)		
(f) Entertainment Tax	368	440	1,147	649	705	1,083	981.25	1,112	1,137	1,531	4.99	0.40
	(1.03)	(0.69)	(0.97)	(0.31)	(0.28)	(0.38)	(0.30)	(0.31)	(0.25)	(0.28)		
(g) Electricity Duty	1,596	2,377	4,431	7,718	8,161	9,239	9,530.30	12,226	16,550	16,069	11.84	0.67
	(4.46)	-3.72	(3.76)	(3.64)	(3.23)	(3.22)	(2.96)	(3.37)	(3.61)	(2.98)		

Source: Reserve Bank of India, *State Finances*, Mumbai (Various Issues).

Note: The figures in parentheses indicate share of individual taxes as percentage of own tax revenue; of total tax revenue as percentage of total revenue, and own tax revenue as percentage of total tax revenue. Growth rate and buoyancy are calculated for the period 1991–2 to 2009–10. RE: Revised Estimates; BE: Budget Estimates; GR: Growth Rate.

negligible. The share kept rising in Assam till 1998–9. But after that it also shows a declining trend. However, in other states the share is not worth mentioning.

The yield from AIT for all the states increased from Rs 98 crore in 1994–5 to Rs 241 crore in 1998–9, but it fell to Rs 151 crore in the next year. From 2000, the yield has shown a steady declining trend. It fell from Rs 107 crore in 2000–1 to Rs 42 crore in 2003–4, and further to a meagre Rs 15 crore in 2006–7. However, the yield from this tax showed some improvement in 2009–10 when it rose to Rs 124 crore. The share of AIT in the gross tax revenue of all the states was less than one per cent from 1991–2 to 2009–10. Both the growth rate and buoyancy of this tax were negative for this period (Table 2.5).

Profession Tax

Profession tax is tax on 'profession, trades, callings and employment'. However, profession tax cannot be used as a major fiscal device owing to the fact that the states cannot levy this tax above the ceiling of Rs 2,500 per annum on any profession as per the restriction imposed by the Constitution.

Trends in yield from profession tax for all the states show an increase from Rs 443 crore in 1991–2 to Rs 2,997 crore in 2001–2, and further to Rs 3,749 crore in 2009–10 with a growth rate of 13.38 per cent per annum during 1991–2 to 2009–10. Also, the buoyancy of the tax to the tune of 0.99 during this period (Table 2.5). Consequently, the share of profession tax in states' own tax revenue (taking all the states together) increased from 1.24 per cent in 1991–2 to 2.34 per cent in 2001–2 but reduced to 1.13 per cent in 2006–7. Even though it improved slightly to 1.15 per cent in 2007–8, it again reduced to 1.03 per cent in 2009–10. This shows that this tax contributes an insignificant portion of revenue to states' own tax revenue. The tax has fared well particularly in the special category states in recent years.

Stamp Duty and Registration Fee

This is another source of direct tax revenue for the states. It is levied on property. Stamp duty and registration fee (SD&RF, as a combined tax) are paid to the government while transferring or registering various financial instruments or deeds relating to financial transactions. Registration is compulsory for certain instruments (mainly movable property) and optional for other financial instruments.

The trends in yield from SD&RF for all the states show an increase from Rs 2,654 crore in 1991–92 to Rs 11,183 crore in 2001–2, and further to Rs 39,576 crore in 2009–10 with a growth rate of 16.59 per cent and and buoyancy of 1.22 during 1991–2 to 2009–10 (Table 2.5). This indicates an upsurge in the fiscal importance of the tax. Consequently, the share of SD&RF in states' own tax revenue also steadily increased from 7.42 per cent in 1991–2 to 10.4 per cent in 2004–5, and fu ther to 10.9 per cent in 2009–10. This tax contributes maximum revenue from among the direct taxes of the states and has also shown the highest growth rate of 16.8 per cent among all the taxes.

Trends in State Taxes on Commodities and Services

There has been a rising trend in states' revenue from taxes on commodities and services. The revenue increased from Rs 31,798 crore in 1991–2 to Rs 112,054 crore in 2001–2, and further to Rs 314,067 crore in 2009–10 (Table 2.5). It increased about nine times the initial level during the entire period, with a growth rate of 13.29 per cent per annum and a buoyancy of 0.99.

The important taxes on commodities and services levied by the states are sales tax, state excise duty, motor vehicles tax, passengers and goods tax, electricity duty, and entertainment tax. Sales tax alone contributes about 72 per cent of the tax revenue from commodities and services, while 23 per cent comes from state excise duty, motor vehicles tax, and passengers and goods tax. Thus, these taxes contribute approximately 95 per cent of the states' revenue from commodities and services.

Sales Tax (State VAT)

Sales tax constitutes a major source of revenue for state governments. The yield from sales tax showed an upsurge from Rs 21,064 crore in 1991–2 to Rs 76,885 crore in 2001–2, and a steady increase to Rs 2,20,644 crore in 2009–10 (Table 2.5). Sales tax fared particularly well in Maharashtra, Tamil Nadu, Punjab, and Assam. Revenue from sales tax collected by all the states, expressed as a percentage of total revenue from taxes on commodities and services rose steadily from 68 per cent in 1994–5 to 68.6 per cent in 2001–2, and further to 70 per cent in 2009–10. The share of sales tax in states' own tax revenue increased from 58.91 per cent in 1991–2 to 60.2 per cent in 2001–2, and further to 60.2 per cent in 2009–10 (Table 2.5). Sales tax is the most buoyant source of revenue for the states with an annual growth rate of 13.85 per cent and buoyancy of 1.03 during 1991–2 to 2009–10.

State Excise Duty

This is the second largest source of revenue collected by state governments. The power of states to levy state excise duties is limited to alcoholic liquor for human consumption, Indian hemp, and other narcotic drugs excluding those used for medicinal purposes or for toilet preparations. The revenues accrue to the states in the form of licence duties from vendors as well as the tax, which can be specific or *ad valorem*. While in western countries the main objective of duties on intoxicants is revenue collection, in India, the overriding consideration in imposing these duties is discouraging the consumption of intoxicants as a matter of public policy. The yield from state excise duty has recorded a steady growth. It increased from Rs 5,439 crore in 1991–2 to Rs 17,110 crore in 2001–2, and further to Rs 48,375 crore in 2009–10 (Table 2.5). However, its share in revenue collected from taxes on commodities and services shows a decline.

While the share was 17.1 per cent in 1991–2, it was 15.3 per cent in 2001–2, and it further fell to 13.7 per cent in 2006–7 but increased slightly to 15.40 per cent in 2009–10. The share of state excise duty in the states' own tax revenue was 15.21 per cent in 1991–2. It fell to 13.4 per cent in 2001–2, and dropped further to 13.52 per cent in 2009–10. It recorded a growth rate of 12.12 per cent during 1991–2 to 2009–10. The buoyancy of state excise was 0.92 (Table 2.5).

Motor Vehicles Tax and Passengers and Goods Tax

Motor vehicles tax and passengers and goods tax are primarily meant to regulate and control motor traffic in the state. Motor vehicles tax is levied on acquisition of vehicles. Passengers and goods tax is treated as user charges or as a charge for constructing and maintaining roads. While some states levy both the motor vehicles tax and the passengers and goods tax, others have merged the two and levy one single tax. It has been observed that these taxes can also serve as a good source of revenue for the states.

Revenue from these taxes increased almost nine times during 1991–2 to 2009–10. It steadily increased from Rs 2,972.7 crore in 1991–2 to Rs 11,089 crore in 2001–2, and further to Rs 28,997 crore in 2009–10. However, its share in the states' own tax revenue remained within the range of 7–9 per cent during this period. It recorded a growth rate of 13.25 per cent and buoyancy of 0.99 during 1991–2 to 2009–10 reflecting an encouraging responsiveness of the tax to changes in GDP.

Electricity Duty

Along with the electricity rates for consuming electricity, consumers pay an additional amount, known as electricity duty. This acts as a good source of revenue for state governments. Electricity duty is levied on the sale or consumption of energy specified either per unit or as a percentage of tariffs. The yield from electricity duty increased at a moderate rate from Rs 1,596 crore in 1991–2 to Rs 4,692 crore in 2001–2, and further to Rs 12,226 crore in 2009–10. Its share in states' own tax revenue, however, showed a fluctuating trend over the years. It was 4.46 per cent in 1991–2 and in the 1990s it hovered around 3 to 4 per cent. The same trend is seen even after 2000. The share of electricity duty in the states' own tax revenue was 3.37 per cent in 2009–10. During this period, the tax recorded a growth rate of 11.84 per cent and a buoyancy of 0.67 (Table 2.5).

Entertainment Tax

Entertainment tax is levied on admission to places of amusement or entertainment, such as cinemas, circus, theatrical performances, exhibitions, sports and games. With the expansion of cinema, the bulk of revenue from this tax is provided by the cinema shows. Though the tax is collected from exhibitors, the ultimate burden is borne by cine-goers. This generated revenue to the tune of Rs 368 crore in 1991–2, which went up to Rs 1,147 crore in 2000–1, but declined to Rs 799 crore in 2001–2. It increased slightly to Rs 1,083 crore in 2007–8 but again reduced to Rs 1,112 crore in 2009–10. It recorded a growth rate of 5 per cent during 1991–2 to 2009–10. Accordingly, its share in states' own tax revenue (all states taken together) reduced from 1.03 per cent in 1991–2 to 0.6 per cent in 2001–2, and further to 0.31 per cent in 2009–10 (Table 2.5).

* * *

As in most developing economies, India also gets substantial revenue from indirect taxes. However, the ratio of indirect taxes to GDP which was 11.75 per cent in 1994–5 went down to 11.11 per cent in 2000–1, and further to 10.52 per cent in 2008–9. Further, trends in tax revenue in India indicate that the union government raises around 65 per cent of the total revenue. Out of this proportion, the ratio of taxes on goods and services to taxes on income and property changed substantially from 71:29 in 1994–5 to 40:60 in 2009–10. In the case of the states, the ratio changed marginally from 87:13 in 1994–5 as also in 2009–10. Also, the composition of revenue from taxes on commodities and services changed significantly. Owing to the opening up of the economy and reforms in the structure of customs duty, the revenue significance of customs duty in total revenue from indirect taxes declined over time. Customs duty and union excise duty contributed about 75 per cent of the gross tax revenue of the centre in 1991–2. This declined to 61 per cent in 2000–1, and further to 29.8 per cent in 2009–10. Among state taxes, sales tax's share in states' own revenue went up from 60.02 per cent in 2001–2 to 60.8 per cent in 2009–10.

CHAPTER 3

TAXES ON INTERNATIONAL TRADE

Taxes on commodities and services are levied on international trade as well as on domestic consumption. With regard to the former, the Indian Constitution empowers the central government to levy 'duties of customs' to have a wedge between domestic prices and the prices of imported goods.[1] This provides a level playing field for domestic producers. Accordingly, the union government has been levying customs duty since Independence. The revenue from this levy recently became part of the divisible pool of taxes that the union government shares with the states.[2] With the increasing volume of imports and exports, the fiscal significance of customs duties has gone up considerably.

REVENUE SIGNIFICANCE OF CUSTOMS DUTY

Customs duty is one of the important sources of indirect tax revenues for the central government. The yield from customs duty was Rs 22,257 crore in 1991–2; contributing 33.04 per cent to the total tax revenue of

---

[1] As per entry 83 in the union list, under the Seventh Schedule of the Constitution, the union government is authorized to levy 'Duties of Customs including export duties'.

[2] This has become part of the divisible pool since 2000 on the recommendations of the Tenth Finance Commission.

the union (Table 3.1). The revenue increased to Rs 57,611 crore in 2004–5, and further to Rs 104,119 crore in 2007–8. Thereafter, due to opening up of the economy and further reduction in the customs duty rates it has declined to Rs 83,324 crore in 2009–10. The growth of this tax during the period 1991–2 to 2009–10 has been 8.40 per cent with a buoyancy of 0.67. However, with the picking up of the imports the revenue from customs duty increased in the later years and by 2011–12 (RE) it reached to Rs 153,000 crore.

The share of customs duty in the total tax revenue of the centre, however, declined over the period primarily due to opening up of the economy and the policy of progressively reducing customs duties from 1990–1. While its share in 1991–2 was 33.04 per cent, this declined to 13.34 per cent in 2009–10 and 16.96 per cent in 2011–12 (Table 3.1).

STRUCTURE OF CUSTOMS DUTY

Customs duty comprises import and export duties. The latter is levied on the export of specified goods out of India. It is mainly levied to discourage the export of any specific commodity or to mop up the windfall export profit. Currently only ores and concentrates of iron and chromium attract this levy. In the 2011–12 budget, an export duty of 10 per cent was levied on de-oiled rice bran to discourage its export. It is levied on FOB (free on board) value. The items on which export duty is leviable and the rates of export duties are provided in the Second Schedule to the Customs Tariff Act, 1975. Section 8 of the Act provides the government the authority to levy or increase export duty. Export duties are normally *ad valorem*.

In addition to export duty there is an export cess leviable on specified articles on their export under various enactments passed by the government. The cess is collected as duty of customs and handed over to the agencies in charge of the administration of the commodity concerned.

Import duty is levied on almost all commodities imported into the country. Import duty rates are either: (1) *ad valorem*, or (2) specific, and/or (3) *ad valorem* cum specific. The statutory rates of import duties, called tariff rates, are fixed by the Parliament. However, the union government has the power, under the law, to provide full or partial duty exemption. Such rates (inclusive of the impact of exemptions) are called 'effective rates'. The more the exemptions, the lower would be effective rate of tax. Over time, the government has been making efforts to lower the number of statutory and effective rates of duties by merging the rates and by removing the exemptions.

The tax base for customs duty is primarily c.i.f. (cost, insurance, and freight) value of the goods imported. The current system of levy and collection of customs duties is governed by two main statutes—the Customs Tariff Act, 1975, and the Customs Act, 1962. These enactments provide the rates at which the customs duties are levied. The First Schedule under the Customs Tariff Act gives the import tariff, based on the Harmonized System of Nomenclature (HSN). The commodities under this Schedule are divided into 99 chapters (13 sections), which are further sub-divided into

Table 3.1 Trends in Revenue from Customs Duty

Year	Customs Duty (Rs Crore)	Share of Customs Duty in Total Tax Revenue of Centre (%)
1991–2	22,257	33.04
1992–3	23,776	31.86
1993–4	22,193	29.30
1994–5	26,789	29.03
1995–6	35,757	32.15
1996–7	42,851	33.02
1997–8	40,193	28.87
1998–9	40,668	28.28
1999–2000	48,419	28.19
2000–1	47,542	25.21
2001–2	40,268	21.53
2002–3	44,852	20.74
2003–4	48,629	19.12
2004–5	57,611	18.89
2005–6	65,067	17.77
2006–7	86,327	18.23
2007–8	1,04,119	17.55
2008–9	99,879	16.50
2009–10	83,324	13.34
2010–11 (p)	1,35,813	17.12
2011–12 (RE)	1,53,000	16.96
Growth Rate	8.40	
Buoyancy	0.67	

Source: Various issues of Union Budget Documents.
Note: P: Provisional; RE: Revised Estimate; Growth Rate and Buoyancy are calculated for the period 1991–2 to 2009–10.

respective sub-headings.[3] Section 8A of the Act provides the authority to levy or increase the rate of import duty.

The structure of customs duty has undergone major changes as India has signed a number of Regional Trading Agreements (RTAs) with various countries. These agreements help in trade promotion. Duty concessions have been extended via these agreements to participating countries. In addition, adopting the policy of an open economy has also had an impact on the rate structure to bring it at comparable levels with the structure prevailing in other countries.

Import Duties

While the main customs duty is known as basic customs duty, there are other forms of duties that are levied along with the basic duty. Specific features of basic customs duty, as well as other duties, are:

Basic duty of customs: It is leviable under section 12 of the Customs Act, 1962, at the rates mentioned in the First Schedule of the Customs Tariff Act, 1975, on goods imported into India. There are preferential rates of duty for goods imported from certain preferential areas/developing countries and other countries under bilateral/multilateral treaties. The duty is levied on the assessable value computed in terms of section 14 of the Customs Act, 1962.[4] The rates of basic customs duty are the standard rates of customs duty.

Standard and preferential rates: Duty at the 'standard rate' is charged where there is no provision for preferential treatment. To be eligible for preferential treatment, the goods should be imported from any preferential or bilateral treaty area. The union government has the power to increase or reduce or discontinue the preferential rate with respect to any article specified in the First Schedule provided it is considered to be necessary in public interest. A preferential rate is applied only when the owner of the article (importer) claims at the time of delivery of the import (with supporting evidence) that the goods are chargeable with the preferential rate of duty.

---

[3] Each chapter and section contains notes to help determine whether the goods are classifiable under the particular chapter or not.

[4] The assessable value is worked out as free on board (FOB) + freight + insurance + landing charges (1 per cent of c.i.f.).

Preferential rates of customs duty have been made applicable also with respect to imports from certain countries, such as Sri Lanka, Mauritius, Seychelles, and Tonga, provided that certain conditions are satisfied. The goods in question must actually be manufactured or produced in such preferential areas as specified under the framed rules. Determining the origin of the goods is crucial to avail of the benefits of these concessional rates of duty.

India views RTAs as 'building blocks' towards the overall objective of trade liberalization. Hence, it is participating in a number of RTAs, which include Free Trade Agreements (FTAs); Preferential Trade Agreements (PTAs); and Comprehensive Economic Cooperation Agreements (CECAs).[5] These agreements are either bilateral or have a regional groupings.[6] To ascertain the applicable rate of duty, one has to refer to customs tariff rates of duties along with the exemption notifications, if any.

Additional duty of custom or countervailing duty: This duty is equal to the central excise duty. Under section 3(1) of the Customs Tariff Act, 1975, goods imported into India are subject to a levy of an additional duty equal to the excise duty leviable on like articles if produced or manufactured in India. It is popularly known as the countervailing duty (CVD). It is levied to counter balance the excise duty leviable on such articles produced or manufactured in India. It includes (1) excise duty leviable under the Central Excise Tariff Act, 1985; (2) additional duties of excise leviable under Additional Duties of Excise (Textile and Textile Articles) Act, 1975, and Additional duties or Excise (Goods of special importance) Act, 1957; and (3) Excise duties and cesses leviable under Miscellaneous Acts. Additional duty of customs is levied on the assessable value of the product plus basic customs duty.

---

[5] The major RTAs that India has entered into are: the South Asia Free Trade Area (SAFTA); Asia-Pacific Trade Agreement (APTA); Bangladesh-India-Myanmar-Sri Lanka and Thailand Technical and Economic Cooperation (BIMSTEC); Global System of Tariff Preferences (GSTP); and tariff preferences for Mauritius, Seychelles, and Tonga.

[6] Other bilateral agreements to which India is a signatory are: the India–Singapore Comprehensive Economic Cooperation Agreement; India–Sri Lanka Free Trade Agreement (ISFTA); India–Chile Preferential Trade Agreement; India–Afghanistan Preferential Trade Agreement; India–Bhutan Trade Agreement; India–Nepal Trade Treaty; framework agreement for establishing free trade between India and Thailand; trade agreement between India and Bangladesh; tariff preference for Myanmar; duty preference scheme for less developed countries and; the free trade agreement concluded with ASEAN.

Special Additional duty of Customs (not exceeding 4 per cent; and for articles of jewellery, 1 per cent)—also called Special CVD: This is levied on all the goods imported into India under section 3(5) of the Customs Tariff Act, 1975. It was levied in Budget 2005 to partially compensate for various domestic taxes like sales tax and value added tax (VAT) and to provide a level playing field to indigenous goods which have to bear these taxes. It is levied on assessable value plus basic customs duty plus additional duty of customs leviable under section 3(1) of the Customs Tariff Act. Special additional duty (SAD) was extended to all imported goods in the 2006 budget. Special Additional Duty was levied at 4 per cent on all imported goods, with few exceptions, to partially compensate the domestic levies. Certain goods are exempted from VAT, basic customs duty, and CVD. Goods imported by export-oriented units (EOUs), kerosene for the public distribution system (PDS), liquefied petroleum gas (LPG) for domestic use, and certain precious metals are exempt from this duty.[7] This duty is not to be included in the assessable value for levy of education cess on imported goods. The manufacturers are also allowed to take credit for this additional duty when they make pay excise duty on their finished products.

National calamity contingent duty (NCCD): This duty was levied under the Finance Act, 2003. The duty is levied at the rate of Rs 50 per MT on imported crude oil and at the rate of 1 per cent on polyester filament yarn. The latter duty was, however, removed in the 2008 budget but was imposed on mobile phones, two-wheelers, motor cars, and multi-utility vehicles.

Education cess: It is leviable at the rate of 2 per cent of aggregate duties of customs (including CVD but excluding the safeguard and anti-dumping duties) with effect from 9 July 2004. The goods, as mentioned in customs notification (69/2004–Cus., dated 9 July 2004), are fully exempt from the levy of this cess.

Secondary and higher education cess: It is leviable at the rate of 1 per cent of aggregate duties of customs (including CVD) with effect from 1 March 2007. The goods, as mentioned in customs notification (69/2004–Cus., dated 9 July 2004), are fully exempted from the levy of this cess.

Anti-dumping duty: It is leviable under section 9A of the Customs Tariff Act, 1975, on the import of specific goods from a specific country. This duty is meant to protect the domestic industry. It is levied when the goods are exported from any country to India at less than their 'normal' price. Investigations for the purpose of levy of anti-dumping duty are carried out by the Ministry of Commerce on the basis of notifications issued by

---

[7] Customs notification numbers 19/2006 and 20/2006.

the Ministry of Finance. Normally, the amount of the anti-dumping duty that is imposed is specific; if it is levied on an *ad valorem* basis then it is calculated on the assessable value of the goods. Anti-dumping duty is leviable on about 132 items, including chemicals, drugs of Chinese origin, CFL, torches, graphite electrodes, iron and steel items, and silk fabrics.

Safeguard duty: It is levied under section 8B of the Customs Tariff Act, 1975, on imports which threaten to cause serious harm to the domestic industry. Investigations for the purpose of levy of safeguard duty are carried out by the Director General of Safeguards in the Ministry of Finance (Central Board of Excise and Customs) and applicable notifications are also issued by the Ministry of Finance (Central Board of Excise and Customs). Normally, the amount of safeguard duty imposed is specific; if it is levied on an *ad valorem* basis then it is calculated on the assessable value of the goods.

CHANGES IN THE PEAK RATE OF BASIC CUSTOMS DUTY

As a result of the tax reforms, efforts have been made to bring down the peak rate of import duty to be in line with the liberalization policy.[8] The peak rate was reduced from nearly 300 per cent to 110 per cent in 1992–3, and then to 85 per cent in 1993–4. Since then, the peak rate (as well as the number of rates) has been brought down steadily (Tables 3.2, 3.3, and 3.4). In 1994–5 and 1995–6 the rate was lowered further to 65 and 50 per cent respectively. The 1994 budget also saw a sea change in customs exemptions with the removal of 'end-use based' exemptions. The current peak rate of duty is 10 per cent on non-agricultural items (except for natural rubber sheets, fish, and cars). The average industrial tariff is about 9.4 per cent.[9] Reduction in duty rates has been accompanied by a reduction in dispersal

---

[8] In this context, the Tax Reforms Committee (TRC) made a three-fold recommendation. First, the very high import duty rates should be brought down in a phased manner (in 1991, many items attracted more than 200 per cent duty). Second, the number of exemptions should be reduced. Third, the tax administration should be strengthened. TRC recommended many other measures including the need to increase the use of information technology in strengthening the tax administration.

[9] For ASEAN countries, the average is much lower. In Philippines it is 6.3 per cent, in Malaysia 8.4 per cent, and in Indonesia 6.9 per cent.

of duty rates as evidenced by the average rate of 9.4 per cent with a peak rate of 10 per cent.

Assessment of the Current Structure of Customs Duty

Notwithstanding the fact that reforms have been introduced in the structure of the customs duty, there exist a large number of rate categories as also a number of exemptions. In all, tariff exemptions can be classified in as many as 20 sections. The total number of notifications is around 130. The notifications incorporate many lists and several conditions to be fulfilled. Existence of too many categories of duties makes the tariff system highly complex. Similarly, the mode of calculating the duty and cess is also not free from doubts and this leads to confusion and disputes. It often takes a long time to issue necessary clarifications to resolve these disputes.

Table 3.2 Changes in Peak Rate of Customs Duty

Year	No. of Major Basic Duty Rates (Ad Valorem)	Peak Basic Rate (Ad Valorem)	Basic Surcharge or SCD	SAD
1990–1	22	More than 300	–	–
1991–2	20	150	–	–
1992–3	16	110	–	–
1993–4	16	85	–	–
1994–5	12	65	–	–
1995–6	9	50	–	–
1996–7	8	50	2% SCD	–
1997–8	7	40	5% SCD	–
1998–9	7	40	5% SCD	4
1999–2000	5	40	10% Surcharge	4
2000–1	4	35	10% Surcharge	4
2001–2	4	35	–	4
2002–3	4	30	–	4
2003–4	4	25	–	4
2004–5	4	20	–	–
2005–6	3	15	4	–
2006–7	3	12.5	4	4
2007–8	3	10	4	–

Notes: SAD = Special additional duty; SCD = Special customs duty.

Table 3.3 Tariff Rates of Customs Duty from 2003–4 to 2007–8

Budget Head	2003–4	2004–5	2005–6	2006–7	2007–8
Animal or vegetable fats, etc.	15, 30, 40, 40, 75, 100	30, 45, 75, 100	15, 30, 45, 75, 100	15, 30, 40, 45, 75, 100	15, 30, 40, 45, 100
Ores, slag, and ash	5	5	5, 15	5, 12.5	5, 10
Petroleum oils, etc.	10, 15, 20, 25	10, 15, 20	10, 15, 55	5, 10, 12.5, 15, 55	5, 10, 55
Inorganic chemicals	5, 15, 30	5, 15, 20	5, 15	10, 12.5	5, 10
Organic chemicals	15, 25, 30	15, 20	10, 15, 20	12.5, 15	10
Miscellaneous chemical products	Free, 25, 30, 50	15, 20, 50	Free, 10, 15, 20	Free, 12.5, 30	
Plastic & articles thereof	30	20	15	12.5	10, 30, 50
Rubber and articles thereof	3, 25, 30	20, 70	3, 15, 20, 70	3, 12.5, 25, 70	3, 10, 25, 70
Pulp paper, paper boards & articles thereof	5, 15, 30	5, 15, 20	5, 15	5, 12.5	5, 10
Primary materials of iron & steel	25, 30, 40	20, 40	15, 20	20	10
Iron & non-alloy steel	30	20, 40	20, 40	12.5	10
Stainless steel	40	40	20	12.5	10
Other alloy steel, hollow drill bars, and rods	40	40	20	12.5	10
Articles of iron & steel	30	20	15	12.5	10
Copper	25	20	15	12.5	5, 10
Aluminium	15, 30	15, 20	10, 15	12.5	5, 10
Tools implements and other misc. articles of base metal	30	20	15	12.5	10

(*contd.*)

Table 3.3 (contd.)

Budget Head	2003–4	2004–5	2005–6	2006–7	2007–8
Machinery excluding machine tools and their parts, etc.	15, 25, 30	NIL, Free, 10, 20	Free, 15%	Free, 12.5	10
Machine tools, parts & accessories	Free, 25	20	15	12.5	10
Electrical machinery	15, 25, 30	Free,5, 10, 15, 20	Free, 15	12.5	7.5, 10
Motor vehicles and parts thereof	Free, 30, 105	20, 105	15, 100	Free, 12.5, 100	Free, 10, 100
Optical, photographic, cinematographic, etc.	Free, 15, 25, 30	Free, 10, 15, 20	Free, 10	12.5	Free, 7.5, 10
Project imports	25, 30, 150	20, 150	15, 100	12.5, 100	10, 100

Table 3.4 Effective Rates of Customs Duty from 2003–4 to 2007–8

Budget Head	2003–4	2004–5	2005–6	2006–7	2007–8
Animal or vegetable fats, etc.	85%, 30%, 75%, 15%, 65%, 50%, 45%,	85%, 65%, 75%, 15%, 50%, 75%, 45%,	20%, 65%, 85%, 75%, 15%, 50%, 45%,	12.5, 20, 65, 85, 75, 15, 80, 50, 75, 45	10, 12.5, 20, 65, 45, 75, 15, 50, 40
Ores, slag, and ash	15%	15%	10%	7.5,	7.5,2
Petroleum oils, etc.	5%, 10%, 15%, 20%, 25%, Nil	5%, Nil, 10%	Nil, 5%, 10%	Nil, 5,10	Nil, 5, 7.5
Inorganic chemicals	Nil, 5%, 15%, 20%	Nil, 5%, 15%	Nil, 5%, 10%	Nil, 5,10	Nil, 5, 10, 7.5
Organic chemicals	Nil, 5%, 15%, 20%	Nil, 5%, 15%, 10%	Nil, 5%, 10%	10, Nil, 5, 2	7.5 20, Nil, 5, 10,2
Miscellaneous chemical products	Nil, 5%, 15%, 25%	5%, Nil, 15%	5%, 15%, 20%, 10%	Nil, 5, 12.5, 15.5,	7.5,20, Nil, 10, 15
Plastic & articles thereof	Nil, 5%, 15%	Nil, 5%, 15%	Nil, 5%, 10%	5, Nil, 7.5	Nil, 5, 10
Rubber and articles thereof	3, 15%,	3%	3%	3%	3%
Pulp paper, paper boards & articles thereof	Nil, 5%	Nil, 5%	Nil, 5%	5, Nil	Nil, 5%
Primary materials of iron & steel	Nil, 5%, 15%, 25%	10%, 5%, 15%,	5%, 10%	5, 7.5	5%
Iron & non-alloy steel		"	"	"	"
Stainless steel	Nil, 5%	5%	5%, 10%	5	5%
Copper		Nil, 10%, 15%	10%		7.5
		15%	10%		7.5

(contd.)

Table 3.4 (*contd.*)

Budget Head	2003–4	2004–5	2005–6	2006–7	2007–8
Tools implements and other misc articles of base metal	25% (ch. 83)	Nil, (Ch. 82)	Nil, Nil (Ch83)	Nil, 7.5	12.5
Machinery excluding machine tools and their parts, etc.	Nil, 5%, 10%, 15%, 20%,	Nil, 5%, 20% 45% 10%	5%, Nil, 10%, 15%,	10, Nil, 5, 12.5	Nil, 5, 10
Electrical machinery	Nil, 5%, 10%, 15%	Nil, 10%, 5%, 15%	Nil, 5, 10%	Nil, 5%, 10	Nil, 5
Motor vehicles and parts thereof	20%, 25%, 60%	15%, 20%, 60	15%, 60%,	12.5, 60	2, 10, 60
Optical, photographic, cinematographic, etc.	Nil, 5%, 15%, 20%, 25%	Nil, 5%, 15%, 10%,	5, 10%, Nil, 15%	Nil, 5%, 12.5, 10,	Nil, 5, 10
Project imports	Nil, 5%, 25%,	Nil, 5%, 10%, 20%,	Nil, 5, 10	10, 5, Nil	Nil, 7.5, 5

Recommended Reforms

The role of customs duty is both of a facilitator and a regulator. Whereas it must facilitate honest importers and exporters, it also has to ensure that the laws of the country are applied strictly. Therefore, there has to be very fine balancing.

In recent years, there have been significant policy reforms and technology upgradation within CBEC. But the work of tax reforms is a never-ending process and not something that can be brought about once for all and then forgotten. The following reforms in customs duty will make the system more efficient and competitive.

Simplification of the Tariff System

There is a great need to simplify the existing tariff system. One step in this direction will be combining the basic and auxiliary rates of customs duty into one protective duty. Further, the general level of import tariffs should be reduced which will force Indian industries to become internationally competitive.

Along with rationalization of tariff rates, existing numerous exemptions and concessions should be abolished and administrative procedures relating to payment of refunds and rebates should also be simplified.

Further, it is suggested that the structure of customs duty could be regrouped into five categories of import duty—basic, CVD, special CVD, national calamity contingent duty, and education cess duties.

Administration of Customs Duty

The Central Board of Excise and Customs (CBEC) is the apex organization for forming and administrating policy with regard to customs duty. The Board consists of five members and is headed by a chairman. Members of the Board of Customs and Revenue Intelligence are two joint secretaries, two commissioners of the rank of joint secretary, four directors, seven under-secretaries, and five senior technical officers and technical officers of the rank of under-secretary. In addition to this, the wing handling the work relating to Customs in the Public Accounts Committee of Parliament (PAC paragraphs, audit paragraphs, etc.) has one commissioner (rank of joint secretary), one director, and one undersecretary (Figure 3.1).

CBEC has the following subordinate and attached offices designated for dealing with the administration of customs.

Director General of Revenue Intelligence (DGRI): It is the apex organization for anti-smuggling and intelligence work in the field of customs. It also undertakes work relating to prevention of smuggling of narcotics. It analyses and disseminates customs related intelligence to field formations. An important function of DGRI is monitoring anti-smuggling work and busting commercial fraud rackets related to the misuse of export incentive schemes.

Director General of Systems: It is the apex organization in charge of all CBEC's computerization projects. DG (systems) works in tandem with the Director General of Foreign Trade (DGFT), banks, the Airport Authority of India, and port authorities. It has developed an Electronic Data Interchange (EDI) module that helps in enforcing the tax.

Director General of Valuation: It functions in the field of customs valuation (of goods imported and exported) and advises the board on proper application of the World Trade Organization (WTO) Agreement on Customs Valuation. It builds a comprehensive valuation database for internationally traded goods and publishes price information on a day-to-day basis to detect undervaluation.

Directorate of Preventive Operations: It evaluates the effectiveness of the staff deployed in anti-smuggling work, and monitors the disposal of confiscated goods. It also studies the requirements for equipment, vehicles, vessels, and communication facilities and arranges repair work.

Director General Safeguard: This organization looks after work relating to the levy of the safeguard duty.

Director General Export Promotion: This organization attends to work relating to ensuring that there is no hindrance to an export initiative. Recently, a large part of the customs work, which was being done in the board's office, was shifted to this directorate.

In addition to these directorates, there are a number of field offices in CBEC attending to customs work mainly through commissionerates.

Steps taken to Modernize Customs Administration

For smooth and effective functioning of the customs administration, all the commissionerates have been computerized and efforts have been

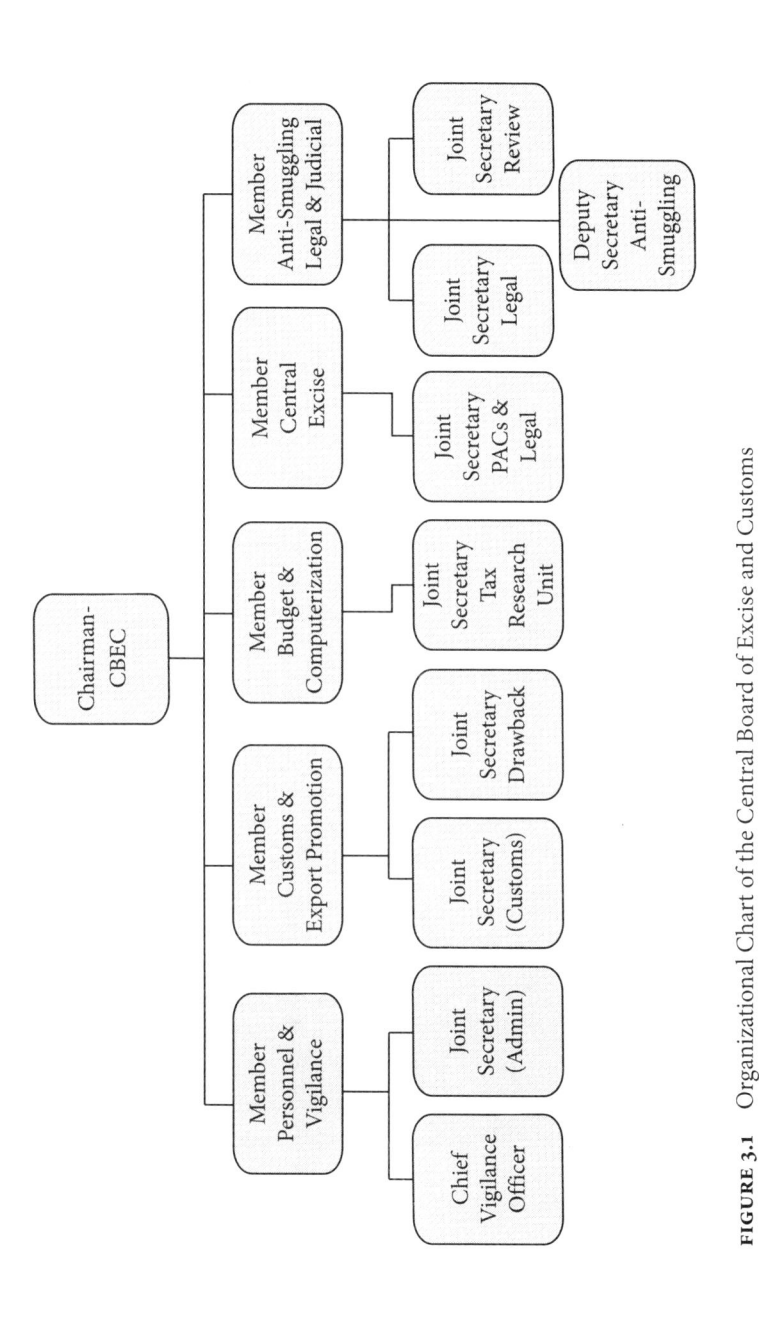

FIGURE 3.1 Organizational Chart of the Central Board of Excise and Customs
Source: Central Board of Excise and Customs, Government of India, New Delhi.

made to provide client services. In this effort most of the procedures for import and export of goods are computerized and the risk management system has been adopted.

By 2006–7, almost 96 per cent of all import documents and close to 94 per cent of all export documents had been filed electronically. Web-based cargo tracking, touch screen kiosks, and SMS-enabled services have been introduced at all major customs ports for providing regular and updated status about import and export declarations. This has significantly enhanced transparency and convenience for the trading community. Online round the clock (24×7) filing of electronic documents is done through the customs e-commerce portal, called ICEGATE (Indian Customs and Excise Gateway). There is also a document tracking system which provides updated information to taxpayers on the status of their electronically filed documents. There is a website (www.icegate.gov.in) to facilitate online filing of documents. This website also contains a helpline and online chat facility to interact with users and assist them in filing electronically. A 24-hour 'help desk' has also been set up to assist importers and exporters. The e-commerce portal also has a facility for message and data exchange with other government departments and agencies involved in customs clearance such as DGFT, banks, and custodians. The Accredited Client Programme (ACP) is operational in 16 major ICES locations. The ACP provides assured facilitation to complaint categories of clients numbering over 170. ACP ensures speedy clearance of highly-compliant clients conforming to national laws and regulations. These automation initiatives have resulted in speeding up the flow of goods while ensuring that effective controls are in place, reducing turnaround and inventory costs, and imparting a vital competitive edge to the Indian industry. There is an online payment of duty drawback, wherein the drawback amount is directly credited to the exporter's account, obviating the need for him to make a separate application for drawback. Online verification of Duty Entitlement Pass Book (DEPB) Scrips is issued to exporters.

Thus, CBEC's efforts have been to simplify and computerize procedures. In its efforts at doing this, it has successfully implemented the 'risk management system' and the ACP schemes to provide customs facilitation. It has also taken steps to facilitate trade through new land customs stations (LCSs) and to improve infrastructure at various LCSs. Also, payment of refunds and rebates is an important function of the customs department. In a competitive market, it is important that these payments are made well in time, especially for exports.

* * *

Taxes on international trade take the form of 'customs duty' on international trade. These are levied so as to have a wedge between domestic prices and the prices of imported goods and to provide a level playing field for domestic producers. The customs duty comprises import and export duties.

Export duty is levied on exports of specified goods. This is mainly levied to discourage the export of any specific commodity or to mop up the windfall export profit. Export cess is also leviable on specified articles.

On the other hand, import duty is imposed on almost all commodities imported into the country. The structure of customs duty in India has undergone major changes with the opening up of the economy. In addition, India has signed a number of RTAs with various countries. Duty concessions are extended via these agreements to the participating countries. The adoption of the policy of liberalization and an open economy also had an impact on the rate structure and brought it to comparable levels with the structure prevailing in other countries.

CHAPTER 4

UNION TAXES ON INCOME AND PROPERTY

In addition to taxation of international trade explained in an earlier chapter, the union government levies broad-based and elastic taxes on income and property. Among these corporation income tax, personal income tax, wealth tax, gift tax, and estate duty are important.

Corporation Tax

Corporation tax is a tax on the income of companies.[1] It broadly covers all incomes that accrue to companies except agricultural income.[2] The union government is empowered by the Indian Constitution to levy corporation tax by virtue of Entry 85 of the Seventh Schedule of the union list.

---

[1] A company, as defined in the Finance Act, refers either to a company registered under the Indian Companies Act, or to any association, Indian or non-Indian, whether incorporated or not, which is declared by the Central Board of Direct Taxes (CBDT) to be a company for the purposes of the Act.

[2] Article 366 of the Constitution states:
  (6) corporation tax means any tax on income, so far as that tax is payable by companies and is a tax in the case of which the following conditions are fulfilled:
    (a) that it is not chargeable in respect of agricultural income;
    (b) that no deduction in respect of the tax paid by companies is, by any enactments which may apply to the tax, authorized to be made from dividends payable by the companies to individuals;
    (c) that no provision exists for taking the tax so paid into account in computing for the purposes of Indian income tax the total income of individuals receiving such dividends, or in computing the Indian income tax payable by, or refundable to, such individuals.

Companies that are domiciled in India are taxed on their global income whereas foreign companies in India are taxed on their income within the Indian territory. Incomes that are taxable in case of foreign companies are interest earned, royalties, income from sale of capital assets located in India, income from sale of equity shares of the company, dividends earned, and fees for technical services.

In the past, some of the domestic companies that have taken advantage of the various exemptions/incentives (such as depreciation and investment allowances) given in the earlier budgets, and which were not paying any corporation tax (known as zero-tax companies) are subjected to a minimum alternate tax (MAT) since 1987–8.[3] In addition to corporation tax on the profits of companies, a dividend distribution tax (DDT) is also payable by the companies on the profits distributed as dividend to their shareholders. Thus, there exist three categories of taxes on the income of companies—corporation tax, minimum alternate tax, and dividend distribution tax.

Fiscal Significance of Corporation Tax

Corporation tax is one of the important sources of revenue for the central government. Also, it is the most buoyant tax among the direct taxes assigned to the centre. Revenue from corporation tax increased from Rs 7,853 crore in 1991–2 to Rs 36,609 crore in 2001–2, and then to Rs 244,725 crore in 2009–10 (Table 4.1 and Figure 4.1). Revenue from corporation tax increased at the rate of 21.5 per cent during the period 1991–2 to 2009–10, which was the maximum increase among the direct taxes collected by the centre. The buoyancy coefficient of corporation tax was 1.6 for 1991–2 to 2009–10. This indicates that the tax revenue was highly responsive to changes in the GDP during this period. The share of corporation tax revenue in the centre's gross tax revenue also increased from 15 per cent in 1994–5 to 19.6 per cent in 2001–2, and further to a whopping 39.19 per cent in 2009–10 (Table 4.1).

The growth in revenue from corporation tax was the combined outcome of policy changes and growth of the corporate sector. Tax reforms underway since the mid-1980s, especially from the mid-1990s, effected the compositional shift in the tax system away from excessive dependence

---

[3] MAT was withdrawn in 1990 and reintroduced in 1996–7 with modifications. For details see the section on Minimum Alternate Tax in this chapter.

Table 4.1 Trends in Revenue from Union Taxes on Income and Property

(Rs Crore)

Years	Corporation Tax	Personal Income Tax	Wealth Tax	Gift Tax
1991–2	7,853	6,731	307	8
	(11.66)	(9.99)	(0.46)	(0.01)
1992–3	8,899	7,888	468	9
	(11.92)	(10.57)	(0.63)	(0.01)
1993–4	10,060	9,123	154	5
	(13.28)	(12.04)	(0.20)	(0.01)
1994–5	13,822	12,025	105	15
	(14.98)	(13.03)	(0.11)	(0.02)
1995–6	16,487	15,592	74	11
	(14.82)	(14.02)	(0.07)	(0.01)
1996–7	18,567	18,231	78	10
	(14.31)	(14.05)	(0.06)	(0.01)
1997–8	20,016	17,097	113	9
	(14.38)	(12.28)	(0.08)	(0.01)
1998–9	24,529	20,240	162	10
	(17.06)	(14.08)	(0.11)	(0.01)
1999–2000	30,692	25,654	133	–3
	(17.87)	(14.94)	(0.08)	(–0.002)
2000–1	35,696	31,764	132	
	(18.93)	(16.84)	(0.07)	
2001–2	36,609	32,004	135	–2
	(19.57)	(17.11)	(0.07)	(–0.001)
2002–3	46,172	36,866	154	–2
	(21.35)	(17.05)	(0.07)	(–0.001)
2003–4	63,562	41,387	136	1
	(24.99)	(16.27)	(0.05)	(0.0004)
2004–5	82,680	49,268	145	2
	(27.11)	(16.16)	(0.05)	(0.001)
2005–6	1,01,277	55,985	250	2
	(27.66)	(15.29)	(0.07)	(0.001)
2006–7	1,44,318	75,093	240	4
	(30.48)	(15.86)	(0.05)	(0.001)
2007–8	1,92,911	1,02,644	340	2
	(32.52)	(17.3)	(0.06)	(0.0003)
2008–9	2,13,395	1,06,046	389	1
	(35.25)	(17.52)	(0.06)	(0.0002)

2009–10	2,44,725	1,22,475	505	1
	(39.19)	(19.61)	(0.08)	(0.0002)
2010–11 (P)	2,98,688	1,39,069	687	0
	(37.66)	(17.54)	(0.09)	0
2011–12 (RE)	3,27,680	1,66,679	1,092	0
	(36.34)	(18.49)	(0.12)	
Growth Rate	21.52	17	4	4.0*
Buoyancy	1.6	1.3	0.31	0.30*

Source: Government of India, Budget Documents, Ministry of Finance, New Delhi, various issues.
Note: P: Provisional; RE: Revised Estimate;
Growth Rate and Buoyancy are calculated for the period 1991–2 to 2009–10;
*Growth Rate and Buoyancy for gift tax are calculated for the period 1991–2 to 1998–9.

on regressive indirect taxes to direct taxes and provided for enhanced competitiveness of the Indian industry.

Rate Structure of Corporation Tax

Corporate income tax rates in India have remained quite high for a long time. The effective corporate income tax rate (including surcharge and super tax), which had been raised from around 22 per cent before the Second World War to a high of 48.4 per cent in 1945–6, rose to an all-time high of 59.13 per cent in 1979–80 after some fluctuations. The corporate income tax structure was very complex during the period 1973–4 to 1982–3. There were many rate categories for domestic companies depending on: (i) the income slab of the company (step system or graduated tax system[4]), (ii) whether the company was widely held (in which the public is interested) or closely held (in which the public is not interested), and (iii) whether or not the company was an industrial (manufacturing) company.

Currently, the corporate tax rate in India is levied on the basis of origin of company, that is, domestic or foreign company. The rate of tax on foreign companies has been kept higher than the tax rate for domestic

---

[4] A step system or a graduated tax system refers to a tax that is larger as a percentage of income for those with larger incomes. In this system, the taxpayer (individual or company) with more incomes pay a higher percentage of it in taxes.

70 HANDBOOK OF TAX SYSTEM IN INDIA

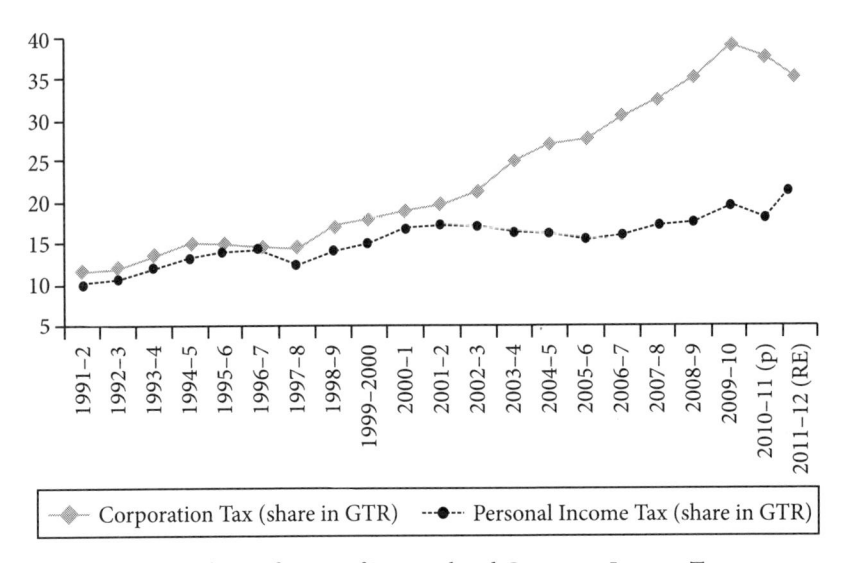

FIGURE 4.1 Fiscal Significance of Personal and Corporate Income Tax (Percentage to Gross Tax Revenue)
Source: Compiled from data from Table 4.1.

companies. This differential is maintained to recoup the potential loss on account of non-declaration of dividends in India by foreign companies. If the company is domiciled in India, the tax rate is flat at 33.21 per cent (inclusive of surcharge). Foreign companies are taxed at the rate of 40 per cent. Trends in corporation tax rates for domestic and foreign companies over a period of time are given in Table 4.2.

The corporation tax rates given in Table 4.2 are statutory rates applicable to the income of a company. The trends given in Table 4.2 indicate that statutory rates have been varying over time. While in the early 1990s, a differential treatment was meted out to 'widely held companies' (in which the public is substantially interested) and 'closely held companies' (in which the public is not substantially interested), since 1994–5, the differential tax rates have been done away with.

In addition to the tax on corporate income, there is a surcharge on the corporation tax levied at the rate of 7.5 and 2.5 per cent on domestic and foreign companies respectively. Through the budget 2013–14, the existing surcharge on domestic companies is proposed to be increased to 10 per cent and for foreign companies to 5 per cent.

To encourage investments in the desired sectors of the economy and to give equal treatment to different types of taxpayers, the Income Tax Act offers a variety of exemptions and concessions. Tax incentives are given

Table 4.2 Rates of Corporate Income Tax

(Rates in per cent)

	1993–4	1994–5	1996–7	1997–8	2002–3	2005–6	2010–11	2012–13
(A) Domestic Companies								
(i) Widely held (in which public is substantially interested)	45	40		35	35	30	30	30
(ii) Closely held (in which public is not substantially interested)	50							
Surcharge on Domestic Companies	15	15	7.5	Abolished	5	10	7.5	5
(B) Foreign Companies	65	55		48	40	40	40	40
Surcharge on Foreign Companies	Nil	Nil		Nil	5	2.5	2.5	2

Source: CBDT, Government of India.

to companies by allowing deduction of certain expenses from the tax base and also allowing accelerated depreciation allowance for calculating tax liability. Such incentives are given for new investments in infrastructure, power distribution, certain telecom services, undertakings engaged in developing or operating industrial parks or special economic zones, producing or refining of mineral oil, and companies carrying on research and development (R&D). These concessions take the form of deductions for both revenue and capital expenditure (other than land) on scientific research in the year in which these are incurred. Incentives are also given for investments in developing housing projects, undertakings in certain hill states, handling food grains, food processing, and rural hospitals. Tax breaks are also available for investments towards backward region development, small-scale industry, and environmental investment. A five-year tax holiday (100 per cent deduction on profits derived) is also given to units set up in free trade zones, software technology parks, and electronic hardware technology parks. Exemptions are also given to export-oriented undertakings.

Liberal deductions are allowed for exports and for setting up new industrial undertakings under certain circumstances. Companies enjoy certain tax incentives like a five-year 'partial' tax holiday (for new industrial undertakings including ships and hotels), lower tax on long-term capital gains, 'priority industry' allowances, provisions for accelerated depreciation, initial depreciation allowances, development allowances, development rebate, and set-off and carry forward of losses. Most of these concessions are directed at new and expanding companies in priority industries, and, taken together, they do reduce the companies' effective tax liability (Gandhi 1970).

Until 2007, tax exemptions were largely profit-linked and these were inherently inefficient and liable to be misused. In 2007, efforts were made to introduce concessions with reference to development. Therefore, in 2007 several tax incentives were introduced to promote research and development in industry, and for the development of the North-Eastern region and agriculture.

In 2009, the tax holiday, which was hitherto available with respect to profits arising from commercial production or refining of mineral oil, was extended to natural gas as well. Thus, the tax benefit was available to undertakings with respect to profits derived from the commercial production of mineral oil and natural gas from oil and gas blocks awarded under the New Exploration Licensing Policy. Therefore, in 2009, to give an incentive to certain businesses, investment-linked tax exemptions were provided. Investment-linked tax incentives were extended to businesses for setting up and operating 'cold chains'—warehousing facilities for storing agricultural produce, and to those in the business of laying and operating cross-country natural gas or crude or petroleum oil pipeline networks—for distribution on the common carrier principle. Under this method, all capital expenditure (other than expenditure on land, goodwill, and financial instruments) was fully allowed as deduction.

Effective rates: The statutory rates discussed earlier are applied to the total income of a company as shown in its profit and loss account after adjusting profit for tax concessions, exemptions, or incentives (explained earlier) available to a company under the Income Tax Act. That is, the amount of tax concessions (exemptions) is deducted from the profits (shown in the profit and loss account) to arrive at the taxable income (the base on which the tax is levied). Thus, the effective tax rate (calculated as the ratio of total taxes paid to the total profits before taxes) is much lower than the statutory tax rates and varies widely among corporations.

For example, the statutory rate of corporation tax in 2010–11 was 30 per cent for domestic companies and 40 per cent for foreign companies. Inclusion of surcharge and the education cess made the total tax rate about 33.66 per cent for domestic companies and 41.82 per cent for foreign companies. Taking into account exemptions and incentives for direct investments, the effective tax rate was about 24.10 per cent only.[5] Also, the effective tax rate for public companies was 22.28 per cent while it was 24.61 per cent for private companies.[6] Also, companies with an average effective tax rate of up to 20 per cent accounted for 39.60 per cent of the total profits before taxes; 19.97 per cent of total taxable income; and 25.53 per cent of total taxes paid. In other words, a large number of companies paid a disproportionately lower amount in taxes in relation to their profits. Only 42,087 companies, accounting for 11.45 per cent of the total profits and 18.80 per cent of the total taxes, had an effective tax rate greater than the statutory rate. Therefore, the tax liability across companies was unevenly distributed (Table 4.3).

---

[5] The effective tax rate for corporates has been gradually rising from 20.6 per cent in 2006–7 to 22.4 per cent in 2007–8 to 22.8 per cent in 2008–9 to 23.5 per cent in 2009–10 and further to 24.1 per cent in 2010–11. This was a result of gradual phasing out of profit-linked deductions and the levy of MAT on companies.

[6] This is based on a sample of 4,59,270 companies (representing 90 per cent of the total corporate returns). See, for details, Government of India (2012).

Table 4.3 Profile of Sample Companies Across the Range of Effective Tax Rate

(2010–11)

Effective Tax Rate (%)	No. of Companies	Share in Total Profits (%)	Share in Total Income (%)	Share in Total Tax Payable (%)
1. 0 or less	1,76,808	2.25	0.34	0.21
2. 0–20	69,405	39.60	19.97	25.53
3. 20–25	16,868	12.75	11.73	11.62
4. 25–30	25,652	16.73	20.00	18.97
5. 30–33.21	97,123	17.22	24.48	23.02
6. More than 33.21	42,087	11.45	19.27	18.80
7. Indeterminate	31,327	0.00	4.22	1.86
8. All Sample Companies	4,59,270	100.00	100.00	100.00

Source: Government of India (2012), Receipt Budget 2012–13, Ministry of Finance, New Delhi.
Note: The effective tax rate is inclusive of surcharge and education cess.

Minimum Alternate Tax

Owing to various concessions and exemptions given to the corporate sector, many of the companies were not paying any tax because their income, computed as per provisions of the Income Tax Act, was either insignificant or negative, although these companies had book profits as per their profit and loss account. These companies were termed as zero-tax companies.[7] To address this problem, Minimum Alternate Tax (MAT) was first introduced on 1 April 1988 through the Finance Act, 1987, by inserting section 115J in the Income Tax Act. The total income of such companies was deemed to be 30 per cent of book profit[8] (subject to certain adjustments), and was charged to tax accordingly. However, sick industrial company, or company located in backward areas entitled to exemption

---

[7] Reliance, TISCO, State Bank of India, Arvind Mill, J.K. Group, etc., were zero-rated companies.

[8] Book Profit = (income tax paid & provisions for tax) + transfer to reserve + provisions made for losses of subsidiary + dividends paid or proposed + exemption against exempt income + provision for contingent liability.

under section 80-IA, or located in Free Trade Zones, or export-oriented units, a company generating power, or in infrastructure sector, was excluded from the purview of MAT. However, the effective rate of tax on companies was 12 per cent only.

This provision of MAT remained in force for a limited period. In 1990, with the balance of payments crisis in full swing the basic corporate tax rate was raised from 40 per cent to 45 per cent and MAT was withdrawn with effect from 1 April 1990.

In 1996–7 a modified version of MAT was re-introduced on the companies which, owing to various concessions and exemptions given to the corporate sector, were not paying any tax to the government. Accordingly, where the total income of a company as computed under the Income Tax Act, after availing all eligible deductions, was less than 30 per cent of the book profit were required to pay MAT.[9] The total income of such companies was deemed to be 30 per cent of book profit (subject to certain adjustments) and was charged to tax accordingly.

MAT was modified in 1997–8 to exempt the exporters from the purview of taxation and payment under the MAT allowed to be carried forward for 5 years against assessments under the regular corporate income tax. In 1997–8, the rate of MAT was 10.50 per cent on book profits. In 2000–1, the rate of MAT was reduced to 7.5 per cent but it was extended to all companies. In 2001–2 the rate of MAT was retained at 7.5 per cent on book profits. In 2001–2 for modernization and fleet expansion of the shipping business, the amounts transferred to a reserve specified under section 33AC of the Income Tax Act 1961 were excluded from the calculations of book profits, for the purpose of determining tax-liability under the MAT. Further, in 2004–5 the income of infrastructure capital companies has been included for assessment under MAT. The rate of MAT remained unchanged in 2002–3 and 2003–4 respectively at 7.5 per cent on book profits. In 2006–7 the rate under MAT was increased from 7.5 per cent of book profits to 10 per cent. Long-term capital gains arising out of securities were included in calculating book profits. MAT paying companies were allowed the credit for MAT over 7 years instead of the 5 years allowed earlier. In 2007–8 the MAT base was widened to include the profits of STPI units and export-oriented units which enjoy a

---

[9] Reliance, TISCO, State Bank of India, Arvind Mill, J.K. Group, etc., were zero-rated companies.

tax holiday. In 2009–10 the rate of MAT was raised further to 15 per cent to improve inter-se-equity in the taxation of corporate taxpayers. In the union budget 2010–11 the rate of MAT was increased to 18 per cent to expand the tax base. In the union budget 2010–11 the rate of MAT was increased to 18 per cent to expand the tax base. In 2011–12 the rate was increased from 18 per cent to 18.5 per cent of book profits and the levy of MAT was extended to Special Economic Zones (SEZs).

Dividend Distribution Tax

In India, until 1997 dividends were taxed in the hands of the recipients (shareholders) as was the case with any other income. However, with the Finance Act, 1997, a dividend distribution tax (DDT) was levied on all domestic companies on the profits distributed as dividends.

Rate Structure of DDT

In 1997–8, DDT was levied at the rate of 10 per cent on distributed profits of companies. It was abolished in 2002, but was again reintroduced in 2003 at a higher rate of 12.5 per cent. In 2006–7 DDT was levied at the rate of 14.025 per cent on dividends distributed by the companies, payable by the companies. In 2007–8, the rate of dividend distribution tax was raised from 12.5 per cent to 15 per cent on dividends distributed by companies.

Equity-oriented funds (with more than 65 per cent of the assets invested in equities) are kept out of the tax net. Since 2005, companies operating in SEZs have been exempt from payment of DDT. Specific cases of dividends—received by a domestic holding company (with no parent company) from a subsidiary that is in turn distributed to its shareholder—are exempted from taxation since 2008–9. Thus inter-corporate dividends are exempted. This exemption is not, however, permitted one step down—that is, if the subsidiary company receives a dividend from its own subsidiary company—as it will create a reverse cascade. DDT exemption does not benefit corporate groups which have multi-layered holding structures.

The prevailing rates of taxes on income of companies, in the form of MAT and DDT for select years are given in Table 4.4.

Table 4.4 Rate of MAT and DDT in India

(Rates in per cent)

Taxes on Company Profits	1997–8	2001–2	2002–3	2003–4	2006–7	2010–11	2012–13
(I) Minimum Alternate Tax (MAT) (on book profits)	10.5	7.5	7.50*	7.5	10	18	18.5
(II) Dividend Distribution Tax	10	20	Abolished	12.5	14.025	15	15

Source: GoI, Budget Documents, various years.
Note: * In 2002–3, shipping companies were taken out of the scope of MAT.

TAX INCENTIVES

Tax incentives take the form of exemptions or deductions under corporation tax as well as under personal income tax. These take the form of business tax expenditures and social tax expenditures. However, the general incentives given under income tax (both under corporate income tax and personal income tax) can be classified under different categories.

Incentives for Industrial Development

Since the advent of planning for economic development, the government has been making concerted efforts for balanced regional growth in the country. Therefore, in addition to the exemptions, various tax incentives have been used from time to time, for encouraging industrial growth in the economy, particularly in the less developed areas of the country. Some provisions have been incorporated in the income tax structure to promote investments and capital formation in specified industries or specific areas. The effort is to give incentive to the industry to plough back its profits into the industry. However, the incentives and exemptions are continuously reviewed so as to eliminate or provide a sunset clause to those that have outlived their life. Some of the important incentives given under the Income Tax Act are:

Tax holiday to new industrial undertakings: Under section 80-IB(4) and (5) of the Income Tax Act, a tax holiday is provided for new industrial undertakings set up in industrially backward states and industrially backward districts before 31 March 2004. To provide adequate stock of hotel rooms for the Commonwealth Games 2010 and also to boost the number of convention centres, tax deduction was allowed with respect to profits and gains derived from the business of hotels and convention centres in the National Capital Territory (NCT) of Delhi and in the districts of Faridabad, Gautam Budh Nagar, Ghaziabad, and Gurgaon from financial year 2007–8. A 10-year tax holiday was provided to developers of SEZs for infrastructure, industry, and exports from 2001–2. With a view to developing backward states, 10-year tax holiday was allowed for industries in the North-Eastern states from 1999–2000. Tax holidays were also provided to undertakings in Jammu and Kashmir.

Incentives for promoting investment in infrastructure: With a view to accelerating economic growth, special emphasis has been laid on developing infrastructure. Recently, some income tax concessions have been introduced for encouraging development of infrastructure—in 2001–2 a provision was made for providing a 10-year tax holiday for core infrastructure sectors of roads, highways, waterways, water supply, irrigation, sanitation, and solid waste management systems. This could be availed of during the initial 20 years. In the case of airports, ports, inland ports, industrial parks, and generating and distributing power, which also become commercially viable only in the long run, a tax holiday of 10 years is provided to be availed of during the initial 15 years.

Similarly, to enable urban local bodies to raise funds for capital investment in urban infrastructure, exemptions were provided on interest on notified bonds issued by a notified state-pooled finance entity on behalf of the urban local bodies in 2007–8. These incentives are expected to boost investment in infrastructure and ease infrastructure bottlenecks.

With a view to creating rural infrastructure and environment friendly alternate means of transportation for bulk goods, investment-linked tax incentives have been provided by inserting a new section 35AD in the Income Tax Act in 2009–10 for the following businesses:

1. setting up and operating cold chain facilities for specified products;
2. setting up and operating warehousing facilities for storage of agricultural produce;
3. laying and operating a cross-country natural gas or crude or petroleum oil pipeline network for distribution/storage;
4. hospitals;
5. fertilizers;

6. affordable housing;
7. bee keeping and production of honey and beeswax;
8. container freight station and in land container depots; and
9. warehousing for storage of sugar.

Incentives for environmental protection: Under sections 35CCA and 35CCB of the Income Tax Act, 100 per cent tax deduction is allowed for donations to associations/institutions for carrying out rural development programmes or programmes of conservation of natural resources and afforestation. In budget 1998–9, 100 per cent tax deduction, subject to a ceiling of Rs 5 lakh, was provided to undertakings engaged in the collection or processing of biodegradable waste and for payments made to eco-friendly projects and schemes producing bacteria-induced fertilizers.

Incentives for developing the social sector: For the development of the social sector in budget 2008–9, a new sub-section (11C) was inserted in section 80–IB to grant a five-year tax holiday to hospitals located outside urban agglomerations, especially in tier 2 and tier 3 towns. Also 100 per cent tax deduction was provided for establishing and running of educational institutions, hospitals, and medical facilities in rural areas exclusively for women and children.

Recommended Reforms

Various reforms adopted since 1991 have paved the way for developing a simple, rational, and stable rate structure of corporate income tax. However, administrative reforms have lagged behind structural reforms. These need to be accelerated. Notwithstanding the reforms attempted since 1991, certain weaknesses remain in the overall structure of corporation tax. We recommend further reforms on the following lines:

Harmonization of personal income tax and corporation tax: It is desirable to have a harmonized structure for different types of taxes on income levied by the union. This will also make the rate more comparable internationally. The rate of corporation tax should not exceed the maximum marginal tax rate of personal income tax (inclusive of surcharge).

Abolition of differential tax rates between foreign and domestic companies: The tax rate for foreign companies should be reduced to the level of tax rate for domestic companies. Foreign companies' corporate income tax rate has been traditionally kept higher owing to the fact that only domestic companies are now paying DDT and foreign companies do not have to declare dividends in India. Thus, once DDT is abolished the tax rate for foreign corporate income can be aligned with that for domestic companies.

Phasing out incentives and exemptions: At present, corporation tax is riddled with tax concessions which take the form of full/partial exemptions and deductions. In spite of economic distortions caused by various tax incentives, these concessions have continued. These concessions may have been justified in an era when marginal tax rates were exorbitantly high. However, over the years, marginal corporate tax rates have been reduced substantially. Therefore, exemptions and notional deductions should be discouraged. It is important that most of the exemptions are withdrawn after their thorough review. The most effective way of overcoming these political economy problems of tax incentives is by ensuring that the incentive-granting process is transparent and has accountability. This will help expanding the tax base and also increase the average tax liability.

Change in MAT's tax base: So far the MAT is being levied on book profits (or, reported commercial profits). However, book profits are substantially lower than the 'real' profits on account of low accounting standards and unclear information system. A major shortcoming of the MAT provisions is that they are based on reported income, virtually unmindful of the prevalent practice of under-reporting. It is recommended that MAT should be equal to an aggregate of 0.75 per cent of the adjusted net worth[10] and 10 per cent of the dividends distributed.

Information about taxpayers' sources of income: According to Raja Chelliah's Interim Report of Tax Reforms Committee, 1991 (Government of India 1991), there is need for generating adequate information about taxpayers' transactions and their sources of income. This collection of information from internal and external sources, and its matching can be done only if this work is computerized.

Need to tone up the tax administration: No tax reform, rationalization or simplification can improve tax compliance unless there is a substantial improvement in public perception regarding the efficiency, technical competence, and integrity of the tax authorities to relentlessly pursue tax evaders, without political or other interference.

---

[10] Adjusted net worth for tax is the average of capital employed as on the first day and last day of the previous year.

To conclude, tax incentives on corporate investments, on the whole, appear more than adequate in the light of ever-increasing needs of the government for more revenue. The question is where does India stand in comparison with other countries in the world in terms of tax incentives and disincentives for corporate investment? With a view to making Indian Corporate Tax structure comparable to other countries, the existing complex corporate income tax laws should be rationalized and simplified.

Personal Income tax

Taxes on income in some form or the other were levied even in primitive and ancient India. References may be found in *Manusmriti* and Kautilya's *Arthashastra* (Kangle 1965).

Evolution

Manu, the ancient sage and lawgiver, stated that king should levy taxes according to *sastra*s. He advised that taxes should be related to income and should not be excessive. He laid down that traders and artisans should pay 1/5th of their profits in gold and silver, while the agriculturists were to pay 1/6th, 1/8th, and 1/10th of their produce, depending upon their circumstances. The detailed analysis given by Manu on the subject clearly shows the existence of a well-planned taxation system, even in ancient times.

Kautilya's *Arthashastra* was the first authoritative text on public finance, administration and the fiscal laws. Collection of income tax was well organized during the Mauryan Empire. Schedule of tax payment, time of payment, manner and quantity were fixed according to *Arthashastra*.

However, the first Income Tax Act in its modern form was introduced in February 1860 by James Wilson, the then first Finance Minister of British India to overcome the financial crisis following the events of 1857. The Act received the assent of the Governor General on 24 July 1860 and came into effect immediately (Pandey 2000). Initially, the government introduced it as a temporary measure of raising revenue for a period of five years. In 1886, a new Income Tax Act was passed with great improvements than the previous Acts.

In the year 1867, it was transformed into a licence tax on trade and profession. Again, in 1869, the licence tax was replaced by Income Tax, which was withdrawn in 1874. After the great famine of 1876–8, the government introduced local Acts for income tax in different provinces. With several amendments, these Acts remained in force till 1886. Thus, the period from 1860 to 1886 was a period of experiments in the context of income tax in India.

In 1918, a new Act was passed, which repealed all the previous Acts. For the first time, this Act introduced the concept of aggregating income under different heads for charging tax.

In 1921, the government constituted an All-India Income Tax Committee and, on the basis of recommendation of this committee, a new Act (Act XI of 1922) came into force. This Act was a landmark in the history of Indian Income Tax system. This Act made income tax a central subject by shifting the tax administration from the provincial governments to the central government.

Owing to a large number of amendments in the Income Tax Act, the law had become very complicated during the early post-independence period. In 1956, the government referred the Act to a Law Commission to make the Income Tax Act simpler, logical, and revenue oriented. The Law Commission submitted its report in September 1958 and, in the meantime, the Government appointed a Direct Taxes Administration Enquiry Committee to suggest the measures for minimizing the inconvenience to the assessees and prevention of tax evasion. Based on these reports, extensive reforms were initiated under the supervision of Professor Nicholas Kaldor and, in 1961, a new Act titled 'Income-tax Act, 1961' was drafted and came into force from 1 April 1962. This Act, with numerous amendments made from time to time by various Finance Acts, is currently in force.

The Existing Tax System

According to the Income Tax Act, 1961, personal income tax is a tax on the gross income of individuals (including non-residents), Hindu undivided families (HUFs), associations of persons/bodies of individuals, artificial juridical persons, local authorities, partnership firms, companies, societies and charitable/religious trusts, and cooperative societies. It broadly covers all incomes (except agricultural income[11]) that accrue to individuals and the above entities. Thus, it is a composite tax on aggregate of income from various sources including salaries, income from house property, profits and gains from business or profession, capital gains, and income from other sources.

Personal income tax is mainly of a global type and makes no discrimination between different sources of income. It has, however, some scheduler type features which differentiate between different sources of income; for example, agriculture is excluded and capital gains are taxed at a different rate (Bedi 2007).

Under Article 270(1) of the Constitution, income tax is levied and collected by the centre, and the proceeds are shareable with the states. However, under Article 271, the cess and surcharges levied on personal income tax by the union are excluded from the divisible pool. The tax is governed by the Indian Income Tax Act, 1961.

Since 1962, it has been subjected to numerous amendments by the Finance Act of each year to cope with changing scenario of India and its economy. As a matter of fact, the Income Tax Act, 1961 has been amended drastically. It has therefore become very complicated both for administration and taxpayers.

The economic crisis of 1991 led to structural tax reforms in India with main purpose of correcting the fiscal imbalance. Subsequently, the Tax Reforms Committee headed by Raja Chelliah[12] and Task Force on Direct Taxes headed by Vijay Kelkar (Government of India 2002) made several proposals for improving the income tax system. These recommendations have been implemented by the government in phases from time to time.

Fiscal Significance

Personal income tax is one of the notable sources of direct tax revenue in India. With rapid industrialization and the consequent rise in personal

---

[11] The Indian Constitution, under its union list, empowers the Parliament to levy personal income tax under Entry 82 of the Seventh Schedule. Accordingly, the Union government is authorized to levy 'taxes on income other than agricultural income'.

[12] See, Government of India (1991, 1992, 1993).

incomes, the yield from personal income tax has increased steadily over the years. More importantly, in the later years, in spite of reduction in the rate of personal income tax, the revenue has shown a significant increase due to increase in per capita incomes, growth of the economy, and better compliance.

Gross revenue collected from personal income tax increased from Rs 6,731 crore in 1991–2 to Rs 41,387 crore in 2003–4, and to Rs 1,22,475 crore in 2009–10. Its share in gross tax revenue of the centre also went up from 9.99 per cent in 1991–2 to 17.11 per cent in 2001–2. Over the years, the tax has attained a growth rate of 17 per cent per annum and a buoyancy value of 1.3 during 1991–2 to 2009–10 (Table 4.1). The percentage share of personal income tax in GDP was 1.03 per cent in 1991–2, which increased to 1.51 per cent in 2000–1, and to 1.9 per cent in 2009–10.

Rate structure

The rates of tax are an important determinant of the compliance behaviour of taxpayers and, hence, revenue collection. The rates also affect the economic behaviour of taxpayers, that is, choice between work and leisure, and choice between consumption and savings.

In India, income tax rates are prescribed by the annual Finance Acts. While a number of changes have been made from time to time in the income tax structure, both with respect to the tax base and tax rates, the tax system, in general, is based on the principle of 'ability to pay', that is, the broadest backs should bear the heaviest burdens. On the basis of this principle, certain people with low incomes are exempted from the tax. The minimum exempted income has been changing from time to time. It was Rs 40,000 in budget 1995–6, which was raised to Rs 50,000 in budget 1998–9, Rs 1,00,000 in budget 2005–6, and to Rs 1,60,000 in 2009–10. The union budget for 2012–13 enhanced the exemption limit for the general category of taxpayers to Rs 2,00,000.

In the past, personal income tax payers witnessed very high marginal tax rates. The maximum marginal tax rate (inclusive of a surcharge) was 84 per cent and 97.75 per cent respectively in fiscal years 1960–1 and 1971–2. This was subsequently reduced to 77 per cent in 1974–5, to 66 per cent in 1976–7, and to 50 per cent in 1985–6 (Aggarwal 1995). After a series of revisions, the maximum marginal rate of individual income tax was reduced to 54 per cent (including an employment surcharge of 8 per cent) from the financial year 1990–1. Consequent to the recommendations in the Interim Report of the Tax Reforms Committee, 1991 (Chelliah Committee), the marginal rate was fixed at 44.8 per cent (including surcharge) from financial year 1992–3. The maximum marginal rate of personal income tax was further reduced to 30 per cent in budget 1997–8 and this continues till date with only marginal modifications in the rate slab and minimum exemption limit.

Currently, individuals are subjected to a rate schedule comprising three rates: 10, 20, and 30 per cent with an initial exemption limit of Rs 200,000. Higher exemption limit of Rs 2,50,000 is available to senior citizens above 60 years and of Rs 5,00,000 to senior citizens above 80 years.[13]

The current personal income tax slabs are as follows:

Income up to Rs 2 lakh	nil
Income above Rs 2 lakh and up to Rs 5 lakh	10%
Income above Rs 5 lakh and up to Rs 10 lakh	20%
Income above Rs10 lakh	30%

Cesses and surcharges are additional levies for a specific purpose. Historically, surcharge on income tax was first levied in India in 1951; this continued till 1985. After that different types of cesses and surcharges were levied by the government from time to time depending on the requirements of the economy (Table 4.5).

The Finance Act, 1994, abolished surcharge from assessment year 1995–6. In 1999–2000, a surcharge of 10 per cent was levied due to the Kargil conflict. In 2000–1, an additional 2 per cent surcharge was levied on account of the Gujarat earthquake. In financial year 2009–10, the then existing surcharge of 10 per cent on personal income tax was removed.

As of now, there is an education cess of 2 per cent to provide universalized quality education, and a cess of 1 per cent for financing secondary and higher education.

Besides the basic exemption limits, the Income Tax Act allows for various types of tax exemptions/rebates/incentives. Sections 10, 10A, 10B, 11, 12, 13, and 13A of the Act describe the types of income that are completely or partially exempt from the payment of income tax. These exclusions are meant to serve various socioeconomic objectives through the medium of tax policy.

---

[13] Prior to 2012–13, women taxpayers were having a higher exemption limit. This has been discontinued with the Union Budget 2012–13.

Table 4.5 Trends in the Maximum Marginal Rate of Personal Income Tax, Cesses and Surcharges

(in per cent)

Financial Year	Marginal income tax rate	Surcharge/Cess
1990–1	50	12
1991–2	50	12
1992–3	40	12
1993–4	40	12
1994–5	40	Nil
1995–6	40	Nil
1996–7	40	Nil
1997–8	30	
1998–9	30	Nil
1999–2000	30	10
2000–1	30	10, 15* + 2% (for Gujarat earthquake)
2001–2	30	2% (for Gujarat earthquake)
2002–3	30	5
2003–4	30	10% (for income above Rs 8.5 lakh)
2004–5	30	10% (for income above Rs 8.5 lakh)
2005–6	30	2.5% (for income above Rs 10 lakh)
2006–7	30	10% (for income above Rs 10 lakh) + 2% education cess
2007–8	30	10% (for income above Rs 10 lakh) + 3% education cess
2008–9	30	10% (for income above Rs. 10 lakh) + 3% education cess
2009–10	30	Education cess of 3%
2010–11	30	Education cess of 3%
2011–12	30	5% surcharge (for income above Rs 1 crore)
2012–13	30	5% surcharge (for income above Rs 1 crore) + Education cess of 3%

Source: GoI, Budget Documents, various years.

Incomes absolutely/partially exempt: Some types of incomes that are exempted from income tax under various clauses of section 10 of the Income Tax Act, 1961 are:

1. Agricultural income [section 10(1)]
2. Receipts received by a member from a Hindu undivided family [section 10(2)]
3. Share of profits from a firm [section 10(2A)]

4. Certain income from interest received by non-residents [section 10(4)].
5. Remuneration to a foreigner and non-resident individual with respect to shooting of a cinematographic film in India [section 10(5A)].
6. Remuneration received by employees of foreign missions, foreign enterprises, foreign philanthropic institutions [section 10(6)].
7. Salaries of a foreign government employee assigned duty in any cooperative technical assistance programme [section 10(8)].
8. Death-cum-retirement gratuity up to prescribed limits [section 10(10)].
9. Scholarships granted to meet the cost of education [section 10(16)].
10. Daily allowance for Members of Parliament [section 10(17)].
11. Any amount received in connection with an award instituted by the central/state governments [section 10(17A)].

Incentives for Savings

In addition to these exemptions, certain provisions have been incorporated in the income tax structure to promote savings and make investments more attractive. These incentives are provided in three forms:

1. Exclusion of income from specified financial assets subject to certain monetary limits (sections 10(15) and 80L).
2. Deduction from income, on a netting principle, of the whole of the funds invested in the National Saving Scheme, certain schemes of the Life Insurance Corporation of India, and equity-linked savings scheme of mutual funds (sections 80-CCA and 80-CCB);
3. Rebate in tax payable as a percentage of the funds invested in specified financial assets or construction of house property (section 88).

Under section 80C of the Income Tax Act, there are certain specified investments which are eligible for tax deduction from income. These are—life insurance premium payments; contributions to the employees provident fund (EPF)/GPF; public provident fund (maximum Rs 1,00,000 in a financial year); National Saving Certificates (NSCs) including accrued interest; Unit Linked Insurance Plan (ULIP); five-year fixed deposits with banks and post offices; repayment of housing loans (principal); Senior Citizens Savings Scheme (SCSS); Equity Linked Savings Scheme (ELSS); National Pension Scheme (NPS); tuition fees including admission fees or college fees paid for full-time education of any two children of the assessee (any development fees or donation or payment of similar nature shall not be eligible for deduction); infrastructure bonds issued by institutions/banks such as IDBI; ICICI, REC, and PFC; interest accrued with respect to NSC VIII issue.

Major initiatives in the field of personal income tax were initiated in financial year 2005–6 including a general rebate on savings in any approved instrument up to Rs 1 lakh. Budget 2010–11 also proposed a deduction of an additional amount of Rs 20,000, over and above the existing limit of Rs 1 lakh on tax savings, for investments in long-term infrastructure bonds. Union budget 2011–12 proposed to extend this window for one more year. In addition, through the Union Budget of 2012–13 an incentive is given in the form of deduction of Rs 10,000 for interest from saving bank accounts. This would exempt a large section of small taxpayers with salary income up to Rs 5 lakh and interest on saving bank account up to Rs 10,000 from paying any income tax on the interest.

Taxation of Capital Gains

According to section 45 of the Income Tax Act, any profits or gains arising from the transfer of a capital asset are chargeable for tax under the head 'capital gains'. Since capital gains are not annual accruals from a given source but represent appreciation in the market value of assets over a period of time, they are treated differently. Capital gain can be categorized as short term or long term, depending on how long the investment has been under possession.

Short-term Capital Gains

According to section 2(42A) of the Income Tax Act, a capital asset held by an assessee for not more than 36 months (immediately preceding the date of its transfer) is known as a short-term capital asset. However, equity or preference shares held in a company; any other security listed in a recognized stock exchange in India; and UTI units or units of a mutual fund specified under section 10(23D) and zero coupon bonds are treated as short-term capital assets if they are held for not more than 12 months.

Short-term capital gains are taxed at normal income tax rates. Capital gains arising on the transfer of equity shares or units of mutual funds were taxed at a flat rate of 10 per cent in 2004–5 and a new tax called securities transaction tax (STT) was introduced in that year. The rate structure of STT was as follows:

(a) For those paying capital gains tax:
    (i) 0.15 per cent of value of transactions, to be split equally between buyer and seller, was payable as STT.
    (ii) For unit holders holding units in equity-oriented mutual funds, 0.15 per cent of value of transactions was payable as STT. Units were to be treated as securities or equity traded on the stock exchange.
(b) For those paying income tax on business profits:
    (i) Day traders and arbitragers were to pay 0.015 per cent of value of transactions as STT. Credit for STT was to be provided on tax on business profits.
    (ii) For derivatives traders (futures and options), 0.01 per cent of the value of transactions was payable with credit for STT against business tax on profits.

Credit for STT against corporate income tax is allowed in cases where business profits are declared on delivery-based transactions. Also, buying and selling of bonds including Government bonds is exempt from STT. Similarly, units of mutual funds other than equity-oriented funds are exempt from STT. While the rate of STT was increased in 2005–6 (by 33.33 per cent) as well as in 2006–7 (by 25 per cent), it was brought down in 2012–13 for cash delivery transactions tax by 20 per cent.

However, budget 2008–9 raised short-term capital gains under section 11A of the Income Tax Act to 15 per cent, to establish parity with dividends.

In the case of short-term capital loss, the same is allowed to be set-off only against gain from the transfer of another short-term or long-term capital asset. However, if the short-term capital loss remains unabsorbed, the same is allowed to be carried forward for set-off only against gain from the transfer of another short-term and long-term capital asset in the subsequent eight years. In other words, a short-term capital loss cannot be set off against income from salaries, house property, business or profession, or income under the head 'other sources'.

Long-term Capital Gains

If a capital asset is held for more than 36 months before selling, the gain arising from the sale is classified as a long-term capital gain. However, if the capital asset is in the nature of equity, it is categorized as a long-term capital asset if it is held for more than one year. Long-term capital gains are taxed at a flat rate independent of the global income of the taxpayer, and are computed by allowing an upward revision of the cost of assets by an inflation index. The Kelkar Task Force on Direct Taxes had recommended abolishing the long-term capital gains tax as it represents capitalization of retained earnings already taxed. Thus, during 2003–4 and 2004–5, this tax was abolished on all transactions related to securities to give a fillip to the capital market. In case of assets other than equity shares or equity mutual funds, long-term capital gain is taxed at 20 per cent. On the other hand, in the case of debt mutual funds, capital gains tax is 10 per cent if the cost of acquisition is not indexed; it is 20 per cent if the cost of acquisition is indexed.

Currently, long-term capital gains from sale of equity shares or units of mutual funds are exempt from tax. Similarly, long-term capital gains are fully exempt if the proceeds are invested in specified savings plans/schemes.

Assessment of the Existing Income Tax System

In the mid-1970s, the personal income tax system of India was in a mess. The income tax was levied at confiscatory rates, which encouraged rampant evasion and generated a parallel economy. The Wanchoo Committee (Government of India 1971) took a forthright position and pointed out that the extraordinarily high income tax rates were the principle cause of tax evasion and recommended reducing the effective top marginal rates.

The reforms of 1990s simplified the tax structure substantially, although the system still suffers from the following weaknesses:

Exemption on agricultural incomes: A glaring weakness of the Indian personal income tax system is the exclusion of agricultural income from the income tax base. Unequal treatment of similar incomes, though from different sources, violates the principle of horizontal equity. Exemption of agricultural income erodes the tax base not only because of non-taxation of agricultural income but also because it provides a loophole for evading tax by declaring non-agricultural income as agricultural income. Also, the exclusion of agricultural income provides an opportunity for tax evasion by camouflaging taxable income and black money as gains from agriculture. Thus, to prevent tax evasion and also to accomplish inter-sectoral equity in the taxation policy, the state governments must tax agricultural income.

Archaic and unstable law: The income tax law in India is pretty old. Also, there is considerable instability in the law due to amendments introduced every year. Frequent amendments related to introduction, withdrawal, and reintroduction of exemptions/concessions for various purposes have made the tax law very complex and have led to uncertainty and confusion among taxpayers and tax administrators.

Multitude of exemptions/concessions and tax incentives: At present, the Income tax Act in India is riddled with tax concessions in the form of full or partial exemptions, deductions, and tax holidays. These concessions may have been justified in an era when the marginal tax rates were exorbitantly high. It is, therefore, important to review all the exemptions/deductions/holidays so as to expand the tax base and also increase average tax liability. The plethora of exemptions/concessions in the existing system has led to complexities in the income tax law, and has obscured its evaluation particularly from the point of equity. Also, the existence of various tax incentives provides an extra challenge and burden to tax administrators in terms of verifications and related activities.

Securities transaction tax: Introduction of STT created an unjustifiable divergence in the taxation of stock market capital gains vis-à-vis capital gains tax on other assets. To ensure adequate liquidity, STT on equity derivative transactions needs to be done away with. The Indian experience has been that volumes in both cash and derivative segment on the exchanges have suffered once the STT was imposed. Those investors who trade derivatives churn their shares many times during the day. They play for smaller profits at greater frequencies. The proportion of STT as part of their profit is, therefore, quite significant.

Recommended Reforms

Reforms in direct taxes have been attempted since the beginning of 1990s. These reforms have greatly simplified the tax structure. Also, the system now fulfils the criteria of equity, economic efficiency, and administrative expediency, more closely. The following reforms should now be adopted to make the system more equitable:

Inclusion of agricultural income tax in the total income of an assessee: Equity in income taxation requires that all the incomes (in whatever form received) should be brought into the tax base and taxed uniformly. It is therefore necessary to ensure that all those having taxable income from agriculture are brought into the tax fold. If for some reasons (may be on political grounds) taxation of agriculture sector is not found feasible, the income from this sector should at least be added to the base of total income to have higher tax bracket for taxpayer. This would have higher tax liability for the persons having agriculture income as compared to another with no such income.

Reducing exemptions to broaden the base of personal income tax: The current tax structure has various types of tax concessions/exemptions. These concessions erode the tax base. It is necessary to review all the existing exemptions and bring them down to barest minimum. This would not only enhance the tax base but also narrow down the discretionary space available to tax administrators to interpret the law or execute statutes.

Improving the tax administration: The tax administration and tax laws should be made as simple as possible. Emphasis on reducing tax evasion through a combination of measures inducing voluntary compliance and a moderate single tax rate (without any tax preferences) will make the administration easy. In union budget 2012–13, a General Anti-Avoidance Rule (GAAR) has been introduced to counter tax avoidance schemes, while ensuring that it is only used in appropriate cases, by enabling a review by a GAAR panel.

Identifying defaulters and levying appropriate penalty: The system of identifying tax defaulters and punishing them needs to be enhanced considerably. The focus should not only be on under-reporters but also on non-filer potential taxpayers. Market/household surveys must be undertaken to ensure bringing in potential taxpayers under the tax net. Also, third-party information and information from other taxes (which are union excise duty, State VAT, profession tax, and stamp duty and registration fee) should be made use of to bring all potential taxpayers into tax fold. More importantly, defaulters and offenders should be appropriately penalized. The amount of penalty should be severe to discourage persons from evading the tax.

Redesigning the scheme of taxation of capital gains: The present system of taxation of capital gains has led to inequitable distribution of the tax burden among the different assessees. All capital gains can be taxed as ordinary income, with long-term gains being suitably indexed for inflation; with a single rate, 'bunching' does not cause any serious problem.

A differential treatment of income from dividend/interest and capital gains introduces opportunities for distorted arbitrage arising from different maturities and different coupons and also leads to window dressing opportunities for tax purposes. Ideally, total returns should form the basis for taxation. Moreover, certain savings instruments are more liquid than others. The resulting misalignment of the term structure of small savings instruments with market rates makes benchmarking more complex. Further, there should be few tax slabs with fairly larger ranges to minimize distortions arising out of bracket creep. Similarly, the maximum marginal tax rate should be moderate so that distortions in the economic behaviour of taxpayers and incentives to evade tax payment are minimized.

Summing up, personal income tax ensures an equitable distribution of tax burden and serves as an effective instrument for achieving the various objectives of economic policy. Revenue from this tax has been increasing steadily as a result of the increasing tax base and decline in rates. However, some structural and administrative changes are the need of the hour to make income tax more equitable and productive.

WEALTH TAX

Wealth tax is an annual tax on 'net wealth'.[14] It is levied on the aggregate capital value, in excess of the specified exemption level. It is payable every

---

[14] Net wealth here refers to the wealth of an individual or family, as the case may be, net of the expenses incurred for earning that wealth.

year on the market value of the assets held by an individual, HUFs, and companies[15], if the 'net wealth' exceeds a certain amount even if such assets do not yield any income.

Evolution of Wealth Tax

This tax was levied in India with the twin objectives of reducing inequalities and helping enforcement of income tax through cross-checks. Since ownership of wealth is the main source of economic inequalities, a tax on wealth was intended to reduce its concentration in a few hands to promote vertical equity. Thus, taxation of wealth is essentially a supplement to taxation of income as income tax does not include non-earning assets.

Following the recommendations of Professor Nicholas Kaldor, an annual tax on net wealth was introduced in India with the enactment of the Wealth Tax Act, 1957, which came into force from 1 April 1957. Till 1992, the total wealth of an assessee included property of every description, that is, movable and immovable—cash, bank balances, shares, jewellery, and other assets. However, following the recommendations of the Tax Reform Committee, 1991, and the subsequent enactment of the Finance Act, 1992, the scope of wealth tax, both in terms of base and rate, was drastically reduced.

As recommended by the committee, to encourage taxpayers to invest in productive assets such as shares, securities, bonds, bank deposits, and mutual funds, these assets were kept outside the tax purview. Thus, the basis of taxation was shifted from unproductive to productive assets. Further, given that a residential house is a universal necessity and should not be subjected to tax, the Finance Act, 1993, exempted the value of one house from the levy of wealth tax. Currently, wealth tax is payable on buildings/houses including farm houses situated within 25 km from the local limits of any municipality (subject to certain exceptions), jewellery, items made of gold, silver or other precious metals, motor cars, yachts, aircraft, urban land, and cash in hand in excess of Rs 50,000.

---

[15] Wealth tax on companies was discontinued from the assessment year 1960–1. The Finance Act, 1983, however, revived the levy of wealth tax on closely-held companies from the assessment year 1984–5. The Finance Act, 1992, extended the scope of wealth tax to all companies.

Revenue Significance

The yield from wealth tax has never been significant. Its yield was Rs 307 crore in 1991–2; contributing 0.46 per cent to the total tax revenue of the centre (Table 4.1).The revenue increased to Rs 468 crore in 1992–3 but has declined since then. Since 1996–7, the yield has shown high fluctuations. In recent years, the yield has improved marginally. The yield was Rs 145 crore in 2004–5, which increased to Rs 250 crore in 2005–6, and further to Rs 505 crore in 2009–10. Consequently, its share in the total tax revenue of the centre declined from 0.46 per cent in 1991–2 to 0.06 per cent in 2008–9 showing a growth rate of 4 per cent and a buoyancy value of 0.31 during 1991–2 to 2009–10.

Rate Structure

Unlike personal income tax, wealth tax in India is levied at a flat rate. The marginal rate of wealth tax was 8 per cent until 1975–6 but has been reduced to 2.5 per cent since 1976–7. Consequent to the recommendations of the Tax Reforms Committee, the marginal rate of wealth tax was reduced in 1992 to a flat rate of 1 per cent with a basic exemption of Rs 15 lakh. However, in 2009, the exemption limit was increased to Rs 30 lakh. No cess and surcharge is levied on wealth tax. The wealth tax liability is affected by the residence and citizenship of the assessee. For an Indian citizen who is also a resident in India, the net wealth consists of all assets in India and outside India.[16] However, if an Indian citizen is a 'non-resident', the foreign wealth is completely exempted.[17] Further, in the case of an assessee who is not a citizen of India, only his wealth in India is taxable.

Exemptions under Wealth Tax

Section 5 of the Wealth Tax Act, 1957, provides for the exemption of certain assets from wealth tax. The exempted assets were broadly divided into two categories—assets which are totally exempt and assets which enjoy only partial exemption.

---

[16] All debts present in India as well as outside India are deductible while calculating net wealth.

[17] For an Indian citizen who is also a 'resident' in India, foreign wealth is chargeable to wealth tax at half the average rate.

Assets completely exempted from wealth tax are:

1. Property held under a trust for any public, charitable, or religious purpose in India
2. Interest of the assessee in coparcenary property of any HUF of which he is a member
3. Occupation of any one building declared by the central government as the official residence of the erstwhile ruler of an Indian state
4. Recognized heirloom jewellery of an erstwhile Ruler
5. Money and the assets brought into India by a citizen of India or persons of Indian origin

In the case of partial exemption, a ceiling was prescribed and the value of the assets in excess of the prescribed limit was included in the net wealth of the assessee.

Weaknesses in the Existing System

Over time, the existing system of wealth tax has not only reduced in fiscal significance but it has also not been serving the purpose of attaining equity in the tax system. In addition, it has the following weaknesses that need to be looked into:

Shrinkage of the tax base: Prior to the enactment of the Finance Act, 1992, the term 'assets', as described in section 2(e), included both movable and immovable property such as cash, bank balances, shares, jewellery, and other assets. However, the Finance Act, 1992, significantly narrowed down the base and the basis of taxation was shifted from wealth to only unproductive assets making wealth tax an unproductive tax.

Lowering of the top marginal rate: The maximum marginal rate of wealth tax was 8 per cent till 1975–6. In the following year it was considerably reduced to 2.5 per cent. In 1985–6, it was further lowered to 2 per cent. The current rate of tax is very low, that is, at the 1 per cent level since 1992.

Cost of administration: The cost of collecting wealth tax is nearly half of the revenue collected. It is estimated that the central government is spending nearly 40 per cent of the amount collected for collecting this tax. Thus, it makes no sense to collect Rs 340 crore and spend more than Rs 100 crore in the process.

Recommended Reforms

The following reforms that could be adopted to provide an integrated direct tax system:

First, a Central Record Office for the listing and valuation of urban property on an all-India basis, as recommended by the Local Finance Enquiry Committee, 1953 should be set up. Similarly, like urban land, something analogous for rural and agricultural property is also recommended to widen the tax base. Further, an interaction with the valuation wing of the State Department of stamp duty and registration fee could also improve the base of the tax.

Second, as inflation has witnessed a steep increase in recent years, the exemption limit for wealth tax has to be raised further. Since out of the total taxpayers, barely 5 per cent come under the purview of wealth tax, including high net-worth individuals (HNIs) and companies with a narrower base, it will be prudent to rationalize the structure of the tax in such a way that both the base and the rate is increased.

Third, wealth tax is not a very important or high revenue yielding tax in India. Revenue collection from this tax has remained at miserably low levels (Rs 240 crore in 2006–7 and Rs 505 crore in 2009–10). Therefore, the system of collection of the tax should be integrated with income tax to reduce the cost of collection.

Finally, an annual tax on wealth encourages current consumption at the cost of saving and capital formation. It also leads to tax evasion as the base of the tax (value of wealth) is subject to valuation based on certain criteria. Thus, the tendency of the taxpayer is to undervalue the base and evade the tax. With a view to avoiding this tendency, the effort should be to strengthen the valuation wing in the department.

GIFT TAX

As part of the process of introducing an integrated tax structure, gift tax was incorporated in the Indian tax system on 1 April 1958 vide Gift Tax Act, 1958, as recommended by Professor Nicholas Kaldor. It is a tax levied on gifts received by individuals and HUFs during the year.

The basic objective of gift tax is to ensure that transfers of wealth which are effected during the lifetime of a person bear tax liability because a gift from one person to another provides a convenient device to avoid or reduce liability under income tax, wealth tax, and estate duty.

It was applicable to gifts made after 1 April 1957, and exceeding Rs 10,000 in a year. As per the Gift Tax Act, 1958, all gifts made in excess of the exemption limit, in the form of cash, draft, cheque, or other gifts from persons who do not have blood relations with the recipient, are taxable. The objective of this tax was to ensure that the base of tax on income and/or wealth was not eroded by transfers to one's relatives and others. However, the meagre revenue collection and high administrative cost forced the government to abolish the tax in 1998. Consequently, all gifts made on or after 1 October 1998 were exempted from the gift tax.

The Finance Act, 2004, however, revived this tax partially with certain modifications. A new provision was introduced in the Income Tax Act, 1961, under section 56(2), according to which gifts received by any individual or HUF in excess of Rs 25,000 in a year are taxable. While before 1998, the tax was levied on the donor, since 2004, it is levied on the donee.

Revenue Significance

From the inception of gift tax in 1958, revenue from this tax has never been of much significance in the central tax structure. The meagre revenue collection from this tax is evident from Table 4.1. Trends indicate that its share in the total central revenue was 0.012 per cent (share of gift tax in total central revenue) in 1991–2, which declined to 0.0002 per cent in 2009–10.

The revenue from this tax in 2004–5 was only Rs 2 crore, which increased marginally in 2006–7, but went down again in 2009–10 (Table 4.1). The fact that revenue has declined over time indicates that the tax has served its objective of curbing transfer of funds to taxpayers with low income through gifts.

Rate Structure

Prior to assessment year 1987–8, the gift tax rate structure was quite progressive, ranging from 5 per cent on the value of taxable gifts not exceeding Rs 20,000 to 75 per cent on the value of taxable gifts in excess of Rs 20 lakh. The basic exemption limit was Rs 5,000. However, from assessment year 1987–8, a flat rate of 30 per cent is applicable on gifts over and above the exemption limits. The exemption limit was Rs 10,000 from the time of inception of the tax.

The exemption limit was increased to Rs 20,000 in budget 1991–2 and to Rs 25,000 in 2004. From 1 October 2009, individuals and HUFs receiving shares or jewellery, valuable artifacts, valuable drawings, paintings or sculptures or even property valued over Rs 50,000 as gifts from non-relatives, are required to pay the tax.

Exemptions under Gift Tax

Apart from the current exemption limit of Rs 50,000 under gift tax, the following gifts are exempt from the tax:

1. Property or money received on the occasion of marriage.
2. Property or money received by way of will or inheritance.
3. Property or money received from local authorities.
4. Received from any foundation, university, or educational institution, hospital or medical institution, or any trust or institution referred to in section 10(23C).
5. Gift given by a blood relative, irrespective of the gift value.
6. Immovable properties located outside the country.
7. Gifts made by a person resident outside India out of the money standing to his credit in a non-resident (external) account maintained in India.
8. Foreign currency gift of convertible foreign exchange, remitted from overseas by a non-resident Indian (NRI) to a resident relative.
9. Foreign exchange asset gifted by an NRI to his/her relatives.
10. Special bearer bonds, 1991.
11. Saving certificates issued by the central government (notified as exempted).
12. Capital investment bonds up to Rs 10,00,000 per year.
13. Relief bonds gifted by an original subscriber.
14. Gifts of certain bonds from an NRI to his/her relatives, which are subscribed in foreign currency (specified by the central government).
15. Gifts made to the central government, any state government, or any local authority.

16. Property or money from any charitable institution registered under section 12AA.

Assessment

From the revenue angle, the yield from gift tax has not been worth the administrative efforts involved in operating it. Right from its inception, the share of gift tax has hovered around 0.05 per cent in the centre's total tax collection. In recent years, revenue collection from this tax has declined rapidly (Table 4.1). Notwithstanding the decline in the yield of the tax, it is important to keep in mind the integrated character of the tax which serves the purpose of checking evasion of personal income tax.

Proportional rate structure: Prior to assessment year 1987–8, the rate structure of gift tax was quite progressive, ranging from 5 per cent on the value of taxable gifts not exceeding Rs 20,000 to 75 per cent on the value of taxable gifts in excess of Rs 20 lakh. However, from assessment year 1987–8, the 5 per cent to 75 per cent range was abolished and was replaced by a flat rate of 30 per cent. Thus, under the present law, whether one makes a taxable gift of Rs 50,000 or Rs 50 lakh or even Rs 5 crore, the rate of tax remains the same.

Recommended Reforms

Under the present gift tax regime, gifts to a wide range of close relatives are exempt without any monetary limit. Thus, the government should consider bringing into the tax net all gifts, including those to close relatives, subject to an annual exemption limit of Rs 5 lakh. This should be a donor-based tax at a rate of 30 per cent.

Estate Duty

One of the taxes related to the income base is estate duty. This is a tax imposed on the value of the estate of the deceased at the time of its transfer to his heirs. The purpose of the tax was to curb the perpetuation of income and to deal with the problem of wealth inequalities through inheritance.

In the Indian Constitution, estate duty is split into: (i) estate duty on non-agricultural estates, and (ii) estate duty on agricultural estates. The former is allocated to the union and latter to state governments.

Estate duty was first introduced in India in 1953. The Estate Duty Act of 1953 imposed a duty on the capital value of all property passing on the death of any person on or after October 1953. Although bearing a sound social philosophy (to promote a more equitable distribution of wealth) and being least objectionable on efficiency grounds, implementation of estate duty was beset with difficult social and economic problems. The estate duty was, therefore, abolished in 1985. In 1985–6, estate duty yielded a meagre revenue of Rs 23 crore (0.08 per cent) to the total central tax collection of Rs 28,671 crore.

Administration of Taxes on Income and Property

All the taxes on income and property levied by the central government are administered by the Central Board of Direct Taxes (CBDT). On the one hand, CBDT provides essential inputs for policy and planning of direct taxes in India, and on the other hand, it is responsible for administering direct tax laws through the Income Tax Department. It is a statutory authority functioning under the Central Board of Revenue Act, 1963.

The chairman, who is also an ex-officio special secretary to Government of India, heads CBDT. In addition, CBDT comprises six members. These members are ex officio additional secretaries to the Government of India, each individually dealing with responsibilities related to income tax, legislation and computerization, revenue, personnel and vigilance, investigations, and audit and judiciary. The chairman and members are assisted by joint secretaries, directors, deputy secretaries, under secretaries, and ministerial staff in their day-to-day functions. Notwithstanding the division of functions among members, CBDT has a collective responsibility to take decisions regarding policies relating to measures for disposal of assessments, collection of taxes, prevention and detection of tax evasion and tax avoidance; and other related matters (Figure 4.2).

In addition, the CBDT chairman and every member are responsible for exercising supervisory control over definite areas of the field offices of the

Income Tax Department, known as zones. There are eight directorates as attached offices of CBDT which play a vital role by developing a positive liaison between the field formations and CBDT. Each directorate is headed by a director general of income tax. Each directorate is responsible for functions related to administration, systems, vigilance, training, legal and research aspects, business process re-engineering, intelligence, and human resource development (HRD). In addition there are three more directorates and also chief commissionerates at the field level, which are dealing individually with investigation, exemption, and international taxation. There are 18 cadre controlling chief commissioners of income tax.

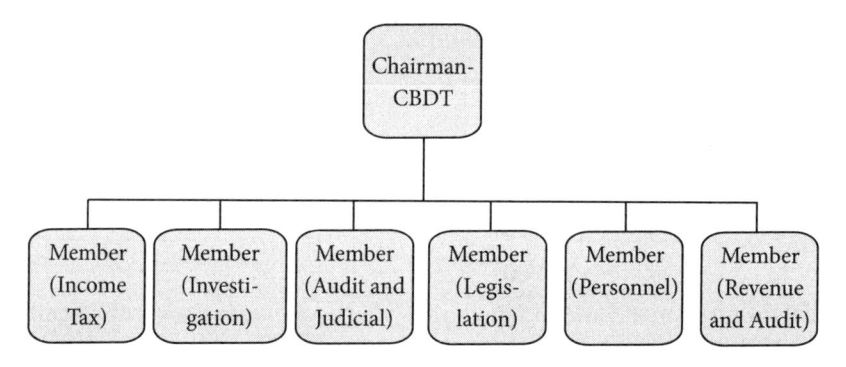

```
                    Chairman-
                      CBDT
    ┌─────────┬─────────┬─────────┬─────────┬─────────┐
  Member    Member    Member    Member    Member    Member
 (Income  (Investi- (Audit and (Legis-  (Personnel) (Revenue
   Tax)    gation)   Judicial)  lation)            and Audit)
```

FIGURE 4.2   CBDT's Organizational Chart

Recently, for better administration, the central government introduced a pilot project named 'Sevottam' in Pune, Kochi, and Chandigarh through Aayakar Seva Kendras in budget 2010–11, which will provide a single window system for registration of all applications including those for redressal of grievances as well as paper returns. This scheme will be extended to more cities in the later year.

PROCEDURES OF TAX ADMINISTRATION

Any *person*[18] having a taxable income in excess of the exemption limit is required to file a tax return. For doing so, all the taxpayers are first

---

[18] A 'person' is defined to include an individual, an HUF, a company, a firm or an association of persons, a local authority, and every artificial judicial person.

required to register with the tax department and obtain a Permanent Account Number (PAN). Payment of tax can be made only at specified branches of designated public sector banks. The system of tax collection comprises methods of: (i) tax deduction at source (TDS) in the case of salary and other payments by employer, etc., and (ii) of advance payment of tax in other cases. The income tax assessment system in India consists of 'intimation' of tax/refund on returned income (section 143(1)(a)) and 'limited scrutiny' (section 143) introduced by the Finance Act, 2002, with effect from 1 June 2002, to disallow inadmissible loss, exemption, deduction, allowance, or relief claimed in the return.

* * *

To conclude, the union government levies broad-based and elastic taxes on income and property. Among these the major taxes are corporate income tax and personal income tax; other taxes include wealth tax, gift tax, and estate duty. Corporation tax, being levied on corporate profits, is the most important source of revenue for the central government and also the most buoyant tax among the direct taxes assigned to the centre.

Tax reforms underway since the mid-1980s, especially from the 1990s, affected a compositional shift in the tax system away from excessive dependence on regressive indirect taxes to direct taxes and provided for enhanced competitiveness of the Indian industry. The growth in revenue from corporation tax is a result of an expanding tax base, increase in the number of companies, and buoyant growth of the corporate sector. Other taxes levied on company profits are MAT and DDT. Foreign companies are taxed at a higher rate of corporation tax as compared to domestic companies.

Personal income tax is a sort of composite tax on aggregate incomes from various sources such as salaries, income from house property, and other sources, with all these heads being mutually exclusive. In recent years, in spite of reduction in the rate of personal income tax, its revenue has shown a significant increase due to increase in per capita incomes, growth of the economy, and better compliance. Keeping in view the current economic slowdown and to revive consumer demand, budget 2010–11 declared an upward revision of the tax slabs keeping the marginal rate and exemption limit the same. After the reforms of the 1990s the tax structure has been substantially reformed, though personal income tax still remains studded with a multitude of tax incentives and exemptions.

Other union taxes include wealth tax, gift tax, and estate duty. While the estate duty has been abolished since 1985, other taxes contribute insignificant revenue to the central kitty.

The administration of taxes on income and property is entrusted to CBDT, which provides essential inputs for policy and planning of direct taxes in India and deals with administration of direct tax laws through the Income Tax Department.

CHAPTER 5

CENTRAL DOMESTIC TRADE TAXES

The Indian Constitution empowers the central government to impose some important domestic trade taxes. These include the union excise duty and service tax.

Union Excise Duty (CenVAT)

Union excise duty (UED) is levied on the manufacture or production of goods. The power to levy and collect excise duty emanates from Entry 84[1] in the union list (Seventh Schedule) of the Constitution. The excise duties levied and collected by the central government are called 'central excise duties' or 'union excise duties.'[2]

---

[1] Entry 84 reads as follows:
'84: Duties of excise on tobacco and other goods manufactured or produced in India except (a) alcoholic liquors for human consumption; (b) opium, Indian hemp, and other narcotic drugs and narcotics, but including medicinal and toilet preparations containing alcohol or any substance included in sub-paragraph (b) of this entry'.

[2] States levy and collect excise duties on alcoholic liquor for human consumption and on narcotic drugs, etc. Entry 51 of the state list states: '51. Duties of excise on the following goods manufactured or produced in the state and countervailing duties at the same or lower rates on similar goods manufactured or produced elsewhere in India: (a) alcoholic liquors for human consumption; (b) opium, Indian hemp and other narcotic drugs and narcotics, but not including medicinal and toilet preparations containing alcohol or any substance included in sub-paragraph (b) of this entry'. See Chapter 7 for details.

Excise as a levy, either in the shape of a tax or a toll, has been collected in India from ancient times. Excise duty on liquor and salt was levied to augment resources even during the Mauryan period. Products like sugar, cloth, leather, and dairy products were subject to excise duty during the Mughal period. The British introduced the modern excise system when in 1894 they imposed a duty at the rate of 5 per cent *ad valorem* on cotton yarn with thread counts of above 20.[3] Thereafter, the tax net was widened gradually, taking note of the recommendations of various expert committees.[4]

By 1974–5, union excise duty was levied on 124 groups of commodities. A major step was taken in the budget of 1975–6, when a residuary entry relating to 'goods not elsewhere specified' was introduced in the central excise tariff in the form of Item No. 68. With this, all commodities (except those under the state list) were brought under the purview of the union excise duty. The duty rate on residuary entry was imposed at 1 per cent *ad valorem*.

Fiscal Significance of Union Excise Duty

Union excise duty (UED) is the largest revenue provider to the central government. The yield from union excise duty was Rs 28,109.80 crore in 1991–2; it contributed 41.7 per cent to the total tax revenue of the union (Table 5.1 and Figure 5.1). The revenue increased to Rs 90,774 crore in 2003–4, and further to Rs 1,02,991 crore in 2009–10 (even though the rate of growth was a little slow in the early 1990s).

Although the total revenue from union excise duty has shown a positive trend over the years—with a growth rate of 9.05 per cent and a buoyancy of 0.71—its share in the centre's total tax revenue almost halved, from 34.45 per cent in 1997–8 to 16.49 per cent in 2009–10. This was due to the relatively higher yield from income tax and customs duty, given the structural changes and growth in the economy.

---

[3] For a more detailed discussion, see Government of India (1978).
[4] The important Committees are Government of India (1955, 1978, 1990, 1993, 2001, 2002, 2004).

Table 5.1 Trends in Revenue from Union Excise Duty and Service Tax

(Rs Crore)

Year	Union Excise Duty	Service Tax
1991–2	28,110	
	(41.73)	
1992–3	30,832	
	(41.31)	
1993–4	31,697	
	(41.85)	
1994–5	37,347	407
	(40.47)	(0.44)
1995–6	40,187	862
	(36.13)	(0.78)
1996–7	45,008	1,059
	(34.69)	(0.82)
1997–8	47,962	1,586
	(34.45)	(1.14)
1998–9	53,246	1,957
	(37.03)	(1.36)
1999–2000	61,902	2,128
	(36.04)	(1.24)
2000–1	68,526	2,613
	(36.33)	(1.39)
2001–2	72,555	3,302
	(38.79)	(1.77)
2002–3	82,310	4,122
	(38.06)	(1.91)
2003–4	90,774	7,891
	(35.69)	(3.10)
2004–5	99,125	14,200
	(32.5)	(4.66)
2005–6	1,11,226	23,055
	(30.38)	(6.30)
2006–7	1,17,613	37,598
	(24.84)	(7.94)
2007–8	1,23,611	51,301
	(20.84)	(8.65)
2008–9	1,08,613	60,941
	(17.94)	(10.07)
2009–10	1,02,991	58,422
	(16.49)	(9.35)

(*contd.*)

Table 5.1 (contd.)

Year	Union Excise Duty	Service Tax
2010–11(P)	1,37,701	71,016
	(17.36)	(8.95)
2011–12 (RE)	1,50,075	95,000
	(16.64)	(10.54)
Growth Rate	9.05	40.52
Buoyancy	0.71	2.9

Source: Various issues of Union Budget Documents.
Note: GR: Growth Rate; P: Provisional; RE: Revised Estimate;
*: Growth Rate and Buoyancy are calculated for the period 1991–2 to 2009–10;
The figures in parentheses indicate the shares of the respective taxes in the total tax revenue of the Union.

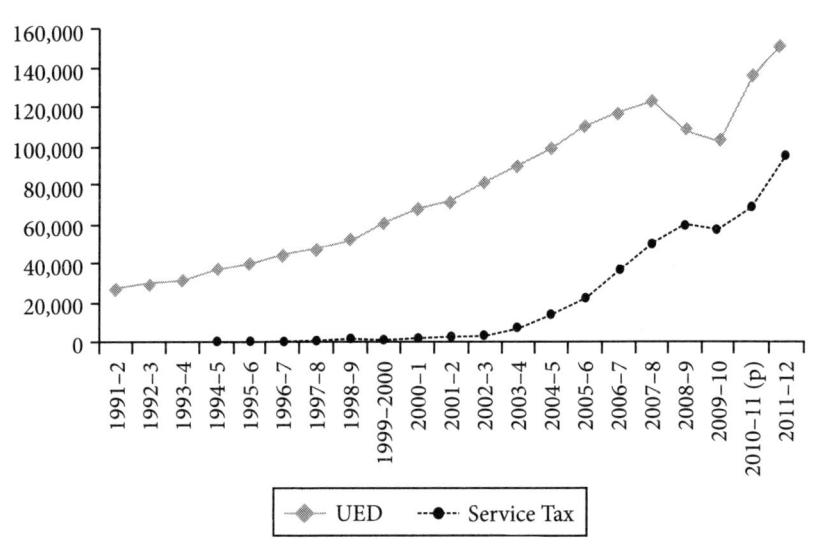

FIGURE 5.1 Trends in Revenue from Domestic Trade Taxes of Union (in Rs crore)
Source: Based on Table 5.1.

Rate Structure

The Indirect Taxes Enquiry Committee (Jha Committee) made a comprehensive study of the indirect tax structure (Government of India 1978). The committee made extremely important recommendations to enlarge the tax base and reform the tax structure. A major breakthrough was attempted by the Tax Reforms Committee (1991–3). It made the following important recommendations:

1. Excise duty should be levied at two or three rates, that is, at 10, 15, and 20 per cent. On non-essential consumption items, a higher rate of excise duty may be charged at 30, 40, or 50 per cent (this implies that the maximum rate on a commodity will not exceed 50 per cent, with a few exceptions like cigarettes).
2. The committee identified certain specific commodities on which exemption from excise duty ought to be removed. The committee recommended that a duty of 10 per cent be imposed on these items.
3. The committee recommended special dispensation for commodities that had been enjoying exemption for a long time. It recommended introduction of a simplified assessment procedure (SAP) for small-scale units whose turnover did not exceed Rs 30 lakh. A nominal duty of 2 per cent (beyond Rs 15 lakh) was also recommended for these tiny units to bring them into the tax net.
4. The committee recommended switching over to *ad valorem* rates of duties, except when it was not feasible for administrative reasons (like petroleum products, tobacco products, textiles, coffee, tea, and marble).

Taking note of the recommendations of the Chelliah Committee, steps were taken to rationalize the rate structure gradually. However, it was not possible to unify the heterogeneous duty structure with one major reform in the excise duty structure as it might have a serious impact on revenue collection. A gradual approach was, therefore, followed; each year witnessed reduction in a number of rates. Thus, reforms in the excise duty structure, that started in 1991–2, continued year after year. These also included switching over from specific rates to *ad valorem* rates in several cases. As a result, the excise duty structure, as it stood in 1995–6, comprised 11 *ad valorem* rates, ranging from 0 to 50 per cent.

In budget 1996–7, the Finance Minister spoke of a four-rate duty structure as the 'ideal' duty structure with the following composition:

1. Zero rate (to apply to 'essential' or 'sensitive' items)
2. A lower rate for goods of mass consumption
3. A single normal rate for all other normal goods
4. A higher rate for luxury items

The four-rate structure was to be put in place in three years' time. With this objective in view, the rates of excise duties were rationalized.

One startling feature of the 1996–7 budget was the imposition of basic excise duty on processed textile fabrics[5] and the extension of the modified value added tax (ModVAT) credit scheme to fabrics also. Excise duty was imposed at the rate of 5 per cent *ad valorem* on processed cotton fabrics and at the rate of 10 per cent *ad valorem* on other processed fabrics. Since grey fabrics were not yet subject to excise duty, independent processors were allowed to take ModVAT credit on their imputed value.[6] Composite mills (mills having all activities related to spinning and weaving in one place) could take ModVAT credit on an actual basis.

The process of rationalization of the rate structure resulted in the reduction of duty on several commodities—toothpaste (from 20 per cent to 10 per cent); detergents (from 30 per cent to 25 per cent); cartons, boxes, and bags made of paper and paperboard (from 20 per cent to 10 per cent); glassware produced by a semi-automatic process (from 20 per cent to 10 per cent); glassware used for table, kitchen, etc. (from 15 per cent to 10 per cent); articles of asbestos cement (from 25 per cent to 20 per cent); and ceramic articles, other than glazed tiles (from 20 per cent to 15 per cent).

It should, however, to be noted that while the rate structure was rationalized in many cases to reduce the dispersal of rates, exemption from duty was also extended to a few more items.[7] The reform process was continued in the following years, and budget 2000–1 contained the historical announcement of the convergence to the three *ad valorem* rates of 8 per cent, 16 per cent, and 24 per cent. In budget 2001–2, while the CenVAT rate of 16 per cent was maintained, the two rates of special excise duties were compressed to a single rate of 16 per cent CenVAT. This was a milestone in the reforms in the excise duty structure.[8] However, the special excise duty rates were increased from two to three rates—8 per cent,

---

[5] Till now, fabrics were subjected to only additional excise duty in lieu of sales tax. Fabrics were exempt from duty under the Central Excise Act, 1944.

[6] ModVAT credit allowed was 50 per cent of the duty payable on fabrics.

[7] The following items were earlier exempt from excise duty: vanaspati and margarine; writing and printing paper supplied to all the state textbook corporations; animal fats and oils; asbestos fibre; metallic ores; and tapioca products.

[8] In his budget speech, the Finance Minister described the achievement thus:

'Mr Speaker, Sir, in the matter of rates of duties of excise I have almost achieved the ultimate with only one basic rate of CenVAT and one rate of special excise duty. The procedures in excise have also been made modern. I can humbly claim that excise duty is now a model of value added tax up to the manufacturing stage'.

16 per cent, and 24 per cent. A moderate excise duty of 4 per cent (without CenVAT credit benefit)[9] was imposed on some of the hitherto exempted items in the hope that the rate will be increased by 4 per cent points in each subsequent year. In budget 2002–3, the special excise duty of 16 per cent on polyester filament yarn, air conditioners, tyres for replacement, and some other items was abolished. The optional rate of 4 per cent that was introduced in the previous year was increased to 8 per cent. At the same time, some more items were included in the 4 per cent category.

Textiles had mostly been kept out of the normal excise duty structure. In budget 2001–2, an option was given to weavers to pay excise duty and take advantage of the CenVAT credit scheme. A similar option was extended to the knitting sector. However, as a deviation from the normal CenVAT rate of 16 per cent, the rate of excise duty on fabrics, made-ups (home textiles), and garments was fixed at 12 per cent.

In 2002, a further boost was given to the reforms in union excise duty through the *Report on the Task Force on Indirect Taxes* (2002), popularly known as Kelkar Committee Report (Government of India 2002). This committee examined the structure of the excise system and made further recommendations on structure and procedures.

The following union budgets gradually geared the rate structure to the rates of goods and services tax (GST).[10] In budget 2003–4, the mean rate of 16 per cent CenVAT rate was still kept undisturbed but the excise duty on certain items was reduced to 8 per cent. A rate of 10 per cent was also created for certain items like garments and woven fabrics. The optional exemption on woven, crocheted or knitted fabrics was withdrawn. Major changes were made in the excise duty structure for the textile sector.

The efforts made in the preceding years to move towards a central VAT rate were recognized and the process was continued in the budget for 2004–5. It was said that 'the most important goods in the manufacturing sector must therefore bear an excise duty of 16 per cent'. Duty rates on certain items were adjusted upwards or downwards, including raising duty on iron and steel to the new rate of 12 per cent. However, the most important change made was with regard to textiles. The mandatory duty on the powerloom sector was withdrawn. Instead, an optional route was opened. This was a major departure from the immediate past. In the process, the

---

[9] The 4 per cent rate of duty was optional. A manufacturer opting for this was not allowed benefit of CenVAT credit. A manufacturer desiring to take benefit of CenVAT credit had to pay duty at the normal rate of 16 per cent.

[10] See Chapter 9 for details of steps taken towards GST.

mandatory CenVAT chain for the textile sector was abolished. Also, there was to be no mandatory duty on pure cotton, wool and silk, irrespective of whether these were in the form of fibre, yarn, fabric, or garment.

In budget 2005-6, the mean rate of 16 per cent excise duty was retained along with the lower rate of 8 per cent and a higher rate of 24 per cent. The same was true of budget 2006-7. However, in this budget, exemption from excise duty was also withdrawn and duty imposed at 8 per cent or 16 per cent. In budget 2008-9, the standard rate of excise duty was reduced from 16 per cent to 14 per cent.

The standard rate of CenVAT got reduced to 10 per cent when a reduction in duty by 4 per cent was announced by the government on 7 December 2008 as a part of the stimulus package to induce demand. When a further stimulus package was announced on 24 February 2009, the standard rate of CenVAT was reduced to 8 per cent *ad valorem*.

Budget 2010-11, however, reversed the CenVAT rate again to 10 per cent to have it at par with the tax rate of services. While the standard rate of UED remained the same, budget 2011-12 enhanced the lower rate from 4 per cent to 5 per cent.

The union budget of 2012-13 revised the standard rate upwards, from 10 per cent to 12 per cent; the lower rate, from 5 per cent to 6 per cent, and from 1 per cent to 2 per cent. However, the lower merit rate of 1 per cent for coal, fertilizers, mobile phones, and precious metal jewellery has been left unchanged.

Types of Union Excise Duties Levied

Excise duty levied and collected under section 3 of the Central Excise Act, 1944, is the most predominant excise duty. It is called Central Value Added Tax (CenVAT).[11] In addition to CenVAT, there are some variants of it that have been levied to fulfil different objectives.

However, some of the duties stand effectively 'abolished'.[12] Given below are the types of excise duties levied and collected by the union government besides the basic excise duty.

---

[11] The name CenVAT was given in 2001. It is also popularly referred to as 'basic excise duty'. See section 3 of the Central Excise Act, 1944.

[12] One such duty is special duty of excise. This duty is leviable on certain goods specified in the Second Schedule of the Central Excise Tariff Act, 1985. The goods are: certain tobacco products, pan masala, aerated waters, soft drink concentrates, special boiling point spirits including petrol, tyres and tubes, certain man-made yarns,

Additional duty under the Additional Duties of Excise (Goods of Special Importance) Act, 1957: The First Schedule to the Additional Duties of Excise (Goods of Special Importance) Act, 1957, specifies three categories of products on which additional excise duty (in lieu of sales tax) was leviable. These are sugar, certain tobacco products, and certain textile articles. However, with effect from 1 March 2006, the duty has been abolished[13] and all goods specified under the Schedule are now exempt.[14] Though the Act itself has not been repealed yet, the additional duty stands merged with CenVAT rates.

Additional duty on motor spirit (petrol): The duty was imposed on petrol by section 111 of the Finance (No. 2) Act, 1998. The duty is for use by the union and is not distributed to the states. In 1998, the duty was imposed at the rate of Re 1 per litre. It was increased to Rs 1.50 per litre by the Finance Act, 2003, and subsequently to Rs 2 per litre by the Finance Act, 2005.

Special additional excise duty on motor spirit (petrol) and high speed diesel oil: By section 147 of the Finance Act, 2002 (20 of 2002), special additional excise duty was imposed on motor spirit (petrol) and high speed diesel oil (HSD) at the rate of Rs 7 per litre on motor spirit and Rs 1 per litre on HSD. The duty was imposed in the form of a surcharge. The effective rate of special additional duty on petrol is Rs 6 per litre. However, 10 per cent ethanol-blended petrol is exempt from this special additional duty. HSD also now stands exempted from this duty.

Additional duty on HSD: In 1999, this duty was imposed at the rate of Re 1 per litre.[15] It was increased to Rs 1.50 per litre by the Finance Act, 2003, and subsequently increased to Rs 2 per litre by the Finance Act, 2005. The duty is for use by the union and is not distributed to the states.

National calamity contingent duty (NCCD) under customs duty: This duty was imposed for use by the union government. It applies to certain specified products. It was imposed by the Finance Act, 2001. The duty imposed in 2001 was increased by the Finance Act, 2005. The Finance Act, 2008 added certain other products within the scope of this levy.

---

air-conditioners, certain categories of motor vehicles, motor cars, certain lorries and trucks, and certain types of chassis. However, all goods were exempt from special duty of excise vide Notification No. 9/2006, dated 1 March 2006, and the special excise duty stands merged with the CenVAT rate for the concerned commodities. Effectively, therefore, special duty of excise is non-existent at present.

[13] Though the Act imposes the duty, for all practical purposes it has been abolished in as much as there is complete exemption granted to all goods since 1 March 2006.

[14] Vide notification No. 11/2006-CE, dated 1 March 2006.

[15] The duty was imposed under section 133 of the Finance Act, 1999 (27 of 1999).

At present, this duty is levied on pan masala, cigarettes, certain other tobacco products like cigarettes of tobacco substitutes, *hookah* or *gudaku* tobacco, smoking mixtures for pipes and tubes, *beedis, zarda,* snuff and some other tobacco products, crude petroleum, high tenacity yarn of polyesters, synthetic filament yarn of polyesters, telephones for cellular networks or other wireless networks, certain categories of motor vehicles and motor cars, and three-wheeler vehicles, certain categories of transport vehicles, lorries and trucks, scooters, motor cycles, and mopeds.

Additional duty of excise (pan masala and certain tobacco products): This duty was imposed, by way of surcharge for the union government, by the Finance Act, 2005. It applies to pan masala, tobacco, cigars, cheroots and cigarillos, cigarettes, and certain other tobacco products like smoking mixture for pipes and tubes, chewing tobacco, snuff, and cut tobacco.

Education cess: The Finance (No. 2) Act, 2004, imposed a cess called the education cess as surcharge for use by the union. This was levied to fulfil the commitment of the central government to provide finance to universalize the quality of basic education. The cess is a duty of excise and is applicable at the rate of 2 per cent on the aggregate of all duties of excise (including special duty of excise or any other duty of excise but excluding the education cess, and the secondary and higher education cess[16] on all excisable goods).

Secondary and higher education cess: The Finance Act, 2007, imposed a cess called the secondary and higher education cess. This is a surcharge for use by the union and is levied to fulfil the commitment of the central government to provide finance for secondary and higher education. The cess is applicable at the rate of 1 per cent of the aggregate of all duties of excise (including special duty of excise or any other duty of excise but excluding the education cess and the secondary and higher education cess on all excisable goods).

The above duties when paid as input duty are CenVATable (that is, CenVAT credit is available), except for additional duty on motor spirit (petrol), special additional excise duty on motor spirit (petrol) and HSD, and additional duty on HSD.

---

[16] The secondary and higher education cess was imposed by the Finance Act, 2007.

CenVAT's Structure

CenVAT rates are prescribed under the First Schedule of the Central Excise Tariff Act, 1985 (No. 5 of 1986). These rates, popularly called tariff rates,[17] are prescribed for commodities classified under chapters 1 to 96 of the First Schedule. The classification of goods under these chapters is broadly designed on the basis of the international harmonized system of classification of commodities, that is harmonized system of nomenclature (HSN).

A commodity can be levied excise duty only if it arises as a result of 'manufacture'.[18] Since excise duty falls on the activity of 'manufacture', that is, the existence of 'manufacture' is a pre-requisite for levy and collection of excise, no CenVAT rate is prescribed under chapter 1 of the Act which covers 'live animals'.

Similarly, no CenVAT rate is prescribed for 'live trees and other plants; bulbs, roots and the like; cut flowers and ornamental foliage' falling under chapter 5 of the Act. Chapter 10 of the Act, relating to cereals, also does not prescribe any excise duty as these are not 'manufactured' goods. For certain other chapters CenVAT rate is prescribed as 'Nil' as there is no intention to levy and collect excise duty on these commodities.

Principal rates of CenVAT

1. *Standard rate of 12 per cent*: For a majority of the commodities covered by the First Schedule of the Central Excise Tariff Act, 1985, CenVAT is levied as the effective duty at the rate of 12 per cent. This may be referred to as the 'standard' rate.
2. *Other rates*: Some commodities are subjected to excise duty at a lower rate of 6 per cent (see Annexure A5.1) and a few commodities are subject to excise duty at a rate higher than the standard rate of 12 per cent. However, the lower merit rate for coal, fertilisers, mobile phones, and precious metal jewellery is taxed at 1 per cent rate.

---

[17] Tariff rate may or may not be the 'effective' rate. If any goods are exempt from part or whole duty, the reduced rate becomes the effective rate of duty.

[18] The Supreme Court has held that an article does not become liable to excise duty merely because of its specification in the Schedule to the Central Excise Tariff Act unless it is saleable and known to the market. See *Commissioner of Central Excise, Chandigarh v Gurdaspur Distillery* 2008 (224) ELT 337 (SC).

Pan masala and pan masala containing tobacco (*gutka*) are not taxed according to the *ad valorem* rate.[19] With effect from 1 July 2008, these two commodities are subject to excise duty on the basis of the number of packing machines installed in the factory of production. The amount payable per machine is specified in Notification No. 42/2008-CE. The quantity of goods produced is immaterial for this purpose. In union budget 2012–13 the rate of excise duty on large cars has been raised by 27 per cent. Excise duty has been lowered in case of branded readymade garments from 4.5 per cent to 3.6 per cent. Excise duty on all processed soya food products has been reduced to the lower rate of 6 per cent. The duty has also been reduced to 6 per cent on iodine. Excise duty on matches manufactured by semi-mechanised units has been reduced from 10 per cent to 6 per cent.

Salient Exemptions in the Excise Duty Structure

The excise duty structure is replete with different kinds of exemptions. The important ones relate to small-scale industries and to some specific areas:

Exemptions for small-scale industries (SSI): The exemption is applicable for the manufacture of specified goods.[20] The exemption is applicable to units whose clearances of excisable goods for home consumption are below Rs 4.5 crore in the preceding financial year. An eligible unit can avail of exemption from excise duty on clearances up to Rs 1.5 crore in a financial year. Some notable features of the exemption scheme are:

1. If a manufacturer has more than one factory, the limit of Rs 1.5 crore applies to total clearances from all his factories.
2. If a factory is run by more than one manufacturer, the limit of exemption applies to clearances by all such manufacturers and not separately.
3. No CenVAT credit is allowed if the clearances remain within the exemption limit of Rs 1.5 crore.

---

[19] Pan masala is one commodity that has been prone to substantial evasion of excise duty. The excise department has been struggling to contain the evasion. In 2008, a new section, 3A, was introduced in the Central Excise Act, 1944, to enable the government to charge excise duty on the basis of capacity of production with respect to notified goods. Under section 3A, the government can levy excise duty on pan masala and pan masala containing tobacco (gutka) on the basis of capacity of production of the packing machines installed in the factory of production. For further details see, Pan Masala Packing Machines (Capacity determination and collection of duty) Rules, 2008.

[20] See Notification No. 8/2003CE, dated 1 March 2003.

4. The exemption does not apply to goods bearing another person's brand name or trade name.[21]

An SSI unit eligible for exemption is also allowed the option of not availing the exemption and thus, pay duty at the normal rate.

Exemptions to health sector: Full exemption from UED/CVD (Countervailing Duty) is provided in union budget 2012–13 to six specified life-saving drugs/vaccines, which are used for the treatment or prevention of ailments such as HIV/AIDS and renal cancer.

Area-based exemptions: The scheme of area-based exemptions was introduced for the first time in 1999[22] for notified areas in the North-East. The scheme was made applicable to specified commodities produced in specified areas and was intended to encourage investment in the North-East. However, the area-based exemption scheme could not remain confined to the North-East. In due course of time, the government extended this exemption scheme to Jammu and Kashmir, Uttarakhand, Himachal Pradesh, and Sikkim.

The structure of exemptions has varied and not remained uniform for all the concerned states. When the scheme was introduced in 1999, an eligible manufacturer was allowed refund of that much portion of the excise duty that was paid by him in cash (that is, other than by utilizing the CenVAT credit). Later on, for tobacco products (for which the scheme was abandoned at one stage but introduced again) manufacturers were required to utilize the amount of exemption in any of the states in the North-East for investments in plant and machinery in a manufacturing unit or for infrastructure or for civil work or for a social project.

Exemption was provided for specified goods manufactured by an eligible unit in the specified state and/or located in a specified industrial growth centre, industrial infrastructure development centre, or export promotion industrial park or industrial estate.

Full Credit Allowed Despite Exemption—A Special Feature

As has been noted earlier, in certain cases the value addition is exempt from excise duty. However, through a special dispensation, in case such a

---

[21] 'Brand name' or 'trade name' means a name or a mark, which includes symbol, monogram, label, signature, or invented word or writing which is used in relation to such specified goods for the purpose of indicating, or so as to indicate a connection in the course of trade between such specified goods and some person using such a name or mark with or without any indication of the identity of that person.

[22] See Notification No. 32/99–CE and 33/99–CE.

product is used as an input by another manufacturer, he is allowed to avail of the full credit that is equivalent to the normal amount of duty payable on such inputs.[23]

Other Exemptions

In addition to those mentioned earlier, exemptions have also been provided for certain specific goods. These exemptions may be unconditional or conditional. For example, an exemption may apply if the product is used for an intended purpose or it is an 'end use' exemption. The other exemptions can be grouped as job work related exemptions—exemption for 'captive use', exemption for cottage and village industry products, repairing work, goods exhibited in exhibition and trade fairs, technical, education and research institutes, goods produced in government factories, mines, mints, defence production, prisons, etc.; solar and other natural energy, chullahs and nuclear fuel; export-oriented exemption; goods meant for use in export goods/services; exemption for ship repair units; exemption for captive use of certain goods; and exemption for certain other specific uses or purposes. According the union budget 2012–13, full exemption is provided to hand-made matches, new and re-treaded aircraft tyres, and branded silver jewellery.

Administration of UEDs

The Central Board of Excise and Customs (CBEC), a part of the Department of Revenue under the Ministry of Finance, Government of India, is the supreme authority dealing with the tasks of forming policy concerning levy and collection of central excise duties and administrative matters relating to it. The Board is the administrative authority for its subordinate organizations, including the Central Excise Commissionerates.

Chief commissioners are the administrative heads of zones under CBEC. The commissionerate of central excise is the fulcrum of excise tax administration. The commissionerate is headed by a commissioner of

---

[23] This can be illustrated by the following example: Assume that a plastic material is produced by a factory in the notified area of Assam and the factory is eligible for exemption. Assume that the normal amount of excise duty payable on a consignment is Rs 1 lakh. Assume that the manufacturer utilizes Rs 60,000 of CenVAT credit and pays Rs 40,000 in cash to discharge the duty liability. In this case, the manufacturer will get a refund of Rs 40,000. However, the user of plastic would get a CenVAT credit of the full amount of Rs 1 lakh.

central excise; the divisions (headed by deputy/assistant commissioners) are the basic contact units dealing with day-to-day excise work (see Figure 3.1 in Chapter 3).

Zones: The country is divided into 23 zones. Each zone is headed by a chief commissioner of central excise. The zonal chief commissioner supervises over the administration of the commissionerates under his jurisdiction. He is overall in-charge of field-level activities in his zone.

Commissionerates: Each zone has certain commissionerates under its jurisdiction. A commissionerate is headed by a commissioner of central excise. The commissionerate is at the fulcrum of the field organization. There are 92 commissionerates of central excise located at different places in the country.

Divisions: A division is the third-tier level of the field organization headed by a deputy commissioner/assistant commissioner of central excise. A commissionerate has five or more divisions. Every division has 4–5 ranges which are headed by the superintendent of central excise.

Large taxpayer units (LTUs): The government has introduced a scheme of LTUs to provide comprehensive facilities with regard to assessment, tax payment liabilities and all other matters pertaining to central excise duty or service tax. The scheme applies to all the business premises of an LTU, even if they are spread out in different places. An LTU's administration is headed by the chief commissioner of central excise and all the work relating to an LTU is done centrally. The returns are also filed and processed centrally. The eligibility condition for an LTU is that in the preceding financial year it ought to have paid more than Rs 5 crore as UED or service tax. At present, the facilities of administration and assessment as LTUs are available in Bengaluru, Chennai, Delhi, and Mumbai.

Generally speaking, excise duty is payable by factories producing excisable goods. Even after independence, the excise procedures were dominated by physical control and supervision by excise officials of the factories producing excisable goods for a considerable period of time.

Currently the procedures of excise administration operate on a self-assessment basis, except in the case of cigarettes for which the superintendent or inspector assesses the duty payable before the removal of goods from the factory by the assessee.

Registration of dealers: Excise duty is collected from factories producing excisable goods. The amount of duty is assessed by the manufacturers on a self-assessment basis. For this purpose, each factory is obliged to get itself registered with the Excise Department. The assessee calculates his duty liability with reference to the value of his clearances and the effective rate of excise duty applicable.

Valuation of goods: If the goods are sold not at the factory gate but from depots, the price charged for the transaction from the depot forms the basis of assessment. The transaction value based policy has significantly reduced the number of disputes on valuation for excise assessment.

Excisable goods that require mandatory affixation of a maximum retail price (MRP) are generally assessed for excise duty under section 4A of the Central Excise Act, 1944. Under this scheme, introduced in 1995, a specified percentage of MRP is deemed to be assessable value. This policy has, by and large, put an end to disputes on interpretation of the valuation law, though sporadic protests continue on the reasonableness of the quantum of abatement with respect to certain commodities.

Payment procedure: An assessee who has paid a duty of Rs 50 lakh or more (excluding the amount paid by utilizing CenVAT credit) in the preceding financial year is required to pay the duty electronically through internet banking. However, other assessees can pay the excise duty by depositing cash in specified banks.

The excise duty is to be paid on a monthly basis. An SSI unit[24] is supposed to pay the duty by the 16th day of the next month, if obliged to pay electronically, and by the 15th day of the next month, if the payment is made non-electronically. However, non-SSI units are required to discharge their payment obligation by the 6th day of the next month, if required to pay electronically, and by the 5th day of the next month if done non-electronically.

Daily stock register: Every assessee is required to maintain proper records, on a daily basis, in a legible format indicating particulars regarding description of the goods produced or manufactured, opening balance, quantity produced or manufactured, inventory of goods, quantity removed, assessable value, the amount of duty payable, and particulars regarding the amount of duty actually paid.

Monthly return: Every non-SSI assessee is required to file a monthly return, in the prescribed format, of production and clearance of goods on a monthly basis. The return is to be filed within 10 days of the end of the month to which the return relates. However, SSI units are required to file returns on a quarterly basis, within 20 days of the close of the quarter to which the return relates.

---

[24] SSI unit here means a manufacture eligible to exemption up to Rs 1.5 crore in a financial year under Notification No. 8/2003–CE.

Adjudication and appellate procedures: Disputes often arise on interpretation of law and procedure. The excise procedures provide for adjudication of disputes by departmental officers, who adhere to the principles of natural justice while issuing adjudication orders. Officers of the rank of assistant commissioner and above, up to the rank of commissioner adjudicate cases on the basis of the powers and functions assigned to them.

The excise procedures provide for an appeal mechanism to an aggrieved party. Against an order passed by an officer below the rank of the commissioner, the appeal lies with the commissioner (appeals). The second appeal lies with the Customs, Excise, and Service Tax Appellate Tribunal (CESTAT).

Appeal against an order in original passed by the commissioner lies directly with CESTAT.

Weaknesses in the Existing System

The existing UED structure and the procedures for its administration are characterized by the following weaknesses:

Multiplicity of duties: In the first place, there are different kinds of excise duties that are levied and collected by the central government. The existence of so many excise duties clutter the tax structure and make it hugely complex in operation.

Numerous CenVAT rates: The simplicity of the structure is marred by the presence of more than one effective rate. There is no strong economic justification for a multi-tier rate structure. While the standard rate is 12 per cent, several commodities are charged excise duty at lower rates of 4 per cent and 8 per cent. This creates distortions and different lobbies exert strong pressure on the government to push commodities into the lower slab rate. The government has often claimed to be moving towards a single rate which is yet to be achieved.

Special levy on pan masala and tobacco-containing pan masala: Manufacturers of pan masala and tobacco-containing pan masala pay excise duty at the notified rate applied to the number of machines installed in the factory of production,[25] and the amount is payable irrespective of the actual production. However, in theory this kind of levy is not in conformity with a conventional VAT structure.

---

[25] See Pan Masala Packing Machines (Capacity determination and Collection of Duty) Rules, 2008.

Existence of numerous exemptions: The large number of exemptions of different kinds poses a serious challenge to the administration for detecting misuse and abuses. There are far too many products that are fully exempt from excise duty:

1. *Area-based exemptions*: Area-based exemptions made an entry into the excise structure with the objective of attracting investments in the North-Eastern states. However, in due course of time, the exemption was extended to several other states. These exemptions put a serious dent on revenue from excise duties. Some manufacturers enjoyed the benefits of exemption by simply resorting to packaging and other trivial processes; they did not contribute to any significant investments. Therefore, the government had to modify[26] the exemption scheme.
2. *SSI exemption*: Over the years, the limit of exemption for SSI units has been increased to Rs 1.5 crore, which is much higher than the threshold exemption limit generally applicable under State VAT. Thus, the higher limit for excise may not only pose adjustment problems under the GST regime but it is also prone to leakage of revenue.
3. *Optional scheme for exemptions*: Under the VAT regime, small dealers are allowed the option of either availing of exemption or registering themselves. The threshold of exemption is also relatively smaller. However, in the textile sector, the government has allowed manufacturers the option to pay excise duty on all manufactures. By and large, all manufacturers have opted to remain out of the tax net. This has tended to break the CenVAT chain. However, as part of base expansion, budget 2011–12 converted the optional levy into a mandatory levy at a unified rate of 10 per cent for branded garments or made-ups. Besides, the levy of CVD on imports (when there is no excise duty payable by a manufacturer opting

---

[26] See, for example, the following amendment that was introduced in Notification No. 32/99–CE by Notification No. 21/2007–CE: 'The exemption contained in this notification shall not apply to such goods which have been subjected to only one or more of the following processes, namely, preservation during storage, cleaning operations, packing or repacking of such goods in a unit container or labelling or re-labelling of containers, sorting, declaration or alteration of retail sale price and have not been subjected to any other process or processes amounting to manufacture in the States of Assam or Tripura or Meghalaya or Mizoram or Manipur or Nagaland or Arunachal Pradesh or Sikkim'.

for exemption) tends to provide illegitimate protection to the domestic industry.

Although the excise administration is manned by professionally trained and qualified officials, there is a lot to comment on the efficiency of the tax administration and its attitude towards problem solving and assisting assessees to comply with tax laws.

Frequency of returns: The requirement of filing monthly excise returns is in contrast to the half-yearly returns filed under VAT and the yearly returns filed under the Income Tax Act. It is believed that the monthly frequency for excise returns is not required and it does not commensurate with the additional compliance cost and paperwork for the assessees. There is no clear evidence of any additional gain that accrues as a result of this rather high frequency of filing excise returns.

Lack of an effective monitoring mechanism: There is no effective monitoring mechanism in place to check the phenomenal growth of frivolous show cause notices. It is common knowledge that a majority of the orders passed by departmental officers are not sustained in appeal before the tribunal. All out efforts are made to somehow confirm the demands even when they are not *prima facie* tenable. Extended period of limitation for raising demands is invoked as a matter of routine when there is no evidence of any necessary legal prerequisites like fraud, collusion, wilful mis-statement, or suppression of facts.

Departmental adjudication does not inspire confidence: Despite being an age old practice, the departmental adjudication of disputes does not inspire confidence of fair play and justice. Assessees often complain that the system has a revenue-biased approach even at the level of senior officers. The fact that the success rate of assessees' appeals in the tribunal is very high lends enough support to this complaint.

Recommended Reforms

Despite the fact that the current system of taxing commodities and services is quite efficient in India, certain recommendations which could be adopted to make the system more vibrant and effective include the following.

Review of exemptions: There is an urgent need for a comprehensive and meaningful review of the existing exemptions. Area-based exemptions are alien to an ideal VAT regime. These exemptions will cause problems if excise is subsumed in GST in the future.

SSI exemption limit needs to be reduced: The SSI exemption limit, which is presently Rs 1.5 crore, is much higher than the threshold for small dealers under state VAT. The limit needs to be reduced for expanding the tax base.

Introduction of quarterly returns: The present system of monthly returns may be replaced by quarterly returns, if not half-yearly returns. This is not likely to pose any risk to revenue.

Training the officers: The officers of the Central Excise Department need to be trained more appropriately to change their mindset and for them to shun a revenue-biased approach. Their actions and decisions should inspire confidence among the assessees. They ought to realize that confirming patently wrong and untenable demands, merely to pretend to safeguard revenue interests, only adds to compliance costs and unproductive work, which, in turn, hampers growth of the economy. It is believed that departmental officers tend to be unduly revenue-biased only to save their skin and pass the buck to the next appellate authority.

The administration needs to do something to remove fear and apprehension among the officers which seem to have firmly set in now. Each commissioner and additional commissioner should be asked to sit in the tribunal for 15 days and watch the court proceedings. This will expose them to the type of queries that come from the benches in the context of the quality of orders passed and the manner in which they are passed as they are subjected to critical scrutiny during the course of these proceedings. This type of training and exposure will help in enhancing their skills in the matter of adjudicating disputes and realizing the responsibility given to them and expected of them to take just and fair decisions.

Effective role by zonal members: Improving the efficiency of the tax administration should start from the top. Each member of the CBEC is assigned some zones and they need to play an effective role in monitoring the performance of each zone under their jurisdiction. As an institutional arrangement, a zonal member should issue a formal performance report that analyses the quality of decisions and disposal of cases, the average time taken in the adjudication of cases, the quality of responses to queries from the trade, etc. A zonal member should also play a proactive role in getting clarifications issued by the Board on technical issues referred to it by the chief commissioners/commissioners under his zones.

Fixing accountability: As there is no accountability for inefficiencies, delays, and patently wrong decisions, the officers tend to be negligent, indifferent, and casual. A suitable mechanism should be set in place to hold erring officials accountable.

Client services: An issue of paramount importance in the VAT regime pertains to the provision of adequate client services. These services not only increase voluntary compliance but also help in reducing dealers' interaction with the department. Experience suggests that provision of these services makes honest taxpayers, who do not know how to comply, fulfil their obligations without delay.

Taxation of Services

The taxation of services in India is a recent phenomenon. It was introduced in July 1994, at the rate of 5 per cent on three services—services relating to general insurance, telephone service, and service provided by stock-brokers. Since then their scope was considerably enhanced and 116 services were being taxed at the rate of 10 per cent by April 2011.

Until 1994 (when service tax was introduced), there was no specific entry in the Seventh Schedule of the Constitution of India; the tax was not assigned to any of the governments. The Parliament's power to levy tax on services was considered to emanate from the Residuary Entry.[27] Subsequently, the Constitution was amended and Article 268A was inserted to provide for levy of service tax by the union government. Article 268A enables the Parliament to make a law for the collection and appropriation of service tax by the states as well.[28] A specific entry for

---

[27] Entry 97 of the union list, which states that 'Any other matter not enumerated in List II or list III including any tax not mentioned in either of those Lists', is treated as a residuary entry.

[28] This was inserted vide the Constitution (88th Amendment) Act, 2003.
The inserted Article 268A reads as:
'Service tax levied by Union and collected and appropriated by the Union and the States
(1) Taxes on services shall be levied by the Government of India and such tax shall be collected and appropriated by the Government of India and the States in the manner provided in clause (2).
(2) The proceeds in any financial year of any such tax levied in accordance with the provisions of clause (1) shall be
   (a) collected by the Government of India and the States;
   (b) appropriated by the Government of India and the States in accordance with such principles of collection and appropriation as may be formulated by Parliament by law.'

taxing services, namely, Entry 92C was also inserted in List I.[29] With the authority drawn from the amendments to the Constitution, the tax base was gradually expanded. The tax on services in India was introduced by the *Interim Report of the Tax Reforms Committee, 1991* (Chelliah Committee) (Government of India 1991). Later, several expert groups and committees contributed to the evolution of service tax in India. Specifically, the *Report of the Fiscal Responsibility and Budget Management Act* (Government of India 2004a) and the *Report of the Expert Group on Services* (Government of India 2001a), recommended a 'general and comprehensive tax to cover all services with a small and clearly defined exemption list'. The group identified services that could be put in the 'negative list' and the services that deserve to be exempt from levy of service tax. The group also favoured eventual integration of CenVAT with service tax, both goods and services being charged at a uniform rate.

The *Report of the Advisory Group* set up by the Planning Commission (Government of India 2001b) recommended that the central government should allow the states to levy tax on all services other than financial services (including all insurance services), telecommunications, postal telecommunications, and transportation of goods and passengers by air, sea, and rail.

Fiscal Significance of Service Tax

Commencing the levy of this tax in 1994–5 to mop up resources, the yield from service tax has been increasing year after year. Its yield increased from a paltry sum of Rs 407 crore in 1994–5 to Rs 3,302 crore in 2001–2, and to Rs 58,422 crore in 2009–10 (Table 5.1); exhibiting a growth rate of 40.52 per cent per annum during 1994–5 to 2009–10. This resulted in an increase in the share of service tax revenue in the centre's gross tax revenue from 0.44 per cent in 1994–5, to 1.77 per cent in 2001–2, and to 9.35 per cent in 2009–10. Service tax revenue as a percentage of GDP also showed an upward trend. It went up from 0.04 per cent in 1994–5, to 0.12 per cent in 2000–1, and to 0.90 per cent in 2009–10.

---

[29] The Entry reads as: '92C. Taxes on services'.

Structure of Service Tax in India

Unlike the structure of UEDs, all taxable services are taxed at the same rate. At the time of its introduction in 1994, the tax was levied on a few select services at a modest rate of 5 per cent. Gradually, the tax rate was increased to 12 per cent. However, the rate of service tax was reduced from 12 per cent to 10 per cent in February 2009 and again raised to 12 per cent from 1 July 2012, which is the current rate of tax. If one takes education cess and secondary and higher education cess into consideration, the effective tax burden of service tax would be equal to 15.6 per cent.

While taxing services, it was a cascade type turnover tax until 2002; there was no mechanism devised to allow for credit of tax paid on services used as inputs. For the first time, in August 2002, credit for service tax paid on an input service was introduced,[30] provided the input service and output service fell in the same category (that is, they were part of the same sub-clause of clause (90) of section 65 of the Finance Act, 1994) of taxable services.[31] In the following year, the credit rules were amended to remove the restriction of input service and output service falling in the same 'category' of services. However, a substantial liberalization in the credit scheme was introduced in September 2004; the CenVAT credit scheme and service tax credit schemes were merged into one scheme. The

---

[30] Service Tax Credit Rules, 2002, vide Notification No. 14/2002-ST, dated 1 August 2002, effective from 16 August 2002.

[31] The following illustrations clarify this:
(1) A photography studio in course of providing photography services avails the service of processing labs for developing and processing exposed films and printing photographs. In this case, both the service provided by the colour lab to the photography studio and by the photography studio to a customer fall in the same category of service, that is, photography service. Therefore, the photography studio is entitled to take credit for service tax paid by the processing lab.
(2) An advertising agency may avail of the services of a photography studio and/or a sound recording studio and/or a video tape production agency during the course of rendering services to its clients. Services provided by the photography studio or the sound recording studio or the video tape production agency, as the case may be, does not fall in the category of services provided by the advertising agency. Therefore, the advertising agency is not entitled to take credit for the service tax paid by a photography studio or a sound recording studio or a video tape production agency.

CenVAT Credit Rules, 2004,[32] thus provided for credit for the tax paid on input services used in providing output services or when used for the manufacture of excisable goods. The definition of input service[33] is wide enough and includes services used in relation to business such as accounting, financing, and modernization of factories.

Taxation on import of services was introduced in 2006. For this purpose, taxable services are categorized into three categories. The import of a taxable service is determined by rules called the Taxation of Services (Provided from Outside India and Received in India) Rules, 2006. The implementation of the tax on import of services has given rise to some disputes. Field officers as well as taxpayers lack clarity on imported services in the absence of a simplified scheme of rules.

Export of individual services is determined by Export of Service Rules, 2005. Taxable services are categorized into three categories. Disputes have arisen in individual cases with regard to whether the service can be said to have been exported out of India or not. The fulfilment of the condition 'used outside India' as a qualification for export have caused a significant amount of confusion. However, in 2009, the Ministry of Finance has come out with a clarification (vide Circular No. 111/5/2009-ST), explaining that if a transaction establishes that the service is exported to another country then there will be no service tax on the transaction.

Prior to 2012, taxation of services was based on a positive list of taxable services. This means that a list of taxable services was notified in the budget or by the department for taxing them. The rest of the services were exempt from taxation. With effect from 1 July 2012, taxation of services is based on a negative list, that is, all services would be taxed except those in

---

[32] Vide CenVAT Credit Rules, 2004 [Notification No. 23/2004-CE (NT), dated 10 September 2004].

[33] 'Input service' means any service-
  (i) used by a provider of taxable service for providing an output service; or
  (ii) used by a manufacturer, whether directly or indirectly, in or in relation to the manufacture of final products and clearance of final products up to the place of removal, and includes services used in relation to setting up, modernization, renovation or repairs of a factory, premises of provider of output services or an office relating to such factory or premises, advertisements or sales promotion, market research, storage up to the place of removal, procurement of inputs, activities relating to business such as accounting, auditing, financing, recruitment, and quality control, coaching and training, computer networking, credit rating, share registry, and security, inward transportation of inputs or capital goods and outward transportation up to the place of removal.

the negative list (as given in Annexure A5.2). This list comprises 38 heads, keeping in view the federal nature of Indian polity, the best international practices, and socio-economic requirements.

The important inclusions in the negative list are all services provided by government or local authorities, except a selected number of specified services where they compete with the private sector. The list also includes pre-school and school education, recognised education at higher levels and approved vocational education, renting of residential dwellings, entertainment and amusement services, and a large part of public transportation including inland waterways, urban railways, and metered cabs. All service related to agriculture and animal husbandry are included in the list.

In addition to negative list, a list of exemptions of 10 services is included by way of the service tax law. These include healthcare services, car services, services provided by charities, religious persons, sportspersons, performing artists in folk and classical arts, individual advocates providing services to non-business entities, independent journalists, and services by way of animal care or car parking. The services of business facilitators and correspondents to banks and insurance companies are also included in the exempted list. Construction services relating to specified infrastructure, canals, irrigation works, post-harvest infrastructure, residential dwelling, and low-cost mass housing under the Scheme of Affordable Housing in Partnership are included in the exemptions. The cinema industry is exempted from service tax on copyrights relating to recording of cinematographic films.

Administration of Service Tax

Service tax is administered by the Central Board of Excise and Customs (CBEC) through commissionerates of central excise (as discussed in the section on union excise duties). CBEC looks after forming policies and procedures and also oversees the implementation and administration of service tax. It also issues circulars to clarify doubts on issues relating to service tax law and procedures. However, in six metropolitan cities (Mumbai, Chennai, Kolkata, Delhi, Bengaluru, and Ahmedabad) commissionerates have been created exclusively for service tax administration.

In general, the commissionerates are grouped into zones and each zone is headed by a chief commissioner of central excise. The commissioner of service tax is the head of the department. A deputy commissioner or assistant commissioner is in charge of the service tax division dealing with day-to-day administration.

Particulars of service tax assessees, their profiles, statistics of service tax collection, etc., are maintained in the division through the concerned superintendent of central excise (in charge of service tax).

The procedures for the administration of service tax are mainly contained in the Service Tax Rules, 1994. These include procedures of registration, the manner of payment of service tax, and procedure and periodicity of filing returns.

Registration: A service provider is required to obtain registration from the department by applying for it in the prescribed format. The department is required to issue the registration within seven days of the receipt of the application, failing which the registration applied for is deemed to have been granted. Business firms operating at more than one place have the option of applying for centralized registration at the place where common billing or accounting is done.

In certain cases, the receiver is liable to pay service tax under the reverse charge mechanism.[34] For instance, when a person receives a taxable service from outside India, the person receiving the service is liable to pay service tax as if he is a provider of a taxable service.

If a manufacturer of final products or provider of output services receives invoices towards purchase of input services centrally, then he is allowed to distribute the CenVAT credit with respect to the service tax obtained on input service to its manufacturing units or units providing output services. Such a manufacturer/service provider is called an 'input service distributor'.[35] An input service distributor who intends to distribute the service tax credit is also required to get a registration. Also, a service provider whose aggregate value of taxable services exceeds Rs 9 lakh in a financial year is required to obtain registration.

Payment of service tax: The liability to pay service tax is calculated with reference to the amount of payments actually received by an assessee and not with reference to the bills/invoices raised for the service provided during the month/quarter.

If an assessee is liable to pay service tax, as an individual or proprietary firm or partnership firm, then the tax is to be paid on a quarterly basis. The other assessees are required to pay the service tax on a monthly basis. The tax is to be paid by the 5th day of the quarter/month, which is immediately

---

[34] A typical example is the 'import' of a service into India.
[35] For details, see rule 7 of the CenVAT Credit Rules, 2004.

following the quarter/month in which payments have been received towards the value of taxable services. If the tax is being paid electronically, then it can be paid by the 6th day of the end of the quarter or month, as the case may be.

However, for the month or quarter ending in March, the service tax liability is required to be paid by the 31st day of March.[36] If an assessee discovers that he has paid any amount in excess of the liability actually due, he is allowed to adjust for this excess amount on his own against his service tax liability for the succeeding month or quarter.

This facility is allowed subject to the condition that the excess amount paid is on account of reasons not involving interpretation of law, taxability, classification, valuation or applicability of any exemption notification; in normal course, excess amount up to a limit of Rs 1 lakh for a relevant month or quarter, as the case may be, is allowed to be adjusted.

However, if an assessee has obtained central registration and the excess amount is on account of delayed receipt of details of payments for taxable services from individual offices/branches, then the excess amount is allowed to be adjusted without any monetary limit. For example, a bank obtains central registration of its regional office in Mumbai for the service provided by its different branches. The bank pays service tax on a monthly basis. It may take time for the regional office to get all the monthly details of receipts of payment for the taxable services from all its branches.

In the meanwhile, the bank pays the service tax on an estimate basis. If the estimated service tax paid is in excess of the actual liability for the month, the excess can be adjusted in the subsequent month. The details and reasons of such adjustment are intimated to the jurisdictional superintendent of central excise within a period of 15 days from the date of such adjustment.

Mode of payment of service tax: In normal course, a taxpayer is required to pay his tax liability through TR-6 challan in a bank. However, if an assessee has paid service tax of Rs 50 lakh or above in the preceding financial year or has already paid service tax of Rs 50 lakh in the current financial year, he is required to deposit the service tax liability electronically through internet banking. The amount of 'Rs 50 lakh' refers to payment by cash plus payment through CenVAT credit.[37]

---

[36] Assume that a dry cleaner, who pays service tax on quarterly basis, receives certain value of taxable service in the quarter ending March 2008 and assume that he is liable to pay an amount of Rs 10,000 on such receipts. In this case, the dry cleaner is required to pay Rs 10,000 as service tax by 31 March 2008.

[37] See rule 6(2) of the Service Tax Rules.

Returns: Every assessee is required to file half-yearly returns in the prescribed form, called ST-3. The return is to be filed by the 25th day of the month following the particular half year. However, if the assessee notices any mistake or omission in the return already submitted, he can file a revised return within a period of 90 days from the date of submission of the original return.

If an assessee does not submit the return by the prescribed date, he is required to submit it on payment of a late fee, which is a pre-determined amount, ranging between Rs 500 and Rs 2,000.

Recovery, interest, and penalties: The service tax provisions emphasize on voluntary compliance on the part of taxpayers. The procedures require a taxpayer to determine the classification of the taxable service provided by him, to determine the value of his taxable service, and to assess the amount of tax payable on a voluntary basis. In normal course, reliance is placed on his self-assessment and the return is accepted.

However, the law provides for recovery of service tax if not paid or short paid by a taxpayer or if any amount has been erroneously refunded.

The service tax provisions also provide for penal consequences on default in the payment of tax. If a person fails to pay service tax by the due date, he is liable to pay a penalty which shall not be less than Rs 200 per day of defaulted payment or at the rate of 2 per cent of such a tax per month, whichever is higher, starting from the first day after the due date till the date of actual payment of the outstanding amount of service tax. However, the total amount of penalty payable shall not exceed the service tax payable.[38]

Similarly, an amount of service tax not paid or short paid or any refund erroneously made is liable to be paid with interest. If any service tax is found due from an assessee and recoverable from him, recovery proceedings are initiated by issuing a show cause notice. In addition to the service tax to be paid, the assessee is also liable to pay interest calculated for the period of delay and till the short payment is made good. Currently, the rate of interest fixed is 13 per cent. If an assessee pays the service tax but a

---

[38] Illustration:

Suppose X, an assessee, fails to pay service tax of Rs 10 lakh payable by 5 March. X pays the amount on 15 March. The default continues for 10 days. The penalty payable by X is computed as:

2 per cent of the amount of default for 10 days = 2 × 10,00,000 × 10/31 × 100 = Rs 6,451.61.

Penalty calculated @ Rs 200 per day for 10 days = Rs 2,000.

Penalty liable to be paid is Rs 6,452.

demand for short payment arises on account of any interpretation of law or error in calculation, action for recovery of short payment can be taken within a period of one year from the 'relevant date'.

However, if the short levy, non-levy, or erroneous refund has arisen on account of fraud, collusion, wilful mis-statement, suppression of facts, or contravention of any provisions of law with intent to evade payment of service tax, then the demand can be raised for a longer period of five years.

Appeals and Remedies: If an assessee feels aggrieved by an order passed as an adjudication order by any officer, he has the right to appeal against such an order. Appeal against an adjudication order passed by an officer below the rank of commissioner lies with the commissioner (appeals). However, an appeal against an adjudication order passed by the commissioner lies with CESTAT, which is also called the tribunal.

Advance Ruling: This refers to determination by the authority, of a question of law or fact specified in the application regarding the liability to pay service tax in relation to a service proposed to be provided by the applicant. An advance ruling enables a non-resident to plan his business in relation to the service proposed to be provided by him. Chapter VA of the Finance Act, 1994, provides for the mechanism of advance ruling for the benefit of non-residents proposing to provide a taxable service in India, either on their own or through collaboration or joint ventures.

Weaknesses in the Existing Tax System

The description of service tax, given in brief in the preceding section, puts light on certain weaknesses:

Organizational weaknesses: Over the years, the administration of service tax has resulted in a large number of disputes and litigations. In many cases, tax officials are reluctant and rather indifferent to providing guidelines and taking decisions. Even the attitude of senior officials does not inspire confidence among taxpayers. Generally speaking, at the ground level, the response to an assessee's queries and references is completely unsatisfactory.

Flaw in the definition of input services: Credit schemes relating to excisable goods and taxable services were merged in 2004 and codified as CenVAT Credit Rules, 2004. Theoretically, the composite scheme promises to relieve the cascading effect of the duties paid on excisable inputs and the service tax paid on input services to manufacturers of excisable goods as also service tax assessees. However, the actual implementation is flawed partly by the inadequacy of the legal text and partly by the Revenue-biased approach of the officials at the ground level. Unfortunately, policy intervention to put an end to doubts, disputes, and controversies has been insufficient and certainly not timely. The definition of 'input service' in the CenVAT Credit Rules, 2004, has been afflicted by the legacy of the definition of 'input' under the ModVAT scheme. The definition of 'input service' in the CenVAT Credit Rules, 2004, is linked with its use in the manufacture of excisable goods or in providing an output service. To that extent its scope has to be examined and determined in each situation. This has led to a number of disputes and litigations.

Recommended Reforms

Despite the fact that the current system of taxing services is quite efficient in terms of revenue generation, the following suggestions can be adopted to make the system more vibrant and effective.

Make credit available upfront on services used as inputs: The definition of 'input service' requires a comprehensive review. Since VAT implies the removal of the cascading effect of taxes and duties paid on the inputs used, the definition of input service needs to sub-serve this objective. In other words, there seems to be a good case for providing credit for the tax paid on all services that are used for business purposes by a manufacturer of excisable goods or provider of services. The only exception ought to be for services used for private use. In other words, CenVAT credit should be allowed upfront for all services used by a manufacturer of excisable goods or provider of services for his business. A relook at the definition of input service seems to be required on the part of the government to reduce interpretational issues.

Combined administration (commissionerates) for both excise and service tax: The present service tax administration calls for reorganization. Under the VAT system, the administration has to deal with the manufacturers of excisable goods as well as providers of services. Since the excise administration is based on geographical jurisdiction, each unit of tax administration has to deal with both manufacturers and providers of services.

It is, therefore, necessary that the tax administration is reorganized and there is no strong justification for the existence of certain commissionerates only for the purpose of service tax. This kind of tax administration where some commissionerates deal with both excise assessees and service tax payers, and some deal exclusively with service tax payers is not suited for the kind of tax administration needed for VAT.

Provision of client services: Provision of proper guidance and assistance to taxpayers is a challenging task for the tax department. CBEC will have to ensure that proper guidance is given to taxpayers. For ensuring this, it is necessary that a suitable mechanism is set in place to respond to taxpayers' queries. The excise department should exploit the potential of information technology to deal with the queries in an efficient manner. A taxpayer should be in a position to trace the movement of his query and the stage at which it is pending.

The department should have a meaningful dialogue with taxpayers, particularly when it involves a taxpayer with credibility, in order to convince him of his tax liability or accept his explanation in case tax is not due. The department's way of remaining silent for months and years on the general doubts and apprehensions of a taxpayer about his liability to pay tax and then driving him to face the consequences of defending a show cause notice must be changed. It must be said that by all standards, the quality of tax administration in guiding taxpayers is far too poor. This needs to be accepted by the department and constructive action has to be taken for introducing drastic reforms in the tax administration.

Change in the procedure for collecting taxes: Service tax payers are required to pay the service tax by the 5th/6th day after the end of the quarter/month. However, for March, the tax has to be paid by the end of the month. This deviation is an anomaly. It needs to be removed. The procedure for payment for March should fall in line with the general procedure.

Implementation of these reforms will make service tax a non-cascade type tax. It will also be administratively convenient and taxpayer friendly. In fact, providing client services and changing the mindset of the administration to treat taxpayers as clients is of utmost importance in a growing economy.

* * *

The analysis of union excise duties (CenVAT) and service tax being levied by the union government indicates that there is a dichotomy in the division of domestic trade taxes in the Indian Constitution. Whereas union excise duties are being levied up to the manufacturing level by the centre, the states are assigned the powers to levy tax on sale and purchase of goods (this is discussed in Chapter 6). That is, a manufacturer pays union excise duty to the central government on the goods cleared by him from the factory and taken to the godown or shop, and another tax (sales tax now known as State VAT) on these goods when sold by him to another dealer or a consumer. Such an assignment of domestic trade taxes in India to the two tiers of government has created a situation where a unified VAT, as being levied by most of the countries, is not feasible unless either of the governments surrenders its taxing powers. Consequently, India has gone in for dual VAT—VAT at the central level as well as the state level. Also, tax on services has evolved over time and the authority to levy this tax has been moved from the Residuary Entry to the union list. Notwithstanding such a move, the separation of service tax from goods in the assignment of taxes has created problems for the introduction of a goods and services tax in India, as discussed in Chapter 9.

Annexure A5.1

Items Attracting Union Excise Duty at 6 per cent

1704 90	Sugar confectionery (excluding white chocolate and bubble gum)
1904 1010, 19041030, 19041090, 19043000, 19049000	Certain prepared foods obtained by the swelling or roasting of cereals or cereal products (includes corn flakes, *paos*, *mudi* and the like, bulgur wheat)
1905 31 00 or 1905 90 20, 19059010, 19053219	Biscuits, wafer biscuits, sweet biscuits, communion wafers—coated with chocolate or containing chocolate and others, pastries and cakes
21069011	Sharbat
21069020	Pan masala containing not more than 15 per cent betel nut, scented *supari*—where the retail sale price is declared on the package and such retail sale price does not exceed Re 1 per package
2106 90 99	Ready to eat packaged food
27111200, 27111300, 27111900	Liquefied petroleum gases

3003, 3004	Certain medicaments including ayurvedic, unani, homeopathic or bio-chemic, other than menthol crystals, penicillin, ampicillin, etc.
3005	Wadding, gauze, bandages and similar articles impregnated or coated with pharmaceutical substances
33	Henna powder, not mixed with any other ingredient
32149090	Ink for writing instruments including for markers and highlighters
35040091	Isolated soya protein
3907, 39239020	Polyester chips, ascetic bags
40070010, 400821	Heat resistant latex rubber thread, heat-resistant rubber tension tape
4301 or 4302	Raw, tanned or dressed fur skins
4408, 4410, 4412, 44	All goods—sheets for veneering, for plywood, particle board, oriented strand board and similar boards of wood, fibre board of wood, plywood, veneered panels and similar laminated wood, articles of wood, articles other than articles of densified wood and flush doors
44182010	Flush doors
48	Paper and paperboard or articles made therein from manufactured paper and paperboard and from pulp in a paper factory, and such pulp contains not less than 75 per cent by weight of pulp made from materials other than bamboo, hard woods, soft woods, reeds (other than sarkanda) or rags
5501, 5502, 5503, 5504, 5505, 5506 or 5507	All goods (sewing thread from man-made filaments, synthetic filament yarn, artificial filament yarn, man-made filament yarn, woven fabrics of synthetic filament yarn) other than nylon filament yarn of 210 deniers or in multiples thereof, with tolerance of 6 per cent
64	Footwear of retail sale price exceeding Rs 250 and not exceeding Rs 750 per pair
6601	Umbrellas and sun umbrellas
68	Goods in which not less than 25 per cent by weight of fly ash or phospho-gypsum or both have been used
7117	Imitation jewellery

732111	LPG gas stoves (with burners only, without other functions such as grill or oven)
7323 or 7615 1910	Pressure cookers of steel or aluminium
842121	Water filtration or purification equipment
85, 8523	MP3/MP4 or MPEG 4 players, with or without radio or video perception facility, recorded video cassettes intended for television broadcasting and supplied in formats such as Umatic, Betacom or any similar format
85279911	Portable receivers for calling, alerting or paging
85393110, 8539	Compact fluorescent lamps (CFL), vacuum and gas filled bulbs of retail sale price not exceeding Rs 20 per bulb
848690 or 9017	Parts of drawing and mathematical instruments used in the manufacture of such drawing and mathematical instruments—on end use basis
9402, 3006	Medical, surgical, dental or veterinary furniture and parts thereof, certain pharmaceutical goods like blood grouping reagents, first-aid-boxes and kits
9603	All goods (brooms, brushes, hand-operated mechanical floor sweepers (not motorized), mops and feather dusters, etc.
4820	Registers, account books, order books, receipt books, letter pads, memorandum pads, diaries and similar articles, blotting-pads, binders (loose-leaf or other), folders, file covers, manifold business forms, interleaved carbon sets and other articles of stationery of paper or paperboard; albums for samples or for collections and book covers of paper or paperboard
6814	Articles of mica
68 (except headings 6804, 6805, 6811, 6812, 6813)	Solid or hollow building blocks, including aerated or cellular light weight concrete blocks and slabs
8413	Power-driven pumps primarily designed for handling water, that is centrifugal pumps (horizontal or vertical), deep tube-well turbine pumps, submersible pumps, axial flow and mixed flow vertical pumps

9004, 9003, 70151010	Sunglasses for correcting vision and goggles, frames and mountings for spectacles, goggles or the like of value below Rs 500 per piece, rough ophthalmic blanks for manufacture of optical lenses
9019, 9022, 9018	Mechano-therapy appliances; massage apparatus; psychological aptitude-testing apparatus; ozone therapy, oxygen therapy, aerosol therapy, artificial respiration or other therapeutic respiration apparatus (other than parts and accessories thereof), all goods for medical, surgical, dental and veterinary use (other than parts and accessories thereof), instruments and appliances used in medical, surgical, dental or veterinary sciences, including scintigraphic apparatus, other electro-medical apparatus and sight-testing instruments (other than parts and accessories thereof)
1507, 1508, 1509, 1511	Soya bean oil, groundnut oil, olive oil, palm oil and their fractions, whether or not refined, but not chemically modified
1516, excluding 15161000	Vegetable fats and oils and their fractions, partly or wholly hydrogenated, interesterified, re-esterified or elaidinised, whether or not refined, but not further prepared, animal or vegetable fats and oils and their fractions, boiled, oxidized, dehydrated, sulphurized, blown, polymerized by heat in vacuum or in inert gas or otherwise chemically modified, excluding those under heading 1516; inedible mixtures or preparations of animal or vegetable fats or oils or of fractions of different fats or oils of this chapter, not elsewhere specified or included
5004, 5007	Silk yarn (other than yarn spun from silk waste) not put up for retail sale; woven fabrics of silk or of silk waste
5105, 5108	Wool and fine or coarse animal hair—carded or combed (including combed wool in fragments); yarn of animal hair (carded or combed) not put up for retail sale
5106, 5107	Yarn of carded wool not put up for retail sale; yarn of combed wool not put up for retail sale

5110, 5113	Yarn of coarse animal hair or of horse-hair (including gimped horse-hair yarn) whether or not put up for retail sale; woven fabrics of coarse animal hair or of horse-hair
5209, 5210	Woven fabrics of cotton—containing 85 per cent or more by weight of cotton and weighing more than 200g/m^2; and woven fabrics of cotton—containing less than 85 per cent by weight of cotton, mixed mainly or solely with man-made fibres, and weighing not more than 200g/m^2
5211	Woven fabrics of cotton—containing less than 85 per cent by weight of cotton, mixed mainly or solely with man-made fibres, weighing more than 200g/m^2
5302, 5305	True hemp (cannabis sativa 1)—raw or processed but not spun; tow and waste of true hemp (including yarn waste and garneted stock), coconut, abaca (manila hemp or *musa textilis nee*), ramie and other vegetable textile fibres (not elsewhere specified or included) raw or processed but not spun; tow, noils and waste of these fibres (including yarn waste and garneted stock)
5306, 5308	Flax yarn; yarn of other vegetable textile fibres; paper yarn (excluding coir yarn)
5309	Woven fabrics of flax; woven fabrics of other vegetable textile base fibres; woven fabrics of paper yarn
54	Certain man-made filament yarn and fabrics
5508, 5204	Cotton sewing thread; sewing thread of man-made staple fibres (whether or not put up for retail sale)
5509, 5510, 5511	Yarn (other than sewing thread) of synthetic, artificial and man-made staple fibres not put up for retail sale
5512, 5513, 5514	Woven fabrics of synthetic staple fibres containing 85 per cent or more by weight of synthetic staple fibres; woven fabrics of synthetic staple fibres containing less than 85 per cent by weight of such fibres, mixed mainly or solely with cotton and of a weight not exceeding 170g/m^2
5601 (excluding 560100 and 56012200)	Wadding and other articles of wadding—made of cotton, etc.

5602, 5603	Felt: non-wovens whether or not impregnated, coated, covered or laminated
5707 (excluding 56075010)	Twine (excluding nylon fish twine), cordage, ropes and cables (whether or not plaited or braided and whether or not impregnated, coated, covered or sheathed with rubber or plastics)
57	Carpets and textile floor coverings
58, 60, 61	Special woven fabrics; tufted fabrics; lace; tapestries; trimmings; embroidery (with some exceptions); knitted or crocheted fabrics; articles of apparel (knitted or crocheted)

ANNEXURE A5.2

Negative List of Services

1. Services provided to the United Nations or a specified international organization;
2. Healthcare services by a clinical establishment, an authorized medical practitioner or para-medics;
3. Services by a veterinary clinic in relation to healthcare of animals or birds;
4. Services by an entity registered under section 12AA of the Income tax Act, 1961 (43 of 1961) by way of charitable activities;
5. Services by a person by way of
   (a) renting of precincts of a religious place meant for general public; or
   (b) conduct of any religious ceremony;
6. Services provided by
   (a) an arbitral tribunal to
      (i) any person other than a business entity; or
      (ii) a business entity with a turnover up to rupees ten lakh in the preceding financial year;
   (b) an individual as an advocate or a partnership firm of advocates by way of legal services to,
      (i) an advocate or partnership firm of advocates providing legal services;
      (ii) any person other than a business entity; or

(iii) a business entity with a turnover up to rupees ten lakh in the preceding financial year; or
(c) a person represented on an arbitral tribunal to an arbitral tribunal;
7. Services by way of technical testing or analysis of newly developed drugs, including vaccines and herbal remedies, on human participants by a clinical research organization approved to conduct clinical trials by the Drug Controller General of India;
8. Services by way of training or coaching in recreational activities relating to arts, culture or sports;
9. Services provided to or by an educational institution in respect of education exempted from service tax, by way of,
    (a) auxiliary educational services; or
    (b) renting of immovable property;
10. Services provided to a recognized sports body by
    (a) an individual as a player, referee, umpire, coach or team manager for participation in a sporting event organized by a recognized sports body;
    (b) another recognized sports body;
11. Services by way of sponsorship of sporting events organised,
    (a) by a national sports federation, or its affiliated federations, where the participating teams or individuals represent any district, state or zone;
    (b) by Association of Indian Universities, Inter-University Sports Board, School Games Federation of India, All India Sports Council for the Deaf, Paralympic Committee of India or Special Olympics Bharat;
    (c) by Central Civil Services Cultural and Sports Board;
    (d) as part of national games, by Indian Olympic Association; or
    (e) under Panchayat Yuva Kreeda Aur Khel Abhiyaan (PYKKA) Scheme;
12. Services provided to the Government, a local authority or a governmental authority by way of construction, erection, commissioning, installation, completion, fitting out, repair, maintenance, renovation, or alteration of
    (a) a civil structure or any other original works meant predominantly for use other than for commerce, industry, or any other business or profession;
    (b) a historical monument, archaeological site or remains of national importance, archaeological excavation, or antiquity

specified under the Ancient Monuments and Archaeological Sites and Remains Act, 1958 (24 of 1958);
  (c) a structure meant predominantly for use as
    (i) an educational,
    (ii) a clinical, or
    (iii) an art or cultural establishment;
  (d) canal, dam or other irrigation works;
  (e) pipeline, conduit or plant for (i) water supply (ii) water treatment, or (iii) sewerage treatment or disposal; or
  (f) a residential complex predominantly meant for self-use or the use of their employees or other persons specified in the Explanation 1 to clause 44 of section 65B of the said Act;
13. Services provided by way of construction, erection, commissioning, installation, completion, fitting out, repair, maintenance, renovation, or alteration of,
  (a) a road, bridge, tunnel, or terminal for road transportation for use by general public;
  (b) a civil structure or any other original works pertaining to a scheme under Jawaharlal Nehru National Urban Renewal Mission or Rajiv Awaas Yojana;
  (c) a building owned by an entity registered under section 12AA of the Income tax Act, 1961 (43 of 1961) and meant predominantly for religious use by general public;
  (d) a pollution control or effluent treatment plant, except located as a part of a factory; or a structure meant for funeral, burial or cremation of deceased;
14. Services by way of construction, erection, commissioning, or installation of original works pertaining to,
  (a) an airport, port or railways, including monorail or metro;
  (b) a single residential unit otherwise than as a part of a residential complex;
  (c) low-cost houses up to a carpet area of 60 square metres per house in a housing project approved by competent authority empowered under the 'Scheme of Affordable Housing in Partnership' framed by the Ministry of Housing and Urban Poverty Alleviation, Government of India;
  (d) post-harvest storage infrastructure for agricultural produce including a cold storages for such purposes; or
  (e) mechanized food grain handling system, machinery or equipment for units processing agricultural produce as food stuff excluding alcoholic beverages;

15. Temporary transfer or permitting the use or enjoyment of a copyright covered under clauses (a) or (b) of sub-section (1) of section 13 of the Indian Copyright Act, 1957 (14 of 1957), relating to original literary, dramatic, musical, artistic works or cinematograph films;
16. Services by a performing artist in folk or classical art forms of (i) music, or (ii) dance, or (iii) theatre, excluding services provided by such artist as a brand ambassador;
17. Services by way of collecting or providing news by an independent journalist, Press Trust of India or United News of India;
18. Services by way of renting of a hotel, inn, guest house, club, campsite or other commercial places meant for residential or lodging purposes, having declared tariff of a unit of accommodation below rupees one thousand per day or equivalent;
19. Services provided in relation to serving of food or beverages by a restaurant, eating joint or a mess, other than those having (i) the facility of air-conditioning or central air-heating in any part of the establishment, at any time during the year, and (ii) a licence to serve alcoholic beverages;
20. Services by way of transportation by rail or a vessel from one place in India to another of the following goods
    (a) petroleum and petroleum products falling under Chapter heading 2710 and 2711 of the First Schedule to the Central Excise Tariff Act, 1985 (5 of 1986);
    (b) relief materials meant for victims of natural or man-made disasters, calamities, accidents or mishap;
    (c) defence or military equipments;
    (d) postal mail or mail bags;
    (e) household effects;
    (f) newspaper or magazines registered with the Registrar of Newspapers;
    (g) railway equipments or materials;
    (h) agricultural produce;
    (i) foodstuff including flours, tea, coffee, jaggery, sugar, milk products, salt and edible oil, excluding alcoholic beverages; or
    (j) chemical fertilizer and oilcakes;
21. Services provided by a goods transport agency by way of transportation of
    (a) fruits, vegetables, eggs, milk, foodgrains or pulses in a goods carriage;

(b) goods where gross amount charged for the transportation of goods on a consignment transported in a single goods carriage does not exceed one thousand five hundred rupees; or

(c) goods, where gross amount charged for transportation of all such goods for a single consignee in the goods carriage does not exceed rupees seven hundred fifty;

22. Services by way of giving on hire
    (a) to a state transport undertaking, a motor vehicle meant to carry more than twelve passengers; or
    (b) to a goods transport agency, a means of transportation of goods;

23. Transport of passengers, with or without accompanied belongings, by
    (a) air, embarking from or terminating in an airport located in the state of Arunachal Pradesh, Assam, Manipur, Meghalaya, Mizoram, Nagaland, Sikkim, or Tripura or at Bagdogra located in West Bengal;
    (b) a contract carriage for the transportation of passengers, excluding tourism, conducted tour, charter or hire; or
    (c) ropeway, cable car or aerial tramway;

24. Services by way of vehicle parking to general public excluding leasing of space to an entity for providing such parking facility;

25. Services provided to Government, a local authority or a governmental authority by way of
    (a) carrying out any activity in relation to any function ordinarily entrusted to a municipality in relation to water supply, public health, sanitation conservancy, solid waste management or slum improvement and upgradation; or
    (b) repair or maintenance of a vessel or an aircraft;

26. Services of general insurance business provided under following schemes
    (a) Hut Insurance Scheme;
    (b) Cattle Insurance under Swarnajaynti Gram Swarozgar Yojna (earlier known as Integrated Rural Development Programme);
    (c) Scheme for Insurance of Tribals;
    (d) Janata Personal Accident Policy and Gramin Accident Policy;
    (e) Group Personal Accident Policy for Self-employed Women;
    (f) Agricultural Pumpset and Failed Well Insurance;
    (g) Premia collected on export credit insurance;

(h) Weather Based Crop Insurance Scheme or the Modified National Agricultural Insurance Scheme, approved by the Government of India and implemented by the Ministry of Agriculture;
(i) Jan Arogya Bima Policy;
(j) National Agricultural Insurance Scheme (Rashtriya Krishi Bima Yojana);
(k) Pilot Scheme on Seed Crop Insurance;
(l) Central Sector Scheme on Cattle Insurance;
(m) Universal Health Insurance Scheme;
(n) Rashtriya Swasthya Bima Yojana; or
(o) Coconut Palm Insurance Scheme;

27. Services provided by an incubatee up to a total turnover of fifty lakh rupees in a financial year subject to the following conditions, namely:
    (a) the total turnover had not exceeded fifty lakh rupees during the preceding financial year; and
    (b) a period of three years has not been elapsed from the date of entering into an agreement as an incubatee;

28. Service by an unincorporated body or a non-profit entity registered under any law for the time being in force, to its own members by way of reimbursement of charges or share of contribution
    (a) as a trade union;
    (b) for the provision of carrying out any activity which is exempt from the levy of service tax; or
    (c) up to an amount of five thousand rupees per month per member for sourcing of goods or services from a third person for the common use of its members in a housing society or a residential complex;

29. Services by the following persons in respective capacities
    (a) sub-broker or an authorized person to a stock broker;
    (b) authorised person to a member of a commodity exchange;
    (c) mutual fund agent to a mutual fund or asset management company;
    (d) distributor to a mutual fund or asset management company;
    (e) selling or marketing agent of lottery tickets to a distributor or a selling agent;
    (f) selling agent or a distributor of SIM cards or recharge coupon vouchers;

(g) business facilitator or a business correspondent to a banking company or an insurance company, in a rural area; or

(h) sub-contractor providing services by way of works contract to another contractor providing works contract services which are exempt;

30. Carrying out an intermediate production process as job work in relation to
    (a) agriculture, printing or textile processing;
    (b) cut and polished diamonds and gemstones; or plain and studded jewellery of gold and other precious metals, falling under Chapter 71 of the Central Excise Tariff Act, 1985 (5 of 1986);
    (c) any goods on which appropriate duty is payable by the principal manufacturer; or
    (d) processes of electroplating, zinc plating, anodizing, heat treatment, powder coating, painting including spray painting or auto black, during the course of manufacture of parts of cycles or sewing machines upto an aggregate value of taxable service of the specified processes of one hundred and fifty lakh rupees in a financial year subject to the condition that such aggregate value had not exceeded one hundred and fifty lakh rupees during the preceding financial year;

31. Services by an organizer to any person in respect of a business exhibition held outside India;

32. Services by way of making telephone calls from
    (a) departmentally run public telephone;
    (b) guaranteed public telephone operating only for local calls; or
    (c) free telephone at airport and hospital where no bills are being issued;

33. Services by way of slaughtering of bovine animals;

34. Services received from a provider of service located in a non-taxable territory by
    (a) Government, a local authority, a governmental authority or an individual in relation to any purpose other than commerce, industry or any other business or profession;
    (b) an entity registered under section 12AA of the Income tax Act, 1961 (43 of 1961) for the purposes of providing charitable activities; or
    (c) a person located in a non-taxable territory;

35. Services of public libraries by way of lending of books, publications or any other knowledge-enhancing content or material;
36. Services by Employees' State Insurance Corporation to persons governed under the Employees' Insurance Act, 1948 (34 of 1948);
37. Services by way of transfer of a going concern, as a whole or an independent part thereof;
38. Services by way of public conveniences such as provision of facilities of bathroom, washrooms, lavatories, urinal or toilets;
39. Services by a governmental authority by way of any activity in relation to any function entrusted to a municipality under Article 243W of the Constitution.

CHAPTER 6

STATE TAXES ON INCOME AND PROPERTY

While assigning direct taxes between the centre and the states, the framers of India's Constitution allocated all-India broad-based taxes such as personal income tax and taxes on corporate income to the centre; taxes that could be better administered at the regional level such as land revenue, agricultural income tax, stamp duty and registration fee, and profession tax were assigned to the states. This chapter presents an analysis of the structure and administrative organization for these state taxes.

LAND REVENUE

Land revenue is the oldest source of tax revenue collected by the states. Item 45 of the state list of the Constitution brings land revenue under the states' powers of taxation. It is levied on agricultural land through land revenue acts administered by revenue departments in the states.

In India, this levy has been there since time immemorial. Since very early times, kings were accustomed to taking a certain share of the produce grown by the owners of land in their dominions (Government of India 1953–4). It also held a dominant position in the early fiscal system and continued to be the main tax in the agricultural sector. Over the years, the old system of revenue collection in kind changed. Currently, different states levy the tax on the basis of the physical configuration and productivity of soil, climate, and rainfall, yield of principal crops and their prices, and the market value and location of land, etc. It was levied in almost all the states on the basis of land surveys, dating generally from pre-independence days. In recent years, however, its fiscal significance has been reduced considerably. Some states like Punjab, Haryana, and Arunachal Pradesh have abolished this tax altogether.

Fiscal Significance

Land revenue had a place of pride in the states' own tax revenue during the pre-independence and even in the early post-independence years. It has, however, lost its importance over the years. The revenue from this tax, for all the states taken together, was Rs 636 crore in 1991–2, it went up to Rs 1,717.52 crore in 2001–2, and further to Rs 5,149.4 crore in 2009–10 (Table 6.1). However, the period 1996–7 to 1999–2000 is characterized by fluctuations in land revenue. Since then it shows an upward trend. Over the years, it has recorded a growth rate of 11.91 per cent.

Table 6.1 Trends in Revenue from Taxes on Income and Property: All States

(Rs Crore)

Years	Agricultural Income Tax	Land Revenue	Profession Tax	Stamp Duty & Registration Fee
1991–2	202	636	443	2,654
	(0.57)	(1.78)	(1.24)	(7.42)
1992–3	111	617	491	2,978
	(0.28)	(1.55)	(1.23)	(7.47)
1993–4	107	732	543	3,555
	(0.23)	(1.58)	(1.17)	(7.66)
1994–5	98	1141	619	5,090
	(0.18)	(2.05)	(1.11)	(9.13)
1995–6	154	1,326	681	5,897
	(0.24)	(2.08)	(1.07)	(9.23)
1996–7	103	1,074	907	6,267
	(0.14)	(1.51)	(1.28)	(8.81)
1997–8	182	1,091	904	7,143
	(0.22)	(1.34)	(1.11)	(8.79)
1998–9	241	1,031	1,180	7,432
	(0.27)	(1.16)	(1.33)	(8.35)
1999–2000	151	1,069	1,619	8,559
	(0.15)	(1.04)	(1.58)	(8.34)
2000–1	107	1,415	1,864	9,675
	(0.09)	(1.20)	(1.58)	(8.20)

2001–2	61	1,717	2,997	11,183
	(0.05)	(1.34)	(2.34)	(8.73)
2002–3	47	1,751	2,116	13,596
	(0.03)	(1.23)	(1.49)	(9.57)
2003–4	42	2,188	2,213	15,963
	(0.03)	(1.37)	(1.38)	(9.98)
2004–5	15	2,530	2,334	19,713
	(0.01)	(1.34)	(1.23)	(10.42)
2005–6	17	2,716	2,547	24,868
	(0.01)	(1.28)	(1.2)	(11.71)
2006–7	15	3,298	2,847	32,452
	(0.01)	(1.31)	(1.13)	(12.85)
2007–8	26	3,969	3,292	37,162
	(0.01)	(1.39)	(1.15)	(12.97)
2008–9	43	4,834	3,511	36,066
	(0.01)	(1.50)	(1.09)	(11.20)
2009–10	124	5,149	3,749	39,576
	(0.03)	(1.42)	(1.03)	(10.73)
2010–11 (RE)	134	6,863	4,044	52,189
	(0.03)	(1.5)	(0.88)	(10.79)
2011–12 (BE)	143	7,633	4,507	62,201
	(0.03)	(1.41)		
GR	–10.06	11.91	13.81	16.79
Buoyancy	–0.78	0.90	0.77	0.88

Source: Reserve Bank of India, *State Finances: A Study of Budgets* (Various Issues), Mumbai: RBI.

Note: GR: Growth Rate; RE: Revised Estimate; BE: Budget Estimate; Growth Rate and Buoyancy has been calculated for the period 1991–2 to 2008–9; The figures within parentheses indicate the percentage shares of the respective taxes in the states' own tax revenue.

The share of total land revenue in states' own tax revenue was 1.78 per cent in 1991–2 which increased to 2.08 per cent in 1995–6. Since then it has moved downwards and reached 1.04 per cent in 1999–2000 after which it shows fluctuation around rising trend.

Yields in individual states also show fluctuations around rising trend[1] although in recent years, in some of the special category states like Sikkim and Uttarakhand, it shows a positive trend. Similarly, in Andhra Pradesh, Bihar, Gujarat, Kerala, Maharashtra, Rajasthan, and Uttar Pradesh, the

---

[1] Some states such as Gujarat, Kerala, Madhya Pradesh, Maharashtra, and Odisha show a rising trend in tax revenue with minor fluctuations.

yield from this tax shows a little improvement in recent years, particularly from 2005–6 onwards (Table 6.2).

Growth rate of land revenue in general was high in each state except Andhra Pradesh, which had the lowest growth rate (4.82 per cent). Among the special category states, the growth rate varied between 4.77 per cent (Assam) and 18.33 per cent (Sikkim) (Table 6.3).

As the higher coefficient of buoyancy indicates a high relative growth of the yield from the tax, we examine whether higher tax efforts fully exploit the existing revenue potential of the states. In doing so, we analyse the average degree of relationship between the tax ratio in different states and the taxable capacity factor through a regression analysis.

The resultant tax ratio represents the ratio that a state will have if it had used its capacity to an average extent. Comparison of an estimated

Table 6.2 States' Tax Effort in Land Revenue

(Rs Crore)

States	Land revenue Average (2006–9)	GSDP* Average (2006–9)	Taxable Capacity	Tax Effort (%)	Rank
Andhra Pradesh	129.41	71,531.08	235.14	55.04	14
Bihar	86.16	29,537.08	119.09	72.35	13
Chhattisgarh	169.49	11,826.06	58.90	287.74	3
Goa	7.60	844.89	7.74	98.24	9
Gujarat	575.10	47,761.24	172.35	333.68	2
Haryana	10.32	31,923.08	126.43	8.16	17
Jharkhand	41.07	7,828.58	42.89	95.76	11
Karnataka	169.91	38,780.18	146.84	115.71	8
Kerala	47.26	22,480.64	96.54	48.95	15
Madhya Pradesh	200.07	37,971.09	144.47	138.48	6
Maharashtra	514.20	56,327.35	195.66	262.80	5
Odisha	283.77	23,563.07	100.10	283.50	4
Punjab	16.01	45,046.40	164.76	9.71	16
Rajasthan	144.84	41,602.86	154.99	93.45	12
Tamil Nadu	135.48	36,283.05	139.51	97.11	10
Uttar Pradesh	376.44	96,261.26	295.47	127.41	7
West Bengal	992.02	54,630.12	191.11	519.07	1

Source: RBI, *State Finances: A Study of Budgets* (various issues); GoI, Central Statistical Organization, New Delhi.

Notes: *GSDP = Gross State Domestic Product from agriculture.
Data in columns related to Taxable Capacity, Tax Effort, and Ranks, are calculated.

Table 6.3 State-wise Trends in Land Revenue

(Rs Crore)

States	1991–2	1996–7	2001–2	2005–6	2007–8	2008–9	2009–10	2010–11 (BE)	2011–12 (BE)	GR	Buoyancy
Non-special Category States											
Andhra Pradesh	30.37	67.95	19.71	68.75	144.39	130.35	222.00	145.00	146.00	4.82	0.42
	(0.99)	(1.39)	(0.16)	(0.36)	(0.50)	(0.39)	(0.63)	(0.31)	(0.26)		
Bihar	13.00	24.86	35.00	55.02	82.10	101.74	124.00	112.00	125.00	10.58	1.00
	(0.99)	(1.10)	(1.43)	(1.55)	(1.61)	(1.65)	(1.53)	(1.06)	(0.99)		
Chhattisgarh			16.57	26.89	88.12	359.49	160.00	170.00	200.00	54.67	2.61
			(0.83)	(0.66)	(1.57)	(5.45)	(2.25)	(2.04)	(2.03)		
Goa	0.88	3.30	7.54	5.08	7.19	9.39	10.60	9.70	12.10	11.85	0.78
	(0.78)	(1.09)	(1.32)	(0.46)	(0.53)	(0.55)	(0.60)	(0.44)	(0.48)		
Gujarat	36.61	87.58	86.95	380.23	683.09	543.5	1,161	1,500.00	1,800.00	18.00	1.33
	(1.27)	(1.44)	(0.94)	(2.42)	(3.12)	(2.31)	(4.34)	(4.33)	(4.61)		
Haryana	1.09	2.43	19.29	13.12	9.38	8.58	9.40	15.60	16.10	16.58	1.13
	(0.08)	(0.11)	(0.39)	(0.14)	(0.08)	(0.07)	(0.07)	(0.09)	(0.08)		
Jharkhand			6.44	30.00	37.46	52.75	60.00	66.00	95.90	36.70	2.35
			(0.31)	(1.04)	(1.06)	(1.04)	(1.08)	(1.11)	(1.22)		
Karnataka	17.17	46.04	49.54	116.50	145.31	255.65	127.80	143.32	190.00	14.80	1.15
	(0.59)	(0.80)	(0.50)	(0.63)	(0.56)	(0.92)	(0.42)	(0.38)	(0.43)		
Kerala	11.44	22.33	34.92	43.88	47.21	47.56	53.90	159.60	162.80	7.88	0.63
	(0.68)	(0.57)	(0.59)	(0.45)	(0.35)	(0.3)	(0.31)	(0.73)	(0.61)		
Madhya Pradesh	30.67	24.04	48.21	77.16	129.15	338.84	180.00	400.20	500.30	28.09	2.17
	(1.45)	(0.59)	(1.03)	(0.85)	(1.07)	(2.49)	(1.04)	(1.96)	(2.16)		

(*contd.*)

Table 6.3 (contd.)

(Rs Crore)

States	1991–2	1996–7	2001–2	2005–6	2007–8	2008–9	2009–10	2010–11 (BE)	2011–12 (BE)	GR	Buoyancy
Non-special Category States											
Maharashtra	44.11	109.96	260.46	428.97	512.22	546.22	714.00	1,195.60	1,497.10	15.33	1.17
	(0.74)	(0.94)	(1.22)	(1.28)	(1.08)	(1.05)	(1.21)	(1.63)	(1.79)		
Odisha	24.77	35.20	84.48	69.62	276.15	348.79	292.10	405.30	465.00	15.47	1.23
	(3.68)	(2.62)	(3.42)	(1.39)	(4.03)	(4.36)	(3.25)	(3.82)	(3.78)		
Punjab	3.50	3.02	8.58	16.29	17.31	15.44	15.30	17.00	19.00	12.37	1.05
	(0.23)	(0.11)	(0.18)	(0.18)	(0.17)	(0.14)	(0.13)	(0.10)	(0.09)		
Rajasthan	32.50	37.74	79.17	84.30	155.29	162.52	147.60	185.00	196.00	10.62	0.90
	(2.10)	(1.21)	(1.40)	(0.85)	(1.17)	(1.09)	(0.90)	(0.95)	(0.92)		
Tamil Nadu	26.50	18.77	50.47	179.48	78.03	207.73	116.60	95.00	70.80	10.15	0.86
	(0.71)	(0.24)	(0.39)	(0.77)	(0.26)	(0.62)	(0.32)	(0.19)	(0.12)		
Uttar Pradesh	42.21	72.63	72.93	108.69	392.53	549.28	663.10	809.60	245.80	35.62	2.54
	(1.21)	(1.15)	(0.71)	(0.58)	(1.57)	(1.92)	(1.96)	(1.99)	(0.49)		
West Bengal	278.23	468.32	711.22	917.11	1,039.58	983.78	928.90	1,260.40	1,694.30	8.84	0.70
	(11.36)	(11.00)	(10.93)	(8.83)	(7.92)	(6.82)	(5.50)	(5.92)	(6.12)		
Special Category States											
Arunachal Pradesh	0.83	1.27	0.99	1.11	2.12	4.90	4.40	5.50	6.00	8.70	0.73
	(20.29)	(14.89)	(2.90)	(1.80)	(2.16)	(3.60)	(2.54)	(2.76)	(2.64)		
Assam	38.67	38.96	63.26	74.65	79.76	113.36	116.90	131.60	141.60	4.77	0.48
	(7.55)	(5.08)	(4.04)	(2.31)	(2.37)	(2.73)	(2.34)	(2.23)	(2.16)		

Himachal Pradesh	0.90	5.96	51.85	1.09	1.89	20.28	14.50	1.60	1.90	9.77	0.80
	(0.47)	(1.45)	(5.66)	(0.07)	(0.10)	(0.90)	(0.56)	(0.05)	(0.05)		
Jammu and Kashmir	0.89	0.81	2.31	1.48	6.49	5.27	5.80	5.20	7.40	13.90	1.18
Manipur	(0.54)	(0.28)	(0.27)	(0.09)	(0.28)	(0.20)	(0.19)	(0.14)	(0.18)		
	0.48	0.76	0.40	1.32	0.75	0.78	0.80	0.90	1.00	4.81	0.44
	(3.34)	(5.35)	(0.77)	(1.39)	(0.51)	(0.46)	(0.41)	(0.36)	(0.31)		
Meghalaya	0.12	0.15	0.67	0.33	2.12	0.50	0.20	2.90	3.20	11.61	0.90
	(0.28)	(0.19)	(0.49)	(0.13)	(0.66)	(0.14)	(0.05)	(0.63)	(0.54)		
Mizoram	0.40	0.80	1.24	1.59	1.48	1.63	2.80	2.80	10.60	8.01	0.72
	(11.98)	(11.99)	(6.49)	(2.89)	(1.91)	(1.72)	(2.60)	(2.26)	(6.12)		
Nagaland	0.08	0.10	0.38	0.55	0.50	0.60	0.60	0.80	0.90	14.54	1.25
	(0.44)	(0.32)	(0.72)	(0.52)	(0.38)	(0.38)	(0.33)	(0.37)	(0.36)		
Sikkim	0.08	0.16	0.51	0.61	2.75	1.95	2.70	3.80	3.80	18.33	1.34
	(0.70)	(0.74)	(0.63)	(0.41)	(1.39)	(1.06)	(1.21)	(1.63)	(1.41)		
Tripura	0.32	0.58	1.14	3.25	2.97	5.55	5.50	5.80	5.80	12.82	0.94
	(1.11)	(0.96)	(0.72)	(1.10)	(0.80)	(1.25)	(1.04)	(0.93)	(0.74)		
Uttarakhand			3.28	9.18	23.40	17.90	8.80	11.70	13.50	21.63	1.02
			(0.37)	(0.51)	(0.85)	(0.59)	(0.25)	(0.27)	(0.28)		
All States	635.90	1,073.72	1,717.52	2,716.25	3,968.75	4,834.35	5,149.40	6,862.60	7,632.70	11.91	0.90
	(1.78)	(1.51)	(1.34)	(1.28)	(1.39)	(1.50)	(1.42)	(1.50)	(1.41)		

Source: Reserve Bank of India, *State Finances: A Study of Budgets* (Various Issues), Mumbai: RBI.

Note: GR = Growth Rate; RE: Revised Estimate; BE: Budget Estimate. Growth Rate and Buoyancy is calculated for the period 1991–2 to 2009–10; Growth Rate and Buoyancy for bifurcated and newly formed States calculated for the years 2001–2 to 2009–10; Figures in parenthesis are expressed as a percentage of the States' Own Tax Revenue.

tax ratio with the actual tax ratio indicates whether the state concerned is making an average degree of effort or is showing a deviation from the norm. We have, therefore, calculated tax effort with reference to the gross state domestic product (GDSP) for all the non-special category states.

For land revenue, the base of the tax is generally the GSDP originating in the agriculture sector. Thus agriculture component of GSDP is taken as the factor influencing the potential revenue that can be obtained from this tax.[2] By using the average figures for the years 2006–7 to 2008–9 estimated from the available data on land revenue and on agriculture component of GSDP, the tax effort is calculated as the percentage share of actual revenue (obtained from land revenue) in the taxable capacity. The results (Table 6.2) indicate that West Bengal, Gujarat, Chattisgarh, Odisha, and Maharashtra are the top five states in the country that put in the highest degree of effort to collect this tax.

Tax Structure

The structure of land revenue is heterogeneous; there is no uniformity either in the rate or in the base of tax. In general, the rate is levied according to whether the land is irrigated or un-irrigated; or the crop sown on the land is commercial or non-commercial. Some of the states, in addition to land revenue, also levy cess and surcharge on land revenue.

In Gujarat, Jharkhand, and Madhya Pradesh, land revenue is collected on the basis of the fertility and productivity of land. In Karnataka, land revenue is fixed keeping in view the physical configuration, climate and rainfall, yield of principal crops and their prices (Rs 5 per *katha* in case of dry land and the tax is double of the rate levied on dry land in the case of garden and wet land). In Kerala, the difference in rates is based on the location of land, that is, whether located in panchayats, or municipality/township/corporation. In Odisha, on non-agricultural land, fixing of rent in urban and rural areas of the state is done with regard to the situation of the land, purpose for which it is used, communication and market facilities, and market value of the land. In Bihar, the rate of land revenue is Rs 10 per acre for irrigated land and Rs 5 per acre for non-irrigated land.[3]

---

[2] The log-linear equation given below uses land revenue as a function of agriculture component of GSDP: log (landrev) = a + b log (GSDPa); where landrev = yield from land revenue; and GSDPa = Agriculture component of Gross State Domestic Product.

[3] Land revenue applicable to irrigated, unirrigated, and partially irrigated land has not been fixed uniformly in Bihar.

In addition, some of the states such as Karnataka, Kerala, Madhya Pradesh, Maharashtra, and Rajasthan levy an additional tax on commercial crops; Kerala levies a tax on plantation crops. In Madhya Pradesh, the rate is Rs 2.50 per hectare for groundnut and tobacco, and Rs 5 per hectare for sugarcane.

In some cases, heterogeneity exists even within a state; the rates vary according to settlements and systems of assessment. In Uttar Pradesh, for example, the rates of land revenue which became payable by tenure holders after the abolition of zamindari varied from district to district according to soil classes and year of settlement as well as according to the manner of acquiring rights of land.

In special category states, the rates of land revenue differ on the basis of category of land. In Tripura the rate is charged on the basis of physical features and economic conditions and trade facilities and communications in the place. In case of agricultural land, the rate is determined on the basis of profit on agriculture and in case of non-agricultural land, on the basis of the value of the land. In Uttarakhand, the rate varies widely depending upon the type of soil and tenants.[4]

In addition to land revenue, states like Odisha, Bihar, Tamil Nadu, Gujarat, Karnataka, Kerala, Madhya Pradesh, and Jharkhand[5] levy cess and surcharge on land revenue for assigning the yield to local bodies/panchayats. For example, Bihar levies cess at the rate of 125 per cent of land rent, while the cess on land revenue in Karnataka and Rajasthan is 45 and 50 per cent respectively. In Uttar Pradesh and Maharashtra, the local bodies are authorized to collect cess/surcharge on land revenue at varying rates (Annexure A6.1).

Exemptions

Like the rate structure, schemes for exemption from land revenue also vary from state to state. In Odisha, land used for agriculture, pisciculture, horticulture, and small-scale industries in the rural areas is exempt from paying land revenue. In Karnataka, dry land up to 10 acres is exempt from tax/

---

[4] In Nagaland, there is no uniform basis for assessing rates of land revenue on different categories of rural land. Except for the Dimapur cadastral area, all other land in the state is not revenue land. Similar is the case in Arunachal Pradesh where land revenue collected from rural land is nil.

[5] In Goa, Uttar Pradesh, West Bengal, and some of the North-Eastern states of Meghalaya, Mizoram, Nagaland, and Tripura, no cess is levied on land revenue.

cess. Similar is the case in Rajasthan, where mainly the un-irrigated land is exempt from payment of land revenue. In some states, exemptions from the payment of land revenue are provided on the basis of land holdings.

In Bihar the holdings exempt from the payment of land revenue vary from two hectares in irrigated areas to ten hectares in non-irrigated areas. Similarly in West Bengal, holdings up to four acres in irrigated and six acres in non-irrigated areas is exempt from payment of land revenue. Also, exemption from land revenue is granted to land up to 3.125 acres in Uttar Pradesh and Uttarakhand, four standard acres in Tripura and five acres in Sikkim. In addition, monasteries in Sikkim are exempt from payment of land revenue.

Administration of Land Revenue

The administrative set-up for the collection of land revenue has a similar pattern with minor variations in all the states. Each state has a Board of Revenue as the supreme revenue authority and all the cases of appeals, revision, etc. are decided by that board. States are divided into divisions and/or districts with commissioners and/or collectors as the chief officers of their areas. The districts are further divided into sub-divisions under sub-divisional officers. The sub-divisions are further divided into 'tehsils'. The grassroots level worker is the village officer; he collects land revenue, prepares accounts, and maintains land records (Angrish 1972). However, variations exist in the administrative system of land revenue in the Eastern sector. For example, in Mizoram, the Sub-divisional Officer (SDO) is in-charge right down to the field level; there are no circle heads and village level functionaries. The SDO is assisted by the assistant settlement officer and field staff. Likewise, in Meghalaya, revenue administration in most of the areas is vested with the district council that enjoys powers with respect to law making, levy and collection of taxes, regulating *jhum*, etc.

Weaknesses in the Existing System

The structure and trend of yield from existing land revenue as presented earlier, indicates certain weaknesses in the land revenue system.

Absence of land revenue in agriculturally developed states: States like Punjab and Haryana, which have witnessed substantial increase in agricultural productivity due to the Green Revolution, do not levy any tax either on land or on its output. Also, states with relatively large holdings and higher per capita income from agriculture do not collect higher revenue from the tax.

Heterogeneity in taxation of commercial crops: Whereas some states like Karnataka, Kerala, Madhya Pradesh, Maharashtra, and Rajasthan levy a tax/cess on commercial crops, the other states have no such provision.

Lacks buoyancy: With many technological changes (such as the Green Revolution and the White Revolution) there has been some increase in the productivity of land resulting in an increase in the yield of agriculture; however, there has been no commensurate increase in the rates of land revenue. In fact, the design of land revenue and general features have remained unchanged. The only change has been some reduction in the tax rates. Therefore, the total share of land revenue, which was 2.08 per cent of states' total own tax revenue in 1995–6, declined sharply and came down to 1.31 per cent in 2006–7. However, it increased marginally (1.50 per cent) in 2008–9. Today, the rates of land revenue are very low; these could be regarded as user charges for maintaining land records by village-level state government functionaries (appointed for revenue collection purposes) rather than as a tax.

Recommended Reforms

In view of the fact that the current system of taxing the agricultural sector is inadequate from the equity and efficiency points of view, it is recommended that the current system of land revenue be replaced by a system of Agricultural Holding Tax (AHT), as recommended by Raj Committee (Government of India 1972). Raj Committee appointed by the Government of India to examine the system of direct taxation of agricultural wealth and income recommended that land revenue, surcharge, and other agricultural income taxes should be replaced by AHT. The main features of the tax are:

1. AHT should be levied on an operational holding basis;
2. The country should be divided into a sufficiently large number of homogeneous tracts so that most of the soil and climatic differences are accounted for in each district/tract;
3. The norms for the value of output of different crops per hectare, for each year, should be worked out on the basis of estimates of yield for the previous 10 years (as revealed in crop cutting experiments)

and the average harvest price of the preceding three years prevailing in the important markets of the area;
4. For each district/tract, the schedule of a rateable value of land per hectare obtained for different crops should be revised every year; the rateable value of an assessed land-holding should be calculated from the schedule so prepared, taking into account the actual crop grown on the holding during the year of assessment and the expenses on irrigation;
5. A development allowance should also be allowed to all agricultural holdings at the rate of 20 per cent of the rateable value subject to a maximum of Rs 1,000; AHT should be levied on the rateable value of a holding minus the development allowance. If the amount of rateable value of a holding minus the development allowance is X thousand rupees, AHT should constitute X/2 per cent of this amount; and
6. Alternatively, land revenue should be supplemented by a crop-specific presumptive levy but grounded by way of field surveys on crop yields (Rajaraman and Bhende 1998). Since field surveys are time-consuming, a supplementary levy of this type can only be implemented in a sequential manner, with an initial focus on the crop/s known to be the most profitable in each area.

Agricultural Income Tax

Agricultural income tax (AIT) is a levy on receipts of agricultural income. It is levied with the twin objective of mobilizing revenue from agriculture for development purposes and for reducing disparity in incomes in rural areas.

The Indian Constitution draws a distinction between agricultural and non-agricultural incomes and empowers the state governments to make laws with respect to taxes on agricultural income vide Entry 46 of list-II (state list) in the Seventh Schedule. Item 82 of the central list (list-I) read with item 46 of the state list (list-II) of the Seventh Schedule of the Constitution specify that taxation of agricultural income should be collected by states while taxation of all other income falls within the purview of the central government. The Constitution, under Article 366, specifies that 'agricultural income' means agricultural income as defined for the purposes of the enactments relating to Indian income tax (Bakshi 2003). All those states which levy AIT adopt the definition contained in the Indian Income Tax Act with slight modifications to suit local conditions. Section 2 of the Indian Income Tax Act, 1961, defines 'agricultural income' as:

1. any rent or revenue derived from land which is situated in India and is used for agricultural purposes, that is, growing of all land produce like grains, fruits, spices, commercial crops, tea, coffee etc.; and
2. any income derived from land by agricultural operations including processing of the agricultural produce, raised or received as rent in kind, so as to render it fit for the market, or sale of such produce; and any income attributable to a farm house is treated as agricultural income provided such conditions are satisfied (Ahuja and Gupta 2006).

Evolution

Agricultural income was subject to taxation in India even when income tax was first levied in 1860. However, the Income Tax Act, 1886, exempted it from the purview of income tax. This continued till the enactment of the Government of India Act, 1935, which segregated agricultural and non-agricultural income and for the first time, provided a separate provincial levy on agricultural income. As explained earlier, this provision was retained in the new Constitution.

Bihar was the first state in India to levy a tax on agricultural income in 1938 while Assam levied the tax in 1939. In course of time, some other states also followed. However, some of the states introduced the tax for a very short period and repealed it subsequently. Presently only five states of the Indian union levy tax on agricultural income: Assam, Karnataka, Kerala, West Bengal, and Tripura. Almost all these states levy tax on plantation crops only.

Fiscal Significance

AIT constitutes a part of direct taxes in India. But in comparison to other direct taxes, the proceeds from this are relatively insignificant. Although agriculture contributes a lot in terms of providing livelihoods and employment to a large section of the people, in terms of its revenue contribution it has always occupied an insignificant position in all the states levying it. Barring Assam, the percentage share of revenue realized from AIT in all the other states' own tax revenue is very negligible (Table 6.4). Assam is the only state which had a significant share till 1998–9. But it has also shown a declining trend after that. It was 20.3 per cent in 1991–2, then it started declining till 1996–97 (4.61 per cent) after which it moved upwards till 1998–9 (10.51 per cent), and since then it has moved downwards and reached the level of 0.22 per cent in 2005–6 and 1.57 per cent in 2009–10. In the other states, AIT's share in states' own tax revenue is less than 1 per cent.

The revenue realized from this tax shows a fluctuating trend with negative growth rates in all the states. The four states of West Bengal, Assam, Karnataka, and Kerala witnessed downward trends with a growth rate of –17.27 per cent in West Bengal, –13.7 per cent in Assam, –11.9 per cent in Karnataka, and –4.1 per cent in Kerala (Table 6.4).

The trends in revenue from AIT and its percentage share in the states' own tax revenue reflect its insignificant contribution towards the state exchequer. High exemption limits, large exclusions, and lower tax rates make it an ineffective source of revenue.

Tax Structure

In the states levying AIT, the tax base is plantation income. The rate of tax, however, varies. In the case of individual taxpayers, the tax rate varies between 5 to 60 per cent while for companies it varies between 30 to 50 per cent.

For individual taxpayers, the exemption limit is Rs 30,000 in Assam; Rs 40,000 in Karnataka and Kerala; and Rs 1,500 in Tripura. The tax rate varies between 20 to 35 per cent in Assam, 10 to 40 per cent in Karnataka, and 10 to 30 per cent in Kerala. However, in Tripura, the tax rate varies between 5 to 60 per cent (Table 6.5).

Corporate taxpayers also have a progressive tax system except in West Bengal and Tripura. In Assam, the tax rate varies between 30 to 35 per cent; in Karnataka, between 30 to 50 per cent with payment of some additional amount of money when the total agricultural income exceeds Rs 1 lakh. Similarly in Kerala, the rate varies between 35 to 50 per cent with an exemption limit of Rs 25,000 (Table 6.6).

Table 6.4 State-wise Trends in Revenue from Agricultural Income Tax

(Rs Crore)

States	1991–2	1996–7	2001–2	2006–7	2007–8	2008–9	2009–10	2010–11 (RE)	2011–12 (BE)	GR	Buoyancy
Assam	103.97	35.36	15.26	2.52	3.14	18.18	78.34	101.2	105.00	−13.70	−1.43
	(20.3)	(4.61)	(0.97)	(0.07)	(0.09)	(0.44)	(1.57)	(1.71)	(1.60)		
Karnataka	9.07	39.53	2.63	1.37	3.04	9.28	8.70	10.00	10.00	−11.90	−0.88
	(0.31)	(0.69)	(0.03)	(0.01)	(0.01)	(0.03)	(0.02)	(0.03)	(0.02)		
Kerala	35.12	12.10	1.87	9.63	22.05	11.97	27.73	12.08	14.49	−6.40	−0.52
	(2.10)	(0.31)	(0.03)	(0.08)	(0.16)	(0.07)	(0.16)	(0.05)	(0.05)		
Tripura	0.24	0.20	0.14	0.15	0.11	0.18	0.01	0	0		
	(0.83)	(0.33)	(0.09)	(0.04)	(0.03)	(0.04)	(0.002)				
West Bengal	27.61	2.18	0.85	1.07	0	3.51	8.86	11.08	13.85	−17.27*	−1.67*
	(1.13)	(0.05)	(0.01)	(0.01)		(0.02)	(0.05)	(0.05)	(0.05)		
All States	202.21	103.24	60.52	14.80	25.89	43.13	123.65	134.36	142.77	−10.11	−0.78
	(0.57)	(0.15)	(0.05)	(0.01)	(0.01)	(0.01)	(0.03)	(0.03)	(0.03)		

Source: Reserve Bank of India, *State Finances: A Study of Budgets* (various issues), Mumbai: RBI.

Note: GR = Growth Rate. RE: Revised Estimate; BE: Budget Estimate; Growth rate and Buoyancy has been calculated for the period 1991–2 to 2009–10; Growth Rate and Buoyancy Value for Tripura has not been calculated because of inadequacy of data; * Calculated for the period 1996–7 to 2006–7.

Table 6.5 Agricultural Income Tax Rates for Individuals in Different States

States	Taxable Income	Tax Rate
Assam	Up to 0.3 lakh	Nil
	0.3–0.5 lakh	0.20%
	0.5–1.0 lakh	0.30%
	Above 1 lakh	0.35%
Karnataka	Up to 0.4 lakh	Nil
	0.4–0.5 lakh	10% of the amount by which total income exceeds 0.4 lakh
	0.5–0.75 lakh	0.01 + 20% of income above 0.5 lakh
	0.75–1.0 lakh	0.06 + 30% of income above 0.75 lakh
	Above 1 lakh	0.135 + 40% of income above 1 lakh
Kerala	Up to 0.4 lakh	Nil
	0.4–0.6 lakh	10% of income above 0.4 lakh
	0.6–1.0 lakh	0.02 + 20% of income above 0.6 lakh
	Above 1 lakh	0.1 lakh + 30% of income above 1 lakh
Tripura	Up to 0.015 lakh	Nil
	0.015–0.05 lakh	0.05%
	0.05–0.1 lakh	0.10%
	0.1–0.15 lakh	0.15%
	0.15–0.2 lakh	0.25%
	0.2–0.25 lakh	0.30%
	0.25–0.3 lakh	0.40%
	0.3–0.4 lakh	0.50%
	Above 0.4 lakh	0.60%
West Bengal		Flat rate of 30%

Source: RBI, *State Finances: A Study of Budgets* (various issues); GoI, Central Statistical Organization, New Delhi.

In Karnataka and Kerala, besides the taxes on individuals and companies, a different rate of tax is levied on firms; this tax is 40 per cent and 35 per cent of total agricultural income in Karnataka and Kerala, respectively. Further, in the case of foreign companies, the prevailing rate is 80 per cent of the total agricultural income in Kerala.

Exemptions

In addition to the exemption limit mentioned earlier, in Kerala, no tax is payable by any person other than a company or a firm where the total

Table 6.6 Agricultural Income Tax Rates for Companies in Different States

Taxable Income	Assam	Karnataka	Kerala	Tripura	West Bengal
Below 0.25 lakh	30%	30% of total income	35% of the total agricultural income	Flat rate of 45%	Flat rate of 30%
0.25–1 lakh	30%	30% of total income	40% of the total agricultural income		
1–3 lakh	35%	Rs 30,000 + 40% of the amount by which the total income exceeds 1 lakh	45% of the total agricultural income		
3–5 lakh	35%	Rs 30,000 + 40% of the amount by which the total income exceeds 1 lakh	50% of the total agricultural income		
Above 5 lakh	35%	Rs 1,90,500 + 50% of the amount by which the total income exceeds 5 lakh	50% of the total agricultural income		

Source: RBI, State Finances: A Study of Budgets (various issues); GoI, Central Statistical Organization, New Delhi.
Notes: Data in columns related to Taxable Capacity, Tax Effort, and Ranks, are calculated.

extent of land, the agricultural income from which is assessable, does not exceed five hectares. Besides, certain types of agricultural income are exempt from the tax net:

1. Any income derived from a house or building which is in actual use and occupation of the receiver of rent or revenue or the cultivator or the receiver of rent-in-kind as the case may be;
2. Any income derived from property held under a trust or any other legal obligation wholly for religious or charitable purposes and in the case of property so held in part only for such purposes, the income applied or finally set apart for application thereto;
3. Any income received by a person as a shareholder out of the agricultural income of a company which has certified that it has paid or will pay the tax with respect to the agricultural income of the company;
4. Any income received by a person as his share out of the agricultural income of a firm or association of individuals if tax has been levied on the agricultural income of such a firm or association; and
5. Any sum received by a person out of the agricultural income with respect to which tax has been assessed on the common manager, receiver or any court of wards, etc. (Government of India 1953–4).

Administration of AIT

In all the states levying AIT, the work of tax administration is entrusted to AIT departments. At the top of the administration is the AIT board as in Assam or the commissioner of AIT as in West Bengal. Then there are other subordinate supervisory officers like deputy commissioners, assistant commissioners, agricultural income tax officers and other junior staff who help in the administration of this tax (Angrish 1972).

Administrative procedures regarding submission of returns, assessments, appeals or revisions remain more or less similar in all the states (Jha 1987). The submission of returns is made within 60 days of the publication of notice for returns. In case the concerned income tax authority has any doubt regarding the return submitted, he can ask for necessary evidence to be supported in support of the return. The assessing officer proceeds to assess the tax on a discretionary basis.

As income from the plantation sector is of a mixed nature, the income from such operations in Assam is subjected to tax levy in a 40:60 ratio.

Thus, the income tax authority of the central government will assess 40 per cent and the remaining 60 per cent will form the basis of assessment and collection under the state Act. In West Bengal, however, if the income is derived from the sale of manufactured tea (black tea), it is treated as mixed income—40 per cent is business income assessable under the central Income Tax Act, 1961, and the balance 60 per cent is agricultural income assessable under the Bengal Agricultural Income Tax Act, 1944. If the income is derived from the sale of green tea leaves, then such an income is treated as 100 per cent agricultural income. In the case of Karnataka, the assessment procedure is similar to that adopted for other direct taxes on income. Under section 18, returns are required to be filed by all persons who had taxable income during the previous year or 15 acres and more of plantation land, within four months from the end of the year (Government of Karnataka 2001).

In view of the coordinated nature of administration of central and state income taxes, the administrative structure is very limited in the states.

Weaknesses in the Existing AIT System

The revenue contribution of existing AIT is quite insignificant. Only five states levy AIT and that too, on plantation crops only. In fact, the system is characterized by a low tax base as allied agricultural activities are not taxed. This increases horizontal inequity. More importantly, this creates a large loophole for the evasion of tax on non-agricultural income since part of one's non-agricultural income can be passed off as agricultural income.

Recommended Reforms

Direct taxation on agricultural income plays a very critical role in the acceleration of economic development because the imposition of a compulsory levy on the agricultural sector helps in the commercialization of agriculture and simultaneously enlarges the supply of savings for economic development. Hence, there is a critical need at the present juncture for reforms in the agricultural sector. It is, therefore, imperative that AIT be rationalized to suit the requirements of economic development of a developing economy like India. To begin with, the tax should be extended to all the large farmers (in all the states) having agricultural income.

Although in the initial years after independence this tax was there in some of the states it was subsequently abolished on the grounds of low productivity and administrative problems.

An analysis of the agricultural component's share in GSDP reveals that even though some major states like Andhra Pradesh, Bihar, Odisha, Haryana, Punjab, Madhya Pradesh, and Uttar Pradesh have a very good share, there are no taxes on agricultural income. In Punjab, as stated earlier, even though the share of agricultural income in the state's GDP is more than 30 per cent, no tax is levied on agricultural income. It is, therefore, recommended that farmers in these states should be brought under the tax net and this will increase the yield of AIT significantly.

The objective of the agricultural tax policy should be taxation to ensure agricultural development and to make agriculture more efficient. This will enable the agricultural sector to increase its share in the general economic development of the country.[6]

For development to take place there should be sustained increase in total production and in productivity per acre in agriculture. Increasing agricultural productivity is a pre-requisite for the creation of surplus in this sector which can easily be siphoned off by agricultural taxes and used for investment.

To conclude, the agricultural sector of the Indian economy, as compared to the non-agricultural sector, has been under-taxed in the past and continues to be so even under the present system of taxation. All classes of income in the agricultural sector have enjoyed a tax advantage over their counterparts working in the non-agricultural sector. Therefore, from the point of view of inter-sectoral equity, it is important that the AIT system is reformed in such a way that the states are able to mobilize the much needed resources for the development of the state.

STAMP DUTY AND REGISTRATION FEE

Stamp duty and registration fee (SD and RF) are two components of a tax on property related to regulation of transactions of instruments.

---

[6] Agricultural development is necessary so that other sectors may be provided with food, foreign exchange, and labour for rapid growth. Many economists have talked of the need for agricultural development as a pre-condition for economic growth.

SD is levied on all documents related to a transaction. It is judicial as well as non-judicial; the former is levied under the Indian Court Fee Act, 1870, and the latter is regulated under the Indian Stamp Act, 1899.

Judicial SD is levied on suits, petitions, applications, etc. filed in courts and public offices. The objective of this duty is not only to cover a part of the administrative cost of justice but also to control frivolous litigation. Non-judicial SD, however, is levied on instruments used for commercial and business transactions. This is calibrated on the ability-to-pay principle.

RF, however, is paid to the government when documents or instruments are presented for registration in return for the safe custody of registered documents.[7] It is a payment made for the service rendered by the government in recording contracts and deeds; for maintaining a permanent database of registered instruments; and for providing information relating to such transactions to members of the public. Registration is compulsory for certain instruments (mainly immovable property) and optional for other financial instruments. Once a document is registered, it becomes a public document and attains a superior evidentiary value.

Constitutional Provisions

Under Article 268 of the Indian Constitution, the power to levy SD lies with the union government, but the revenue is collected and retained by the states. Vide Entry 91 of the union list, the central government is empowered to legislate the SD rate on most of the documents that are normally executed in the course of transactions in banking, industry, trade, and commerce including bills of exchange, cheques, promissory notes, transfer of shares, bills of lading, letters of credit, debentures, and insurance policies. This prevents competitive exploitation of this tax by the states and facilitates the smooth conduct of inter-state and international trading through uniform and low rates. States have the exclusive powers (vide entry 63 of list-II) to fix SD rates for all other documents—conveyance deeds, gifts, exchange, mortgages, lease, bonds, awards, settlements, trust, and partition. While exercising this power, the state governments have added new schedules to the main Act applicable to their jurisdictions; amended articles of the schedules in the main Act; or enacted their

---

[7] Registration fee is levied under the Indian Registration Act, 1908.

own Stamp Acts. Karnataka, for instance, enacted its own Stamp Act of 1957 (which came into force from June 1958) along with Maharashtra, Gujarat, and Kerala.

Fiscal Significance

The combined tax of SD&RF is one of the important state taxes having the highest growth rate. The total yield from this tax in all the states was Rs 2,654 crore in 1991–2, this went up to Rs 24,867.75 crore in 2005–6, and further to Rs 39,576.17 crore in 2009–10 showing a growth rate of 16.59 per cent and a buoyancy of 1.22. This indicates an upsurge in the fiscal importance of the tax. Consequently, SD&RF's share in states' own tax revenue increased from 7.42 per cent in 1991–2, to 10.42 per cent in 2004–5, and to 10.90 per cent in 2009–10 (Table 6.7).

However, the trends in tax revenue have not been in the same direction for all the states. In the case of individual states, except Andhra Pradesh, Assam, Chhattisgarh, Odisha, Rajasthan, West Bengal, and Jammu and Kashmir, tax revenue from stamp duty shows fluctuations in all the other states. In 2009–10, SD&RF accounted for 18.23 per cent of the state's own tax revenue in Maharashtra, 12.88 per cent in Punjab, 13.47 per cent in Uttar Pradesh, and 10.76 per cent in Kerala. However, the contribution of this tax is very low in some of the special category states.[8]

The growth rate of tax revenue during 1991–2 to 2009–10 is very high in many states. Among non-special category states, Chhattisgarh registered the highest growth rate of 22.85 per cent during the period 2001–2 to 2009–10, while, among special category states, Uttarakhand registered the highest growth rate of 22.10 per cent in the same period. The coefficient of buoyancy for the tax falls short of unity in Bihar (Table 6.7) while it is more than one in all the other non-special category states. Revenue from SD&RF turns out to be buoyant even in low income states like Odisha and Rajasthan, and in special category states like Assam, Jammu and Kashmir, and Meghalaya.

As the higher coefficient of buoyancy indicates a high relative growth of yield from the tax, we examine whether the higher tax effort fully exploits the existing revenue potential of the states. In doing so, we analyse the average degree of relationship between the tax ratio in different states and

---

[8] It is 0.49 per cent in Mizoram, 0.65 per cent in Nagaland, and 0.92 per cent in Arunachal Pradesh.

Table 6.7 State-wise Trends in Stamp Duty and Registration Fee

(Rs Crore)

States	1991–2	1996–7	2001–2	2005–6	2007–8	2008–9	2009–10	2010–11 (RE)	2011–12	GR	Buoyancy
Non-Spl. Cat. States											
Andhra Pradesh	170.05	435.16	804.89	2,013.45	3,086.06	2,930.99	2,638.63	3,600.00	4,240.00	18.53	1.39
	(5.57)	(8.91)	(6.41)	(10.48)	(10.72)	(8.79)	(7.50)	(7.59)	(7.51)		
Bihar	118.00	227.41	340.00	505.29	654.15	716.19	997.90	1,215.00	1,600	9.44	0.84
	(9.01)	(10.10)	(13.92)	(14.19)	(12.86)	(11.60)	(12.34)	(11.48)	(12.72)		
Chhattisgarh			121.35	312.80	462.72	495.59	583.13	650.35	750.00	22.85	1.20
			(6.09)	(7.72)	(8.24)	(7.52)	(8.19)	(7.81)	(7.63)		
Goa	5.24	16.96	26.38	60.49	117.59	115.37	111.25	130.39	148.10	18.16	1.14
	(4.62)	(5.60)	(4.63)	(5.52)	(8.65)	(6.81)	(6.31)	(5.98)	(5.82)		
Gujarat	166.94	399.13	539.41	1,153.16	2,018.43	1,728.50	2,556.72	3,449.98	5,000.00	15.12	1.12
	(5.77)	(6.58)	(5.83)	(7.35)	(9.22)	(7.34)	(9.56)	(10.10)	(12.81)		
Haryana	97.72	273.10	488.29	1,339.73	1,763.28	1,326.39	1,293.57	1,900.00	2,350.00	17.77	1.32
	(7.52)	(12.74)	(9.82)	(14.76)	(15.18)	(11.38)	(9.79)	(10.95)	(11.75)		
Jharkhand			80.00	125.00	108.11	372.61	274.94	302.50	450.00	15.94	1.12
			(3.85)	(4.33)	(3.05)	(7.33)	(4.94)	(5.07)	(5.74)		
Karnataka	206.01	487.63	855.04	2,212.20	3,408.83	2,926.72	2,627.57	3,500.35	4,030.00	17.39	1.32
	(7.10)	(8.45)	(8.68)	(11.87)	(13.12)	(10.59)	(8.59)	(9.20)	(9.20)		
Kerala	152.19	360.30	394.28	1,101.42	2,027.97	2,002.99	1,896.41	2,617.05	3,252.17	14.70	1.13
	(9.09)	(9.24)	(6.66)	(11.26)	(14.84)	(12.53)	(10.76)	(11.94)	(12.21)		
Madhya Pradesh	151.78	318.89	444.96	1,009.48	1,531.54	1,479.29	1,783.15	2,200.00	2,000.00	19.90	1.53
	(7.17)	(7.77)	(9.46)	(11.08)	(12.74)	(10.87)	(10.32)	(10.79)	(8.65)		

(contd.)

Table 6.7 (contd.)

(Rs Crore)

States	1991–2	1996–7	2001–2	2005–6	2007–8	2008–9	2009–10	2010–11 (RE)	2011–12	GR	Buoy-ancy
Non-Spl. Cat. States											
Maharashtra	369.78	1,274.57	2,442.67	5,265.86	8,549.57	8,287.63	10773.65	14,140.27	15,667.14	18.63	1.43
	(6.21)	(10.88)	(11.47)	(15.70)	(17.99)	(15.93)	(18.23)	(19.24)	(18.73)		
Odisha	35.43	68.52	109.76	236.06	404.76	495.66	359.96	450.00	510.00	14.9	1.18
	(5.26)	(5.11)	(4.45)	(4.72)	(5.90)	(6.20)	(4.01)	(4.24)	(4.14)		
Punjab	119.46	182.44	444.31	1,670.50	1,567.84	1,730.29	1550.94	2,500.00	2,900.00	17.87	1.52
	(7.74)	(6.67)	(9.22)	(18.58)	(15.84)	(15.52)	(12.88)	(14.37)	(14.21)		
Rajasthan	118.51	276.26	478.89	1,031.80	1,544.35	1,356.63	1362.94	1,750.00	1,900.00	16.08	1.34
	(7.65)	(8.84)	(8.44)	(10.44)	(11.63)	(9.08)	(8.30)	(9.01)	(8.90)		
Tamil Nadu	296.46	590.60	1,137.89	2,084.86	3,804.74	3,793.68	3662.16	4,599.47	6,492.54	15.77	1.26
	(7.94)	(7.40)	(8.75)	(8.94)	(12.85)	(11.26)	(10.02)	(9.36)	(10.86)		
Uttar Pradesh	445.19	87506	142929	299678	397668	4,138.27	4562.23	6,081.73	6,993.99	14.89	1.09
	(12.73)	(13.88)	(13.84)	(15.89)	(15.93)	(14.44)	(13.47)	(14.95)	(13.9)		
West Bengal	173.03	309.81	555.39	1,177.59	1,416.96	1,509.49	1,814.22	2,358.57	3,002.92	14.59	1.15
	(7.06)	(7.27)	(8.54)	(11.34)	(10.79)	(10.47)	(10.74)	(11.07)	(10.84)		
Spl. Cat. States											
Arunachal Pradesh	0.07	0.38	0.27	0.41	0.86	1.25	1.88	2.06	2.27	15.37	1.24
	(1.71)	(4.45)	(0.79)	(0.66)	(0.88)	(0.92)	(1.08)	(1.03)	(1.00)		
Assam	11.74	22.56	41.97	85.88	109.91	111.16	108.45	123.09	145	14.24	1.35
	(2.29)	(2.94)	(2.68)	(2.66)	(3.27)	(2.68)	(2.17)	(2.08)	(2.21)		

Himachal Pradesh	7.98	15.44	34.27	82.43	86.99	98.33	113.40	124.47	142.76	17.03	1.25
	(4.14)	(3.75)	(3.74)	(5.51)	(4.44)	(4.38)	(4.40)	(3.65)	(3.53)		
Jammu and Kashmir	3.99	6.15	23.10	43.35	67.10	60.28	64.88	72.73	75.58	19.22	1.59
	(2.43)	(2.13)	(2.69)	(2.57)	(2.92)	(2.24)	(2.11)	(2.00)	(1.81)		
Manipur	0.92	1.40	1.48	2.81	2.93	3.18	4.26	4.85	15.52	8.63	0.81
	(6.41)	(9.86)	(2.85)	(2.96)	(1.99)	(1.87)	(2.17)	(1.93)	(4.88)		
Meghalaya	0.72	1.16	3.49	5.47	5.99	5.54	11.02	8.60	12.29	15.10	1.22
	(1.69)	(1.50)	(2.57)	(2.16)	(1.88)	(1.50)	(2.48)	(1.86)	(2.09)		
Mizoram	0.02	0.02	0.08	0.17	0.23	0.46	0.39	0.70	2.50	17.84	1.45
	(0.60)	(0.30)	(0.42)	(0.31)	(0.30)	(0.49)	(0.36)	(0.56)	(1.44)		
Nagaland	0.12	5.60	1.80	0.89	1.02	1.01	1.19	1.17	1.26	8.54	0.89
	(0.67)	(17.86)	(3.43)	(0.84)	(0.78)	(0.65)	(0.66)	(0.54)	(0.50)		
Sikkim	0.16	0.42	1.30	2.27	4.26	4.35	4.48	3.13	3.26	22.59	1.59
	(1.41)	(1.94)	(1.62)	(1.54)	(2.15)	(2.36)	(2.01)	(1.34)	(1.21)		
Tripura	2.42	3.62	9.61	14.21	14.98	17.03	18.15	19.97	19.97	13.42	0.99
	(8.39)	(5.98)	(6.06)	(4.80)	(4.04)	(3.85)	(3.44)	(3.19)	(2.55)		
Uttarakhand		89.45	333.39	424.27	357.46	398.70	425.65	483.85	22.10	1.16
		(10.00)	(18.68)	(15.49)	(11.74)	(11.20)	(9.84)	(10.17)		
All States	2,653.90	6,267.20	11,182.80	24,867.70	37,162.10	36,066.30	39,576.00	52,189.00	62,201.00	16.59	1.22
	(7.42)	(8.81)	(8.73)	(11.71)	(12.97)	(11.20)	(10.90)	(11.39)	(11.53)		

Source: Reserve Bank of India, *State Finances: A Study of Budgets* (Various Issues), Mumbai: RBI.

Note: GR = Growth Rate; RE: Revised Estimate; BE: Budget Estimate.Growth Rate and Buoyancy is calculated for the period 1991–2 to 2009–10; Growth Rate and Buoyancy for the bifurcated and newly formed states is calculated for the years 2001–2 to 2009–10; Figures in parenthesis are expressed as a percentage of the States' Own Tax Revenue.

the taxable capacity factor through a regression analysis. The resultant tax ratio would represent the ratio that a state would have if it had used its capacity to an average extent. Comparison of an estimated tax-ratio with the actual tax ratio indicates whether the State concerned is making an average degree of effort, or is showing a deviation from the norm.

We have, therefore, calculated tax effort[9] with reference to states' GSDP for all the non-special category states.

For SD&RF, the base of the tax is generally the value of property transactions in the state. However, due to non-availability of data relating to various categories of property transactions, a GSDP component (real estate ownership of dwellings and business premises) is taken as the factor influencing the potential revenue that can be obtained from this tax.[10] By using the average figures for 2006–7 to 2008–9 estimated from available data on SD&RF and on real estate ownership of dwellings and business premises, the tax effort is calculated as the percentage share of actual revenue (obtained from SD&RF) in the taxable capacity. The results (Table 6.8) indicate that Punjab, Uttar Pradesh, Madhya Pradesh, Goa, and Haryana were the top five states in the country that put in the highest degree of effort to collect this tax.

Structure of Stamp Duty and Registration Fee

The Indian Stamp Act, 1899, regulates SD's base and rate. Schedule I of the Act prescribes the rates of tax applicable to all the states. The items enumerated in this Schedule are under the jurisdiction of the union government and have an all-India importance for trade and commerce. The states are not authorized to change the rate of the tax given in this Schedule. However, if any state considers it necessary to change the rates of duty on any item falling in this Schedule, the President's assent has to be obtained for the law prescribing the new rates.

The rates levied under the Indian Stamp Act and the various amendments made by the states (vide separate enactments) indicate that, in general, there is uniformity of rates throughout the country with regard

---

[9] Tax effort is a relative concept. It is defined as a ratio of tax revenue to its taxable capacity. Such a measure involves the implicit assumption that the total income of a State is an appropriate indicator of taxable capacity.

[10] The following log-linear equation uses stamp duty and registration fee as a function of GSDP: $\log(STAMP) = a + b \log(GSDP)$; where STAMP = yield from stamp duty and registration fee, and GSDP = Gross State Domestic Product.

Table 6.8 States' Tax Effort in SD&RF

(Rs Crore)

States	S&R Average (2006–9)	GSDP* Average (2006–9)	Taxable Capacity	Tax Effort (%)	Rank
Andhra Pradesh	2,960.81	41,212.33	3,536.37	83.72	14
Bihar	608.45	6,833.96	614.72	98.98	9
Chhattisgarh	449.27	4,857.06	440.83	101.92	7
Goa	116.29	1,117.86	105.44	110.29	4
Gujarat	1,723.99	20,268.49	1,771.90	97.30	12
Haryana	1,618.22	17,420.21	1,528.96	105.84	5
Jharkhand	191.99	3,258.48	298.85	64.24	15
Karnataka	3,180.45	39,058.00	3,356.23	94.76	13
Kerala	1,850.30	21,194.07	1,850.64	99.98	8
Madhya Pradesh	1,420.64	14,598.57	1,287.26	110.36	3
Maharashtra	7,750.97	90,387.37	7,597.81	102.02	6
Odisha	386.97	6,746.78	607.08	63.74	16
Punjab	1,866.04	7,996.22	716.31	260.51	1
Rajasthan	1,398.22	16,180.45	1,422.90	98.27	10
Tamil Nadu	3,531.96	42,227.04	3,621.13	97.54	11
Uttar Pradesh	4,209.54	31,508.41	2,722.80	154.60	2
West Bengal	1,395.01	25,977.49	2,256.25	61.83	17

Notes: SD&RF = Stamp Duty & Registration Fee; GSDP* = Gross State Domestic Product from Real Estate Ownership of Dwellings and Business services

to the instruments falling under Schedule I of the Indian Stamp Act, 1899. However, changes have been made in Schedule I in Tamil Nadu, Assam, and the North-Eastern states. Gujarat, Maharashtra, Karnataka, Kerala, and Rajasthan have enacted separate Acts for SD rates. Therefore, there exists a wide divergence in the rates on several instruments.

An analysis of the SD rates on conveyances, which is the main component of the revenue from SD, indicates that the current rates in different States have large variations (Box 6.1). While Maharashtra, Haryana, and Punjab differentiate between rural and urban areas with regard to rates of duties on conveyances, the states of Karnataka, Madhya Pradesh, and Punjab have special rates for certain sections (Annexure A6.2).

Box 6.1 Rate of Stamp Duty on Conveyance in Major States

S.No.	State	Rate of Stamp Duty	Special Rates for certain sections
1	Andhra Pradesh	5%	
2	Bihar	6%	
3	Gujarat	2% to 3.5%	
4	Haryana	5% (rural), 7% (urban)	
5	Karnataka	7.50%	7% for insurance
6	Kerala	6% to 8.5%	
7	Madhya Pradesh	7.50%	5.5% in case of females
8	Maharashtra	1%–5%	
9	Odisha	3%–8%	
10	Punjab	5% (rural), 8% (municipal & corporation area)	3% in case of females/ agriculture
11	Rajasthan	0.5%–11%	
12	Uttar Pradesh	8%	6% for women
13	West Bengal	5%	

SD rates are more or less uniform across the high income states; however, they vary widely across special category states. In Tripura, for instance, the rate is Rs 10 and in Uttarakhand, it ranges between Rs 20 and Rs 125. In Meghalaya, it is Rs 3 to Rs 99 per thousand. Similarly in Manipur, it is 7 per cent to 8 per cent while in Himachal Pradesh it is 5 per cent per thousand (Annexure A6.2).

In addition, some of the states levy additional duties or surcharges on basic SD. Madhya Pradesh, for example, levies an additional duty of 1 per cent on the value of property situated in a municipal and panchayat area and a surcharge of 5 per cent is levied on the transfer of vacant agricultural land. Bihar and Uttar Pradesh also levy additional duty as well as a surcharge on conveyance and on some other documents.

This analysis of SD rates relates to statutory rates. The effective rate of tax has to be determined after taking into account exemptions and concessions announced through various notifications issued by the government.

One of the important concessions applicable in the case of conveyance relates to documents submitted by a woman. This concession is now given in many of the states to promote empowerment of women in society. The states offering such a concession include Delhi, Andhra Pradesh, Madhya Pradesh, Uttar Pradesh, Haryana, Chhattisgarh, Uttarakhand, and Rajasthan. The revenue implications of this concession are also important. In the case of Madhya Pradesh, the revenue loss is approximately 7.7 per cent (Box 6.2). SD is reduced by nearly 25 per cent with respect to transfer of immovable property valued at Rs 10 lakh in favour of one or more women (individually or severally) in Uttarakhand. In addition to this special concession, there are a large number of other exemptions that also affect the base of this tax.

Another instrument that contributes to revenue from SD is exchange of property. Rates on this instrument in different states indicate that there are variations in the high income states of Maharashtra, Gujarat, and Haryana. In Maharashtra, SD rate on the exchange of property is between 1 and 5 per cent while in Haryana, the rate is quite high, that is, 6 per cent in rural and 8 per cent in urban areas (Annexure A6.2).

Structure of Registration Fee

A document is registered as proof of its authenticity. It can be used as legal evidence to show that a particular transaction has taken place between the concerned parties. While the Indian Registration Act, 1908, leaves it to the parties concerned to get a document registered, generally the parties prefer to do so to give legal validity to the document and to minimize cases of fraud, cheating, and legal disputes.

When a document is registered under the Indian Registration Act, a particular fee is required to be paid for the service provided. The RF structure stipulated in different states indicates that there is no uniformity either in the structure or in the classification scheme; RF rate on instruments like

Box 6.2 Revenue Implications of Concessions Given to Women on Account of Registered Documents in Madhya Pradesh

Year	No. of Registered Documents in the Name of Women	As a % of Total No. of Documents Registered	Amount of Concessions (in Rs Crore) Given to Women for Registration of Documents	As a % of Total Revenue Collected from Stamp Duty & Reg. Fee
2003–4	36,849	9.70	9.24	1.50
2004–5	91,523	21.48	27.07	3.42
2005–6	1,70,442	36.17	72.84	7.21
2006–7	2,05,145	40.73	97.40	7.77

conveyance is 1 per cent in Gujarat, Jharkhand, Karnataka, Maharashtra, and Rajasthan but in other states it ranges between 0.5 and 2 per cent (Annexure A6.3).

Assessment of the Existing Structure

The given structure of SD and RF indicates that there are variations in the rates on many of the documents and that this has led to a diversion of economic activity and also loss of legitimate revenue to the states concerned.

In some of the states, the SD and RF rates are on the higher side. In view of the fact that in addition to SD and RF, the owner of a property has also to pay property tax and capital gains tax, the high rates of tax make people resort to under-valuation of transactions which not only affects the buoyancy of the tax but also has a cascading effect on other taxes imposed by other levels of government—property tax by the local government (Alm James et al. 2004).

High SD also has an effect on the circulation of 'black money'. It is widely believed that due to the high SD, many immovable property sales transactions are deferred, others are not recorded, while those recorded are recorded for a value less than the actual consideration. For 'under declaration', individuals involved in the transaction pay a part of the value of the property in cash which simply goes unrecorded. As this money continues to circulate in the economy, other transactions also take place in the black market and this money escapes the tax net. Empirical exercises indicate that the union government stands to lose about 62 per cent of every rupee of these additional tax leakages of which about 17 per cent is shared with the states. Experiences of some of the states that reduced SD and RF indicate that the revenue from SD did in fact increase.

In the absence of any scientific method for valuing the property at market price, a large number of disputes arise leading to cases being referred to the district collector. This often results in the proliferation of corrupt practices as people make every possible effort to influence the officer by greasing his palm, either in cash or in kind, to get a favourable valuation of their property.

There have been complaints from trade and industry, as well as from ordinary citizens, that the manner of levy of SD and its collection imposes hardships as well as harassment leading to an increase in transaction costs.

The cost of collection of SD and RF is on the higher side in some states like Madhya Pradesh where it ranges between 5 and 6 per cent of the revenue collected as compared to 1 to 2 per cent in other states.

Finally, the existing SD and RF system is based on registration of 'deeds' and not on 'title of ownership'. This drawback in the system stems partly from the Transfer of Property Act, 1882, under which there is no need for the title to be issued by a public authority. As a result, a person wishing to enter into a transaction concerning immovable property must himself investigate the title of that property. Under the present system, a person (with no title to the property) may sell even a well-known public place such as Connaught Place (New Delhi). In fact, such provisions have in the past led to many fraudulent documents being registered.

Administration of SD and RF

The desired objectives of a tax can be achieved only when it is administered according to the law. Failure to properly administer the tax defeats its purpose and threatens the canon of equity as full payment of the tax is done by those who cannot avoid it.

In this context, this section analyses the administration and organizational structure of Department of SD&RF. However, as there are similarities in tax organization in most of the states, the analysis of each of the aspects of the administration is presented simultaneously for all the states. Variations, if any, are indicated.

The Inspector-General of Registration and Collector of Stamps (IGR) is the head of administration of registration and stamps. Under IGR's superintendence there are two units of the departments: (i) headquarters organization, and (ii) field organization. The administration at the headquarters is under the direct supervision of IGR. IGR, drawn from the Indian Administrative Service, provides the organizational leadership to the department.

In the hierarchy (immediately under the IGR), joint IGRs /deputy IGRs supervise the work of registration and stamps. Assistant IGRs supervise the work of the divisions.

Field organization: Field establishment is another wing under IGR. At the field level, district registrars and sub-registrars work in a hierarchy. These officers work directly under the supervision of IGR.

While this administrative structure is common to all the states, Karnataka has two deputy IGRs to supervise the functioning of the intelligence wing.

Weaknesses in SD and RF Operations

There are a number of important issues with regard to SD's and RF's administrative aspects:

Non-availability of stamps of requisite denomination: It is generally felt that there is a shortage of stamps and stamp paper of various denominations. Adhesive judicial stamps are printed in denominations of 10/60 paise and Rs 1, 2, 4, 5, 10, 20, 25, 30, 35, 40, 45, 50, 60, 75, 100, 200, 300, 500, 1,000, 3,000, 5,000, and 25,000. Due to this varied structure of stamps and their non-availability in the required quantity, people often affix stamps of higher value to the documents. Generally, there are only limited outlets and very often the required denominations are out of stock. Authorized vendors are the only agency for selling certain stamps. Given the absence of alternative arrangements for sale or some provision for the payment of SD through other means (such as cash or demand draft), these vendors create an artificial scarcity for stamps.

Discretion in determining the value of property: The law gives immense discretionary powers to the officer concerned in fixing the value of a property. This 'absolute' authority vested in the officer provides immense scope for its abuse. Also, the registering officer has the authority to use his discretionary powers for impounding documents, or making a reference of the case for enquiry by the collector. This, in some cases, could lead to harassment of citizens.

Cumbersome procedures and mushrooming of middlemen: The procedure for registering and collecting tax is outdated and cumbersome and requires a plethora of documents such as clearance certificates, no objection certificates, and photographs for registration entailing repeated visits to different offices by taxpayers. This causes harassment to the taxpayers, and results in a considerable delay in registration.

Also, there is no coordination between the Income Tax Department and the Department of Stamp Duty and Registration Fee for the sharing information on valuation. Owing to this, a variety of middlemen have proliferated around the Department of SD&RF which affects honest taxpayers and puts hurdles in the way of normal commercial activity.

Understaffed and inadequate infrastructure: The Department of SD&RF is understaffed and unable to provide requisite services to customers with the existing manpower. In many states, the posts of key functionaries at the grassroots level are lying vacant. As a result, the SD&RF Department makes use of 'volunteers' who are paid out of 'unaccounted' funds. This is an appalling situation that often leads to corruption.

Also, the SD&RF Department lacks basic infrastructural facilities. Many sub-registrars' offices operate from rented premises, which are often very cramped. These do not have adequate water supply and sanitary facilities for the public.

Lack of training for officials: Most of the officers are not adequately equipped in the intricacies of assessment procedures (as laid down by law) and the legal problems that have arisen in relation to registration of documents. In fact, at no stage of recruitment or promotions are the officers of the SD&RF Department sent for appropriate training in the administration of SD&RF. Advance training in SD&RF policy and administration is characterized by its absence.

Inadequate management information system (MIS): While efforts are on, currently the SD&RF departments are not in full preparedness for MIS. Because of poor MIS, the information obtained is often not computerized. The available scattered information does not facilitate effective management. Karnataka has made headway in this aspect but could not supply data for this study relating to the revenue realized from each type of document due to lack of proper computerization.

Recommended Reforms

An analysis of SD&RF's present structure and administration indicates that the following reforms are the need of the hour:

Reducing the tax rate: The SD&RF tax rate should be fixed keeping in view the combined incidence of this tax along with property tax and capital gains tax during the transfer of property. High tax rates act as a powerful incentive for its avoidance and evasion. Also, it may be judicious to impose a low tax rate for low-value properties and a moderate rate for properties of higher value. If it is not possible to have a uniform rate of duty on conveyance across all the states, the states should at least agree to fix rates within a fairly narrow common band; this can be further narrowed down over time after consultations with each other (National Institute of Public Finance and Policy 1996).

While a few states have expressed their fear of loss of revenue due to reduction in the rate of stamp duty, the experience of some states indicates that increase in overall tax revenues will compensate for the revenues loss resulting from the reduced rate of stamp duty (Alm James et al. 2004). Stamp duty rates in UK are very low and range from 0.5 per cent to 1.5 per cent which explains why under-valuation almost never takes place there. This can be taken as an exemplary case.

Rationalizing rate slabs: In addition to the high tax rate, there are also a large number of slabs for duties fixed on an instrument. This is not only an impediment to transparency in the system but also makes compliance difficult for citizens. Thus, for administrative convenience, the number of rate slabs should be reduced considerably, particularly for instruments which are not significant from the point of view of revenue.

Availability of stamps: In order to obviate difficulties arising from the sale of stamps/stamp paper, nationalized banks and the postal department should be involved in setting up special counters for selling stamps.[11] The printing press should upgrade its technology and use it to eliminate the problem of fake stamps. In this context, it is useful to note that the security press has developed new designs for high value stamp paper. State governments can place orders for stamp paper six months in advance by paying 30 per cent of the value of the indent placed with the press.

Setting up valuation committees: Setting up valuation committees and their proper functioning is crucial for proper SD&RF administration as the value of property is the base for this tax. Currently, valuation committees are functioning in Karnataka and Madhya Pradesh. While establishing such committees in all the states will be an important step in facilitating valuation, it is noticed that in spite of the existence of such committees, there exist deviations in the valuation of property from the real value. It is, therefore, important that the department hires professional valuers. Alternatively, experts in town and country planning should undertake this task.

Alternative methods to stamps: Some alternative method (other than affixation of stamps) should be devised for making payment for SD. For instance, in Karnataka, traditional SD has been done away with and in many cases, SD for registerable documents is collected by nationalized

---

[11] In fact, as per the government notification, buying and selling of judicial and non-judicial stamp paper on a commercial basis is a permitted activity in terms of notification No. F.4 (6)-BC/68 dated 25 March 1968, and DBOD. No.Leg59/6.90 (H) dated 19 April 1968. Therefore, banks can provide the service of selling stamps/stamp paper.

banks in the form of DDs/POs/bankers cheques. Maharashtra and some other states have switched over to the use of franking machines and payment of composite duty. This not only avoids delays due to the non-availability of particular varieties of stamps but also reduces printing costs and the corruption involved and benefits consumers.

The system of e-stamping, as being developed in Madhya Pradesh, is superior to the normal system of payment of stamp duty, and can usefully be adopted by all the states.

Decentralization of executing authority: To impart speedy and efficient justice to the public, it is essential that the powers of execution under the Act be decentralized. According to the Act, the power to consolidate SD vests in the state government and thus, the powers vested in the superintendent of stamps and IGR can be decentralized. This will facilitate the early disposal of stamp cases.

Computerization: Computerization of the SD&RF Department is indispensable for its transformation into a well-organized, competent, and proficient department with greater accountability for anti-evasion activities. Computerization of the entire registration process will result in the simplification of existing time-consuming and cumbersome procedures of registration of documents and the collection of SD&RF. People-friendly procedures should be adopted to disseminate information about various aspects of the system. Tax rates and procedures should be made available on the internet.[12] This will reduce the interaction between citizens and department officials.

Andhra Pradesh has taken such an initiative with the launching of the computer-aided administration of registration department (CARD). All the states should adopt the system of e-stamping for registration.

Training for officials: Another essential reform is focusing on training of departmental personnel. As of now, at no stage of recruitment or promotions, are the officers of the department sent for appropriate training. It is of paramount importance that the officers posted in the SD&RF Department be given intensive training in the field of economics of taxation, accounts, financial rules, tax laws, and procedures of administration of SD&RF. The volume and nature of training per year should be estimated and incorporated into the manpower plan of the department.

---

[12] Tamil Nadu, for example, has disseminated the information on stamp duty and registration fee in the local language while information on guidance value is available on public demand. Karnataka has also computerized its Department of Stamps and Registration with the application of software 'Kaveri' for the convenience of the public.

Transparency and simplicity of laws and rules: There should be clarity in the provisions of the Stamp Act. The provisions in the Act should be explained in a simple language so that the people who desire to pay proper duty on their documents understand their obligations. Every effort should be made to rationalize the law, to simplify its working, and to avoid deficiencies in its implementation. In addition, the Stamp Act should also focus on prescribing more stringent penalties for offences.

Vigilance system: For checking corrupt practices prevalent in the department, a small internal vigilance system should be developed. It could be headed by an officer at the level of the district registrar, and include representatives from different departments as its members. The district registrar should be made directly accountable to IGR for its investigations.

IGR should, in turn, coordinate these internal anti-corruption investigations with external anti-corruption bodies such as the Vigilance Commission.

Performance Indicators: To assess the performance of the department, some indicators could be devised to determine the effectiveness and efficiency of the department in accomplishing its objectives. These performance indicators reveal the manner in which annual targets for different activities are set for enhancing the revenue collection. A well-organized and systematic plan to achieve the target can yield not only more revenue collection but also improve the service delivery.

The Torrens system: To have a proper record of title in the properties owned by residents in the states, it is imperative that we switch over from the system of registration of 'deeds' to a system of 'title of ownership'. Given the various merits of the system, more than 50 countries have already switched over to it (Box 6.3). In the long run, adopting the Torrens system of registration will be the best possible reform in SD&RF.

Citizens charter: Finally, the department should have a citizen's charter to enable taxpayers to know the dos and don'ts in SD&RF. In addition, a feedback system should be in place that can act as a performance indicator regarding improving the quality of service to citizens. In such a feedback system, the citizens could be provided with a questionnaire containing multiple choice questions regarding the service provided by the officers. These could include:

1. Time taken for completion of task
2. Whether the staff was helpful or not
3. Whether the services of a middleman were used

Box 6.3 Torrens System of Registration

Torrens system, which was first adopted in South Australia in 1858, is prevalent in more than 50 countries including Australia, Canada, England, some states in USA, Thailand and many European countries.

This system of registration notifies the transfer and also vests the title of land with the transferee. In this system, the State guarantees the title of the land to the purchaser and in case a purchaser finds that he has been defrauded regarding the title to the land, the State compensates him. For compensation purposes, the registration department of the State maintains a fund such as Torrens Assurance Fund of New South Wales, Australia.

A major advantage of Torrens system over Deed system is that the chances of legal disputes and litigations regarding ownership rights of land are much less under it. In addition, this will make the assessment and collection of property taxes easier. To make the Torrens system work more efficiently, all the land/property records and registration of property transactions would have to be computerized. This will make the authentication of property titles much easier. A pre-requisite for successful transition needs coordination between land records, land revenue, property tax, and SD&RF Department.

Maharashtra has already implemented the Torrens system on an experimental basis in 10 villages in Pune and Punjab is planning to switch over to this system of registration. The switchover from the system of registration of deeds to the Torrens system will help in protecting property rights in India.

4. Whether a bribe was given to the staff or middleman
5. Any other related queries

Such a questionnaire should be printed both in regional languages and in English for better understanding of the concept for initiating this system. The responses can then be directed to the SROs or DROs, whoever the citizen approached for the service. It is, however, important that there should be no mention of the citizen's identity in such a feedback system.

PROFESSION TAX

Profession tax is a tax on a profession, trade, calling, and employment. States are empowered to levy this tax by virtue of Entry 60 of list-II of the Seventh Schedule to the Constitution of India.

At present, this tax is levied by 17 states. These include Gujarat, Maharashtra, Andhra Pradesh, Karnataka, West Bengal, Chhattisgarh, Madhya Pradesh, Odisha, Uttar Pradesh, Assam, Manipur, Meghalaya, Mizoram, Nagaland, Sikkim, Tripura, and Uttarakhand.

Fiscal Significance

Profession tax cannot possibly be used as a major fiscal tool owing to the fact that the Constitution of India imposes a limitation that the maximum rate that the states can levy on any profession should not be over Rs 2,500 per annum.[13] Given this limitation, the states have been able to mobilize some resources from this tax. The trends in yield from profession tax for all the states show an increase from Rs 443 crore in 1991–2, to Rs 1,864 crore in 2000–1, and further to Rs 3,749 crore in 2009–10; a growth rate of 13.38 per cent per annum during 1991–2 to 2009–10. Also, the buoyancy of the tax was of the order of 0.99 during the same period. Consequently, the share of profession tax in states' own tax revenue increased from 1.24 per cent in 1991–2 to 1.58 per cent in 2000–1 and fell down slightly to 1.03 per cent in 2009–10. Thus, the contribution of this tax to states' own tax revenue is insignificant for all the states taken together. In 2009–10, Nagaland was the only state that had more than 10 per cent of its own tax revenue from profession tax (12.49 per cent). In the non-special category states, the share fluctuated between 1 to 3 per cent in 2009–10. Some of the states such as Chhattisgarh and Madhya Pradesh showed a declining trend during 2000–1 to 2009–10 (Table 6.10).

As the higher coefficient of buoyancy indicates a high relative growth of the yield from the tax, we examine whether the higher tax effort fully exploits the existing revenue potential of the states. In doing so, we analyse the average degree of relationship between the tax ratio in different states and the taxable capacity factor through a regression analysis. The resultant tax ratio represents the ratio that a state will have if it had used its capacity to an average extent. Comparison of an estimated tax ratio with the actual tax ratio indicates whether the state concerned is making an average degree of effort, or is showing a deviation from the norm. We

---

[13] Article 276(2) of the Constitution states that the total amount payable in respect of any one person to the state or to any one municipality, district board, local board, or any other local authority in the state, by way of taxes on profession, trades, callings, and employments should not exceed Rs 2,500 per annum.

have, therefore, calculated tax effort with reference to GSDP of states for all the non-special category states.

For profession tax, this study takes the yield from it as a function of GSDP generated by all sectors except agriculture. GSDP drawn from the agricultural sector has been excluded from the base for this tax because there is no tax levied by any of the states on employees in this sector. Thus, for estimating the taxable capacity of states in this study the following regression equation has been used: log (PROF_TAX) = a + b log (GSDP–GSDPa). By using average figures for 2006–7 to 2008–9 estimated from the available data on profession tax and on GSDP–GSDPa, the tax effort is calculated as the percentage share of actual revenue (obtained from profession tax) in the taxable capacity. The results (Table 6.9) indicate that Karnataka, Madhya Pradesh, Odisha, Maharashtra, and West Bengal were the top five states in the country that put in the highest degree of effort to collect this tax.

Structure of the Tax

Profession tax is levied both on wage/salary earners and on self-employed persons (like small traders, professionals, and owners of video libraries/

Table 6.9 States' Tax Effort in Profession Tax

(Rs Crore)

States	Profession Tax Average (2006–9)	GSDP* Average (2006–9)	Taxable Capacity	Tax Effort (%)	Rank
Andhra Pradesh	347.46	2,76,29,682.00	244.92	141.87	6
Chhattisgarh	11.82	64,41,279.35	27.65	42.75	8
Gujarat	155.54	2,71,66,345.00	238.80	65.14	7
Karnataka	460.91	2,21,29,629.29	175.64	262.42	1
Madhya Pradesh	181.30	1,21,57,508.00	71.60	253.20	2
Maharashtra	1,432.10	6,04,32,075.27	791.06	181.04	4
Odisha	90.74	95,27,139.63	49.70	182.59	3
Uttar Pradesh	18.26	2,77,76,922.67	246.88	7.40	9
West Bengal	293.84	2,32,04,561.33	188.57	155.82	5

Note: GSDP* = Gross State Domestic Product from all sectors except for agriculture.

Table 6.10 State-wise Trends in Revenue from Profession Tax

(Rs Crore)

States	1991–2	2001–2	2005–6	2007–8	2008–9	2009–10	2010–11 (RE)	2011–12 (BE)	GR	Buoyancy
Non-special Category States										
Andhra Pradesh	31.40	1,137.17	227.07	355.72	374.46	430.36	540.00	648.00	16.60	1.30
	(1.03)	(9.05)	(1.18)	(1.24)	(1.12)	(1.22)	(1.14)	(1.15)		
Chhattisgarh		47.62	20.57	11.54	7.68	8.82	9.90	12.30	−22.10	−1.50
		(2.39)	(0.51)	(0.21)	(0.12)	(0.12)	(0.12)	(0.13)		
Gujarat	38.93	93.31	119.32	149.67	185.84	196.87	227.24	249.96	9.70	0.70
	(1.35)	(1.01)	(0.76)	(0.68)	(0.79)	(0.74)	(0.66)	(0.64)		
Karnataka	47.89	167.23	330.25	451.37	538.79	527.21	550.00	610.00	13.60	1.00
	(1.65)	(1.70)	(1.77)	(1.74)	(1.95)	(1.72)	(1.45)	(1.39)		
Madhya Pradesh	10.46	182.18	158.45	192.97	182.18	216.13	222.00	240.00	0.90	0.10
	(0.49)	(3.87)	(1.74)	(1.61)	(1.34)	(1.25)	(1.09)	(1.04)		
Maharashtra	212.42	981.98	1,157.72	1,488.35	1,561.22	1612.35	1,608.14	1,700.00	12.90	1.00
	(3.57)	(4.61)	(3.45)	(3.13)	(3.00)	(2.73)	(2.19)	(2.03)		
Odisha		39.86	66.46	86.44	112.18	135.55	145.00	165.00	22.70	1.30
		(1.62)	(1.33)	(1.26)	(1.40)	(1.51)	(1.37)	(1.34)		
Uttar Pradesh		14.53	11.80	18.96	20.90	20.94	25.84	31.01	17.50	1.50
		(0.14)	(0.06)	(0.08)	(0.07)	(0.06)	(0.06)	(0.06)		
West Bengal	80.18	215.87	249.15	295.06	321.60	362.40	453.00	566.25	8.80	0.70
	(3.27)	(3.32)	(2.40)	(2.25)	(2.23)	(2.14)	(2.13)	(2.04)		

Special Category States

State									
Assam	12.08	73.27	99.80	124.68	137.73	150.15	160.58	166.00	13.80	1.30
	(2.36)	(4.68)	(3.09)	(3.71)	(3.32)	(3.01)	(2.72)	(2.53)		
Manipur	2.14	12.87	11.97	14.72	15.46	17.63	25.10	30.00	11.70	0.90
	(14.91)	(24.76)	(12.61)	(9.99)	(9.09)	(8.99)	(10.00)	(9.44)		
Meghalaya	0.53	0.89	1.16	1.46	−6.47	2.06	2.39	2.78	14.60	1.30
	(1.25)	(0.65)	(0.46)	(0.46)	(−1.75)	(0.46)	(0.52)	(0.47)		
Mizoram	0.92	3.63	4.53	5.32	5.93	7.93	8.01	10.00	12.80	1.10
	(27.54)	(18.99)	(8.23)	(6.86)	(6.27)	(7.37)	(6.45)	(5.77)		
Nagaland	2.25	12.00	14.87	17.72	19.86	22.54	26.00	29.00	16.10	1.40
	(12.50)	(22.88)	(14.09)	(13.49)	(12.73)	(12.49)	(12.10)	(11.55)		
Sikkim			47.81	49.10	1.56	2.13	2.00	2.00	−48.60	−4.50
			(32.48)	(24.82)	(0.85)	(0.96)	(0.86)	(0.74)		
Tripura	3.38	11.59	21.95	23.74	25.98	29.17	30.00	31.50	13.70	1.00
	(11.72)	(7.31)	(7.41)	(6.40)	(5.87)	(5.53)	(4.79)	(4.02)		
Uttarakhand		2.18	3.49	5.18	6.09	7.13	8.00	12.00	17.70	1.00
		(0.24)	(0.20)	(0.19)	(0.20)	(0.20)	(0.18)	(0.25)		
All States	442.59	2,997.43	2,546.62	3,291.85	3,510.98	3,749	4,044	4,507.00	13.38	0.99
	(1.24)	(2.34)	(1.20)	(1.15)	(1.09)	(1.03)	(0.88)	(0.84)		

Notes: GR = Growth Rate; RE: Revised Estimate; BE: Budget Estimate; 1. The figures in parentheses indicate the percentage share of profession tax in SOTR for each state; 2. The growth rate and buoyancy for the States are calculated for the period 1991–2 to 2009–10. For the bifurcated States and newly formed States, the growth rate and buoyancy is calculated for the period 2001–2 to 2009–10. In Odisha, the growth rate and buoyancy are for the period 2000–1 to 2009–10, and for Sikkim it is for the period 2004–5 to 2009–10 (according to the year of levy of the tax).

theatres), including legal persons. The tax rate is generally specific with several slabs and ranges from Rs 720 to Rs 2,500 per annum. The tax rate varies considerably among the states (Annexure A6.4).

The tax is not levied in Haryana, Bihar, Goa, Jharkhand, and Punjab among the non-special category states and in Himachal Pradesh, Arunachal Pradesh, and Jammu and Kashmir among the special-category states. The profession tax was levied in Uttar Pradesh from 1966–7, but was withdrawn in 1971–2. Since then the tax is assigned to local bodies. In Rajasthan, the tax was levied only on persons having a salary/wage more than Rs 1.50 lakh p.a. and also paying income tax. But the tax has been abolished since 2004.

Exemptions

In all the states, certain categories of persons are exempt from the tax. This includes agricultural labourers and farmers, persons above the age of superannuation, members of the armed forces, physically handicapped persons, and ex-servicemen.

Administration of Profession Tax

In most states, the Commissioner of Commercial Taxes looks after the administration of profession tax. Generally, the administrative responsibility is distributed among jurisdictional commercial tax officers and specialized profession tax officers (PTOs). For all registered employees, including registered sales tax dealers, PTOs are assessing authorities.

Taxpayer identification and collection are the most important areas of administration of this tax since it has to be collected in small amounts from a large number of individuals. This information is usually gathered from the registering authority for each type of assessee. However, for those in the informal sector, a door-to-door survey is attempted in some cases.

Recommended Reforms

One of the reforms required for making profession tax an important fiscal tool with the states is to increase the ceiling of Rs 2,500 fixed in the Constitution on the levy of this tax. As has already been discussed in the

Empowered Committee of State Finance Ministers, the ceiling of this tax must be increased to Rs 25,000.

The two-way classification of professionals like doctors, lawyers, and architects on the basis of years of practice and location requires modification. If only professionals with a minimum period of practice are defined as liable for the levy of this tax, the location may not have much to do with the ability to pay the tax.

Further, a rate like Rs 200 per annum or Rs 25 a month is not worth collecting if the collection costs exceed the revenue collection from this tax.

With a view to bringing in potential professional taxpayers into the tax net, the states must undertake periodic surveys of different occupational groups. It is also necessary that the staff strength in the administrative system is augmented. Despite registers being prescribed for watching the performance under profession tax, in most of the states data about the number of enrolled persons who have paid their dues on time, the number of registered persons who have filed returns on time, assessments pending and the extent of delays, etc. is not readily available. Since more effort is required to raise revenue from profession tax, lesser attention is paid at all levels and the tax has not been given priority in the department's computerization programme.

* * *

Among state taxes, land revenue is the oldest source of tax revenue for the states. It is levied on land and the method of levying the tax varies from state to state due to variations in tax criteria which could be based on location of land, soil productivity, yield, or the value of the crop. Besides, some states levy cess and surcharge on land revenue and the yield is assigned to local bodies. In some of the states, this tax is collected by local bodies. This tax has been abolished in Punjab, Haryana, and Arunachal Pradesh.

AIT is imposed on receipts of agricultural income. It is applicable only in five Indian states. Its share is negligible in the states' own tax revenue. For individual taxpayers, the rate of tax varies from 5 per cent to 60 per cent; it varies from 30 per cent to 50 per cent for private companies. In general, the system is characterized by the low tax rate, narrow base, high exemption limits, and a large number of exemptions and exclusions. Also, non-imposition of this tax in most states and the lack of integration of AIT with personal income tax create a loophole for evasion of tax on non-agricultural income: part of one's non-agricultural income can be passed off as agricultural income. The system of AIT should be reformed in such a way that the states are able to mobilize the much needed resources and at the same time maintain inter-sector equity in the levy of tax.

Profession tax is levied on wage and salary of employed persons and honorarium or fee for the self-employed persons. It is levied on a specific basis in 17 states. Since there is a ceiling on the maximum rate of the tax imposed by the Constitution of India, the states have not been able to utilize this tax as a fiscal tool. Also, there are many exemptions under the tax for certain categories of persons. The need of the hour is to increase the ceiling on the rate of the tax and to conduct periodic surveys for different occupational groups to bring potential taxpayers into the tax net.

Stamp duty (SD) is levied on all judicial as well as non-judicial transactions of instruments. Registration fee (RF) is collected by the Government when the documents or instruments are registered. The share of stamp duty and registration fee (SD and RF) has increased over time and currently, it contributes 10 per cent of the states' own tax revenue. However, there are huge variations in the current rates amongst the States. Imposition of additional duties or surcharges on the basic SD is also contributing to variations in SD rates. In addition, there is a difference between statutory rate and effective rate owing to the large number of exemptions and concessions in the tax structure. To promote empowerment of women, many of the states have provided concessions for conveyance deeds, related to valuation of property. The large number of exceptions have affected the base of the tax. The existing unscientific system of valuation of property gives rise to disputes. Reforms in structure and administration are required to bring transparency into the system and to modernize the tax department. Adoption of e-stamping and setting up of valuation committees could be a major reform for the system.

Annexure A6.1

Comparative Picture of Land Revenue in Different States

States	Land used for Agri./Allied activities	Irrigated/Unirrigated land	Cess/Surcharges	Tax on commercial crops
Non-special category states				
Andhra Pradesh		Varies between Rs 100 to 500 when water is supplied through all major and medium irrigation projects. And between Rs 60 to 500 in case of all other sources of irrigation.		
Bihar		Rs 10.00 per acre for irrigated land and Rs 5.00 per acre for non-irrigated land	Cess @ 145% of the land rent	
Chhattisgarh			Rs 0.50 per rupee of land revenue	
Goa	100 paisa per hectare			
Gujarat			Varies between Rs 0.50–3 according to districts and type of land use.	

(contd.)

Annexure A6.1 (*contd.*)

States	Land used for Agri./Allied activities	Irrigated/Unirrigated land	Cess/Surcharges	Tax on commercial crops
Jharkhand			145% of land revenue	
Karnataka		Rs 5 per Katha in case of dry land and the rate is double of the rate levied on dry land in case of garden and wet land.	75% of land revenue	Tax on commercial crop is called as AIT
Kerala		Rs 0.50 per acre/p.a up to 20 acres and Rs 1 per acre/p.a above 20 acres in Panchayat; Rs 1 per acre/p.a up to 6 acres and Rs 2 per acre/p.a above 6 acres in Municipality and Rs 2 per acre/p.a up to 2 acres and Rs 4 per acre/p.a above 2 acres in corporation area.	Irrigation cess which varies between Rs 17–Rs 148.5	Tax on commercial crop is known as plantation tax

Madhya Pradesh		50 paisa on every one rupees rent	Rs 2.50 per hectare on ground nut, tobacco etc. and Rs 5 per hectare on sugarcane.
Maharashtra	Varies between Rs 2.02 to Rs 62.50 according to rental divisions in case of paddy land.	In case of irrigated land the rate varies between Rs 2.50 to Rs 50 and in case of un-irrigated land the rate varies between Rs 0.31 to Rs 26.07	Under Maharashtra Education and Employment Guarantee (Cess) Act, 1962, there is a special assessment levied on commercial crops which varies between Rs 40–Rs 380 depending on the type of commercial crop.
Rajasthan		In irrigated land the minimum rate varies between Rs 1.88 to Rs 13.00 and the maximum rate varies between Rs 4.15 to Rs 112.50 per hectare (district-wise	A surcharge of 50 paisa per rupee on the total amount of land revenue is levied when the amount is between Rs 75 to

(*contd.*)

Annexure A6.1 (*contd.*)

States	Land used for Agri./Allied activities	Irrigated/Unirrigated land	Cess/Surcharges	Tax on commercial crops
		variation). In case of un-irrigated land the minimum rate varies between Rs 0.13 to Rs 3.75 and the maximum rate varies between Rs 0.63 to Rs 37.48 per hectare (district-wise variation).	Rs 100; 75 paisa per rupee when the amount is between Rs 100 to Rs 150 and the amount of surcharge is equal to the total amount of land revenue when the amount is Rs 150 or more.	
Tamil Nadu		In case of wet area the minimum rate varies between Rs 0.37 to Rs 3.00 and the maximum rate varies between Rs 3.50 to Rs 32.50 per acre (district-wise variation). In case of dry area the minimum rate varies between Rs 0.19 to Rs 0.62 and the maximum rate varies between Rs 2.75 to Rs 8.25.	Water cess at the rates ranging upto Rs 20 per acre for first wet crop and up to Rs 30 for Dufussal crops in respect of project which are designated for irrigation of dry crops or for short-term crops only. However, the usual rates of water cess in respect	

		of new tanks under the special minor irrigation projects varies between Rs 7.50 to Rs 22.50 depending upon crop intensity. Local cess was levied at the rate of two rupee on every rupee of land revenue payable to government.
Uttar Pradesh		Varies between Rs 10 and Rs 20 per acre for irrigated land and Rs 5 and Rs 10 per acre for un-irrigated land.
West Bengal	Rs 20 per acre/per annum for agricultural purpose, Rs 30 for activities allied to agriculture and tea cultivation.	

(contd.)

Annexure A6.1 (*contd.*)

States	Land used for Agri./Allied activities	Irrigated/Unirrigated land	Non-agricultural Use
Special Category States			
Assam	In rural areas the rate varies between Rs 5 to Rs 8.		
	In case of tea land the rate of land revenue is Rs 12 for Brahmaputra valley and Rs 9 for Barak valley.		
	In case of special land bearing green tea leaves the rate of tax is 32 paise per kg. for Assam valley, 29 paisa for Barak valley and 30 paisa for Brahmaputra valley.		
Himachal Pradesh		In case of irrigated land the rate varies between Rs 2 to Rs 15 per hectare and in case of un-irrigated land the rate varies between Rs 1.50 to Rs 14.	

(contd.)

Manipur	The rate varies between Rs 61.90 to Rs 84.40 on the basis of class of land.
Mizoram	Rate on patta land varies between Rs 40 to Rs 100, on agriculture land LSC varies between Rs 100 to Rs 200 per hectare per annum and there is progressive increase of rate per hactare beyond 2 hectare.
Meghalaya	In the Garo district the rate of land revenue is Rs 60, Rs 80 and Rs 120 per bigha for garden lands, tea lands and Fishery land respectively.
	In Jaintia Hills district the rate of land revenue for paddy cultivation in dry area is 80 paisa per bigha and for wet area it is 60 paisa. For orange crones the rate is Re 1.

Annexure A6.1 (*contd.*)

States	Land used for Agri./Allied activities	Irrigated/Unirrigated land	Cess/Surcharges	Tax on commercial crops
Sikkim		In case of wetland the rate varies between Rs 9 to Rs 30 and in case of dry land the rate varies between Rs 5 to Rs 15 according to different circle.		
Tripura			For Viti land the rate is Rs 6 for Nal land it is Rs 7.50 and for Lunga land the rate is Rs 6 per acre.	
Uttarakhand		In case of irrigated land the rate varies between Rs 10 to Rs 20 and for un-irrigated land rate is Rs 5 for un-irrigated land.		

Source: Data collected from the relevant State Departments.

Annexure A6.2

Rates of Stamp Duty in Indian States

States	Conveyance	Mortgage of Property - With Possession	Mortgage of Property - Without Possession	Lease for more than 30 years or in perpetuity	Power of attorney
Andhra Pradesh	5% of market value (MV) of property	5% of loan amount	3% of loan amount	5% MV of Property or 10 times of AAR, whichever is higher.	1. For registration of documents Rs 20 2. For authorizing person Rs 20 – Rs 75 3. For construction on/development of/sale/transfer of immovable property 5% of MV of the property
Bihar	6% of consideration set forth or MV of the property	2% of the amount secured	1% of the amount secured	For 30 to 100 years 6% on 4 times of AAR	1. For registration of documents Rs 100

(contd.)

Annexure A6.2 (*contd.*)

States	Conveyance	Mortgage of Property – With Possession	Mortgage of Property – Without Possession	Lease for more than 30 years or in perpetuity	Power of attorney
				For more than 100 years or in perpetuity 6% of 1/6th of the whole amount of rent to be paid for first 50 years.	2. For authorizing person Rs 200–Rs 500 3. For construction on/development of/sale/transfer of immovable property 5% of MV of the property
Gujarat	(a) Relating to immovable property 3.5% of MV of property	3.5% of the amount secured	1. where the loan or debt does not exceed Rs 10 crore 0.25% (max. Rs 1 lakh)	For 30 to 98 years 3.5% on 3 times of AAR	1. For registration of documents Rs 100
	(b) Relating to movable property 2% of MV of property		2. where it exceeds Rs 10 crore 0.50% (max. Rs 3 lakh)	For the lease in perpetuity 3.5% of 1/5th of the whole amount of rent to be paid for first 50 years.	2. For authorizing person Rs 100

Haryana	1. For rural areas 5% on market value	3% (in Rural areas) & 5% (in Urban areas)	1.5% of the amount secured	For 30 to 100 years same duty as on conveyance on 4 times of AAR	1. For registration of documents Rs 1.50
	2. For Urban areas 7% (including 2% for Municipal duty in Urban areas)			For more than 100 years or in perpetuity same duty as on conveyance of $1/6^{th}$ ($1/10^{th}$ if lease granted for agricultural purposes) of the whole amount of rent to be paid for first 50 years.	2. For authorizing Person Rs 3 – Rs 30
	3. (2%)*				3. For construction on/ development of/sale/ transfer of immovable property 1.5% of MV of the property

3. For construction on/ development of/ sale/ transfer of immovable property 1% of MV of the property

(*contd.*)

Annexure A6.2 (*contd.*)

States	Conveyance	Mortgage of Property — With Possession	Mortgage of Property — Without Possession	Lease for more than 30 years or in perpetuity	Power of attorney
Jharkhand	4% of market value of property	4% of market value	Where amount secured exceeds Rs 5000 2.5%–3% of amount secured	For 30 to 100 years same duty as on conveyance on 8 times of AAR For more than 100 years or in perpetuity same duty as on conveyance of 1/4th of the whole amount of rent to be paid for first 50 years.	1. For registration of documents Rs 60 2. For authorizing person Rs 15.75 to Rs 31.50 3. For construction on/development of/sale/transfer of immovable property 4% of MV of the property

Karnataka	7.5% of MV of property	7.5% of the amount secured	0.50% of the amount secured	7.5 of MV of the property	1. For registration of documents Rs 100 2. For authorizing Person Rs 100–Rs 200 3. For construction on/development of/sale/transfer of immovable property 7.5% of MV of the property
Kerala	1. If property situated within municipalities corporations 8.5% of MV of property 2. If other property 6% of MV of property	Same duty as conveyance	5% of the amount secured	For 30 to 100 years same duty as on conveyance on 4 times of AAR For more than 100 years or in perpetuity same duty as on conveyance of 1/6th of the whole amount of rent to be paid for first 50 years.	1. For registration of documents Rs 25 2. For authorizing person Rs 50–Rs 500

(*contd.*)

Annexure A6.2 (*contd.*)

States	Conveyance	Mortgage of Property — With Possession	Mortgage of Property — Without Possession	Lease for more than 30 years or in perpetuity	Power of attorney
Madhya Pradesh	7.5% of MV of the property (5.5%)*	7.5% of the amount secured	4% of the amount secured	7.5% of MV of the property	1. For registration of documents Rs 50 2. For authorizing person Rs 50–Rs 100 3. For construction on/development of/sale/transfer of immovable property 7.5% of MV of the property

3. For construction on/development of/sale/transfer of immovable property same duty as on conveyance

Maharashtra	1%–5% of MV of property (varying according to area and municipal council)	Same duty as on conveyance	0.5% on the amount (subject to min. of Rs 100 and max. of Rs 10 lakh).	Same as conveyance duty on 90% of the MV of the property	1. For registration of documents Rs 100 2. For authorizing person Rs 100 3. For construction on/development of/sale/transfer of immovable property same duty as on conveyance on MV of the property
Odisha	3%–8% of MV of property (varying according to whether movable or immovable and multi unit houses)	Same duty as is leviable on conveyance	Same duty as is leviable on conveyance	Same duty as is leviable on conveyance	1. For registration of documents Rs 100 2. For authorizing person Rs 5–Rs 100

(*contd.*)

Annexure A6.2 (contd.)

States	Conveyance	Mortgage of Property — With Possession	Mortgage of Property — Without Possession	Lease for more than 30 years or in perpetuity	Power of attorney
Punjab	1. For immovable properties: Rs 3 to Rs 30 (varying according to the value of such conveyance from Rs 50 to in excess of Rs 1,000)	Rs 2 to Rs 20 (varying according to the amount secured from Rs 50 to in excess of Rs 1,000)	Rs 10 to Rs 20 (varying according to the amount secured from Rs 500 to in excess of Rs 1,000)	For 30 to 100 years same duty as on conveyance on 4 times of AAR	3. For construction on/development of/sale/transfer of immovable property 7.5% of MV of the property 1. For registration of documents Rs 100

	2. For other conveyances: Rs 2 to Rs 15 (varying according to the value of such conveyance from Rs 50 to in excess of Rs 1,000)	For more than 100 years or in perpetuity same duty as on conveyance of 1/6th (1/10th if lease granted for agricultural purposes) of the whole amount of rent to be paid for first 50 years.	2. For authorizing person Rs 300–Rs 600
			3. For construction on/ development of/sale/ transfer of immovable property same duty as on conveyance for amount of consideration
Rajasthan	1. If relating to immovable property 11% of the MV of the property	Same duty as on conveyance	5% of the amount secured	For lease not less than 20 years same duty as on conveyance on value of average rent of 2 years	1. For registration of documents Rs 10

(*contd.*)

Annexure A6.2 (*contd.*)

States	Conveyance	Mortgage of Property (With Possession)	Mortgage of Property (Without Possession)	Lease for more than 30 years or in perpetuity	Power of attorney
	2. If relating to movable property 0.5 % of the MV of the property			For lease more than 20 years or in perpetuity Same duty as on conveyance on MV of the property	2. For authorizing person Rs 10 to Rs 50 3. For construction on/development of/sale/transfer of immovable property same duty as on conveyance on MV of the property
Tamil Nadu	6% of MV of the property	3% of the amount secured	1% of the amount secured (subject to max. Rs 20,000)	For 30 to 100 years 4% of the amount of rent, fine, premium or advance, if any payable	1. For registration of documents Rs 5

				2. For authorizing person Rs 15 to Rs 175
		For more than 100 years or in perpetuity 8% of the amount of rent, fine, premium or advance, if any payable (subject to max. Rs 20)		3. For construction on/development of/sale/transfer of immovable property 4% on MV of the property
		Same duty as on conveyance [clause (a)] on MV of the property		1. For registration of documents: Rs 10
				2. For authorizing Person Rs 20 to Rs 100
		Rs 10 to Rs 70, varying according to the amount secured		
	Same duty as on conveyance [clause (a)] but on property of greater value			
Uttar Pradesh	1. If relating to immovable property:			
	• If MV of property does not exceed Rs 500–Rs 60			

(*contd.*)

Annexure A6.2 (*contd.*)

States	Conveyance	Mortgage of Property — With Possession	Mortgage of Property — Without Possession	Lease for more than 30 years or in perpetuity	Power of attorney
	• If MV of property exceeds Rs 500–Rs 125 2. If relating to movable property: Rs 20 3. 6% on MV of property (reduced rate)*				3. For construction on/development of/sale/transfer of immovable property: same duty as on conveyance [clause (a)] for the MV of the property
West Bengal	For Panchayat areas: 5% on MV of the property	Same duty as on conveyance on amount secured	2% of the amount secured	For 30 to 100 years: same duty as on conveyance on 4 times of AAR	1. For registration of documents Rs 5

For municipality and development authority areas: 6% on MV of the property

For more than 100 years or in perpetuity: same duty as on conveyance of $1/6^{th}$ ($1/10^{th}$ if lease granted for agricultural purposes) of the whole amount of rent to be paid for first 50 years.

2. For authorizing person: Rs 6 to Rs 100

3. For construction on/development of/sale/transfer of immovable property same duty as on conveyance for the MV of the property

Source: Data collected from the relevant State Departments.
Note: 1. * The rates in parentheses are reduced rates of Stamp Duty for women.
2. AAR: Average Annual Rent; MV= market value.

Annexure A6.3

Rates of Registration Fee in States

States	Conveyance	Exchange	Mortgage of property	Gift	Power of attorney
Andhra Pradesh	0.5% on every Rs 1000 or part thereof		0.5% on every Rs 1000 or part thereof	0.5% on every Rs 1000 or part thereof	Rs 100 to Rs 1,000
Bihar	1. For instrument for sale: 2% of the MV of the property 2. For other conveyances: 4% of the MV of the property	4% of the MV of the property of greater value under exchange	2% on the amount secured by such deed.	4% of the MV of the property, which is the subject matter of gift.	1. For registration of documents: Rs 250 2. For authorizing person: Rs 250 3. For construction on/development of/sale/transfer of immovable property: Rs 250

Chhattisgarh	Rs 970 for every Rs 1 lakh of the market valued of the property.		1% of the MV of the property, which is the subject matter of gift.
Gujarat	1% of the MV of the property		1% of the MV of the property, which is the subject matter of gift.
Jharkhand	1% of the MV of the property	1% of the MV of the property of greater value under exchange	
Karnataka	1% of the MV of the property	1% of the MV of the property	1% of the MV of the property, which is the subject matter of gift.
Kerala	2% on the value of consideration for such conveyance	2% of the amount secured by such deed	2% on the value of consideration for such conveyance, which is the subject matter of gift.

(contd.)

Annexure A6.3 (*contd.*)

States	Conveyance	Exchange	Mortgage of property	Gift	Power of attorney
Madhya Pradesh	Up to Rs 50,000: 1.1% of the market value On amount exceeding Rs 50,000: 0.8% of the market value				
Maharashtra	1% of the MV of the property (Subject to min. Rs 100 and max. Rs 30,000)	1% of the MV of the property of greater value under exchange (Subject to min. Rs 100 and max. Rs 30,000)	1% of the MV of the property (Subject to min. Rs 100 and max. Rs 30,000)	1% of the MV of the property, which is the subject matter of gift (Subject to min. Rs 100 and max. Rs 30,000)	1% of the MV of the property (Subject to min. Rs 100 and max. Rs 30,000)
Odisha	2% on the value of consideration for such conveyance	2% of the MV of the property of greater value under exchange	2% of the amount secured by such deed	2% on the value of consideration for such conveyance, which is the subject matter of gift.	Rs 300

State	Conveyance	Exchange	Mortgage	Gift	Power of Attorney
Punjab					Rs 25–50
Rajasthan	1% of the value of consideration subject to max. of Rs 25,000	Same as on conveyance	Same as on conveyance	Same as on conveyance	Same as on conveyance
Tamil Nadu	1% on the value of consideration for such conveyance		1. If possession not given: Rs 5,000 2. If possession given: Rs 2,00,000		Rs 50
Uttar Pradesh	2% of the value of consideration subject to max. of Rs 5,000		2% of the amount secured subject to max. of Rs 5,000		
West Bengal	1.1% on the value of consideration for such conveyance	1.1% of the MV of the property of greater value under exchange		1.1% on the value of consideration for such conveyance, which is the subject matter of gift.	

Source: Data collected from the relevant State Departments.

ANNEXURE A6.4

Rate Structure of Profession Tax Across Different States

State/Class of Assessees	Salary and Wage Earners	Legal Practitioners	Medical Practitioners	Directors of Companies registered under Companies Act, 1956	Technical and professional consultants like engineers, chartered accountants, architects	Postal agents or chief agents, principal agents, special agents, insurance agents and surveyors or loss assessors registered or licensed under the Insurance Act 1938 (4 of 1938)	Estate agents or promoters or brokers or commission agents or delcredere agents or mercentile agents	% age share in SOTR in 2006–7
Andhra Pradesh	Rs 60–200 PM for salary of Rs 5,001–20,000	Rs 500–1,000 PA for Hyderabad and Secunderabad and Rs 300–750 PA for other areas	Rs 1,000–2,500 PA for Hyderabad and Secunderabad and Rs 500–1,500 PA for other areas	Rs 2,500 PA	Rs 550–2,500 PA in Hyderabad and Secunderabad and Rs 330–1,000 PA in other areas	Rs 550 PA	Rs 550–1,000 PA	1.3

Gujarat	Rs 20–200 for monthly salary of Rs 3,000–12,000 and above	Rs 500–2,000 levied by local bodies and Rs 1,000 levied by State Govt.	Rs 500–2,000 levied by local bodies and Rs 1000 levied by State Govt.	Rs 500–2,000 levied by local bodies and Rs 1,000 levied by State Govt.	Rs 500–2,000 levied by local bodies and Rs 1,000 levied by State Govt.	Rs 500–2,000 levied by local bodies and Rs 1,000 levied by State Govt.	0.71
Karnataka	Rs 60–200 PM for salary of Rs 5,000–15,000 and above	Rs 1,500–2,500 PA for Bengaluru and Rs 1,000–1,500 PA for other areas	Rs 1,000–2,500 PA for standing in profession of 2 yrs–10 yrs or more	Rs 1,000–2,500 PA for Bengaluru and Rs 1,000–1,500 for other areas	Rs 1500 PA	Rs 2,500 for Bengaluru and Rs 1,000–1,500 for other areas	1.68
Maharashtra	Rs 720–2,500 PA for salary of Rs 2,500–10,000 and above	Rs 2,500 PA	Rs 2,500 PA	Rs 2,500 PA	Rs 2,500 PA	Rs 2,500 PA	3.11

(contd.)

Annexure A6.4 (*contd.*)

State/Class of Assessees	Salary and Wage Earners	Legal Practitioners	Medical Practitioners	Directors of Companies registered under Companies Act, 1956	Technical and professional consultants like engineers, chartered accountants, architects	Postal agents or chief agents, principal agents, special agents, insurance agents and surveyors or loss assessors registered or licensed under the Insurance Act 1938 (4 of 1938)	Estate agents or promoters or brokers or commission agents or delcredere agents or mercentile agents	% age share in SOTR in 2006–7
Odisha	Rs 30–200 PM for salary of Rs 5,001–20,000 and above	Rs 360–2,400 PA for annual gross income of Rs 60,000–Rs 2,40,000 and above	Rs 360–2,400 PA for annual gross income of Rs 60,000–2,40,000 and above		Rs 360–2,400 PA for annual gross income of Rs 60,000–2,40,000 and above	Rs 200–500 PA for annual gross income of Rs 15,000–96,000	Rs 1,000–1,200 PA	1.21

West Bengal	Rs 30–200 PM for salary of Rs 3,001–40,001 and above	Rs 216–2,400 PA for annual gross income of Rs 18,001–4,80,001 and above	Rs 216–2,400 PA for annual gross income of Rs 18,001–4,80,001 and above	Rs 216–2,400 PA for annual gross income of Rs 18,001–4,80,001 and above	Rs 216–2,400 PA for annual gross income of Rs 18,001–4,80,001 and above	Rs 2,500 per annum	2.26

Special Category States

Assam	Rs 30–208 per mensem for salary of Rs 3,500–9,000 and above	Rs 480–2,500 per mensem for annual gross income of Rs 40,000–1,00,000 and above	Rs 480–2,500 per mensem for annual gross income of Rs 40,000–1,00,000 and above	Rs 2,500 PA	Rs 480–2,500 per mensem for annual gross income of Rs 40,000–1,00,000 and above	Rs 480–2,500 per mensem for annual gross income of Rs 40,000–1,00,000 and above	Rs 2,500 PA	3.11
Manipur	Rs 300–2,500 PA for gross annual income of Rs 15,001–1,25,000	Rs 1,000–2,500 for standing in profession for 3–5 yrs or more	Rs 1,000–2,500 for standing in profession for 3–5 yrs or more	Rs 1,000	Rs 1,000–2,500 for standing in profession for 3–5 yrs or more	Rs 1,000–2,500 for standing in profession for 3–5 yrs or more	Rs 2,000	10.93

(*contd.*)

Annexure A6.4 (*contd.*)

State/Class of Assessees	Salary and Wage Earners	Legal Practitioners	Medical Practitioners	Directors of Companies registered under Companies Act, 1956	Technical and professional consultants like engineers, chartered accountants, architects	Postal agents or chief agents, principal agents, special agents, insurance agents and surveyors or loss assessors registered or licensed under the Insurance Act 1938 (4 of 1938)	Estate agents or promoters or brokers or commission agents or delcredere agents or mercentile agents	% age share in SOTR in 2006–7
Mizoram	Rs 100–2,500 for gross annual income of Rs 10,001–250,000 and more	Rs 350–1,000 PA for standing in the profession of 3–10 yrs or more	Rs 350–1,000 PA for standing in the profession of 3–10 yrs or more	Rs 1,000 PA	Rs 350–1,000 PA for standing in the profession of 3–10 yrs or more	Rs 250–1,000 PA for standing in profession of 3–10 yrs and above	Rs 1,000 PA	7.39

Sikkim	Rs 125–200 PM for salary of Rs 20,001–40,001 and more	Rs 100–2,500 PA for gross annual income of Rs 25,001–2,70,001 and above	Rs 100–2,500 PA for gross annual income of Rs 25,001–2,70,001 and above	Rs 100–2,500 PA for gross annual income of Rs 25,001–2,70,001 and above	Rs 100–2,500 PA for gross annual income of Rs 25,001–2,70,001 and above	Rs 100–2,500 PA for gross annual income of Rs 25,001–2,70,001 and above	Rs 1,500 PA	26.98
Tripura	Rs 55–180 PM for salary of Rs 2,500–10,001 and above	Rs 300–1,500 for practicing in Tripura town or other place, with 1 lakh or more population, having standing in profession of 5–15 yrs or more	Rs 300–1,500 for practicing in Tripura town or other place, with 1 lakh or more population, having standing in profession of 5–15 yrs or more	Rs 1,500 PA	Rs 300–1,500 for practicing in Tripura Town or other place, with 1 lakh or more population, having standing in profession of 5–15 yrs or more	Rs 300–1,500 for practicing in Tripura town or other place, with 1 lakh or more population, having standing in profession of 5–15 yrs or more	Rs 1,500 PA	6.51

Source: Data collected from the relevant State Departments.

CHAPTER 7

STATES' DOMESTIC TRADE TAXES

As per the state list of the Constitution (as given in Annexure A1.2 to Chapter 1), the important taxes that are assigned to the states include sales tax (now State VAT), state excise duty (SED), motor vehicles tax (MVT), passengers and goods tax (P&GT), electricity duty, and entertainment tax. Sales tax alone contributes about 72 per cent of the tax revenue from commodities and services, while 23 per cent comes from SED, MVT, and P&GT. Thus, these taxes contribute approximately 95 per cent of the states' own tax revenue from taxes on commodities and services.

SALES TAX (STATE VAT)

Sales tax has its evolution in India dating back to Kautilya's *Arthashastra*[1]. However, its revival as a fiscal measure is an outcome of the present century when, for the first time, the Indian states were empowered to impose sales tax through the autonomy provided by the Government of India Act, 1935. The first state to resort to a general sales tax was Tamil Nadu[2] that introduced a multi-point sales tax in 1939. Following Tamil Nadu, many states resorted to this form of taxation during and after the Second World

---

[1] References of taxes on sales and citation of rules thereof provide ample evidence of a first-point sales tax being in existence in ancient India. See for details Purohit, Mahesh (1975).

[2] The tax was levied in erstwhile Province of Madras which included the present state of Tamil Nadu and parts of many of the present southern States. For the details of evolution of sales tax in India see Purohit, Mahesh (1991).

War. As there has been no specific rationale behind the introduction of a particular form of sales tax, models adopted initially underwent many changes.

The Indian Constitution clearly provided the authority to the states vide Entry 54 of the state list which states that the states are authorized to levy 'tax on the sale or purchase of goods other than newspapers, subject to the provisions of entry 92A of List I'. Entry 92A authorises Parliament to levy tax on the sale or purchase of goods (other than newspapers) in the course of inter-state trade. As a result, the Central Sales Tax Act, 1956, was enacted. The revenue from this tax was assigned to the states.

While sales tax has been in vogue in Indian states for nearly 50 years, efforts have been made in recent years to replace this by a value added tax (VAT). In this context, the Union Government took the lead and appointed committees of the states' Finance Ministers as also of the Chief Ministers[3]. These committees deliberated on this issue over a long period of time and finally sales tax has been replaced by a system of value added tax (known as State VAT). This heralded a paradigm shift in the states' tax system. Although CST continues at the moment, efforts are continuing to replace it by a destination-based tax.

Fiscal Significance

State VAT constitutes a major source of revenue for the state governments. Its yield has shown an upsurge from Rs 21,064 crore in 1991–2 to Rs 76,885 crore in 2001–2 and to Rs 2,20,644 crore in 2009–10, with a growth rate of 13.85 per cent and buoyancy of 1.03 over the period (Table 7.1). Sales tax revenue collected by all the states, expressed as a percentage of states' own tax revenue, has remained stable around 60 per cent in most of the years. Its share was 62.2 per cent in 2000–1 but came down to 60.8 per cent in 2009–10.

In states like Maharashtra, the sales tax revenue has increased from Rs 3,809 crore in 1991–2 to Rs 12,131 crore in 2001–2, and to Rs 32,676 crore in 2009–10 (Table 7.2). With a share of 55.3 per cent in the state's own tax revenue; it had a growth rate of 12.74 per cent and buoyancy of 0.99 over the period. Similarly, in Tamil Nadu sales tax contributes 62.01 per cent in the state's own tax revenue in 2009–10. In case of special category

---

[3] Committees have been appointed from 1995 onwards. See Annexure A9.1 to Chapter 9 of the book.

Table 7.1 Yield from State Taxes on Commodities and Services

(Rs Crore)

Year	Sales Tax	State Excise	Motor Vehicles Tax	P&GT	Electricity Duty	Entertainment Tax
1991-2	21,064	5,439	1,837	1,136	1,596	368
	(58.9)	(15.2)	(5.1)	(3.2)	(4.5)	(1.0)
1992-3	23,349	6,265	2,194	1,278	1,748	470
	(58.6)	(15.7)	(5.5)	(3.2)	(4.4)	(1.2)
1993-4	27,638	7,106	2,583	1,480	1,726	522
	(59.5)	(15.3)	(5.6)	(3.2)	(3.7)	(1.1)
1994-5	33,154	7,747	3,081	1,483	2,242	447
	(59.5)	(13.9)	(5.5)	(2.7)	(4.0)	(0.8)
1995-6	35,477	8,516	3,726	1,508	2,377	440
	(55.5)	(13.3)	(5.8)	(2.4)	(3.7)	(0.7)
1996-7	43,927	8,805	4,117	1,663	2,718	606
	(61.8)	(12.4)	(5.8)	(2.3)	(3.8)	(0.9)
1997-8	48,842	11,271	4,854	2,004	3,194	665
	(60.1)	(13.9)	(6.0)	(2.5)	(3.9)	(0.8)
1998-9	53,116	13,387	5,024	1,979	3773	660
	(59.7)	(15.0)	(5.6)	(2.2)	(4.2)	(0.7)
1999-2000	62,301	15,032	6,153	2,099	3,667	828
	(60.7)	(14.7)	(6.0)	(2.0)	(3.6)	(0.8)
2000-1	73,364	16,036	6,666	2,075	4,431	1,147
	(62.2)	(13.6)	(5.6)	(1.8)	(3.8)	(1.0)
2001-2	76,885	17,110	7,644	3,671	4,692	799
	(60.0)	(13.4)	(6.0)	(2.9)	(3.7)	(0.6)
2002-3	86,038	18,994	8,441	3,569	5,256	800
	(60.5)	(13.4)	(5.9)	(2.5)	(3.7)	(0.6)
2003-4	97,590	19,638	10,138	4,190	5,580	756
	(61.0)	(12.3)	(6.3)	(2.6)	(3.5)	(0.5)
2004-5	1,16,754	21,940	10,811	5,206	7,255	862
	(61.7)	(11.6)	(5.7)	(2.8)	(3.8)	(0.5)
2005-6	1,28,769	25,036	11,964	6,450	7,718	649
	(60.7)	(11.8)	(5.6)	(3.0)	(3.6)	(0.3)
2006-7	1,53,573	29,316	13,238	6,808	8,161	705
	(60.8)	(11.6)	(5.2)	(2.7)	(3.2)	(0.3)

2007–8	1,73,422	34,127	15,143	6,808	9,239	1,083
	(60.5)	(11.9)	(5.3)	(2.4)	(3.2)	(0.4)
2008–9	1,98,327	40,989	16,446	8,541	9,530.30	981
	(61.61)	(12.7)	(5.1)	(2.7)	(2.96)	(0.3)
2009–10	2,20,644	48,375	19,140	9,857	12,226	1,112
	(60.77)	(13.32)	(5.3)	(2.7)	(3.37)	(0.31)
2010–11 (RE)	2,81,928	57,649	22,802	11,296	16,550	1,137
	(61.52)	(12.58)	(5.0)	(2.5)	(3.61)	(0.25)
2011–12 (BE)	3,34,025	69,767	28,007	11,663	16,069	1,531
	(61.9)	(12.93)	(5.2)	(2.2)	(2.98)	(0.28)
GR	13.85	12.12	13.36	13.12	11.84	4.99
Buoyancy	1.03	0.92	0.99	0.97	0.67	0.40

Source: Reserve Bank of India, *State Finances: A Study of Budgets* (Various Issues), Mumbai: RBI.
Note: 1. P&GT = Passengers and Goods Tax and GR = Growth Rate; 2. The figures within parentheses indicate as a percentage of states' own tax revenue.

states like Assam, the sales tax revenue increased from Rs 293 crore in 1991–2 to Rs 3,535 crore in 2009–10.

As the higher coefficient of buoyancy indicates a high relative growth of the yield from the tax, it is necessary to know whether the higher tax effort[4] fully exploits the existing revenue potential of the states. In doing so, the average degree of relationship between the tax ratio in different states and the taxable capacity factor is generally analysed through regression analysis. The resultant tax ratio represents the ratio that a state would have if it had used its capacity to an average extent. Comparison of an estimated tax ratio with the actual tax ratio indicates whether the state concerned is making an average degree of effort, or is showing deviation from the norm. Tax effort for sales tax is estimated as the percentage share of actual revenue (from sales tax) with reference to its base in the taxable capacity.

---

[4] Tax effort is a relative concept. It is defined as a ratio of tax revenue to its taxable capacity. Such a measure involves the implicit assumption that the total income of a state is an appropriate indicator of taxable capacity. Tax effort is estimated through the equation: log (STAX) = a + b log (GSDP); where STAX = Revenue from total state VAT minus CST; and GSDP = Gross State Domestic Product.

Table 7.2 Fiscal Significance of Sales Tax in States

(Rs Crore)

States	1991–2	1996–7	2001–2	2005–6	2007–8	2008–9	2009–10	2010–11 (RE)	2011–12 (BE)	GR	Buoyancy
Andhra Pradesh	1,674 (54.80)	3,526 (72.22)	7,741 (61.60)	12,542 (65.30)	19,026 (66.10)	21,852 (65.51)	23,640 (67.21)	31,838 (67.14)	38,306 (67.87)	15.76	1.21
Bihar	940 (71.80)	1,496 (66.48)	1,450 (59.40)	1,734 (48.69)	2,535 (49.80)	3,016 (48.87)	3,849 (47.46)	5,663 (53.33)	6,508 (51.72)	11.11	0.81
Chhattisgarh			940 (47.20)	2,089 (51.56)	3023.69 (53.80)	3,611 (54.76)	3,712 (52.11)	4,524 (54.32)	5,488 (55.82)	20.67	1.10
Goa	81 (71.70)	220 (72.77)	401 (70.50)	743 (67.79)	879 (64.7)	1,132 (66.82)	1,142 (64.81)	1,495 (68.54)	1,780 (69.96)	15.02	0.92
Gujarat	2,011 (69.50)	4,026 (66.37)	5,857 (63.30)	10,561 (67.28)	15,105 (69.00)	16,811 (71.36)	18,200 (68.06)	23,996 (69.22)	26,000 (66.59)	12.35	1.03
Haryana	620 (47.70)	1,380 (64.40)	2,945 (59.20)	5,604 (61.73)	7,721 (66.50)	8,155 (69.97)	9,032 (68.33)	12,300 (70.88)	14,100 (70.48)	17.17	0.97
Jharkhand			1,515 (73.00)	2,150 (74.43)	2,790 (78.60)	3,715 (73.07)	4,200 (75.53)	4,503 (75.46)	5,897 (75.22)	14.38	1.03
Karnataka	1,653 (57.00)	3,510 (60.86)	5,269 (53.50)	9,870 (52.97)	13,894 (53.50)	14,623 (52.89)	15,833 (51.78)	20,540 (53.98)	24,170 (55.16)	13.28	1.04

Kerala	1,122 (67.00)	2,772 (71.11)	4,441 (75.00)	7,038 (71.97)	9,372 (68.60)	11,377 (71.15)	12,771 (72.46)	15,835 (72.23)	19,428 (72.92)	13.71	1.07
Madhya Pradesh	948 (44.80)	1,731 (42.19)	2,361 (50.20)	4,508 (49.46)	6,045 (50.30)	6,843 (50.26)	7,724 (44.72)	10,200 (50.05)	11,830 (51.17)	15.84	1.12
Maharashtra	3,809 (64.00)	7,290 (62.23)	12,131 (57.00)	19,677 (58.67)	26,753 (56.30)	30,681 (58.97)	32,676 (55.28)	40,815 (55.53)	46,000 (54.97)	12.74	0.99
Odisha	394 (58.50)	894 (66.58)	1,402 (56.80)	3,012 (60.21)	4,118 (60.10)	4,803 (60.08)	5,409 (60.22)	6,500 (61.27)	7,564 (61.46)	15.65	1.23
Punjab	753 (48.80)	1,265 (46.24)	2,684 (55.70)	4,627 (51.47)	5,342 (54.00)	6,436 (57.72)	7,577 (62.94)	10,000 (57.49)	11,800 (57.82)	13.73	1.21
Rajasthan	824 (53.20)	1,599 (51.18)	3,069 (54.10)	5,594 (56.61)	7,751 (58.40)	8,905 (59.59)	10,164 (61.92)	12,300 (63.35)	13,490 (63.19)	15.07	1.26
Tamil Nadu	2,442 (65.40)	5,341 (66.90)	8,386 (64.50)	15,555 (66.68)	18,156 (61.30)	20,675 (61.38)	22,662 (62.01)	30,371 (61.82)	37,196 (62.21)	13.08	1.06
Uttar Pradesh	1,898 (54.30)	3,473 (55.08)	6,163 (59.70)	11,285 (59.84)	15,023 (60.20)	17,482 (61.00)	20,825 (61.47)	24,466 (60.13)	32,000 (63.58)	16.78	1.27
West Bengal	1,415 (57.80)	2,704 (63.49)	3,802 (58.40)	6,109 (58.80)	8,060 (61.40)	8,955 (62.11)	10,510 (62.19)	13,275 (62.32)	17,024 (61.48)	10.97	0.89

(contd.)

Table 7.2 (contd.)

(Rs Crore)

States	1991–2	1996–7	2001–2	2005–6	2007–8	2008–9	2009–10	2010–11 (RE)	2011–12 (BE)	GR	Buoyancy
Special Category States											
Arunachal Pradesh	0.43	0.4	17	48	77.06	106	130	151	173	48.27	3.30
	(10.50)	(4.69)	(50.00)	(77.28)	(78.60)	(77.59)	(75.10)	(75.59)	(76.23)		
Assam	293	517	1,073	2,568	2,691	3,111	3,535	4,319	4,875	16.24	1.52
	(57.20)	(67.47)	(68.50)	(79.46)	(80.10)	(74.95)	(70.89)	(73.07)	(74.25)		
Himachal Pradesh	67	146	355	727	1,092	1,246	1,487	2,004	2,444	18.99	1.39
	(34.70)	(35.49)	(38.80)	(48.56)	(55.80)	(55.58)	(57.77)	(58.84)	(60.50)		
Jammu and Kashmir	62	123	400	1,092	1,480	1,853	2,130	2,573	3,025	23.00	1.85
	(37.80)	(42.49)	(46.60)	(64.64)	(64.40)	(68.78)	(69.27)	(70.62)	(72.32)		
Manipur	8	2	30	71	121	141	163	201	242	19.73	1.74
	(57.10)	(14.44)	(57.70)	(74.95)	(81.90)	(83.13)	(83.29)	(80.15)	(76.20)		
Meghalaya	18	31.4	81	173	235	282	321	324	418	18.40	1.45
	(41.90)	(40.58)	(59.60)	(68.62)	(73.60)	(76.29)	(72.34)	(70.19)	(71.08)		
Mizoram	0.34	1.99	10	42	62	78	86	102	135	33.89	2.58
	(11.30)	(29.84)	(52.60)	(75.54)	(80.00)	(81.92)	(79.88)	(82.05)	(78.09)		

Nagaland	13	19	30	77	95	115	132	155	186	15.43	1.26
	(72.20)	(59.65)	(57.70)	(73.12)	(72.20)	(73.52)	(73.25)	(72.16)	(73.85)		
Sikkim	3	8.22	35	57	81	101	121	139	160	23.25	1.63
	(27.30)	(37.88)	(43.80)	(38.48)	(41.10)	(54.79)	(54.31)	(59.80)	(59.50)		
Tripura	15	35.69	106	203	265	315	375	450	598	20.62	1.47
	(51.70)	(58.99)	(66.70)	(68.69)	(71.50)	(71.14)	(71.14)	(71.83)	(76.33)		
Uttarakhand			486	1,014	1,627	1,911	2,247	2,888	3,188	22.53	1.27
			(54.30)	(56.84)	(59.40)	(62.75)	(63.13)	(66.75)	(66.97)		
All States	21,064	43,926	76,885	1,28,769	1,73,421	1,98,327	2,20,644	2,81,928	3,34,025	13.85	0.75
	(58.91)	(61.78)	(60.02)	(60.65)	(60.52)	(61.61)	(60.77)	(61.52)	(61.90)		

Source: Reserve Bank of India, *State Finances: A Study of Budgets* (Various Issues), Mumbai: RBI.

Note: GR = Growth Rate. Growth Rate and Buoyancy for the states are calculated for 1991–2 to 2009–10. Figures within parenthesis indicate percentage of states' own tax revenue. For the bifurcated and the newly formed states, the growth rate and buoyancy are calculated for the period 2001–2 to 2009–10.

While all other components under state VAT relate to intrastate transactions, CST is a tax on exports out of the state and it is a tax included in the union list. Since its revenue is not dependent upon the efforts of the state of origin, it is excluded in measuring tax effort. The ideal way would be to obtain data on turnover relating to consumption of various types of commodities and to estimate the turnover of inputs used in the industries. However, owing to non-availability of required information from all states, the gross state domestic product (GSDP) is generally used as the determinant or the potential base of sales tax.

In this study, tax effort is calculated with reference to GSDP of states for all non-special category states.[5] In doing so, the average of three-years (that is, 2006–7 to 2008–9) for the tax as well as the related base is taken. The tax effort is estimated as the percentage share of actual revenue (obtained from sales tax) in the taxable capacity. The results (Table 7.3) indicate that Kerala, Goa, Andhra Pradesh, Tamil Nadu, Karnataka, and Haryana are the top six states in the country that put in the highest degree of effort to collect this tax. However, Bihar, West Bengal, Jharkhand, and Odisha have low ranks.

Structure of State VAT

VAT—a multi-point sales tax with set-off—is collected at each stage of the production and distribution process. It provides tax credit for all taxes paid on inputs (including capital goods) and therefore, does not have any cascading effect. The standard rate of VAT is 13.5 per cent, that is, all the goods that are not enumerated in any of the lists are taxed at this rate. In addition, VAT has four rate categories.

The first category consists of all those goods which are taxed at 'zero rate', that is, exempted from levy of tax. These goods, as given in Annexure A7.1, fall under 46 categories, comprising natural and unprocessed products, goods which are legally barred from taxation, and goods which have social implications. While the list is common for all the states, each state has the authority to identify and add a maximum of ten goods to the list of exempted items. These goods must be of local social importance for the individual state and should not have any inter-state implication;

[5] Special category states of the north (like Jammu and Kashmir and Himachal Pradesh) and of the north-east (such as Manipur, Meghalaya, Mizoram, Nagaland, Sikkim, and Tripura) have not been included in calculating tax effort of the states. The tax effort of these states is constrained due to their status of special category.

Table 7.3 Tax Effort of States: Sales Tax

(Rs Crore)

States	ST Average 2006-9	GSDP* Average 2006-9	Taxable Capacity	Tax Effort %	Rank
Andhra Pradesh	17,470.85	3,60,560.00	13,345.60	130.91	3
Bihar	2,493.79	1,21,946.67	4,345.85	57.38	17
Chhattisgarh	2,530.06	80,103.33	2,813.04	89.94	13
Goa	911.57	19,390.33	648.00	140.67	2
Gujarat	13,076.37	3,26,907.67	12,058.64	108.44	7
Haryana	6,237.29	1,55,779.33	5,599.27	111.39	6
Jharkhand	2,307.75	82,127.00	2,886.62	79.95	15
Karnataka	12,156.24	2,67,244.00	9,788.64	124.19	5
Kerala	9,176.98	1,76,648.67	6,377.35	143.9	1
Madhya Pradesh	5,502.31	1,64,197.00	5,912.70	93.06	12
Maharashtra	24,639.22	6,77,891.33	25,650.99	96.06	11
Odisha	3,626.08	1,23,394.33	4,399.25	82.42	14
Punjab	5,227.56	1,51,542.33	5,441.73	96.06	10
Rajasthan	7,353.34	1,97,010.67	7,139.63	102.99	8
Tamil Nadu	16,976.14	3,54,615.00	13,117.93	129.41	4
Uttar Pradesh	14,090.65	3,84,316.33	14,256.67	98.84	9
West Bengal	7,225.60	3,00,467.00	11,050.70	65.39	16

Source: Computed.
Notes: ST = Sales Tax; GSDP* = Gross State Domestic Product; LGSDP = Log of GSDP; LST = Log of Sales Tax.

for example, *kumkum* or bell metal (*kansa*) in Maharashtra or *gamocha* in Assam.

The second category comprises those special items that are taxable at the rate of 1 per cent. These include gold, silver, gold and silver ornaments, precious stones (including semi-precious stones) and real, artificial or cultured pearls.

Another category is that of basic necessities, which include food items, agricultural products, medicines and drugs, and declared goods.[6] This category also includes chemicals, inputs and capital goods. Hence, the list

---

[6] Under the Additional Duties of Excise (Goods of Special Importance) Act, 1957, certain goods were declared of special importance in inter-state trade. These goods are known as declared goods.

of goods in this category is very long, covering more than 270 items. This category is taxed at the rate of 5 per cent (Annexure A7.1).

There is also a category of goods taxable at the rate of 20 per cent (or more) but the commodities listed in this schedule are not covered under VAT, instead a first-point sales tax is levied on these items. This category covers items such as motor spirit (petrol, diesel, and aviation turbine fuel) and liquor.

While there exists a general uniformity among all the states, variations do exist amongst some of the states. Efforts are being made by the Empowered Committee of state Finance Ministers to ensure that there is complete uniformity in the rates. In Punjab, there is a specific provision for levying purchase tax on five commodities, which include paddy, wheat, cotton, sugarcane, and milk (when purchased for use in the manufacture of any goods other than tax-free goods). The tax shall be leviable on the first purchase of these goods from within the state. In the case of milk, however, first purchase shall be when the purchase is made by a manufacturer of taxable goods. The purchase tax paid by the dealer is admissible as input tax credit when the goods are sold in the state or are used for the manufacture of taxable goods in the state, which are for sale or sold in the course of inter-state trade or in the course of export.

Luxury tax or hotel tax is levied on luxuries provided in hotels (accommodation and other services) and lodging houses in the states.

Sales Tax Incentives for Industrial Development

Most states have provided in their sales tax laws some attractive incentives to lure industries. These incentives had taken various forms and applied to different industrial units for varying periods depending upon the location of industry in backward or developed areas of the state.[7] The variants of the concessions offered were the following:

- *Tax exemption,* that is, exemption of sales tax on purchase of inputs or sale of finished goods;
- *Tax waiver,* that is, payment of sales tax on sale of finished goods is waived;
- *Tax deferral,* that is, payment of sales tax to the government on sale of finished goods is deferred for a certain period of time;

[7] See for details Mahesh Purohit (2005).

- *Tax loan,* that is, the dealer is assumed to have been given the due amount of sales tax as loan; and
- *Refund of sales tax,* that is, the dealer first pays the tax to the government which is later refunded to him, or given a set-off for the amount paid.

These incentives were offered generally to all 'new' industrial units that were set up after a notified date. The quantum and scope of the incentives differed according to the area in which the industries were set up. Sometimes the incentives were offered on a selective basis for a group of specified industries only. In many states, however, the exemptions were offered for the purpose of regional development. That is, the incentives were offered for certain identified backward regions where a new industrial unit was being set up or to an existing industrial unit if it goes in for expansion or diversification.

The above incentives have affected the revenue of the states by over 25 per cent; they conform to the tenets of "beggar thy neighbour policy". It was, therefore, resolved in the Empowered Committee, as recommended by the *First Report of the Finance Ministers on Introduction of VAT,* that no new incentives would be granted under sales tax. However, as a sound social policy, the states have promised to continue the incentives granted earlier (under the sales tax regime) with deferment for the unexpired period of exemption. The details of the treatment of such incentives under VAT are given in Annexure A7.2.

In addition to discontinuation of the industrial incentives, the introduction of VAT has been accompanied by the abolition of all other taxes such as turnover tax, surcharge, additional surcharge and special additional tax. However, many of the states continue to levy a purchase tax (for example, Punjab, Tamil Nadu, Gujarat, Bihar and Madhya Pradesh). This tax is leviable (i) on goods taxable under VAT but purchased from unregistered dealers; (ii) goods purchased from any other person on which no taxes are payable by that registered dealer on the sale price of such goods and sent on consignment; (iii) on those taxable goods that are used in the production or packing of tax-free goods; or (iv) on goods consumed in the manufacture of other goods for sale.

Taxation of Inter-state Trade

While state VAT is a state subject, as given earlier, taxation of inter-state sales is included under the union list. It is taxed under the provisions of the Central Sales Tax Act, 1956, enacted by the Parliament under the powers drawn from the union list of the Constitution. Presently CST is levied on the basis of 'origin' and collected by the exporting state; it is inconsistent with the principles of VAT. Such a system was initially introduced to regulate inter-state trade. To ensure an equal tax treatment for commodities entering into inter-state trade and on those locally produced, the CST prescribes two different rates of tax: 2 per cent on inter-state sales to registered dealers and 10 per cent on sales to unregistered dealers; the rates are different as the registered dealer pays state VAT on his sales while no state VAT is charged on the sales of the unregistered dealer.

In spite of the low rate of CST on registered dealers, the levy of CST on the basis of 'origin' goes against the principle of a unified market. It is in conflict with the principle of inter-jurisdictional equity. CST levied on inputs cascades and results in higher prices. The producing states use this measure to 'export' their tax to the consumers in other states. Such a tax also encourages consumers to buy locally produced goods at the expense of the interests of the national economy.

Resolving the long-drawn controversy, the union and states have agreed to phase out CST. Accordingly, CST has by now been brought down to 2 per cent. It will be brought down to 0 per cent when GST is introduced in India[8].

Administration of State VAT

Since VAT replaced the then prevailing sales tax in the states, the organization for tax administration prevalent under sales tax has been adapted for VAT, with the necessary changes to suit the system.

In almost all the states, VAT administration has four components, which includes headquarters organization, administrative organization, enforcement organization, and appellate organization.

Headquarters organization is under the direct supervision of the Commissioner of Commercial Taxes (CCT). In the hierarchy, immediately under the CCT are the Additional Commissioners of Commercial Taxes (Additional CCT) who exercise the power delegated to them by the CCT. These Additional CCTs look after work related to the Headquarters,

---

[8] The rate of tax on inter-state transactions was 4 per cent until recently. It was brought down to 3 per cent on 1 April 2007 and to 2 per cent on 1 June 2008.

zones (that is regions), vigilance, management information system (MIS), and legal aspects related to administration of state VAT. There are Joint Commissioners (JCCT) supervising the work of intelligence including vigilance and monitoring; transactions, audit, and appeals including tribunal and court cases. These officers work directly under the Commissioner.

The administrative organization of the department follows a two-tier system: (i) the division and (ii) the circle. The division is headed by a person of the rank of JCCT (administration) and the circle is generally headed by an Assistant Commissioner of Commercial Taxes (ACCT). The work related to assessment is done by the ACCT and the Commercial Tax Officer (CTO).

The enforcement work is undertaken at the divisional level. The organizational structure of the enforcement wing shows that the ACCT is in overall charge of the enforcement work at the field level. However, at the headquarters level, the ACCT has to report to the DCCT or to the CCT. The work of the enforcement personnel at the field level involves survey, investigation, visit to and the search of places of business, seizure of books of accounts, and reporting of malpractices. To fulfil these tasks, this wing collects information from different sources such as railways, transport organizations, other government departments etc.

The tax administration provides for the right to appeal, revision and reference. According to the existing arrangements, there are three tiers of administration of appeal prior to court appeal. The initial appeal is made to the JCCT (appeals), who works as an appellate authority. The work is territorially distributed. A revision petition against the orders of the JCCT (appeals) can be filed before the commercial taxes tribunal. The tribunal consists of members drawn from the judicial, accounts and taxation services. Besides these regular channels of appeals, the CCT can exercise *suo moto* powers of revision either on his own motion or on the basis of the petitions filed before him.

Procedures of Tax Administration

It is widely recognized that a streamlined registration process, automated return processing, electronic clearance of refunds, and extensive use of internet technologies for tax payment, processing, and accounting are the hallmarks of any leading VAT administration. Given the intensity of citizen interaction in the processes of tax administration, it is expected that transformation of these key processes would lead to improved service delivery and help in exploitation of the true revenue potential of commercial activity in various states.

Registration of Dealer: Registration of dealers enables the department to control taxpayers' payment of VAT, submission of returns and all other administrative aspects. Under this process, some of the states subject the dealers to pre-verification while others issue registration certificate and undertake verification afterwards. In some states, there is a provision for a security deposit before issuance of the registration certificate. For example, Delhi and Gujarat prescribe a security deposit of Rs 1 lakh and Rs 50 thousand, respectively for dealers for VAT registration. However, there is no such provision for security deposits in Andhra Pradesh, West Bengal and Madhya Pradesh for registration. The process of collection of security deposit is a one time activity during the process of registration.

While registering a dealer, the department issues a Taxpayer Identification Number (TIN)—a unique 11-digit number for each dealer in a state. The first two digits are designed to represent the state; next two are charge code; next four digits give the serial number of the dealer; next digit refers to the Act; and the last two digits are check numbers. To illustrate the formats, the TIN formats of West Bengal and Gujarat are given in Box 7.1. From the illustrative TIN formats, it is evident that in an 11-digit TIN, only four digits are available for giving the serial number of a dealer in West Bengal and five digits for Gujarat. This limits the maximum number of dealers that can be given a unique TIN within a district. When the number of dealers within a district exceeds this number it would become necessary to split the district.

Submission of Returns: Registered dealers have a declarative obligation to submit a return showing their turnover, as well as gross and net VAT liability. At present, the return procedures adopted across the states—in terms of periodicity of returns and design of return forms—vary. Many of the states require returns to be submitted quarterly but in the case of new dealers and potential taxpayers, the periodicity of filing of returns is monthly. In addition to the quarterly returns, in some states there is a provision for an annual return. For dealers with a small turnover and small tax liability, there is a simplified return which may be filed annually.

Payment of Tax: Tax is paid along with submission of returns. The procedure for payment of tax requires the filing of the challan form in quadruplicate. When the challan is given to the bank/treasury, the third and fourth copies are returned by the bank/treasury after being endorsed for payment. The original copy is sent to the respective assessing authority,

Box 7.1 TIN Formats

West Bengal TIN format

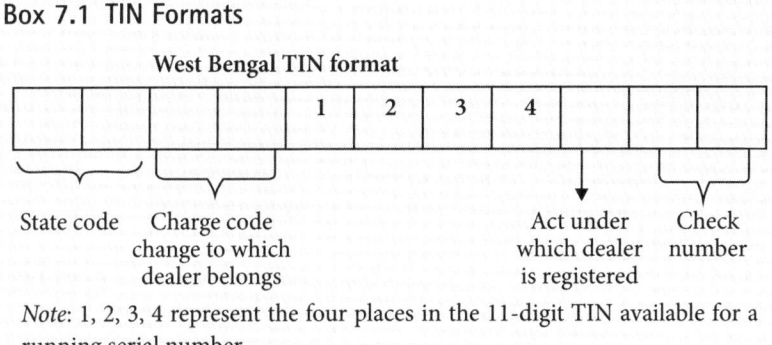

			1	2	3	4			

State code   Charge code   Act under   Check
                change to which   which dealer   number
                dealer belongs   is registered

Note: 1, 2, 3, 4 represent the four places in the 11-digit TIN available for a running serial number.

Gujarat TIN format

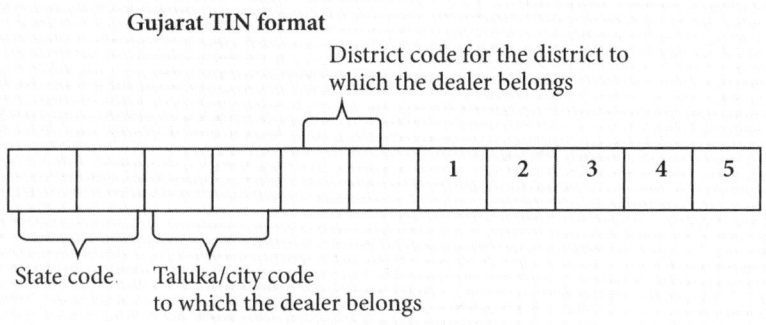

District code for the district to which the dealer belongs

					1	2	3	4	5

State code   Taluka/city code
                 to which the dealer belongs

Note: 1, 2, 3, 4, 5 represent the five places in the 11-digit TIN available for a running serial number.

while the bank/treasury retains the duplicate copy. The dealer submits the copy marked 'quadruplicate' along with the return to the assessing authority. In most of the states, a system of e-payment also exists.

Procedure of Assessment: VAT is a self-assessed tax, based primarily on voluntary compliance. When a registered dealer submits his return and pays the tax, the assessing authority assumes that the assessment is complete. However, the department has the authority to make an assessment when it suspects that incorrect details are given in the return. In addition, emphasis is given to the system of selective audits. Every year, a certain percentage of the dealers are selected on a scientific basis to be audited on the basis of 'risk assessment'.

Appeals and Revision: Because of the possibility of abuse of discretionary powers by the assessing authorities and of errors in the interpretation of the law, the tax administration provides for the right to appeal, revision and reference. According to the existing arrangements there are three tires of appeal. First appeal against the order of assessing authority is made to the Appellate Assistant Commissioner or Appellate Deputy Commissioner. Second Appeal is made to the Appellate Tribunal and the third Appeal against the order of Appellate Tribunal to the High Court or to the Special Taxation Tribunal. The Tribunal consist of members drawn from different walks of life. Normally these members are from the judiciary, accounts and taxation services.

Besides these channels of appeal, the Commissioner of Commercial Taxes can exercise *suo moto* powers of revision. Most of the states such as Madhya Pradesh, Chhattisgarh, Rajasthan, West Bengal, Andhra Pradesh, Haryana, and Uttarakhand have provision of *suo moto* revision. The appellate organization of the Department is generally under the supervision of the Commercial Tax Department at its initial stages and in most of the states, the first appeal is heard by the Deputy Commissioner/Joint Commissioner (appeals). In order to provide for quick justice, there is a time limit at each appellate stage for disposal of appeal/revision cases.

Motor Vehicles Tax

Motor vehicles tax (MVT) is within the ambit of the state's legislative powers. Under entry 57 of List II in the Seventh Schedule, state governments are assigned this power. However, regulation and taxation being treated as two distinct powers in the Indian Constitution, the former falls within the concurrent list (List III, entry 35) and the power is exercised by both the central and the state governments. However, the taxation powers and the revenue from the tax are assigned to the States.

Fiscal Significance

Revenue from MVT for all states in the 1950s and the 1960s was inconsequential. However, during recent years, it has increased considerably. It has increased from Rs 1,837 crore in 1991–2 to Rs 6,666 crore in 2000–1. By 2009–10, the yield from MVT increased to Rs 19,140.04 crore (Table 7.1). The revenue from the MVT has increased at an annual growth rate of 13.23 per cent and exhibited a buoyancy value of 1.0 during the period 1991–2 to 2009–10.

However, its share in the states' own tax revenue has remained around 6 per cent over the years. Revenue growth has fallen in the year 1998–9 in relation to the preceding year for the states of Assam, Bihar, Goa, Karnataka, and Maharashtra. Among the states, the highest yield from this tax in 2009–10 was in Maharashtra (Rs 2,682.3 crore), followed by Tamil Nadu (Rs 2024.64 crore) and Andhra Pradesh (Rs 1,995.3 crore). The yield from this tax rose throughout from 1993–4 to 2009–10 in a majority of the states. Chhattisgarh and Uttarakhand recorded quite high revenue from MVT which increased at a steady rate of 12.7 per cent and 14.5 per cent, respectively. Among the non-special category states, Bihar has recorded the lowest growth rate, that is, 9.6 per cent (Table 7.4).

The growth rate of revenue from the motor vehicles tax in a majority of non-special category states was within the range of 10 to 21 per cent; Jharkhand exhibited the highest growth rate of 20.8 per cent followed by Goa (16.8 per cent) and Gujarat (15.3 per cent). Revenue from the tax in the special category states recorded growth rates as high as 23.2 per cent in Tripura, 19.8 per cent in Himachal Pradesh, and 17.7 per cent in Sikkim during the period 1991–2 to 2009–10 (Table 7.4). Also, the tax is buoyant during the period 1991–2 to 2009–10 for all the states. In the case of individual states also, the tax indicates buoyant revenue in all the states.

Tax Effort in Motor Vehicle Tax and Passengers and Goods Tax

Tax effort is defined as a ratio of actual tax revenue of a government to its taxable capacity.[9] The MVT and P&GT are levied independently in some states while both these taxes have been merged together (as one tax) in some states. In view of this, in this study the tax effort is estimated for

---

[9] For estimating the tax effort of MVT the study requires data relating to gross revenues of transport companies and the fare rate as well as the freight chart.

For P&GT, data on the volume of passenger traffic (measured in passenger kilometres), freight volume, quantity, as well as value, is required. Unfortunately, such data are not available especially from private transport companies.

Table 7.4 Yield from Motor Vehicles Tax in Different States

(Rs Crore)

States	1991–2	1996–7	2001–2	2005–6	2007–8	2008–9	2009–10	2010–11 (RE)	2011–12 (BE)	GR	Buoyancy
Andhra Pradesh	203.40 (6.66)	553.80 (11.34)	939.20 (7.48)	1,355.70 (7.06)	1,603.80 (5.57)	1,800.60 (5.40)	1,995.30 (5.67)	2,778.00 (5.86)	3,433.60 (6.08)	12.64	0.99
Bihar	75.00 (5.73)	160.80 (7.15)	141.50 (5.79)	302.40 (8.49)	273.20 (5.37)	297.70 (4.80)	345.13 (4.27)	450.00 (4.25)	537.00 (4.58)	9.56	0.63
Chhattisgarh			124.90 (6.27)	206.00 (5.08)	276.90 (4.93)	313.80 (4.80)	351.88 (4.94)	410.00 (4.92)	450.00 (4.58)	12.74	0.73
Goa	5.30 (4.67)	15.00 (4.96)	32.80 (5.77)	63.80 (5.82)	82.00 (6.03)	90.20 (5.30)	78.05 (4.43)	90.00 (4.13)	125.00 (4.91)	16.84	1.07
Gujarat	113.00 (3.91)	333.90 (5.51)	676.60 (7.32)	1,154.00 (7.35)	1,310.10 (5.99)	1,381.70 (5.90)	1,542.60 (5.77)	1,725.00 (4.98)	1,900.00 (4.87)	15.31	1.12
Haryana	68.50 (5.27)	61.60 (2.87)	103.60 (2.08)	172.10 (1.90)	233.80 (2.01)	239.30 (2.10)	277.10 (2.10)	350.00 (2.02)	515.00 (2.57)	10.07	0.72
Jharkhand			86.10 (4.15)	138.30 (4.79)	135.70 (3.82)	400.60 (7.90)	400.00 (7.19)	440.00 (7.37)	556 (7.09)	20.76	1.45
Karnataka	227.50 (7.84)	325.80 (5.65)	712.40 (7.23)	1,105.40 (5.93)	837.30 (3.22)	1,681.20 (6.10)	1,961.60 (6.41)	2,250.00 (5.91)	2,630.00 (6.00)	12.15	0.95

Kerala	94.80 (5.66)	247.60 (6.35)	452.20 (7.63)	628.50 (6.43)	853.20 (6.24)	937.50 (5.90)	1,131.10 (6.42)	1,233.39 (5.63)	1,410.73 (5.30)	13.35	1.04
Madhya Pradesh	123.80 (5.85)	338.20 (8.24)	393.30 (8.36)	556.00 (6.10)	702.60 (5.85)	772.60 (5.70)	919.01 (5.32)	1,130.00 (5.54)	1,285.00 (5.56)	11.06	0.93
Maharashtra	233.30 (3.92)	613.70 (5.24)	947.80 (4.45)	1,309.10 (3.90)	2,143.10 (4.51)	2,220.20 (4.30)	2682.30 (4.54)	3,471.00 (4.72)	4,000.00 (4.78)	14.10	1.10
Odisha	59.80 (8.88)	128.30 (9.56)	216.40 (8.77)	405.9 (8.11)	459.40 (6.70)	524.40 (6.60)	611.23 (6.80)	715.00 (6.74)	842.30 (6.84)	13.27	1.05
Punjab	40.50 (2.62)	195.20 (7.14)	318.40 (6.61)	431.20 (4.80)	499.50 (5.05)	524.10 (4.70)	554.74 (4.61)	700.00 (4.02)	800.00 (3.92)	12.46	1.13
Rajasthan	139.30 (8.99)	276.90 (8.87)	566.30 (9.99)	908.20 (9.19)	1,164.40 (8.77)	1,213.60 (8.10)	1,372.87 (8.36)	1,500.00 (7.73)	1,650.00 (7.73)	13.75	1.16
Tamil Nadu	248.20 (6.65)	425.40 (5.33)	648.40 (4.98)	1,124.90 (4.82)	1,483.20 (5.01)	1,709.60 (5.10)	2,024.64 (5.54)	2,576.76 (5.25)	3,235.25 (5.41)	11.66	0.95
Uttar Pradesh	93.00 (2.66)	139.50 (2.21)	503.00 (4.87)	965.2 (5.12)	1,145.80 (4.59)	1,124.70 (3.90)	1,403.50 (4.14)	1,135.21 (2.79)	2,329.95 (4.63)	12.79	0.97
West Bengal	75.00 (3.06)	134.30 (3.15)	208.70 (3.21)	537.60 (5.17)	532.10 (4.05)	608.00 (4.20)	774.34 (4.58)	1,006.64 (4.73)	1,358.97 (4.91)	14.34	1.13

(*contd.*)

Table 7.4 (contd.)

(Rs Crore)

States	1991–2	1996–7	2001–2	2005–6	2007–8	2008–9	2009–10	2010–11 (RE)	2011–12 (BE)	GR	Buoyancy
Special Cat. States											
Arunachal Pradesh	0.40	1.10	1.60	3.00	6.40	7.80	13.07	15.00	17.00	16.64	1.36
	(9.78)	(12.77)	(4.70)	(4.84)	(6.55)	(5.70)	(7.54)	(7.52)	(7.47)		
Assam	12.80	52.00	93.60	155.90	138.60	145.20	177.26	220.19	270.00	14.10	1.34
	(2.50)	(6.78)	(5.98)	(4.82)	(4.13)	(3.50)	(3.55)	(3.73)	(4.11)		
Himachal Pradesh	8.80	14.50	132.70	101.50	113.70	135.50	133.97	150.03	173.08	19.81	1.45
	(4.56)	(3.51)	(14.49)	(6.78)	(5.81)	(6.00)	(5.20)	(4.40)	(4.28)		
Jammu and Kashmir	7.10	11.70	28.20	49.20	72.60	77.70	92.70	113.10	123.20	16.13	1.34
	(4.32)	(4.03)	(3.29)	(2.91)	(3.16)	(2.90)	(3.01)	(3.10)	(2.95)		
Manipur	1.40	1.30	2.80	3.30	3.60	4.00	4.35	6.43	15.65	7.54	0.69
	(9.76)	(9.46)	(5.34)	(3.52)	(2.42)	(2.40)	(2.22)	(2.56)	(4.92)		
Meghalaya	2.40	3.00	4.70	8.70	11.30	13.20	13.61	15.64	18.59	10.92	0.88
	(5.64)	(3.82)	(3.47)	(3.46)	(3.56)	(3.60)	(3.06)	(3.39)	(3.16)		
Mizoram	0.57	0.90	2.10	4.30	5.40	5.50	6.71	6.80	8.76	16.43	1.35
	(17.07)	(13.87)	(10.98)	(7.90)	(6.92)	(5.80)	(6.24)	(5.48)	(5.06)		
Nagaland	2.00	3.90	5.30	8.70	12.30	14.10	16.73	25.60	27.86	11.97	1.00
	(11.11)	(12.37)	(10.20)	(8.26)	(9.36)	(9.10)	(9.27)	(11.92)	(11.09)		

Sikkim	0.40	1.20	2.00	4.20	6.20	6.90	7.88	9.00	10.00	17.67	1.28
	(3.52)	(5.61)	(2.45)	(2.88)	(3.14)	(3.80)	(3.53)	(3.87)	(3.72)		
Tripura	1.10	1.40	5.30	17.40	23.20	29.8	37.14	44.57	44.57	23.15	1.61
	(3.81)	(2.31)	(3.33)	(5.89)	(6.26)	(6.70)	(7.05)	(7.11)	(5.69)		
Uttarakhand			67.40	114.80	155.30	167.00	184.56	225.30	249.53	14.46	0.83
			(7.53)	(6.44)	(5.67)	(5.50)	(5.19)	(5.21)	(5.24)		
All States	1,837.10	4,117.30	7,644.40	11,964.10	15,143.00	16,446.40	19,140.00	22,801.70	28,007.00	13.36	1.00
	(5.14)	(5.79)	(5.97)	(5.64)	(5.28)	(5.10)	(5.27)	(4.98)	(5.19)		

Source: Reserve Bank of India, *State Finances: A Study of Budgets* (Various Issues), Mumbai: RBI.
Note: GR = Growth Rate.
Growth rate and buoyancy for the states are calculated for 1991–2 to 2009–10.
Figures within parenthesis indicate percentage of States' own tax revenue.
For the bifurcated and the newly formed states, the growth rate and buoyancy are calculated for the period 2001–2 to 2009–10.

the two taxes together. Accordingly, the following regression equation is estimated[10]:

log (MVT_P&GT) = a + b_1 log (NO_2_W) + b_2 log (NO_OT_W)
where,

MVT_P&GT = Revenue received from motor vehicles tax and passengers and goods tax,

NO_2_W = Number of two-wheelers, and

NO_OT_W = Number of other vehicles including number of taxis, buses and trucks.

All data relating to number of motor vehicles and their categories have been obtained from the publications of the Ministry of Road Transport and Highways and from the website of the Ministry of Road Transport and Highways, Government of India for the years 2006–7 to 2008–9. Accordingly, for estimating taxable capacity, numbers of two-wheelers and other vehicles have been taken as the potential base. The regression equation, estimated for the two taxes together, gives the following fit:

Log (MVT_P&GT) = −3.38 + 0.65 ln (2W) + 0.37 ln (NO_OT_W)
t-ratio's = (−1.71) (1.98) (0.11)
R-Square = 0.66

The results of the regression given above indicate that none of the t-ratios are significant. However, due to non-availability of a suitable alternative, this equation is used for assessing potential revenue generated from this tax.

The results of the taxable capacity and tax effort, as given in Table 7.5, suggest that Bihar, Karnataka, and Odisha stand at ranks 1, 2 and 3,

---

[10] An attempt was also made to fit the equation separately for motor vehicles tax and for the passengers and goods tax. However, the fit was not found to be good. For motor vehicles tax the following equation has been attempted:

log (MVT) = a + b log (NO2) + b log (NO4) + b log (NOT)+ b log (NOB) + b log (NOTR) + b log (NOO)
where

MVT = Revenue received from motor vehicles tax; NO2 = Number of two-wheelers; NO4 = Number of four-wheelers; NOT = Number of taxis; NOB = Number of buses; NOTR = Number of trucks; NOO = Number of other vehicles. Similarly, for passengers and goods tax the equations attempted is as follows:

log (P&GT) = a + b log (NOB) + b log (NOTR)
where

P&GT = Revenue received from passengers and goods tax; NOB = Number of buses; and NOTR = Number of trucks.

Table 7.5 Tax Effort of States: Motor Vehicles Tax and P&GT

(Rs Crore)

States	RMVT* Average (2006–9)	TW* Average (2006–9)	Others* Average (2006–9)	Taxable capacity	Tax Effort %	Rank
Andhra Pradesh	1,635.53	52,66,841	19,44,409	1,475.54	110.84	8
Bihar	1,250.87	12,13,404	5,45,288	538.09	232.46	1
Chhattisgarh	692.34	15,45,154	3,82,602	622.13	111.29	7
Goa	218.29	4,37,586	1,87,954	265.18	82.32	11
Gujarat	1,403.28	75,56,911	27,04,770	1,892.24	74.16	13
Haryana	728.28	24,68,179	15,07,421	889.71	81.86	12
Jharkhand	330.93	12,98,918	3,81,311	555.20	59.61	16
Karnataka	2,320.85	42,61,057	19,57,604	1,284.65	180.66	2
Kerala	832.79	23,45,472	20,70,341	870.71	95.64	10
Madhya Pradesh	1,701.03	42,93,141	12,33,939	1,269.00	134.04	4
Maharashtra	2,569.70	93,93,636	39,25,451	2,212.47	116.15	6
Odisha	1,083.20	18,76,535	4,98,834	713.56	151.80	3
Punjab	497.20	33,80,119	11,85,869	1,083.45	45.89	17
Rajasthan	1,333.21	42,70,425	16,38,967	1,278.03	104.32	9
Tamil Nadu	2,719.71	94,53,193	24,80,543	2,184.03	124.53	5
Uttar Pradesh	1,257.65	77,99,075	20,97,806	1,913.55	65.72	15
West Bengal	550.37	19,48,935	10,52,333	752.07	73.18	14

Source: Computed.
Note: RMVT: Revenue from MVT and P> TW: Number of Two-wheelers; Others: Number of Other Vehicles; P&GT= Passengers and Goods Tax.

respectively. However, the tax effort varies from 233 in Bihar, 181 in Karnataka, 152 in Odisha, to 66 in Uttar Pradesh and 46 in Punjab.[11] Of all the major states, about six states are already generating revenue from this tax above their capacity.

Thus, despite the low growth rates in the 1990s, MVT and P&GT have of late gained momentum and the states can increase their revenue substantially by effectively mobilizing resources from this tax.

Structure of Tax

Motor vehicles tax is levied on acquisition of vehicles and includes one-off payment under the Indian Motor Vehicles Act, 1939. The main objective of this Act is to control and regulate the vehicular traffic in the country[12]. The levies charged under this Act are for (i) registering motor vehicles (ii) obtaining driving licences (iii) transfer of ownership of motor vehicles (iv) trade certificates issued to manufacturers, dealers and repairers of vehicles (v) permit for transport vehicles and (vi) certificate of fitness for transport. The levies include fees for registration, permit and driving licence. The fees are raised and restructured from time to time. The states also levy tax on mechanically propelled vehicles.

MVT is being levied in all states and union territories (UTs) except the UT of Lakshadweep. The existing tax structure shows wide variations in tax rates (Table 7.6). In fact, it is difficult to make comparisons of rates levied on different types of vehicles in different states. There are different bases for computation and different rates, leading to differing incidence of taxes per vehicle in different states. First, there are different schemes for the classification of vehicles. Second, there is no uniformity in the bases of various levies. Third, the tax is sometimes specific and some times *ad valorem*. Finally, in some states there is a one-off levy[13] and in others, there is an *ad valorem* levy payable every year.

---

[11] We have also tried to use regression approach, but the t-ratios for both the intercept and the coefficient of the independent variable (number of buses and trucks) turned out to be insignificant, so we have applied representative tax system approach.

[12] The tax was initially introduced through the Indian Motor Vehicles Act, 1914. Over time, with the growth in the vehicular traffic and the expansion of the system of road transport, various amendments were introduced. Finally, a new law called the Indian Motor Vehicle Act, 1939, was introduced.

[13] Except Sikkim, Mizoram, Meghalaya, Jammu and Kashmir, and Assam, other States levy a life-time tax on motorcycles.

Table 7.6 Rates of Motor Vehicles Tax

States	Structure of Motor Vehicle Tax		
	Cars	Buses (Stage Carriage)	Trucks
Andhra Pradesh	ULW up to 2286 kg 9% of the cost (Life-time Tax); Additional tax for drawing trailers Rs 3906 (Life-time Tax)	100 to 120 kms: Rs 330/PQ 120 to 160 kms: Rs 350/PQ 160 to 240 kms: Rs 435/PQ	Vehicles exceeding 3,000 kg but not exceeding 4,500 kg in laden weight: Rs 954.45/PQ
Gujarat	6% of the sale price (lump sum compulsory)	Stage carriage: Seating capacity up to 9: Rs 1200/PY; Seating capacity exceeding 9: Rs 1,200 + 80 per Seating + 40 per Standing	For all types of goods vehicle – Rs 2,000 + 400 per every 1,000 kg or part thereof if exceeding 3,000 kg
Haryana	Value up to Rs 4 lakh: Rs 2,000; Rs 4 lakh to Rs 10 lakh – 1% of the value of the car Value exceeding Rs 10 lakh – 1.5% of the value of the car	Token tax of Rs 550/PY per seat subject to a maximum of Rs 35,000/PY	Gross vehicle weight exceeding 1.2 tonne but not exceeding 6 tonnes Rs 1,200/PY
Himachal Pradesh	Personal Motor Vehicles having engine capacity up to 1000 cc – 2.5 % Above 1000 cc – 3 % of the price of motor vehicle at the time of registration	Rs 500/seat per annum (subject to the maximum of Rs 35,000/ PY)	Light Goods Vehicle: Rs 1,500/PY

(contd.)

Table 7.6 (contd.)

States	Structure of Motor Vehicle Tax		
	Cars	Buses (Stage Carriage)	Trucks
Karnataka	Having floor area up to 5 sq. mtr, (i) cost of which does not exceed Rs 5 lakh: 12 per cent of cost of the vehicle; (ii) cost exceeds Rs 5 lakh but not exceeding Rs 10 lakh, 13 per cent of cost (iii) cost exceeding Rs 10 lakh, 16 per cent of the cost (Life-time Tax)	Having floor area exceeding 5 sq mtr but not exceeding 6 sqr mtr: For every sqr mtr Rs 800/PQ Exceeding 6 sqr mtr but not 9 sqr mtr: Rs 850/PQ Exceeding 9 sqr mtr but not 12 sqr mtr: Rs 950/PQ Above 12 sqr mtr Rs 1,100/PQ	Laden weight exceeding 1,500 kg but not exceeding 2,000 kg Rs 10,000 (Life-time Tax); exceeding 2,000 kg but not 3,000 kg: Rs 15,000 (Life-time Tax)
Maharashtra	7% of the cost (One-time Tax)	Rs 71/seat per annum + Rs 18 per standee per annum; contract carriage: Ordinary Buses: Rs 1,500/seat per annum	Registered laden weight exceeding 1,500 kg and up to 3,000 kg: Rs 2,700/PY
Manipur	NA	Bus (>34 seats): Rs 2,200/PY or Rs 550/PQ; Medium Bus (>23 seats <34): Rs 1,580/PY or Rs 395/PQ	Registered laden weight exceeds 2.5 tonne but does not exceed 3 tonne: Rs 1,240/PY
Meghalaya	NA	Mini Bus (up to 30 seats) - for every seat authorised to carry passenger: Rs 100/PY or Rs 25/PQ Omni Bus (above 30 seat) -for every seat authorized to carry passenger: Rs 80/PY or Rs 20/PQ	One metric tonne or less: Rs 680/PY For every additional 1/2 metric tonne or part thereof of authorized load of goods: Rs 180/PY

State			
Mizoram	NA	Rs 500/PY	LCV (Goods) Above 1-5 MT payload: Rs1,300/PY
Odisha	Not exceeding 762 kg ULW- 5% of the cost of the vehicle or ten times of annual tax, whichever is higher; Exceeding 762 kg not exceeding 1,524 kg ULW - 5% of the cost of the vehicle or ten times of annual tax, whichever is higher; Exceeding 1,524 kg not exceeding 2286 kgs ULW - 5% of the cost of the vehicle or ten times of annual tax, whichever is higher	Up to 160 Rs 172/PM; 161 to 240 km: Rs 196/PM; 241 to 320 km: Rs 245/PM Above 320 km: Rs 294/PM Per standee: Rs 152/PY	Laden weight between 5001-10,000 kg: Rs 2,446/PQ; Annual Rate of Addl. Tax Rs 446/PQ
Rajasthan	NA	NA	Cost of chassis/vehicle up to Rs 1,000,000 - 2% of the cost of the horse
Sikkim	Engine capacity up to 900 cc: Rs 1,000/PY; Above 900 cc, up to 1,490 cc: Rs 1,200/PY; Above 1,490 cc, up to 2,000 cc: Rs 2,500/PY; Above 2,500 cc: Rs 3,000/PY	Rs 125/seat per year	Exceeding 2,000 kg but not exceeding 4,000 kg gross vehicle weight - every additional 250 kg or part thereof above 2,000 kg: Rs 1,465 plus Rs 124
Tamil Nadu	NA	Per passenger Rs 400 /PY	Vehicles not exceeding 3,000 kg in laden weight – Rs 600 (Life-time Tax)
Tripura	Rs 275/PY or Rs 2,750 (One-time Tax)	Rs 1420 for 27 seats plus Rs 42 for every addl. seat beyond 27	Up to 3,000 kg registered laden weight - Rs 500/PY

(contd.)

Table 7.6 (contd.)

States	Structure of Motor Vehicle Tax		
	Cars	Buses (Stage Carriage)	Trucks
Uttarakhand	NA	Seating capacity for more than thirty-five persons Rs 1,115 + Rs 45 for every seat in excess of thirty-five seats; Additional tax up to 4,500 km for: (i) plain routes Rs 154 per seat; (ii) hill routes Rs 146 per seat and For each kilometer exceeding 4,500 kms Rs 0.04 per seat per km to be added to the above amount	Unladen weight exceeding 2,000 kilograms but not exceeding 3,000 kilograms – 2.5% of cost of the vehicle and additional tax of Rs 210 per metric tonne of the gross vehicle weight of the vehicle or part thereof operating on hill routes; Rs 85 per metric tonne of the gross vehicle weight of the vehicle or part thereof operating on plain routes; Rs 5,000 for each year or thereof for vehicles operating under the national permit
Uttar Pradesh	For petrol vehicles Rs 5,000 (One-time Tax); For diesel vehicles, 5% of the cost (One-time Tax);	Seating capacity for more than thirty-five persons Rs 1,115 + Rs 45 for every seat in excess of thirty-five seats	Unladen weight exceeding 2,000 kg but not exceeding 3,000 kg: Rs 748/PY

Lack of uniformity exists even in the case of scooters (two wheelers). Some states levy this tax on the basis of engine capacity defined in terms of c.c. (cubic centimetres); in others states it is on the basis of unladen weight (ULW) and cost of the vehicle. Some states like Andhra Pradesh and Maharashtra levy this tax on an *ad valorem* basis.

The MVT on personal cars has been levied on the basis of ULW, cost of vehicle and also on the basis of seating capacity. In some states the tax is paid on a one-time basis while in certain other states it is an annual payment; in Kerala and Jammu and Kashmir, the tax is paid on a quarterly basis.[14]

In case of passenger transport vehicles, like stage or contract carriage, the seating capacity and route length on which the carriage plies forms the tax base. The period of payment also varies; some states charge the tax quarterly[15] while others charge the tax annually. The tax on goods transport vehicles is primarily based on weight, that is registered laden weight (RLW) or ULW and gross vehicle weight. In some states the mode of payment is annual while in others it is quarterly payment. Apart from using it as a source of revenue, MVT is used as an instrument for regulating and controlling vehicular emissions. This is done to protect the environment.

Administration of Motor Vehicle Tax

As stated earlier, the MVT is levied under the Indian Motor Vehicles Act, 1939. It includes fees levied for registration, permits, and driving licences. In addition to the tax under the Central legislation, motor vehicles tax is levied by the states under their respective Motor Vehicle Taxation Acts. In most of the states, this tax is administered by the transport department. The regulatory activities relating to MVT, such as the registration of vehicles, is done by the Inspectors and the Transport Officers. The work relating to assessment of tax primarily depends upon the structure provided by law. In some states, the returns are required to be submitted to the assessing authority. In many states, the tax is levied on the basis of the

---

[14] In Assam, the tax on motor cars is levied every 15 years.

[15] In Andhra Pradesh, Chattisgarh, Jammu and Kashmir, Karnataka, Kerala, Tamil Nadu, and Uttar Pradesh, the tax levy on private stage carriages is on a quarterly basis.

purchase price of the vehicle and in others it is related to registered laden weight or ULW.

In the case of passenger buses, the tax is assessed on the basis of sitting capacity and/or occupancy ratio. However, the law also provides for tax on the basis of compounded levy. In most states, the tendency is to provide transparency concerning the administration of tax; in some states, the criterion of laden/unladen weight, number of seats/occupancy ratio, and compounded levy, give considerable scope to the transport officer to levy the tax according to his discretion resulting in corruption in the tax department.

Assessment of the Existing Taxes

The tax collected by the transport department in the form of motor vehicle tax is ultimately collected from the owner of the vehicles. An assessment of the existing structure of MVT suggests that the current system is characterized by the following features:

Variations in Rates: The existing structure shows wide variations in tax rate. In fact, it is difficult to make comparisons of rates levied on different types of vehicles in different states. First, there are differing schemes for classification of vehicles. Second, there is no uniformity in the bases of various levies. Third, the tax is at times specific while in some cases it is *ad valorem*. Finally, in some States there is a one time levy and in others, there is an *ad valorem* levy payable every year.

Separation of Motor Vehicles Tax from Passengers and Goods Tax: An analysis of the motor vehicles tax shows that MVT in some states is either very high or very low as compared to the MVT in other states. This is mainly because some states have two different taxes—MVT and P&GT—while in the other states, the two taxes have been merged. The current system of taxation, therefore, does not make the MVT comparable amongst the states.

High Incidence of taxes: While considering the overall burden of taxes on the road transport industry, we have to take into account the burden of all the taxes levied directly on the vehicles, on its important components (spares), on fuel, and the operational taxes, such as the registration fee, MVT, licence fee, P&GT, and permit fees. The rates of taxes levied by the Central Government are uniform throughout the country. However, variations exist in the rates of vehicle taxes levied by the states. The estimates of combined incidence of tax on passengers and goods vehicle in the different states show that the tax burden is in the range of Rs 3 to 4 lakh per vehicle per annum.[16]

Recommended Reforms

The assessment of the MVT and other taxes on goods and vehicles indicates that it is important to take note of the above aspects and introduce reforms in the existing rate structure of road user taxation. In view of the varying structures of bases, rates, nature and the types of taxes levied in different states, it is important that the tax system should be reformed in such a way that it is (i) neutral, (ii) efficient in allocation of resources, (iii) administratively expedient, and (iv) non-cascading. Keeping these objectives in view, the following reforms are recommended in the rates and the base of the motor vehicles tax:

Uniformity in the structure: Lack of uniformity in the structure of MVT and P&GT as well as the discretion exercised in assessing the actual tax payable by the owner of vehicle not only causes disregard for the need to register vehicles, but also intensifies corruption in the system. It is, therefore, essential to have uniformity in the tax system in all the states.

One-time tax: Some of the taxes, such as road tax, which are levied on most of the users not involved in commercial activities, could be collected as a one-time tax. This would not only reduce the administrative costs of handling the same taxpayer perpetually but also save time and lower the compliance costs for the taxpayers. Many states have already implemented a one-time (life-time) tax. It is high time that others also follow suit. However, keeping in view the issue of pollution emission through vehicles, the one-time tax should be limited to the first ten years of the life of the vehicle. Thereafter, based on the emission of the vehicle and its age, the charge should be graduated over time. The vehicle should be condemned after 20 years of life.

A combined tax on vehicles, passengers and goods: Although the objectives of MVT and P&GT were initially different, over a period of time both the taxes were structured with primarily the same objectives. It is, therefore, important that MVT and P&GT are levied through one tax,

---

[16] The combined tax burden on goods vehicles is computed on the basis of a compounded levy. For motor cycles we assume engine capacity of 60cc, with ULW of 95 kg, and a purchase price of Rs 45,000. It is further assumed that the vehicle covers 6,300 km per year. The cost of a car is assumed to be Rs 1 lakh. See for details, Mahesh C Purohit and Vishnu Kanta Purohit (2010).

as is being done in some of the states. The combined incidence of tax could be worked out to have one rate and one administration. It could be called as Vehicle Tax for personal vehicles and Road Tax for the commercial vehicles.

Ad valorem rate: The rate of the tax must be *ad valorem*. The comparative picture of different taxes levied by all the states indicates that to have buoyancy in the tax system, it is useful to resort to a tax system that is based on cost of purchase of vehicles with additional factors of (i) occupancy and (ii) length of routes or goods carried. The purchase price, which automatically flows in from the manufacturers, would take away the discretion of the Administrative Assistant (RTI) or the Officer (RTO) dealing with assessment of tax liability of vehicles. The tax liability should be indicated through a ready reckoner.

Encouraging use of National Permit: The national permits for stage and contract carriages, as well as for public and private carriers, are fixed for three to five years. The procedure for grant of such permits for private carriers is relatively simple than that for stage carriages and public carriers. For issue of the national permits, an annual composite fee per state (other than the home state, where full taxes have to be paid) is charged in lieu of the counter-signature fee. Thus, the prescribed fee is marginally lower than the full tax liability for other inter-state permits and single-point taxation. In spite of the low tax incidence of the national permits, to ensure the smooth flow of goods and passengers across states, it would be desirable to encourage the use of national permits. It is suggested that there should be no freezing of the number of such permits. Also, attempts must be made to have a proper evaluation of the incidence of tax from the issue of national permits. If necessary, the composite tax could be increased to have parity with the existing state taxes on vehicles. Above all, the procedure for issue of such permits must be further simplified. This would help in augmenting movement of long-distance goods in the country.

Pollution-abatement incentives: Some incentive could be built into the tax system to give initiative for the use of non-polluting instruments in each of the vehicles. The structure of tax on motor vehicles as prevalent in other countries point out the fact that most countries have differentiated tax structure based on the type of fuel or on the basis of use of catalysts. It is, therefore, useful to adopt built-in fiscal incentives for pollution abatement.

Tax incentives for other policy objectives: In addition to incentives for pollution abatement, it is advisable to use taxes on road transport as an instrument to achieve certain policy objectives. First, these taxes could be introduced in such a way that they encourage the use of multi-axle vehicles (MAVs). This is important in the context of over-loading of two-axle vehicles (TAVs) and the consequent damage to the roads. Here it is important to note that the damaging power of vehicles increases exponentially with their weight. A nominal increase of 10 per cent over the permissible load weight can lead to a reduction of about one-third in the road life, necessitating a much earlier investment for road strengthening. While movement of goods by road has increased over time, the introduction of MAVs has been rather slow. TAVs continue to account for a major proportion (approximately 96 per cent) of the total goods fleet in the country. Transportation of heavy loads without causing excessive damage to the roads can be best achieved by using MAVs as they can distribute the load on the road uniformly. Also, these vehicles are fuel-efficient, economical and facilitate container movement. Studies indicate that MAVs can generate savings ranging between 4 and 6 per cent for transport operators and reduce road cost by 8 per cent. Second, the tax concession should be given to encourage the use of noise-reduction in vehicles and a surcharge could be added for high value vehicles. That is, the tax rate could be inversely related to noise pollution and positively to the value of vehicles.

The reforms suggested above would set in place a rational and efficient tax policy for the transport sector. At the state level, it is needed to have a free flow of inter-state trade and commerce.

Passengers and Goods Tax

The P&GT is levied on passengers and goods carried by road or by inland waterways. Both the MVT and P&GT, as stated earlier, are similar in nature; these taxes fall on the same base and are paid ultimately by the same group of people. Some of the states levy both these taxes while others have merged the two and levy a single tax.

Fiscal Significance

The P&GT has gained prominence recently. The yield from P&GT (for all the states) increased at a slow pace in the 1990s but picked up in the later period.

The yield from the tax has increased from Rs 1,136 crore in 1991–2 to Rs 2,075 crore in 2000–1 and further to Rs 9,857 crore in 2009–10 (Table 7.1). Accordingly, the tax has recorded a growth rate of 13.1 per cent and buoyancy of 1.0 during the period. P&GT has contributed in the range of 1.8 per cent to 3.2 per cent to States' own tax revenue. The tax share, in general, has fluctuated over the years.

The yield from the P&GT, amongst different states, shows considerable variations. In 2009–10, it was at a maximum in Madhya Pradesh (Rs 1,332.90 crore), followed by Bihar (Rs 1,613.20 crore), Karnataka (Rs 1,291.10 crore) and Tamil Nadu (Rs 1,091.90 crore). The yield from this tax has been quite low throughout the period in the special category states of Manipur, Mizoram, and Uttarakhand. Gujarat, Kerala, and Odisha have also seen a decline in the revenue. Thus, the revenue from P&GT exhibited a very high growth rate in certain states but showed a declining trend in others (Table 7.7).

Tax Structure

The pattern of levy of this tax in different states is as follows:

1. Some states levy tax on actual collection of fare and freight. In Haryana, for example, the passenger tax is levied at the rate of 25 per cent of the value of the fare; Manipur at the rate of 10 per cent of the fare charged, and in Himachal Pradesh, it is 40 per cent of the passenger fare, as shown in Table 7.8.
2. Some states levy a composite passenger tax. That is, the tax is a compounded levy based on the criteria of seating capacity, occupancy ratio, etc. In some states, the tax is collected as a percentage of the purchase price of the vehicle. The states following the system of lump sum tax are Haryana (for smaller vehicles), Meghalaya, and Mizoram. Manipur gives the option to the owners of vehicle to pay according to the *ad valorem* rate or follow the compounded levy scheme.
3. Some states, such as Bihar, Delhi, Karnataka, Odisha, Rajasthan, Tamil Nadu, and West Bengal, do not levy this tax.

With regard to goods tax also different methods of levy are followed. In states like Himachal Pradesh the tax is levied at the rate of 5 per cent of

Table 7.7 Yield from Passengers and Goods Tax in States

(Rs Crore)

States	1991-2	1996-7	2001-2	2005-6	2007-8	2008-9	2009-10	2010-11 (RE)	2011-12 (BE)	GR	Buoyancy
Andhra Pradesh	0.21	1.51	5.29	50.35	80.29	15.90	10.30	11.30	12.40	50.8	3.3
	(0.01)	(0.031)	(0.042)	(0.262)	(0.28)	(0.05)	(0.03)	(0.02)	(0.02)		
Bihar		28.94	153.32	613.38	937.87	1,279.40	1,613.20	1,623.80	1,940.00	32.5	2.0
		(1.29)	(6.28)	(17.23)	(18.44)	(20.70)	(19.94)	(15.35)	(15.42)		
Chhattisgarh			196.27	395.33	510.72	420.70	696.10	616.00	700.00	14.7	0.8
			(9.85)	(9.76)	(9.09)	(6.40)	(9.77)	(7.40)	(7.12)		
Goa	1.83	4.76	36.19	130.80	112.72	157.50	160.70	147.00	162.00	33.7	1.9
	(1.61)	(1.57)	(6.36)	(11.93)	(8.29)	(9.30)	(9.12)	(6.74)	(6.37)		
Gujarat	75.55	96.19	99.11	156.30	151.62	169.40	6.90	275.00	280.00	-4.5	-0.4
	(2.61)	(1.59)	(1.07)	(1.00)	(0.69)	(0.70)	(0.03)	(0.79)	(0.72)		
Haryana	119.82	259.64	498.56	757.60	379.39	370.30	391.50	400.00	425.00	8.6	0.6
	(9.22)	(12.12)	(10.03)	(8.34)	(3.27)	(3.18)	(2.96)	(2.31)	(2.12)		
Jharkhand			22.23	96.66	71.07	93.00	64.10	65.40	30.00	13.1	0.9
			(1.07)	(3.35)	(2.00)	(1.80)	(1.15)	(1.10)	(0.38)		
Karnataka	82.06	199.44	498.11	1,041.45	837.34	1,085.00	1,291.10	1,440.00	1,510.00	16.9	1.3
	(2.83)	(3.46)	(5.06)	(5.59)	(3.22)	(3.90)	(4.22)	(3.78)	(3.45)		
Kerala	0.01	0.001	0.001	0.002	0	0	0	0	0		
	(0.0006)	(0.00003)	(0.00002)	(0.000018)							

(contd.)

Table 7.7 (contd.)

(Rs Crore)

States	1991–2	1996–7	2001–2	2005–6	2007–8	2008–9	2009–10	2010–11 (RE)	2011–12 (BE)	GR	Buoyancy
Madhya Pradesh	173.67 (8.20)	297.17 (7.24)	262.40 (5.58)	578.58 (6.35)	916.44 (7.63)	1,332.60 (9.80)	1332.9 (7.72)	1,575.00 (7.73)	1,815.00 (7.85)	11.6	1.1
Maharashtra	199.07 (3.34)	200.87 (1.71)	1,027.39 (4.83)	504.63 (1.50)	388.27 (0.82)	892.00 (1.70)	976.6 (1.65)	738.60 (1.00)	812.40 (0.97)	6.1	0.5
Odisha	0.02 (0.003)	0.005 (0.0004)	252.04 (10.22)	463.34 (9.26)	626.90 (9.14)	638.30 (8.00)	815.30 (9.08)	875.00 (8.25)	1,000.00 (8.13)	136.2	6.9
Punjab	80.64 (5.23)	0.008 (0.00029)	0	0	0	0	0	0	0	–88.2	–16.4
Rajasthan	–0.01 (û0.001)	0	23.10 (4.08)	236.71 (26.06)	160.61 (1.21)	189.90 (1.30)	176.10 (1.07)	160.00 (0.82)	265.00 (1.24)	192.2	9.3
Tamil Nadu	26.4 (0.71)	187.26 (2.35)	282.65 (2.17)	984.94 (4.22)	1,483.21 (5.01)	978.70 (2.90)	1091.90 (2.99)	1527.5 (3.11)	1,788.40 (2.99)	22.2	1.7
Uttar Pradesh	161.40 (4.61)	221.44 (3.51)	76.65 (0.74)	105.19 (0.56)	109.65 (0.44)	266.50 (0.90)	271.10 (0.80)	890.80 (2.19)	0	17.5	1.4
West Bengal	138.60 (5.66)	–0.06 (–0.0015)	1.06 (0.0164)	0.63 (0.006)	1.07 (0.01)	–0.04 (–0.0003)	0.02 (0.0001)	0.03 (0.0001)	0.03 (0.0001)	85.5	6.0
Special Category States											
Assam	10.05 (1.96)	20.53 (2.68)	9.71 (0.62)	61.52 (1.90)	12.39 (0.37)	284.70 (6.90)	545.40 (10.94)	480.40 (8.13)	411.20 (6.26)	13.1	1.3

Himachal Pradesh	26.98	65.26	34.27	42.61	55.12	62.40	88.70	102.10	117.40	2.2	0.2
	(13.98)	(15.84)	(3.74)	(2.85)	(2.81)	(2.80)	(3.45)	(3.00)	(2.91)		
Jammu and Kashmir	37.58	12.07	147.24	236.27	264.59	297.00	315.50	358.10	382.30	25.6	2.0
	(22.86)	(4.17)	(17.17)	(13.99)	(11.51)	(11.00)	(10.26)	(9.83)	(9.14)		
Manipur	0.43	0.38	0.44	0.68	0.76	0.80	0.80	1.90	1.10	5.0	0.5
	(3.00)	(2.66)	(0.84)	(0.71)	(0.51)	(0.50)	(0.41)	(0.77)	(0.33)		
Meghalaya	1.03	5.71	1.61	2.76	3.58	3.30	3.50	4.60	5.00	6.2	0.5
	(2.42)	(7.38)	(1.18)	(1.09)	(1.12)	(0.90)	(0.79)	(1.00)	(0.84)		
Mizoram	0.31	0.31	0.53	0.99	1.07	1.40	1.40	1.40	3.20	10.2	0.9
	(9.28)	(4.59)	(2.76)	(1.81)	(1.38)	(1.50)	(1.29)	(1.10)	(1.86)		
Nagaland				1.34	2.19	2.30	4.00	2.50	2.70	23.2	2.7
				(1.27)	(1.67)	(1.50)	(2.19)	(1.18)	(1.09)		
Uttarakhand			0.003	0.0001	0.0004	0	0	0	0	−66.3	−8.5
			(0.00031)	(0.00001)	0	0	0	0	0		
All States	1,135.60	1,662.60	3,671.40	6,449.60	6,808.00	8,540.90	9,857.00	11,296.40	11,663.10	13.1	1.0
	(3.18)	(2.34)	(2.87)	(3.04)	(2.38)	(2.70)	(2.71)	(2.46)	(2.16)		

Source: Reserve Bank of India, *State Finances: A Study of Budgets* (Various Issues), Mumbai: RBI.

Note: The figures in parentheses indicate the percentage share of passengers and goods tax in the state's own tax revenue; The growth rate and buoyancy of all the states are calculated for 1991–2 to 2009–10 but for bifurcated and newly formed states it is calculated for 2001–2 to 2009–10; for Uttarakhand for 2001–2 to 2005–6; for Nagaland for 2002–3 to 2009–10; for Punjab for 1991–2 to 1998–9; Rajasthan for 1993–4 to 2009–10; and for West Bengal for 1997–8 to 2007–8.

Table 7.8 Rates of Passengers and Goods Tax

State	Rate of tax
Assam	Passenger and Goods Tax is levied on commercial vehicles registered in other states and plying in Assam on the strength of permits issued by the states. The basis of taxation for passenger carrying vehicles is as per seating capacity and for goods carrying vehicles as per actual permissible load carrying capacity.
Goa	Passengers tax: (a) Sitting capacity × Rs 30 per month; (b) Standing capacity—1/3 of the sitting capacity × Rs 30 per month.
Gujarat	The passenger tax is 1% of the amount of fare collected for municipal areas and 17.5% for the area outside the municipal areas.
Himachal Pradesh	Passengers tax at 40% of the fare and goods tax at 5% of the freight.
Haryana	Passengers tax at 25% of the value of the fare is charged on passengers carried by a motor vehicle.
Maharashtra	Passengers tax is levied at 17.5% of the revenue in the state.
Manipur	For passenger vehicle, the tax rate varies between Rs 300 to Rs 3,000 per annum on the basis of type of vehicle. In case of goods vehicle the tax varies between Rs 500 to Rs 3,000 per annum on the basis of the load of the vehicle. Vehicles with load of above 10 tonnes are charged with Rs 200 for every additional tonne.
Meghalaya	Passengers and goods tax is levied at the rate of 10 paise per rupee value of the fare subject to the minimum of 1 paise in any one case, the amount of tax being rounded to the next higher whole paise.
Mizoram	The rate of tax varies between Rs 400 to Rs 2,900, according to the type of the vehicle.
Rajasthan	In Rajasthan, a special road tax is levied in lieu of passengers and goods tax. It is levied on all kinds of transport vehicles. In the case of goods carriers registered in the state, the tax is based on the cost of the chassis/vehicle, whereas for passenger vehicles registered in the state, the tax is broadly based on the cost of vehicle/chassis and its seating capacity. In the case of vehicles registered outside the state, the tax is based on the basis of load carrying capacity for goods vehicles and on the basis of seating capacity for the passenger vehicles.

the freight charged; and Manipur levies 10 per cent of the freight charged (with the option for compounded levy).

The rest of the states follow the system of compounded levy. Haryana, for example, levies a lump sum tax varying from Rs 1,200 to Rs 14,400 per annum. Manipur levies a lump sum tax on the basis of the type of vehicle (with consideration to whether the vehicle plies within the state or interstate); Meghalaya also follows a system similar to Manipur; and Mizoram follows the system of age of vehicle to fix the compounded tax.

Rajasthan has introduced a special road tax in lieu of P&GT. It is also levied on all transport vehicles. In case of goods vehicle registered with the state, the tax is levied primarily according to the cost of purchase of vehicle; in the case of passenger vehicles, the tax is based on both the cost and the seating capacity. For the vehicles registered outside the state, for the goods vehicles the tax is levied on the basis of load carrying capacity and for the passenger vehicles it is on the basis of seating capacity.

It is felt that in the states where the tax is collected on the basis of actual passengers carried or goods transported, the tax official gets the power to determine tax and thus, the interaction between the officials and transporters increases. In most cases, they connive to have a reduced tax to be levied on the vehicles.

Some states, in addition to this tax, levy surcharge. Himachal Pradesh levies a surcharge of 20 per cent on passenger tax.

Administration of Passengers and Goods Tax

In most states, this tax, whether levied separately or jointly with MVT, is administered by the Transport Department. In many states, the tax on passengers is levied on the basis of the seating capacity and the percentage of fare. However, in Rajasthan it is levied on the purchase price of the vehicles. The tax collected by the Transport Department from passengers and goods tax is ultimately borne by the owner of the vehicles and is collected from the passengers and consignees of the goods. For this purpose, each owner is required to maintain separate accounts for the passenger tickets issued and goods received in respect of each vehicle. In the case of public goods vehicles, many state governments accept a lump sum amount in lieu of tax chargeable on freight.

Weaknesses of the Existing Tax System

An important feature of the existing tax system is the existence of a large number of check points for passengers and goods tax. Studies undertaken regarding the efficiency of the check points in different states reveal that the existence of many internal check points is not contributing significantly to the checking of tax evasion. Further, the larger the number of check points, the higher is the wastage of time arising from the stoppage of traffic. Even a conservative estimate shows that the money value of the loss of time suffered by the transporters due to the check points is tremendous.

As pointed out earlier, the present procedures of assessment and collection cause considerable time wastage and allow for a high degree of discretion in the assessment of these taxes. Further, these procedures generate an agency of intermediaries and consequently encourage corruption.

Recommended Reforms

The existing structure of the P&GT, as presented in Table 7.8, shows wide variation in tax rates. In fact, it is difficult to make comparisons of rates levied on different type of vehicles in different states. While in some states it is an *ad valorem tax*, in others it is a specific tax. In view of the varying structures of base and rates of taxes levied in different states, it is important that we aim at having a tax system which is neutral, efficient in the allocation of resources, administratively expedient; and non-cascading. Keeping in view these objectives, the following reforms are suggested.

Uniformity in the rate structure and the base of tax: As it is in Rajasthan, the base of the passengers and goods tax should be the purchase price of the vehicle instead of the seating capacity and rate should be a percentage of the purchase price.

A combined tax on vehicles, passengers and goods: Although the objectives of the MVT and the P&GT were different initially, currently both the taxes are structured with similar objectives. It is, therefore, important that the MVT and P&GT be levied through one tax, as is already being done in certain states like Tamil Nadu and Punjab.

To conclude, the existing system of passengers and goods tax performs the important function of raising resources for the states levying this tax. There could be further improvement in revenue by simplifying the tax procedures. However, in those states where the rates of motor vehicles tax have been kept adequately low, a tax on passengers and goods may be levied; but if the motor vehicles tax is itself very high, the levy of a separate tax on passengers and goods would be unjustifiable.

State Excise Duty

State excise duty (SED) is levied on production and consumption of spirituous beverages that include (a) alcoholic liquor for human consumption; (b) opium, Indian hemp and other narcotic drugs and narcotics; but not including medicinal and toilet preparations containing alcohol or any substance included in point (b).

The Constitution of India, vide Entry 51 of state list in Seventh Schedule, empowers the states to levy SED under the state list. Accordingly, the states have the absolute power to regulate and exercise comprehensive control over all activities in relation to intoxicants. They regulate and control manufacture and distribution of excisable articles by charging prescribed fees, fixing the number of licences, and also by prescribing the terms and conditions on which licences may be granted. However, under Article 268 of the Constitution, the Government of India levies SED on medicinal and toilet preparations but the states collect and retain the revenue.

The state government also fixes the wholesale prices of plain country spirit and spiced country spirit on the basis of tenders submitted by tender seekers. In addition to manufacture of these items, the state government exercises complete control over the import and export (including transport) of excisable articles; lays down the guidelines for the distribution of alcohol for potable and industrial purposes, and also makes allocation for the above purposes. Also, to promote alcohol-based industries, alcohol is supplied to them after denaturing it so that it may not be diverted for use as alcoholic beverages.

The state government monitors activities relating to the supply of rectified spirit, manufacturing of medicinal preparations, storage of finished products and arrangement of manufacture etc. While regulating manufacture and consumption of all these items for the masses, the Government does not interfere in the matter of alcoholic drinks used by tribal society on different social and festive occasions.[17] Similarly the Government of Maharashtra initially gave 100 per cent exemption of excise duty on wines if manufactured from grapes produced in the state for a period of 10 years—from 2001 to 2011. This exemption has now been extended by another 10 years, till 31 December 2021.

---

[17] In MP, for example, the government has exempted *pachwai*, a popular drink amongst the tribals.

Fiscal Significance

The SED continues to be a significant source of revenue for the states. Its yield in absolute terms was Rs 5,439 crore in 1991–2 and increased to Rs 17,110 crore in 2001–2; it has more than doubled by 2009–10 (Rs 48,734.6 crore) showing a growth rate of 12.12 per cent over the period. However, in terms of states' own revenue, its share has gone down from 15.2 per cent in 1991–2 to 13.3 per cent in 2009–10 (Table 7.1). In some states such as Andhra Pradesh, Chhattisgarh, Karnataka, MP, Rajasthan, Tamil Nadu, and Uttar Pradesh, the percentage share of SED in state's own tax revenue is much higher in comparison to the all-state average (Table 7.9). This is reflected in the buoyancy coefficient of the tax which is more than unity in most states.

The yield from SED is mainly a function of the prohibition policy. The states that have gone in for prohibition earn negligible revenue from this tax, as is the case with Gujarat (share in state's own tax revenue was 0.25 per cent in 2009–10). For states not having prohibition, the yield has shown an increase over time. However, there is no consistency in the trend of revenue (in absolute term). The states getting more than 10 per cent of their own tax revenue from SED in 2009–10 include Andhra Pradesh, Bihar, Chhattisgarh, Haryana, Karnataka, Madhya Pradesh, Punjab, Rajasthan, Tamil Nadu, and Uttar Pradesh. On the other hand, among the special category states, barring Assam, Jammu and Kashmir, Manipur, Mizoram, and Nagaland, all other states are getting more than 10 per cent of their own tax revenue from SED in 2008–9. Among the special category states, Assam has the highest growth rate followed by Arunachal Pradesh, Tripura, and Sikkim. The coefficients of buoyancy fall short of unity in many non-special category states—Chhattisgarh, Goa, Gujarat, Haryana, Jharkhand, Kerala, Maharashtra, Punjab, Rajasthan, and West Bengal. Amongst the special category states also, except for Arunachal Pradesh, Assam, and Manipur, the other states have a buoyancy value of less than one.

Structure of State Excise Duty

The SED is levied on the production and regulation of liquor. The objective of levy of this duty (in addition to revenue) is to control and regulate illegal manufacturing and trading which has grave repercussions on the

Table 7.9 Revenue from State Excise Duty

(Rs Crore)

States	1991–2	1996–7	2001–2	2005–6	2007–8	2008–9	2009–10	2010–11 (RE)	2011–12 (BE)	GR	B
Andhra Pradesh	811.95	63.90	1,651.90	2,684.57	4,040.69	5,752.60	5,848.60	7,912.00	9,014.40	17.56	1.28
	(26.58)	(1.31)	(13.15)	(13.98)	(14.03)	(17.24)	(16.63)	(16.68)	(15.97)		
Bihar	125.00	218.72	275.00	318.59	525.42	679.10	1,081.70	1,400.00	1,790.00	18.28	1.32
	(9.54)	(9.72)	(11.26)	(8.95)	(10.33)	(11.00)	(13.37)	(13.23)	(14.23)		
Chhattisgarh			313.61	634.50	843.10	964.10	1,187.70	1,390.00	1,626.00	18.49	1.00
			(15.73)	(15.66)	(15.01)	(14.62)	(16.67)	(16.69)	(16.54)		
Goa	14.97	26.75	46.13	55.35	75.94	88.70	104.50	130.00	147.00	9.52	0.62
	(13.19)	(8.84)	(8.10)	(5.05)	(5.59)	(5.24)	(5.93)	(5.96)	(5.78)		
Gujarat	13.08	24.32	47.32	48.06	47.20	48.70	65.90	62.20	66.60	8.19	0.61
	(0.45)	(0.40)	(0.51)	(0.31)	(0.22)	(0.21)	(0.25)	(0.18)	(0.17)		
Haryana	341.87	64.13	875.39	1,106.86	1,378.81	1,418.50	2,059.00	2,200.00	2,400.00	11.73	0.82
	(26.29)	(2.99)	(17.60)	(12.19)	(11.87)	(12.17)	(15.58)	(12.68)	(12.00)		
Jharkhand			200.00	155.00	211.11	357.50	500.00	525.00	700.00	8.88	0.69
			(9.63)	(5.37)	(5.95)	(7.03)	(8.99)	(8.80)	(8.93)		
Karnataka	510.32	843.87	1,976.94	3,396.79	4,766.57	5,749.60	6,946.30	8,125.00	9,115.00	16.03	1.23
	(17.60)	(14.63)	(20.06)	(18.23)	(18.34)	(20.80)	(22.72)	(21.35)	(20.80)		

(contd.)

Table 7.9 (contd.)

(Rs Crore)

States	1991–2	1996–7	2001–2	2005–6	2007–8	2008–9	2009–10	2010–11 (RE)	2011–12 (BE)	GR	B
Kerala	210.30 (12.56)	418.53 (10.74)	541.46 (9.14)	841.00 (8.60)	1,169.25 (8.55)	1,397.60 (8.74)	1,514.80 (8.59)	1,799.80 (8.21)	2059.10 (7.73)	9.87	0.79
Madhya Pradesh	375.36 (17.73)	742.54 (18.10)	704.68 (14.99)	1,370.38 (15.03)	1,853.83 (15.43)	2,302.00 (16.91)	2,951.90 (17.09)	3,525.00 (17.30)	4,050.00 (17.52)	17.96	1.46
Maharashtra	600.88 (10.09)	1,068.50 (9.12)	1,787.26 (8.40)	2,823.85 (8.42)	3,963.05 (8.43)	4,433.80 (8.52)	5,056.60 (8.56)	5,800.00 (7.89)	8,500.00 (10.16)	11.27	0.93
Odisha	55.07 (8.17)	90.77 (6.76)	197.46 (8.00)	389.33 (7.78)	524.93 (7.66)	660.10 (8.26)	849.10 (9.45)	1,000.00 (9.43)	1,200.00 (9.75)	16.46	1.14
Punjab	479.64 (31.09)	1,000.72 (36.59)	1,350.06 (28.01)	1,568.16 (17.44)	1,861.52 (18.80)	1,810.00 (16.23)	2,100.90 (17.45)	2,640.00 (15.18)	3,250.00 (15.93)	6.59	0.43
Rajasthan	356.32 (23.01)	784.57 (25.12)	1,110.27 (19.58)	1,521.80 (15.40)	1,805.12 (13.60)	2,169.90 (14.52)	2,300.50 (14.02)	2,460.00 (12.67)	2,623.00 (12.29)	9.70	0.76
Tamil Nadu	483.12 (12.94)	1,063.07 (13.32)	2,058.22 (15.82)	3,176.65 (13.62)	4,764.06 (16.08)	5,755.50 (17.09)	6,740.70 (18.44)	7,930.00 (16.14)	1,091.20 (1.83)	14.92	1.26
Uttar Pradesh	715.62 (20.46)	1,322.90 (20.98)	1,961.38 (18.99)	3,088.54 (16.38)	3,948.40 (15.82)	4,720.00 (16.47)	5,666.10 (16.73)	6,770.10 (16.64)	8,124.10 (16.14)	12.94	1.01

West Bengal	183.11	326.80	512.43	743.46	935.47	1,082.90	1,443.80	1,812.50	2,418.80	11.13	0.90
	(7.47)	(7.67)	(7.88)	(7.16)	(7.13)	(7.51)	(8.54)	(8.51)	(8.74)		
Special Category States											
Arunachal Pradesh	2.00	4.89	10.55	9.51	11.60	16.60	23.80	26.20	28.80	14.01	1.11
	(48.9)	(57.33)	(30.87)	(15.41)	(11.83)	(12.19)	(13.72)	(13.11)	(12.65)		
Assam	15.60	29.42	150.91	160.39	188.71	198.70	239.20	323.10	400.00	16.40	1.54
	(3.05)	(3.84)	(9.64)	(4.96)	(5.62)	(4.79)	(4.80)	(5.47)	(6.09)		
Himachal Pradesh	66.25	132.46	236.28	328.97	389.57	431.80	500.30	577.40	709.70	11.53	0.88
	(34.34)	(32.14)	(25.81)	(21.97)	(19.89)	(19.26)	(19.43)	(16.95)	(17.57)		
Jammu and Kashmir	46.80	74.00	178.47	190.00	238.00	250.00	270.00	307.00	333.00	9.69	0.87
	(28.47)	(25.58)	(20.81)	(11.25)	(10.35)	(9.28)	(8.78)	(8.43)	(7.96)		
Manipur	0.47	1.80	1.47	3.26	3.75	3.90	4.70	10.40	12.10	11.57	1.10
	(3.28)	(12.68)	(2.83)	(3.43)	(2.54)	(2.30)	(2.40)	(4.13)	(3.81)		
Meghalaya	17.62	31.28	41.69	59.16	58.62	69.80	90.30	100.20	124.40	8.77	0.73
	(41.42)	(40.43)	(30.66)	(23.41)	(18.37)	(18.89)	(20.32)	(21.70)	(21.15)		
Mizoram	0.74	0.89	1.35	1.46	1.70	1.90	2.10	2.20	2.30	6.56	0.57
	(22.16)	(13.34)	(7.06)	(2.65)	(2.18)	(1.98)	(1.95)	(1.73)	(1.33)		
Nagaland	0.80	1.00	1.80	1.96	2.83	3.30	3.10	3.60	3.90	7.34	0.65
	(4.44)	(3.19)	(3.43)	(1.86)	(2.15)	(2.14)	(1.74)	(1.69)	(1.56)		

Table 7.9 (contd.)

(Rs Crore)

States	1991–2	1996–7	2001–2	2005–6	2007–8	2008–9	2009–10	2010–11 (RE)	2011–12 (BE)	GR	B
Sikkim	6.65	10.54	17.59	32.96	37.94	46.50	57.30	55.50	67.40	13.25	0.97
	(58.59)	(48.57)	(21.88)	(22.39)	(19.18)	(25.17)	(25.69)	(23.84)	(25.06)		
Tripura	5.23	12.41	22.03	32.30	38.50	48.30	61.10	75.00	82.50	13.35	0.99
	(18.13)	(20.51)	(13.90)	(10.91)	(10.37)	(10.91)	(11.59)	(11.97)	(10.53)		
Uttarakhand			232.04	292.75	441.56	528.40	704.60	686.90	727.70	14.15	0.87
			(25.94)	(16.40)	(16.12)	(17.35)	(19.80)	(15.88)	(15.29)		
All States	5,438.77	8,805.32	17,110.10	25,035.60	34,127.22	40,989.70	4,8374.60	5,7649.00	6,9767.00	12.12	0.92
	(15.21)	(12.38)	(13.36)	(11.79)	(11.91)	(12.73)	(13.32)	(12.58)	(12.93)		

Source: Reserve Bank of India, *State Finances: A Study of Budgets* (Various Issues), Mumbai: RBI.

Note: GR = Growth Rate and B = Buoyancy.

Growth rate and buoyancy for all the states are calculated for the years 1991–2 to 2009–10. For the bifurcated and newly formed states these are calculated for the years 2001–2 to 2009–10;

Figures with in parenthesis are expressed as a percentage of the state's own tax revenue.

quality of liquor. The state governments, therefore, issue permits or licence for manufacturing, trading and consumption.

To prevent leakages, a few states have taken over the wholesale distribution of liquor and auctioning of vending rights to ensure that only that liquor is consumed which is routed through the institutional network.

State excise duty is collected in two components, which are excise duty and licence fee. While the former is levied on the basis of manufacture or consumption of alcoholic drinks, the latter is determined through auction-cum-tender generally, issued separately for country liquor (including spiced country liquor) and for Indian Made Foreign Liquor[18] (IMFL). The criterion for fixing the licence fee is tender price and the minimum guaranteed quantity (MGQ) to be off-loaded by the licencees for consumption and varies according to the type of liquor. Also, fixed fee system is adopted for country liquor, IMFL, beer, etc., after inviting applications and going by the draw of lottery if there are more than one applicants. Bhang shops are settled by the tender-cum-auction rule. While in Bihar and Tripura, the retail vending of country liquor is settled through auction and tender, in Rajasthan, the licence for country liquor is granted by inviting applications and then having a draw of lots whenever there was more than one application for a liquor shop. Similar procedure is followed for IMFL and beer in Rajasthan.

A fixed fee system is followed for the issue of licences for retail sale of country liquor and spiced country liquor in Uttar Pradesh (UP), Maharashtra, and Madhya Pradesh (MP). Similarly, in Himachal Pradesh, the licence fee is fixed for foreign liquor and beer. In the case of IMFL, fixed fee is paid for wholesale licence in Rajasthan, Bihar, Odisha, Andhra Pradesh, and Tamil Nadu. In Haryana, however, the quota of country liquor as well as IMFL is fixed by the government every year.

Retail sale of IMFL is granted through fixed licence fee system in UP, Maharashtra, Odisha, and MP. On the other hand, the licence for retail sale of IMFL follows auction-cum-tender method in Bihar and Tripura.

The method of fixing the rate of excise duty, as presented in Table 7.10, varies from state to state. The excise duty is charged progressively based on increase in price range for IMFL in Andhra Pradesh, Karnataka, Kerala, Rajasthan, and Arunachal Pradesh. However, in MP and UP, it is charged according to the ex-distillery price.

In the case of country liquor, the excise duty is charged according to proof strength in the states of UP and Himachal Pradesh. In Maharashtra,

---

[18] IMFL includes whiskey, brandy, gin, rum, or vodka made in India.

Table 7.10 Methods of Levying State Excise Duty in States

Excisable Item	Fixed Fee - Whole sale Licence	Fixed Fee - Licence for retail sale	Auction cum tender	Auction-Cum-lottery	Rate of Excise Duty	Excise Duty on wholesale price	Excise Duty on MRP	Excise duty charged acc. to proof strength	Excise Duty based on successive increase in price range
Country Liquor and Spiced Country Liquor	Rajasthan Bihar Odisha AP Tamil Nadu	UP Maharashtra Odisha MP	Tripura Bihar (Retail Vend)	Rajasthan	Ad valorem (Maharashtra) Specific (other States)	Haryana Bihar MP Odisha	Maharashtra	UP Himachal Pradesh	
IMFL	Rajasthan Bihar Odisha Andhra Pradesh Tamil Nadu	UP Maharashtra Odisha MP	Tripura Bihar (Retail Vend)	Rajasthan	Ad valorem (Maharashtra) Specific (Other States)	Manipur Sikkim Bihar Tamil Nadu* Tripura Kerala Meghalaya Odisha Mizoram	Maharashtra		Kerala Karnataka Arunachal Pradesh Andhra Pradesh Rajasthan

Beer	Himachal Pradesh	UP Maharashtra Odisha	Rajasthan	Ad valorem (Maharashtra, Rajasthan) Specific (Other States)	Manipur Meghalaya Sikkim Tripura Tamil Nadu Kerala Haryana MP Meghalaya Mizoram	Maharashtra Rajasthan	Himachal Pradesh UP Odisha Bihar	Karnataka

Source: Data collected from the relevant State Developments

Note: In Tamil Nadu, the vend fee for IMFL is merged with excise duty; In Karnataka, sale of country liquor is banned; no duty is levied in Bihar.

it is levied on the manufacturing cost. The excise duty on beer is charged according to proof strength in the states of Bihar, UP, Himachal Pradesh, and Odisha.

Rate Structure of SED

The rates of SED, as given in Table 7.11, indicate that there is a great divergence amongst the states. In Maharashtra, SED on beer is levied according to the manufacturing cost (at 100 per cent of the manufacturing cost or Rs 15 per bulk litre[19] (BL) in case of mild beer; and at 125 per cent of the manufacturing cost or Rs 20 per BL for fermented beer). Similarly, in Odisha, the rate is Rs 10–20 per BL of fermented beer. While in Himachal Pradesh, the rate of SED on beer is Rs 4.67 per bottle of 650 ml or Rs 6.20 per BL, in UP it is Rs 25.38 to 46.15 per BL, depending upon the strength of the beer. Bihar levies this duty between Rs 6 and Rs 18 per BL (according to the percentage of alcohol) MP has the SED of Rs 25 per BL.

Regarding country liquor, it is integrated with the licence fee in Bihar. In Haryana and Himachal Pradesh, it is taxed at Rs 5 and Rs 7, respectively, per proof litre (PL); in Rajasthan, SED on country liquor is Rs 116.67 per London proof litre (LPL).[20] In UP, the SED on country liquor is Rs 59 to Rs 85 per BL (Table 7.11).

The rate of SED on wine in Haryana varies from Rs 3 to Rs 4 per BL according to the strength; in Kerala, from Rs 3 to Rs 12 per PL. In UP, the excise duty on a bottle of 750 ml of wine is levied either at a specific rate of Rs 66.66 or at an *ad valorem* rate of 25 per cent of Maximum Retail Price (MRP) of the bottle, whichever is higher. Karnataka levies an additional excise duty ranging from Rs 10 per BL to Rs 70 according to the declared price (DP) range on bottled wine, and Rs 3.85 per BL to Rs 8.85 according to the DP range on bulk wine.

Madhya Pradesh levies a whopping Rs 250 per PL. It is followed by Gujarat, where the SED on wine is Rs 100 per PL. In Odisha, the SED on wine is Rs 35–140 per LPL.

In the case of IMFL, Karnataka levies a basic excise duty of Rs 40 while the additional excise duty varies according to the DP range; Bihar and Madhya Pradesh levy duty on the wholesale price according to brand of

---

[19] A bulk litre is the volume of a liquid as measured,
[20] LPL has the same meaning as PL. It is the percentage of proof alcohol in alcoholic liquor.
LPL = Bulk × (proof strength/100)

Table 7.11 Rates of State Excise Duty in Select States

States	Wine	Beer	Bhang/KG	CL	IMFL	Rum for Army
Bihar				Rs 70 per LPL	Company's maximum	
Gujarat	Rs 100 per PL	Rs 6 per BL	Rs 60			
Haryana	Rs 3–4 per BL			Rs 5 per PL	Rs 25 per PL	Rs 25 per PL
Himachal Pradesh	Rs 1.50–2.00 per BL	Rs 4.67 per bottle of 650 ml or Rs 6.20 per BL	Rs 20	Rs 7 per PL	Rs 23 per PL	Rs 19–23 per PL
Karnataka	Rs 3.85–70 per PL*					
Kerala	Rs 3–12 per PL				Rs 34.50–100 per PL	
Maharashtra	100–200% of mfg. cost	100–125% of the mfg. cost or Rs 15–20 per BL		Rs 10–60 per PL	200% of mfg. cost or Rs 160 per PL whichever is higher	40% of mfg. cost or Rs 20 per BL whichever is higher
Manipur	Rs 14 per BL				Rs 50 per LPL for Army	Rs 30
Mizoram	Rs 30 per PL		Rs 60		Rs 8–52 per PL	
MP	Rs 250 per PL		Rs 300	Rs 125 per PL		
Odisha	Rs 35–140/LPL	Rs 10–20 per BL		Rs 16 per LPL	Rs 140–200 per LPL	Rs 50 per LPL
Rajasthan				Rs 116.67 per LPL	Rs 170–500 per LPL	Rs 50 per LPL
Tamil Nadu		Rs 0.25–4.36/BL			Rs 30–113.24 per PL	Rs 22 per PL
Uttar Pradesh	Rs 66.6 or 25% of max. retail price of bottle whichever is more/BL	Rs 25.38–46.15 per BL	Rs 20	Rs 59.03–85 per BL	Rs 130–496 per bottle of 750 ml	Rs 53.33 per BL
Uttarakhand		Rs 13	Rs 20	Rs 25–75 per BL		Rs 43 per AL

Source: Data collected from the relevant State Departments.

Note: * In Karnataka, the Sales Tax is merged with SED and renamed as Additional Excise Duty.; LPL: London Proof Litre, BL: Bulk Litre, AL: Alcoholic Litre and PL: Proof Litre, IMFL: Indian Made Foreign Liquor, CL: Country Liquor.

the liquor. In Haryana, SED on IMFL is Rs 25 per PL, whereas in Kerala, the rate ranges progressively from Rs 34.50 to Rs 100 according to the different price ranges of the IMFL. In Odisha, SED on IMFL varies between Rs 140 and Rs 200 per LPL and in Tamil Nadu it varies between Rs 30 and Rs 113.24 per PL.

In Kerala, civilians are charged higher rates of excise in comparison to the army. The maximum rate charged for a civilian is Rs 100 on IMFL and for an army personnel, it is Rs 21 per PL. This concessional rate is applicable solely for IMFL supplied through the canteen stores department (CSD) to the army personnel. However, no duty is levied on IMFL to naval personnel on board the ships. Likewise, in Manipur, a low rate excise duty is levied on IMFL procured by the armed forces and para-military forces—Rs 50 per LPL. Manipur has been under prohibition, and manufacturing and distribution of liquor is not allowed in the state. There are also concessional rates of SED for rum supplied through CSD to the army. In Maharashtra, SED on rum for army is 40 per cent of the manufacturing cost or Rs 20 per BL, whichever is higher; in Uttarakhand, SED is Rs 43 per alcoholic litre (AL).[21] While in Odisha, the rate is Rs 50 per LPL, in UP, it is Rs 53.33 per BL.

The licence fee for possession of liquor in star hotels varies across states. The fees are Rs 3 to 6 lakh in Bihar, whereas in Odisha it varies between Rs 2 and 3 lakh. Within the states also the licence fee for possession of liquor in hotels varies according to the location of hotels. For the hotels in the six major cities of Odisha, it is Rs 2.50 lakh and for other areas, it is Rs 2 lakh. Similarly, in Bihar, licence fee for hotels in corporation area of Patna and Muzzafarpur is Rs 5 lakh whereas in the other areas it is Rs 4 lakh. In Himachal Pradesh, the licence fee varies from Rs 35,000 to Rs 60,000 (Table 7.12).

Administration of State Excise Duty

The State Excise Commissioner (SEC), who is an officer from the IAS cadre, heads the department of State Excise. Directly below the SEC, at the headquarters organization, there is a deputy SEC who helps in the formulation of policy and directs the overall administration under the superintendence of the SEC. Through the mechanism of licence fee,

---

[21] AL = percentage of pure alcohol in alcoholic liquor. It is calculated as follows:
AL = Bulk × [(v/v)/100], where v/v = 1

Table 7.12 Licence Fee in Select States

State	Denatured Spirit	Bottling of IMFL	Manufacture of Wines	Distillery	Brewery	Possession of liquor for Star Hotels	Club Licence	Beer Bar Licence
Bihar						Rs 3–6 lakh	Rs 300,000	Rs 30,000–100,000
Himachal Pradesh	Rs 1,000–2,000/BL		Rs 2,000	Rs 75,000	Rs 10,000	Rs 35,000–60,000	Rs 1,000–5,000	
Kerala				Rs 25,000–2,00,000	Rs 50,000–Rs 200,000			
Maharashtra			Rs 25,300				Rs 55,000–234,300	Rs 53,400–199,700
Meghalaya				Rs 9,000				
Odisha		Rs 3/BL		Rs 1,000,000–3,500,000	Rs 25–50 lakh	Rs 2–3 lakh	Rs 75,000–150,000	Rs 75,000–100,000
Tamil Nadu	Rs 200–25,000		Rs 200	Rs 4,000		Rs 1,000	Rs 1,000	
Tripura		Rs 5/BL						
Uttar Pradesh		Rs 0.20–1.35						

Source: Data collected from the relevant State Development.
Note: BL: Bulk Litre; IMFL: Indian Made Foreign Liquor.

the deputy SEC and the administrative units (spread over all the districts) regulate production, distribution and consumption of liquor in the state.

The administrative unit at the field level consists of districts headed by a person of the rank of assistant SEC. The distribution of administrative work by districts is on a territorial basis. However, in some of the states, a number of revenue districts have been merged into one.

As in the other states, the Department of State Excise in Maharashtra is also headed by the SEC. However, administratively, the department is governed by the Home Department of the Government of Maharashtra. At the headquarters, the commissioner is assisted by one additional commissioner of SED (Excise Policy and Related Matters) and two joint commissioners—one dealing with the administration and the other with the issue of alcohol and molasses. In addition, there are two deputy commissioners (senior scale) at the headquarters assisting the commissioner—one dealing with excise policy regarding retail sale of toddy and the other dealing with medicinal & toilet preparations. There are two deputy commissioners (junior scale) and four assistant commissioners who assist the senior officers.

The excise law provides for the right to appeal, revision and reference. According to the existing arrangements, there are three tiers of appeal prior to a court appeal. The initial appeal is made to the DyETC (Appeals) who works as an appellate authority. The work is territorially distributed. A revision petition against the orders of the DyETC (appeals) can be filed before SEC. The revision is filed before the Board of Revenue which also has *suo moto* powers. The Tribunal consists of members drawn from the judicial, accounts and taxation services. In cases involving points of law, reference can be made to the High Court; otherwise the findings of the Revenue Board are final.

The government of Maharashtra has sanctioned flying squads for enforcement-related work. All such flying squads and the rest of the executive officers deal with enforcement activities like controlling distillation activities of illicit liquor; detecting excise duty evasion and smuggling of non-excise paid goods. In addition, the state government has sanctioned twelve check-posts at key locations in order to prevent inter-state smuggling and illegal transportation.

As stated, the Department of State Excise collects excise duty on the alcoholic products and regulates their trade. This objective is achieved by the issuance of various types of licences for the manufacture, possession, sale, transport, import, and export of these alcoholic products.

Even after the licence is issued, the regulation for movement of liquor in the state among the licenced dealers is controlled through the issue of licence for imports within the state. The importing licence first applies for the licence to the Superintendent of Excise of the district declaring the quantity required by him from out of the state. The same procedure applies for obtaining liquor from the warehouses within the state. In either case, the licencee is required to deposit the duty, licence fee, and the cost price in the treasury by challan and produce the challan to the Superintendent of Excise who will then authorize the import (or issue) of the liquor.

For import of liquor, the licence is sent out of the state and the Excise Officer in the exporting state looks into it. In the case of domestic sale, the officer-in-charge of the warehouse issues the liquor on the basis of the endorsement on the challan.

Weaknesses of the Existing System

The structure of SED in different states indicates that the present system is heavily biased towards licence fee and characterized by the following weaknesses:

Divergence in types and rates of SED: Divergence in types of duties and rates of SED makes it difficult to know the incidence of tax on liquor in any particular state. Also, it is very difficult to estimate the effective rate of tax in any state and knowing whether the state is realizing its full potential. It makes inter-state comparison of duty/fee structures difficult and inter-state commerce cumbersome. It provides huge incentives for inter-state smuggling and leads to unhealthy competition among the states to generate revenue at the expense of others.

Narrow base of SED: The current structure of SED has a narrow base and yields very low revenue. There seems to be no relationship between the auction price of licences and the sale price of the liquor, etc. This is partly due to connivance between the producer, wholesaler and retailers. This seems possible due to the existence of monopoly allocations of licences in a district. Also, the government is currently fixing the minimum selling price rather than the MRP. The licence fee has been increased manifold, making the excise duty less important.

Non-existing MIS: One of the important causes of poor performance of the Department of Excise is the lack of computerization and adoption of new techniques for managing SED.

Though there has been overall regulation of the liquor trade. Evasion of tax is attempted by the dealers through under payment of tax; adulteration of intoxicants; misuse of import licences; sale of alcohol meant for industrial use in open market; and the showing of greater percentage of wastage.

Absence of effective leadership: One of the important causes of poor performance of the Department of Excise is the absence of effective leadership. In some of the states, the SEC has other additional responsibilities and therefore he is hardly able to devote his time to look into the policies or operations of the tax. For instance, in Bihar, the SEC currently shoulders responsibility as Inspector General of Stamps and Registration, and Secretary of Department of Personnel, which takes away considerable amount of his time and attention. It is, therefore, important that the SEC should be a full-time person.

Further, the State Excise Acts were generally enacted in the early twentieth century and characterized by a plethora of rules. There is an urgent need for updation and consolidation of these Acts and Rules so as to make them concise, easy to comprehend and apply to meet the needs of the modern globalized world and also ensure efficient tax systems, procedures and forms amenable to online transaction on a national network. Also, excise administration needs strengthening and modernization through training and incentives.

Recommended Reforms

An analysis of the present structure and administration of SED indicates that the following reforms are the need of the hour to make the system more vibrant and effective:

Computerization of the department: It is important to introduce new techniques for managing SEDs by setting up computerized norms and prescribing a standard computer package to be mandatorily installed in all distilleries from which required data can be fed into the departmental MIS systems. E-governance measures need to be introduced for a better tax administration and tax structure that would provide some incentive for better compliance on the part of the targeted taxpayers.

Simplification of the procedures: The rules and procedures of the Excise Act need to be simplified, rationalized, and put on the departmental website which should be user-friendly. Proper regulatory measures are needed to curb evasion by establishing a strong system of penalties and prosecution.

Provision of adequate client services: Adequate client services play an important role in the tax regime. These services not only help increase voluntary compliance but also reduce interaction of the dealers with the department. The department should lay special emphasis on providing requisite client services to all the taxpayers. In fact, the department should provide printed brochures and leaflets, including return forms, well in advance of the due date of submission of the return. Also, requisite information should be made available electronically, mostly online.

Introduction of a competitive licensing system: In order to have overall control on import, production and sale of liquor in the state, and to check the misuse of liquor and evasion of tax in the state, the current practice of monopoly licensing needs to be replaced by a competitive licensing system wherein there could be many dealers. To encourage more persons to enter into the field, the present practice of asking for a huge sum as security money must be replaced by a new policy with a relatively low sum as security money and a higher excise duty. The current policy of monopoly licensing in a district has not only created a big cartel of such dealers but has also discouraged production of liquor in the State.

The price of the liquor could be taken into account while fixing the excise duty. Today, it is the licence fee which is being accorded top priority. This needs to be revisited. It is recommended that the tax base be rationalized. It should be levied on the MRP linking the same to the manufacturing cost (MC) of the product. The MC has to be determined and declared with reference to the principles enunciated in the law. The MRP must be printed on the bottles sold. It is imperative on the part of the state government to enact a new legislation to levy this tax on MRP.

A differential tax as per the place of consumption, strength of quality and the manufacturing cost must be levied by the state to yield requisite revenue for its developmental activities.

Finally, the licence fee or auction/tender for giving licence must be kept independent of SED. This could be based on criteria different from those for licence fee.

Electricity Duty

Electricity duty is a tax on the sale or consumption of energy. It is one of the service taxes specifically allotted to the states. The power to tax the sale and consumption of electricity is enunciated in entry 53 of List II (the state list) under the Seventh Schedule of the Constitution. Mumbai (then Mumbai) was the first state to levy an electricity duty in 1932 in the form of a tax on the sale or consumption of electricity.[22] Other states also followed suit in course of time.

Fiscal Significance

The consumers pay an additional amount, known as electricity duty, along with the electricity rates for consuming electricity. This tax acts as a good source of revenue for the state governments. The revenue from this tax was Rs 1,596 crore in 1991–2, but it went up to Rs 4,692 crore in 2001–2 and further to Rs 12,226 crore in 2009–10 (Table 7.1), recording a growth rate of 11.8 per cent during 1991–2 to 2009–10. Accordingly, its buoyancy coefficient was 0.67 during the period.

The receipts from electricity duty in different states indicate that in Andhra Pradesh, the share of electricity duty in the state's own tax revenue has declined from 2.52 per cent in 1991–2 to 0.45 per cent in 2009–10. In Maharashtra, Rajasthan, and West Bengal; the yield from electricity duty shows a positive trend with high growth rates. The growth rate has shown a decline over the years in Jharkhand (–3.52 per cent), Kerala (0.72 per cent), and Haryana (4.52 per cent). The states, which had more than 5 per cent of their own tax revenue from electricity duty in 2009–10, include Chhattisgarh, Gujarat, Punjab, and Jammu and Kashmir.

The trend in the yield from electricity duty shows fluctuations in all the special category states. In spite of high fluctuations in revenue except for Manipur, Meghalaya, Nagaland, and Tripura, the other special category states, such as Assam, Himachal Pradesh, and Jammu and Kashmir, show very high growth rates (Table 7.13). The buoyancy, however, falls short of unity in many States.

Structure of Electricity Duty

Electricity duty is levied on the sale or consumption of energy specified either per unit or as a percentage of tariffs. The rate, bases of levy and exemptions differ widely from state to state. While in most states the duty is not included in the basic electricity tariff rate, and is charged over and

---

[22] Government of India (1953–4).

Table 7.13 Revenue from Electricity Duty

(Rs Crore)

State	1991–2	1996–7	2001–2	2005–6	2007–8	2008–9	2009–10	2010–11 (RE)	2011–12 (BE)	GR	Buoyancy
Andhra Pradesh	76.90	1.80	109.70	151.90	195.30	218.50	159.30	264.00	277.20	10.18	0.77
	(2.52)	(0.04)	(0.87)	(0.79)	(0.68)	(0.66)	(0.45)	(0.56)	(0.49)		
Bihar	23.00	70.50	34.90	18.10	64.10	67.60	66.60	90.30	60.70	20.81	1.52
	(1.76)	(3.14)	(1.43)	(0.51)	(1.26)	(1.10)	(0.82)	(0.85)	(0.48)		
Chhattisgarh			226.10	362.30	394.80	415.10	416.90	554.30	600.00	9.10	0.51
			(11.34)	(8.94)	(7.03)	(6.30)	(5.85)	(6.66)	(6.10)		
Gujarat	376.30	900.60	1,656.50	1,899.60	2,046.50	2,369.90	2,643.70	2,900.00	3,200.00	10.08	0.76
	(13.01)	(14.85)	(17.91)	(12.10)	(9.35)	(10.06)	(9.89)	(8.36)	(8.20)		
Haryana	38.50	35.50	29.50	61.50	107.40	106.30	119.60	143.00	155.00	4.52	0.37
	(2.96)	(1.66)	(0.59)	(0.68)	(0.92)	(0.91)	(0.90)	(0.82)	(0.77)		
Jharkhand			74.30	73.30	68.10	74.00	52.50	53.60	100.00	−3.52	−0.32
			(3.58)	(2.54)	(1.92)	(1.46)	(0.94)	(0.90)	(1.28)		
Karnataka	76.10	106.50	171.30	277.10	449.50	370.60	678.7o	608.00	689.50	12.91	0.98
	(2.63)	(1.85)	(1.74)	(1.49)	(1.73)	(1.34)	(2.22)	(1.60)	(1.57)		
Kerala	41.10	46.70	5.20	31.50	39.00	56.00	24.80	27.90	29.30	0.72	0.03
	(2.46)	(1.20)	(0.09)	(0.32)	(0.29)	(0.35)	(0.14)	(0.13)	(0.11)		
Madhya Pradesh	282.20	516.30	268.20	842.20	626.10	343.10	2,146.50	1,102.60	1,370.00	0.88	0.64
	(13.33)	(12.58)	(5.70)	(9.24)	(5.21)	(2.52)	(12.43)	(5.41)	(5.93)		

(contd.)

Table 7.13 (contd.)

(Rs Crore)

States	1991–2	1996–7	2001–2	2005–6	2007–8	2008–9	2009–10	2010–11 (RE)	2011–12 (BE)	GR	Buoyancy
Maharashtra	296.3	403.3	1,034.20	1,660.80	2,687.80	2,394.90	3,289.30	4,685.70	4,400.00	14.78	1.13
	(4.98)	(3.44)	(4.86)	(4.95)	(5.66)	(4.60)	(5.57)	(6.38)	(5.26)		
Odisha	99.40	120.00	136.90	353.10	327.40	365.00	460.00	460.00	500.00	9.12	0.75
	(14.76)	(8.95)	(5.55)	(7.06)	(4.78)	(4.57)	(5.12)	(4.34)	(4.06)		
Punjab	60.50	79.9	2.80	669.40	603.80	631.30	230.10	1,519.80	1,400.00	14.33	1.17
	(3.92)	(2.92)	(0.06)	(7.45)	(6.10)	(5.66)	(1.91)	(8.74)	(6.86)		
Rajasthan	53.30	91.90	250.80	471.30	584.20	654.00	700.00	770.60	846.60	17.59	1.44
	(3.45)	(2.94)	(4.42)	(4.77)	(4.40)	(4.38)	(4.26)	(3.97)	(3.97)		
Tamil Nadu	82.90	150.60	259.70	95.20	37.20	355.70	37.10	1,766.40	552.00	1.11	0.09
	(2.22)	(1.89)	(2.00)	(0.41)	(0.13)	(1.06)	(0.10)	(3.60)	(0.92)		
Uttar Pradesh	57.10	78.30	9.20	182.20	206.60	216.70	272.20	281.50	323.70	27.28	0.86
	(1.63)	(1.24)	(0.09)	(0.97)	(0.83)	(0.76)	(0.80)	(0.69)	(0.64)		
West Bengal	22.50	88.30	354.70	382.40	506.70	587.50	664.60	774.00	1,041.00	20.52	1.60
	(0.92)	(2.07)	(5.45)	(3.68)	(3.86)	(4.07)	(3.93)	(3.63)	(3.76)		
Special Category States											
Assam	2.80	2.30	2.90	13.30	4.60	22.40	27.10	41.60	41.10	16.72	1.58
	(0.54)	(0.30)	(0.18)	(0.41)	(0.14)	(0.54)	(0.54)	(0.70)	(0.63)		
Himachal Pradesh	2.70	18.60	8.30	89.30	81.50	78.80	39.10	220.00	190.00	16.88	1.19
	(1.43)	(4.52)	(0.91)	(5.96)	(4.17)	(3.52)	(1.52)	(6.46)	(4.7)		

Jammu and Kashmir	4.00	6.70	45.70	70.00	152.70	150.70	195.90	214.00	236.00	27.74	2.19
	(2.43)	(2.32)	(5.33)	(4.14)	(6.64)	(5.59)	(6.37)	(5.87)	(5.64)		
Manipur			2.17	0.27	0	0.40	0.01	0.01	0.01		
			(4.18)	(0.28)		(0.23)	(0.01)	(0.004)	(0.003)		
Meghalaya		0.01	0.01	0.04	0.03	0	0.10	1.30	1.40		
		(0.01)	(0.01)	(0.02)	(0.01)	(0.01)	(0.01)	(0.27)	(0.23)		
Nagaland				0.01	0.02	0	0.11	0.03	0.04		
				(0.01)	(0.02)	(0.02)	(0.06)	(0.01)	(0.02)		
Tripura			0.20	0.02	0.01	0	0.02	0.02	0.03		
			(0.13)	(0.01)			(0.004)	(0.003)	(0.004)		
Uttarakhand			7.94	12.24	55.22	51.60	2.10	72.00	75.00	1.40	−0.44
			(0.89)	(0.69)	(2.02)	(1.69)	(0.06)	(1.66)	(1.58)		
All States	1,596.10	2,718.20	4,691.60	7,717.60	9,239.10	9,530.30	12,226.00	16,550.50	16,068.60	11.84	0.67
	(4.46)	(3.82)	(3.66)	(3.64)	(3.22)	(2.96)	(3.37)	(3.61)	(2.98)		

Source: Reserve bank of India, *State Finances: A Study of Budgets* (Various Issues), Mumbai: RBI.

Note: GR = Growth Rate.

Growth rate and Buoyancy are calculated for the period 1991–2 to 2009–10.

Growth rate and Buoyancy, for bifurcated and newly formed states calculated for the years 2001–2 to 2009–10.

Growth rate and Buoyancy could not be calculated for Manipur, Meghalaya, Nagaland, and Tripura due to the irregularity in availability of data.

Figures within parentheses are expressed as a percentage of state's own tax revenue.

above the electricity tariff rate, in Manipur the amount of tax is in-built in the electricity tariff.

In Andhra Pradesh there are two rates of duty, one is for captive consumption, which is 25 paise per unit, and another is 6 paise per unit (Table 7.14). In Chhattisgarh, Himachal Pradesh, and Odisha, the rate varies according to the type of use; for example domestic consumption, mines, commercial, or industrial use. However, in Kerala, there is a different duty structure for consumers who generate energy for self-consumption. In Rajasthan, while the rate of duty is the same for domestic, commercial, industrial and mining use, a lower rate of duty is charged for agricultural use.

While in Karnataka and Punjab the rate of electricity duty is 5 per cent and 10 per cent, respectively, on the electricity charges payable, in Gujarat it varies according to the type of use. In Gujarat, however, the rate structure is *ad valorem* only for consumption other than self-generation (purchase of power) and it is *specific* for self-generation. For both domestic consumers and educational institutions of rural areas, the rate is 10 per cent of the tariff and for urban it is 20 per cent.

In some states, there is a different rate structure for metered and unmetered connections. In UP, for example, the duty is 20 per cent of the rate charged for unmetered connections and the duty varies according to the use of energy for metered connections. In Meghalaya, while the domestic consumers are charged at 5 paise per unit, the industrial users are charged at two varying rates according to the units consumed. The rate is 1 paisa per unit for the first 15,000 units and 1.5 paise for the next 25,000 units. The electricity duty is not levied in Arunachal Pradesh, Mizoram, Nagaland, Sikkim, and Tripura. Detailed rate structure of different states is given in Table 7.14.

Exemptions

Exemptions from electricity duty are linked to provisions in the Constitution. Article 287 specifically exempts electricity sold for consumption to the Central Government and prohibits taxation of electricity used for construction, maintenance or operation of railways.

In addition, many states have different exemptions under the state Acts. In UP, for example, energy consumed by a cultivator in agricultural operations such as pumping of water for irrigation, crushing, milling, etc., is exempted. The duty is also not levied on Special Economic Zones

Table 7.14 Rates of Electricity Duty

Name of State	Type of Use			
	Domestic	Industrial	Commercial	Agricultural
Andhra Pradesh	6 paise per unit (except privileged and exempted categories)	6 paise per unit (except privileged and exempted categories)	6 paise per unit (except privileged and exempted categories)	
Kerala	10 paise per unit	10 paise per unit	10 paise per unit	
Rajasthan	40 paise per unit	40 paise per unit	40 paise per unit	4 paise per unit (in case of metered supply) and 5% of the flat rate in case of non-metered supply
Odisha	4% of the energy charge in case of LT non-industrial category.	4% of the energy charge for SSI and 6% of the energy charged in case of other LT industrial category.		2% of the energy charge
Punjab	10% (ad valorem) on sale of power for all categories of consumers			
Karnataka	5% on the electricity charges			
Bihar	6% of the value of energy.	6% of the value of energy.	6% of the value of energy.	
Uttar Pradesh	9 paise per unit		3 paise per unit (when consumed by the state)	0.04 paise per unit
Tamil Nadu				Exempted

(contd.)

Table 7.14 (contd.)

Gujarat	In case of consumption other than self-generation 10% of electricity tariff in rural areas and 20% of electricity tariff in urban areas. For self-generation: 10 paisa per unit in rural areas and 20 paisa for urban areas	For HT, the rate is 15% of electricity tariff and for LT, the rate is 10% 40 paisa per unit	For Hall, Cinema, Hotel and Restaurant and residuary the rate is 25%. 25 paisa for Hall and Cinema, 30 paisa for Hotel and Restaurant, 20 paisa for Co-operative Sugar Factory and 40 paisa for residuary.
Meghalaya	5 paisa	1 paisa per unit for first 15,000 unit and 1.5 paisa per unit for the next 25,000 units.	Exempted
Manipur	2 paise per kilowatt-hour with a surcharge of 10% (paid by the generating unit)		

Source: Data collected from the relevant State Development.
Note: LT = Low tension; HT = High tension.

(SEZs) for ten years. Similarly, in Tamil Nadu, the sale of electricity for agricultural purposes, hut service connection, and SEZs is exempted. In Punjab, scheduled caste domestic consumers, having connected load up to 500 watts, are given free electricity up to 200 units per month and non-scheduled-caste BPL consumers, having connected load up to 1,000 watts, are given free electricity up to 200 units per month. In Haryana, energy supplied for tube wells and pumping sets installed for agricultural purposes are exempted from payment of electricity duty, while in Odisha, no electricity duty is levied on the energy consumed by the public water works, sewerage and pumping, and railway traction. On similar lines, in Punjab, the captive generating plant owners have been exempted from levy of electricity duty.

Recommended Reforms

Although electricity duty could be a good source of revenue for the state governments, as of now the yield from the tax shows fluctuations in the yield for some of the states. The following reforms are recommended to make this tax an important fiscal tool:

- The duty of electricity should be made progressive, as in the case of entertainment tax (see the next section). A higher rate must be fixed for those people who consume more.
- It is also suggested that the duty should be collected from those people who run shops at railway platforms and use electricity. The use of electricity by these persons is meant for profit purposes and not for the consumption by Indian Railways; therefore, it is justified to levy duty on such users. Changes according to the above suggestions will bring in more revenue to the state government.
- There is no reason for exempting agriculture from the payment of electricity duty. The tax may, however, be levied at a lower rate.
- The duty should also be levied on captive generation of electricity by the industry for own consumption or for sale.

Entertainment Tax

Entertainment tax is one of the few taxes on services assigned to the states under the Constitution (entry 62 of List II of the Seventh Schedule). It is a tax levied on the price charged for admission to any place of entertainment or amusement which includes cinemas, theatrical performances, exhibitions drama/music performances, games and sports, Cable TV, and cinematographic, or video shows. Besides these, horse races, betting, performances and pageants, and dance bars are also included in the tax base by some of the states.[23]

While most states use the tax for general purposes, Tamil Nadu assigns 90 per cent of collection from this tax to local bodies. Kerala and Uttar Pradesh have assigned this tax to the local bodies which collect and use the amount of tax for their purposes.

Fiscal Significance

Entertainment tax is not a major source of revenue. Its contribution to the states' exchequer in 1991–2 was Rs 368 crore, which went up to Rs 1,147 crore in 2000–1, but has shown a declining trend with some fluctuations. Its yield in 2009–10 was Rs 1,112.05 crore. The share of entertainment tax in states' own tax revenue has declined to 0.3 per cent in 2009–10 from 1.03 per cent in 1991–2 (Table 7.1). Likewise, the trend in revenue from entertainment tax in most of the states also indicates a declining trend during the period 1991–2 to 2009–10. The share of entertainment tax in the states' own tax revenue (for all states) was 0.69 per cent in 1995–6. This has increased to 0.97 per cent in 2000–1. Since then it has moved downwards and reached 0.28 per cent in the year 2006–7. However, in the year 2007–8, it increased marginally to 0.38 per cent of the states' own tax revenue and again dropped to 0.30 per cent in 2009–10. Among individual states, except for certain non-special category states (Maharashtra, Haryana, Karnataka, Kerala, Chhattisgarh, Goa, and UP), and certain special category states (Meghalaya, Sikkim, and Uttarakhand), all other states exhibited negative growth rate in tax revenue (Table 7.15).

This phenomenon is due to the proliferation of means of home-based entertainment and a qualitative change in people's entertainment preferences during the recent period. Film shows, which are the principal contributors to entertainment tax revenue, have now been substituted by other forms of entertainment, within and outside the home. This has also made it difficult for the government to revise tax rates upwards.

---

[23] Entertainment tax on dance bar is levied in Maharashtra; tax on performance and pageants is levied in Karnataka.

Table 7.15 Revenue from Entertainment Tax

(Rs Crore)

States	1991–2	1996–7	2001–2	2005–6	2007–8	2008–9	2009–10	2010–11 (RE)	2011–12 (BE)	GR	Buoyancy
Andhra Pradesh	37.93 (1.24)	64.94 (1.33)	67.44 (0.54)	56.32 (0.29)	61.95 (0.22)	65.83 (0.20)	71.56 (0.20)	87.00 (0.18)	95.70 (0.17)	-1.00	-0.10
Bihar	13.10 (1.00)	20.53 (0.91)	15.19 (0.62)	13.76 (0.39)	14.24 (0.28)	13.66 (0.22)	18.03 (0.22)	13.75 (0.13)	14.00 (0.11)	-1.20	-0.10
Chhattisgarh			1.14 (0.06)	3.41 (0.08)	5.38 (0.10)	5.82 (0.09)	6.86 (0.10)	4.29 (0.05)	4.29 (0.04)	23.20	1.20
Goa	0.73 (0.64)	1.36 (0.45)	2.72 (0.48)	5.18 (0.47)	0	0.96 (0.06)	37.10 (2.11)	45.00 (2.06)	40.00 (1.57)	8.40	0.50
Gujarat	32.64 (1.13)	58.98 (0.97)	64.80 (0.70)	44.24 (0.28)	28.76 (0.13)	34.11 (0.14)	47.28 (0.18)	54.61 (0.16)	80.50 (0.21)	-5.10	-0.40
Haryana	8.27 (0.64)	2.29 (0.11)	7.99 (0.16)	13.54 (0.15)	17.43 (0.15)	24.40 (0.21)	35.55 (0.27)	36.50 (0.21)	37.95 (0.19)	11.70	0.80
Jharkhand			18.81 (0.91)	2.81 (0.10)	11.27 (0.32)	0	9.24 (0.17)	12.26 (0.21)	12.26 (0.16)	-16.50	-1.60
Karnataka	48.33 (1.67)	34.2 (0.59)	48.93 (0.50)	88.06 (0.47)	352.90 (1.36)	157.75 (0.57)	116.14 (0.38)	110.00 (0.29)	130.00 (0.30)	7.60	0.60
Kerala	0.01 (0.0006)	0.07 0	0.24 0	1.06 (0.01)	123.00 (0.01)	0.17 (0.001)	0.48 (0.003)	0.69 (0.003)	0.85 (0.003)	20.50	1.30

(*contd.*)

Table 7.15 (contd.)

(Rs Crore)

States	1991–2	1996–7	2001–2	2005–6	2007–8	2008–9	2009–10	2010–11 (RE)	2011–12 (BE)	GR	Buoyancy
Madhya Pradesh	18.76 (0.89)	17.10 (0.42)	31.96 (0.68)	9.22 (0.10)	12.42 (0.10)	14.88 (0.11)	3.44 (0.02)	24.00 (0.12)	26.90 (0.12)	−13.60	−1.30
Maharashtra	78.80 (1.32)	101.31 (0.86)	247.15 (1.16)	244.89 (0.73)	409.74 (0.86)	436.96 (0.84)	491.60 (0.83)	400.00 (0.54)	440.00 (0.53)	11.10	0.90
Odisha	4.99 (0.74)	5.72 (0.43)	27.62 (1.12)	0.10	2.22 (0.03)	18.58 (0.23)	9.28 (0.10)	11.44 (0.11)	12.06 (0.10)	−12.50	−1.00
Punjab	0.52 (0.03)	5.54 (0.20)	9.19 (0.19)	5.62 (0.06)	5.44 (0.05)	0.81 (0.01)	230.13 (1.91)	1,519.78 (8.74)	1,400.00 (6.86)	3.60	0.60
Rajasthan	14.76 (0.95)	2,1.45 (0.69)	22.29 (0.39)	11.19 (0.11)	15.50 (0.12)	17.59 (0.12)	14.03 (0.09)	20.00 (0.10)	24.00 (0.11)	−2.30	−0.20
Tamil Nadu	29.34 (0.79)	117.16 (1.47)	88.00 (0.68)	12.58 (0.05)	9.09 (0.03)	12.24 (0.04)	37.06 (0.10)	1,766.43 (3.60)	532.03 (0.89)	−7.80	−0.60
Uttar Pradesh	83.58 (2.39)	95.39 (1.51)	5.47 (0.05)	83.10 (0.44)	94.34 (0.38)	129.85 (0.45)	186.60 (0.55)	216.43 (0.53)	275.50 (0.55)	23.30	1.40
West Bengal	18.67 (0.76)	45.01 (1.06)	50.28 (0.77)	44.83 (0.43)	30.07 (0.23)	38.19 (0.26)	41.60 (0.25)	52.00 (0.24)	65.00 (0.23)	−2.50	−0.20
Special Category States											
Assam	11.21 (2.19)	13.35 (1.74)	31.59 (2.02)	2.31 (0.07)	2.65 (0.08)	2.22 (0.05)	2.63 (0.05)	4.51 (0.08)	5.00 (0.08)	−9.80	−1.10

Himachal Pradesh	0.55	0.39	0.12	0.10	0.11	0.15	0.26	0.30	−15.00	−1.40
	(0.13)	(0.04)	(0.01)	(0.01)	0	(0.01)	(0.01)	(0.01)		
Jammu and Kashmir	0	2.50	0	0.02	0	0	0	0		
	0	(0.29)	0	0	0	0	0	0		
Meghalaya	0.55	0.86	1.26	0.83	0	1.23	1.11	1.30	6.70	0.60
	(1.29)	(0.63)	(0.5)	(0.26)	0	(0.28)	(0.24)	(0.22)		
Sikkim	0.10	0.42	0.56	0.56	0.57	0.61	0.76	0.79	2.20	0.10
	(0.13)	(0.52)	(0.38)	(0.28)	(0.31)	(0.27)	(0.33)	(0.29)		
Tripura	0	1.34	0.03	0.26	0.41	0	0	0	−10.40	−0.80
	0	(0.85)	(0.01)	(0.07)	(0.09)					
Uttarakhand	0.82	5.69	4.46	6.45	5.87	6.27	8.00	10.00	1.80	0.10
	(2.84)	(0.64)	(0.25)	(0.24)	(0.19)	(0.18)	(0.18)	(0.21)		
All States	367.58	605.79	648.65	1,082.87	981.25	1,112.05	1137.25	1,531.43	4.99	0.30
	(1.03)	(0.85)	(0.62)	(0.31)	(0.38)	(0.30)	(0.31)	(0.25)	(0.28)	

Source: Reserve Bank of India, *State Finances: A Study of Budgets* (Various Issues), Mumbai: RBI.

Note: The figures within parentheses indicate as a percentage of states' own tax revenue; GR =Growth Rate; The GR and buoyancy of the states are calculated for 1991–2 to 2009–10; For Andhra Pradesh, both are calculated for 1999–2000 to 2009–10. For Chhattisgarh, both are calculated for 2003–4 to 2009–10. For Goa both are calculated for 1991–2 to 2006–7. For Gujarat and Haryana, GR and buoyancy are calculated for 1996–7 to 2009–10. For Kerala, both are calculated for 1998–9 to 2009–10. For Odisha and Meghalaya, both are calculated for 1994–5 to 2009–10. For Punjab, West Bengal and Himachal Pradesh, both are calculated for 1996–7 to 2009–10. For UP, both are calculated for 2005–6 to 2009–10. For Sikkim, both are calculated for 2001–2 to 2009–10 and for Jharkhand both are calculated for 2001–2 to 2007–8.

Structure of Entertainment Tax

In some states, the entertainment tax is imposed on a slab basis with a progressive rate structure. In states like Rajasthan, Tamil Nadu, Haryana, UP, and Odisha, it is levied on a proportional basis. For instance, in Rajasthan, the rate of tax is 30 per cent of the payment for admission to entertainment in cinema halls and 10 per cent of the monthly subscription charges per subscriber in the case of a direct to home (DTH) broadcast service provider (Annexure A7.3). Similarly, in Haryana, the entertainment tax is levied at 30 per cent of the admission fee on cinema and 25 per cent on other entertainment. In Andhra Pradesh, the rate of tax on cinema varies according to the location (municipal corporation area, different grades of municipalities, and *Gram Panchayat*s) and the type of theatres (air-conditioned or not, permanent/touring/temporary), whereas in Chhattisgarh and Bihar, the tax rate depends on the population size. In Uttarakhand, the tax on cinematographic exhibition varies according to the location and the size of the population. However, in Odisha it varies according to the location only. In Maharashtra, the rate varies according to different zones. Although, the usual practice is to charge the tax on the tickets sold, in some states like Andhra Pradesh, Uttarakhand and Himachal Pradesh, the tax is collected on the basis of a specified percentage of the gross collections or on the basis of occupancy ratio.

In addition to the tax on cinema, show tax at a specific rate ranging from Rs 2 to Rs 12 is levied in Andhra Pradesh, depending on the location. However, in Karnataka, the show tax differs on the basis of the language of the film. In Bihar, there is a provision to pay a tax of Rs 100 for every show. In Meghalaya, the show tax is 10 per cent per show and, in Tripura, the tax is collected at 20 per cent of the face value of the ticket (Annexure A7.3).

In some states, a tax on horse races and betting is also levied. In Andhra Pradesh, the rate of tax on horse races is 35 per cent of total payment, while in Karnataka it is 70 per cent on the rate of admission. In Tamil Nadu, the tax on horse races is levied according to the price of the ticket. In addition, some states levy additional duties or surcharges on the basic entertainment duty. Goa, for example, levies a surcharge of 10 per cent on the entertainment provided by cinematographic films. A surcharge of 5 per cent is levied on horse races and betting in Tamil Nadu. Similar is the case of Uttarakhand, where a surcharge of 10 paisa is levied on horse race and betting.

Tax Concessions and Exemptions

Entertainment devoted to philanthropic, religious and charitable purposes, or those provided or sponsored by non-profit institutions, or organized in aid of the promotion of health, agriculture, industry, and scientific development, are generally exempted from taxation. In addition, there are certain state-specific exemptions. In Karnataka and Odisha the regional language films are exempted from the tax, while in Uttarakhand and Uttar Pradesh, certain events such as Drama, *Nautanki*, and *Kavi Sammelan* are exempted. In Tripura, entertainment, which is of an educational character, or with a scientific purpose, or for a charitable purpose, is exempted. Similar is the case in Tamil Nadu where exemption from entertainment tax is granted in respect of film shows conducted for raising funds for cultural, educational, and charitable purposes.[24]

In Tamil Nadu and West Bengal, a tax concession is provided for certain regional language films. In West Bengal, the rate of tax is 10 per cent on admission fee for Bengali, Nepali, or Santhali films and 30 per cent on admission fee for other language films. In UP, certain tax concession is provided to the owners of cinema halls for the revival of closed cinema halls and for the renovation of the existing cinema halls.

Administration of Entertainment Tax

In most of the states, the entertainment tax is administered by the commercial tax department. However, in UP there is a separate department for entertainment tax.

The pattern of payment and the method of collection of the tax are uniform in all the states of the Indian Union.

Assessment of entertainment tax is made on the basis of returns. These returns are submitted by the proprietor of the place of entertainment to the assessing authority with a treasury receipt or a crossed cheque in favour of the assessing authority. But in case of non-submission of returns or incorrect or incomplete returns, the assessing authority, after making an enquiry, assesses the tax for that period to the best of his judgment. However, before taking such an action, the proprietor is given a reasonable

---

[24] Entertainment tax on cable TV has also been exempted in Tamil Nadu with effect from 1 April 2008.

opportunity of proving the correctness and completeness of any return submitted by him or that no return was due from him.

Assessment of the Existing System

The existing rates of entertainment tax are very high; they are higher than even the rates of the sales tax and the betting tax in some states. In Bihar, for example, the rate of tax is 50 per cent at present and it was 110 per cent till 2005. The rate of tax is 60 per cent in UP and in many states, it is more than 30 per cent.

Recommended Reforms

Entertainment tax has lost its fiscal significance in recent years due to the proliferation of means of home-based entertainment. However, the following steps could be taken to revive this source of revenue:

- Tax concession should be provided to owners of cinema halls for upgrading/renovation of existing old theatres.
- Rural market should be explored since the availability of home-based entertainment is lesser there in comparison to urban areas and cities.
- Sports, games, musical performance, etc., should be brought under the tax net in all the states.
- The tax should be extended to newer forms of amusement like theme parks, consumer exhibitions, bowling alleys, dance bars, and pool parlours. Simultaneously, traditional forms of art, drama, and sports, could be preserved and encouraged by making them tax exempt.
- The cinema owners should not be allowed to enhance admission rates without prior approval of the government at the time of release of a good movie.

To conclude, the scope of the tax needs to be expanded to comprehensively cover all forms of entertainment.

* * *

Few important taxes on commodities and services assigned exclusively to the state governments include sales tax (now state VAT), SED, MVT, P&GT, electricity duty, and entertainment tax. Among these taxes sales tax has surfaced as the major contributor to the state exchequer and nearly 72 per cent of the tax revenue from commodities and services is collected through this tax. While 23 per cent comes from SED, MVT and P&GT. Thus these taxes together contribute to approximately 95 per cent of the state's revenue from taxes on commodities and services. Sales tax has now been replaced by State VAT. This has been a paradigm shift in the states' tax system. The GST would be replacing the existing state VAT and services would be eventually brought within the purview of state taxation by virtue of this new tax.

Both MVT and P&GT are structured with primarily the same objectives. Both the taxes fall on the same base and are paid ultimately by the same group of people. Thus some states have merged these two into one tax. It is time that the entire system of taxes on vehicles has to be revamped for all states so that a new tax system evolves which would be neutral, efficient in allocation of resources, administratively expedient and non-cascading.

State excise duty is primarily levied to control the activities in relation to intoxicants. States regulate and control manufacture and distribution of excisable articles by charging fees, fixing the number of licences and also by prescribing the terms and conditions on which licences may be granted. Electricity duty is levied on the sale or consumption of energy. The rate, bases of levy and exemptions vary widely among states. Finally, entertainment tax is one of the few taxes on services assigned to the states. While most states use entertainment tax for general purposes, Tamil Nadu and UP have assigned this tax to local bodies. With the introduction of GST, this tax would be subsumed in GST and the rate structure would be different.

Annexure A7.1

Rates of State VAT in States

A. Commodities exempted from VAT

S. No.	Description of Goods
1	Agricultural implements manually operated or animal driven
2	Aids and implements used by handicapped persons
3	Aquatic feed, poultry feed and cattle feed, including grass & hay

4	Betel leaves
5	Books and periodicals & journals
6	Bread
7	Charcoal
8	Charkha, Amber Charkha, Handlooms and Gandhi Topi
9	Coarse grains other than paddy, rice and wheat
10	Condoms and contraceptives
11	Cotton and silk yarn in hanks
12	Curd, Lassi, butter milk, separated milk
13	Earthen pot
14	Electrical energy
15	Fishnet and fishnet fabrics
16	Fresh milk and pasteurized milk
17	Fresh plants, saplings and fresh flowers
18	Fresh vegetables and fruits
19	Garlic and Ginger
20	Glass bangles
21	Human blood and blood plasma
22	Indigenous handmade musical instruments
23	Kumkum, Bindi, Alta and Sindur
24	Meat, fish, prawn and other aquatic products when not cured or frozen, eggs and livestock and animal hair
25	National Flag
26	Non-judicial stamp paper sold by Govt. Treasuries, postal items like envelope, postcard, etc., sold by Govt., rupee note & cheques
27	Organic manure
28	Raw wool and its waste -Waste of wool
29	Seeds
30	Semen including frozen semen
31	Silk worm laying, cocoon, and raw silk and its waste -Silk waste
32	Slates, slate pencils and chalks -Slates -Slate pencils -Writing or drawing chalks and tailor chalks
33	Sugar and Khandasari

34	Tender green coconut
35	Textiles fabrics
	-Silk fabric
	-Cotton
36	Tobacco
37	Toddy, Neera and Arrack
	Unprocessed salt
39	Water other than aerated, mineral, distilled, medicinal, ionic, battery, de-mineralized and water sold in sealed container

B. Commodities Taxable at 1% Rate

S. No.	Description of Goods
1	Bullion
2	Gold, Silver, Platinum Ornaments, new and old
3	Precious Stones
4	Paddy
5	Rice (other than paddy)
6	Wheat

C. Commodities Taxable at 5% Rate

S. No.	Description of Goods
1	Agricultural implements not operated manually or not driven by animal
2	All equipment for communications such as private branch exchange and Electronic Private Automatic Branch Exchange (EPABX)
3	All intangible goods like copyright, patent, R.E.P. Licence
4	All kinds of bricks including brickbats, jhama, fly ash bricks, refractory bricks, asphaltic roofing, earthen tiles
5	All types of yarn other than cotton and silk yarn in hank and sewing thread
6	Aluminum utensils and enamelled utensils
7	Arecanut powder and betel nut
8	Asbestos
9	Bamboo, rattan, reed, and canes
10	Bearings
11	Beedi leaves
12	Belting of all varieties and descriptions

13	Bicycles, tricycles, cycle rickshaws and their parts
14	Biomass briquettes
15	Bio-fertilizers and Micro-nutrients, etc.
16	Bitumen
17	Castings
18	Centrifugal and monoblock and submersible pumps and parts
19	Cereal oats, meal and pellets; cereal grains otherwise worked
20	Coal, including coke in all its forms but excluding charcoal
21	Coffee beans and seeds, cocoa pod and chicory
22	Chemical fertilizers, pesticides, weedicides, insecticides
23	Clay including fireclay
24	Coir and coir products excluding coir mattresses
25	Common salt including iodized salt
26	Cotton and cotton waste
27	Crucibles
28	Crude petroleum oils and Crude Oils obtained from bituminous minerals
29	Degras: Residues resulting from the treatment of fatty substances or animal or vegetable waxes
30	Drugs, Medicines and Bulk drugs
31	Edible oils (non-refined and refined), but excluding coconut oil sold in sachets, bottles or tins of 200 grams or 200 millilitre each or less, including consumer containers when these are sold in bulk in a common container; oil cake
32	Electrodes
33	Embroidery or zari articles, that is, imi, zari, kesab, saima dabka, chumki, gotta sitara, nasqi, kora, glass bead, badia
34	Exercise book, graph book and note book/laboratory note book
35	Non-ferrous metals and alloys; non-ferrous metals such as aluminum, copper, zinc and extractions of these Ferrous metals and alloys
36	Fibres of all types and Fibre waste
37	Flour, atta
37A	Maida, suji, besan
38	Fried grams
39	Gur, jaggery and edible variety of gur
40	Hand pumps, parts, and fittings
41	Herb, bark, dry plant, dry root (commonly known as jari booti) and dry flower

42	Hides and skins, whether in raw or dressed state, other than fur skins and artificial fur
43	Hosiery goods
44	Hurricane lanterns
45	Husk of cereals unprepared, whether or not chopped, ground, pressed or in the form of pellets
46	Ice
47	Imitation jewellery and Synthetic gems
48	Incense sticks commonly known as agarbati
48A	Dhupkathi or dhupbati
50	Industrial cables (high voltage cables, XLPE cables, jelly-filled cables)
51	IT products
52	Kerosene oil sold through PDS
53	Knitting wools
54	Lac and shellac
55	Leaf plates and cups
56	Lignite
57	Lime, limestone, clinker and dolomite
58	Mica, including splitting; Mica waste
59	Natural graphite
60	Natural honey
61	Natural sands of all kinds, whether or not coloured
62	Natural sponge of animal origin
63	Newars
64	Napa slabs (rough flooring stones)
65	Oil cake not used as cattle feed
66	Oil seeds
67	Pulses
68	Paper, Paper Board and Newsprint
69	Pipes and pipe fittings of all varieties including G.I. pipes, C.I. pipes, ductile pipes, and PVC
70	Plastic footwear, Hawai chappals and their parts
71	Plastic granules
72	Printed material including diary and calendar
73	Printed ink excluding toner and cartridges
74	Raw cashew
75	Readymade garments
76	Renewable energy devices and spare parts

77	Residues of starch manufacture and similar residues, beet pulp. Bagasse and other wastes of sugar manufacture, brewing or distilling dregs and waste whether or not in the form of pellets
78	Safety materials
79	Sewing machines
80	Sewing thread of man-made staple fibre
81	Ship and other water vessels
82	Spices of all varieties and forms including cumin seed, aniseed, turmeric and dry chillies
83	Sports goods excluding apparels and footwear
84	Starch
85	Sulphur of all kinds, other than sublimed sulphur, precipitated sulphur and colloidal sulphur
86	Tamarind
87	Tea
88	Tractors, threshers, harvesters, and attachments and parts thereof
89	Transformers having a power-handling capacity exceeding 16KVA but not 500KVA
90	Transmission towers
91	Umbrella except garden umbrella
92	Vegetable oil including gingelly oil and bran oil
93	Vegetable plaiting materials and other vegetable products not elsewhere specified or included
94	Writing instruments

D. Commodities Taxable at 20% or More

S. No.	Description of Goods
1	Foreign liquor as defined from time to time in rule 3(6)(1) of the Mumbai Foreign Liquor Rules, 1953
2	Country liquor as defined in Maharashtra Country Liquor Rules, 1973
3	Liquor imported from any place outside the territory of India, as defined from time to time in rule 3(4) of Maharashtra Foreign Liquor (Import and Export), Rules, 1963
4	Molasses and rectified spirit
5	High Speed Diesel Oil (a) When delivered-

(i) to a retail trader for trading from a place of business situated within the geographical limits of the Municipal Corporations of Brihan Mumbai, Thane and Navi Mumbai; and

(ii) to a person other than the retail trader having place of business situated within the geographical limits of the Municipal Corporations of Brihan Mumbai, Thane and Navi Mumbai.

(b) In circumstances other than those mentioned in clause (a) above.

6	Aviation Turbine Fuel (duty paid) (other than that covered by entry 3)
7	Aviation Turbine Fuel (bonded)
8	Aviation Gasoline (duty paid)
9	Aviation Gasoline (bonded)
10	Any other kind of motor spirit

(a) When delivered-

(i) to a retail trader for trading from a place of business situated within the geographical limits of the Municipal Corporations of Brihan Mumbai, Thane and Navi Mumbai; and

(ii) to a person other than the retail trader having place of business situated within the geographical limits of the Municipal Corporations of Brihan Mumbai, Thane and Navi Mumbai.

(b) In circumstances other than those mentioned in clause (a) above.

11	Petrol
12	Diesel oil
13	Aviation spirit
14	Bhang
15	Opium
16	Narcotics
17	Tendu leaves
18	Natural gas
19	Arms and ammunition
20	Lottery tickets
21	Lime-stone (non-L.D. grade)

22	Timber (excluding converted timber)
23	Lime-stone (L.D. grade)
24	Light Diesel Oil (LDO)
25	Naptha
26	Medicines and drugs including vaccines, syringes and dressings, medicated ointments produced under drugs licence, light liquid paraffin of I.P. grade

ANNEXURE A7.2

Tax Incentives under VAT for the Units Availing Exemption under Sales Tax

	Exemption from Payment of Output Tax	Deferment of Tax	Remission of Tax
Andhra Pradesh		Unit availing exemption will be converted to the unit availing deferment. The balance period, as on 31.3.2005, to such a unit will be doubled.	The deferment unit shall continue to avail the benefits for the period as mentioned in the Eligibility Certificate.
Himachal Pradesh	Any dealer who manufactures and sells goods and who was enjoying the benefit of any incentive of sales tax leviable on the sale of manufactured goods and who would have continued to be eligible for such an incentive on the date of commencement of this Act, had this Act not come into force, may be allowed by the State Government, by notification, -	(b) to opt, in the prescribed manner, for the facility of making deferred payment of tax for the unexpired period of incentive instead of availing the exemption specified in clause (a), or	

(contd.)

Annexure A7.2 (*contd.*)

	Exemption from Payment of Output Tax	Deferment of Tax	Remission of Tax
	(a) to continue to avail of the benefit of exemption from payment of tax on the sale of manufactured goods made by such a dealer himself for the unexpired period, subject to the condition that no input tax credit shall be allowed to the subsequent dealer purchasing goods manufactured and sold by such a dealer (industrial unit).	(c) to continue to avail of the facility of making deferred payment of tax on the sale of manufactured goods made by such a dealer himself for the unexpired period; such a dealer (industrial unit) shall be eligible to issue tax invoice and to claim input tax credit subject to the provisions of section 11 of this Act.	
Madhya Pradesh	Unit availing exemption will be allowed exemption of output tax for the balance of the un-expired period	The deferment unit shall continue to avail the benefits for the period as mentioned in the Eligibility Certificate	
	The dealer shall compute tax liability by deducting Input Tax Credit from tax collected on sales in MP and be eligible to retain the amount of tax collected in excess of Input Tax Credit.	Both category of dealers shall make purchases from the Registered Dealer after payment of tax.	

Maharashtra	Exemptions and deferment to continue for un-expired period. Inputs will be purchased after full payment of tax. In case of exemption, input tax payment will be claimed as refund in the return. No output tax is payable.	In deferment cases also, refund of input tax will be claimed in the return and the output tax will be deferred. The purchasing dealer will pay the tax on value addition
Karnataka	Exemptions and deferment to continue for un-expired period. Inputs will be purchased after full payment of tax. In case of exemption, input tax payment will be claimed as refund in the return. No output tax is payable.	In deferment cases also, refund of input tax will be claimed in the return and the output tax will be deferred. The purchasing dealer will pay the tax on value addition
Tamil Nadu	Any industrial unit availing a tax holiday or tax exemption on the date of commencement of the Act shall be treated as a unit availing tax deferment.	The unit availing tax deferment shall be eligible to issue tax invoices and to claim input tax credit.
Uttar Pradesh	The industrial unit availing benefit of exemption from or reduction in the rate of tax on the turnover of sales before the date of commencement of this Act or an industrial unit which is granted the facility	The industrial unit availing the benefit of tax deferment under the erstwhile Act or under the Central Sales Tax Act, 1956, before the commencement of this Act, or a unit which is granted the facility

(contd.)

Annexure A7.2 (contd.)

Exemption from Payment of Output Tax	Deferment of Tax	Remission of Tax
of exemption from or reduction in the rate of tax on the turnover of sales on or after the commencement of the erstwhile Act or the Central Sales Tax Act, 1956, shall be entitled for exemption by way of refund of the net tax paid along with the return for the tax period in the prescribed manner on fulfilling the conditions of holding a valid registration certificate and a valid certificate of entitlement. The amount of refund shall not be more than an amount equal to the net tax paid for the relevant tax period, and the net tax payable has been deposited along with return. The facility of refund shall cease on the day when the amount or the period mentioned in the Certificate of Entitlement, whichever is earlier, and the tax payable on the turnover of sales of goods mentioned in the Certificate of Entitlement and which is manufactured	of tax deferment under the erstwhile Act or under the Central Sales Tax Act, 1956, shall continue to avail the facility of deferment for net tax payable under this Act and the Central Sales Tax Act, 1956. The industrial unit availing the benefit of tax deferment or availing the facility of refund shall be eligible to issue tax invoices and to claim input tax credit.	

		in the industrial unit shall be deducted from the total amount mentioned or described in the Certificate of Entitlement,
Uttarakhand		Any exemption from or any concession in payment of tax or concession or reduction of tax in respect of any sale or purchase of any goods granted to any industrial unit or such facility, allowed under the relevant provisions of the Repealed Act, shall continue for the remaining unexpired period.
West Bengal	Unit availing exemption will be allowed exemption of output tax for the balance un-expired period.	Unit enjoying benefit of remission for specified period may be allowed remission of 95% of output tax payable for the balance un-expired period. The deferment unit shall continue to avail the benefits for the period as mentioned in the EC

ANNEXURE A7.3

Rates of Entertainment Tax in States

States	Tax on Cinema Shows	Show Tax	Cable TV	Horse Racing and Betting	Totalization Tax	Others
Andhra Pradesh	20% on the sale of tickets in case of air conditioned and air cooled theatres. And 18% in the case of others	Varies between Rs 2 to Rs 12 per show	In the case of Municipalities, the rate varies between Rs 2 to Rs 5 per connection per month. In major Gram Panchayats, the rate is Rs 200 per month and in the case of minor Gram Panchayats, the rate is Rs 100 per month (irrespective of number of connections)	35% of all payments	15%	

Bihar	Varies between 8 to 24% of gross collection capacity per show	Rs 100 for every show	No betting tax
Chhattisgarh	0–30%		Varies between 0 to Rs 20
Goa	Varies between 10% to 35% (according to the amount of payment) + 10% surcharge		Rs 15 per month per connection	5 paisa on a rupee in case of entertainment provided by way of cyber café and pool parlour; 15% of the amount paid for admission when payment exceeds Rs 10 in the case of theatrical performance and drama

(*contd.*)

Annexure A7.3 (*contd.*)

States	Tax on Cinema Shows	Show Tax	Cable TV	Horse Racing and Betting	Totalisation Tax	Others
Karnataka	40% on the rate of admission for non-regional films		Varies between Rs 15 to Rs 20 per month	70% on the rate of admission		For Video parlours, the tax varies between Rs 5,000 to Rs 15,000 per month Amusement tax of 5% on the rate of admission above Rs 50
Kerala	20%					
Madhya Pradesh	50% in the case of Municipal Corporation areas and 40% in the rest of the areas		Rs 20 per month per subscriber in Urban and Cantonment areas			

Odisha		5% of monthly gross receipt	No betting tax
Rajasthan	30% of the payments	Rs 20 per month per subscriber	No betting tax	10% of the monthly subscription charges per subscriber in case of DTH service providers
Tamil Nadu	15% of the gross payment in the case of new films and 10% of gross payment for old films	Exempted	5% surcharge on betting tax	20% of every sum paid in Guindy 15% of every sum paid in Uthagamandalam + 5% surcharge	10% tax on amusements and for recreation parlours the rate of tax is 20% on each payment of admission
Uttar Pradesh	60% + maintenance fee at Rs 3 per ticket + Film Development Fund levy at 50 paise per ticket			

(contd.)

Annexure A7.3 (contd.)

States	Tax on Cinema Shows	Show Tax	Cable TV	Horse Racing and Betting	Totalisation Tax	Others
West Bengal	10% on admission fee for Bengali/Nepali/Santhali Films and 30% for other language films	Rs 200	On cable operators, rate is 5% of the gross receipts and on sub-cable operators, the rate is Rs 1,500 per year in Kolkata metropolitan area and Rs 1,000 for others	15%	For horse race 5% and for others 10%	Rate of entertainment tax for hotel/restaurants is 30% of the total sum paid by a person if the admission fee includes the cost of food and drinks. If it is only an entertainment programme then the rate of tax is 60% of admission fee

Assam		12.5% in case of games, sports, music or dramatic performances organized by a State Body (or any other body affiliated to it), or affiliated to an All India body constituted for similar purpose
	20% of the payment for admission received by the proprietor per connection per month	For television exhibition and admission to an aerial ropeway carrier, the rate is 20% and 25% of the payment, respectively
Himachal Pradesh	20% of the payment for admission	For horse race the tax rate varies between 100% to 125% depending upon the payment for admission. The betting tax is 10% of all money paid

(*contd.*)

Annexure A7.3 (*contd.*)

States	Tax on Cinema Shows	Show Tax	Cable TV	Horse Racing and Betting	Totalisation Tax	Others
Manipur	1st class, Rs 7.5 per ticket; for 2nd class Rs 6.50 per ticket; and for 3rd class Rs 5.60 per ticket	Rs 100 per show	Rs 500 per month and Rs 100 per month for video parlours			
Meghalaya	10%		Rs 10 per connection per month	Betting tax on arrow shooting is 40% of the amount received as stake money		12.5% in case of games/sports/music or dramatic performances organized by registered organizations under the Societies Registration Act

Mizoram	20% of the payment for admission received by the proprietor per connection per month	12.5% in case of games, sports, music or dramatic performances organized by a State Body (or any other body affiliated to it), or affiliated to an All-India body constituted for similar purpose
Sikkim	40 to 75% of the admission charge	25% of the total collection. Video parlours are taxed at Rs 1,000 to Rs 3,000 per month. Pool parlours at Rs 200 to Rs 5 per month. VCD libraries at Rs 100–Rs 300 per month

(*contd.*)

Annexure A7.3 (*contd.*)

States	Tax on Cinema Shows	Show Tax	Cable TV	Horse Racing and Betting	Totalisation Tax	Others
Uttarakhand			20%	10 per cent of all money paid into any totalistic or horse races by way of stakes and also money paid or agreed to be paid as a bet to a licenced book-maker by a backer + surcharge of 10 paise on each stake of bet levied afterwards		

CHAPTER 8

LOCAL TAXES

The functions of the local bodies are well indicated in the Constitution of India under Article 243W and the Twelfth Schedule, but no tax power has been assigned to them. Normally, state governments assign some taxes from the state list, wholly or partially, to local bodies. In general, the local bodies have used property tax (house tax) and octroi as two important sources of revenue.

PROPERTY TAX

The Seventh Schedule to the Constitution places the levy of tax on property in the state list. However, the states have authorized local governments to levy, collect, and appropriate the tax.

Structure of Property Tax

Property tax is an *ad valorem* tax levied by local bodies on the owners of real property within their jurisdiction based on the value of such property. There are provisions for rebates for owner-occupied houses; rebates for senior citizens; women, and physically challenged persons; rebates on early payment; vacancy remissions; depreciation as per the age of the building; and rebates for repairs and maintenance. In addition, there are exemptions given in the property tax through which the gross estimated tax base gets reduced. These are based on factors including ownership (such as government-owned property), the use of the property (such as properties used for charitable purposes), or on characteristics of the owner or occupier (such as age or disability). For example, property owned and occupied by colleges and universities, churches and cemeteries, public hospitals, charitable institutions, public roads, parks, schools, libraries, foreign embassies, and property owned by international organizations are exempt. In some states, agricultural land and principal residences are also exempt. Vacant land is also exempt in certain cases.

Since the base of the tax is the value of the property, it is important to determine the value in a proper way. For this purpose, two approaches are adopted—area-based approach and value-based approach (Table 8.1).

Under the area-based system, a charge is levied per square metre of land area, per square metre of building (or sometimes 'usable' space), or some combination of the two. Where a measure of the area is used for

Table 8.1 Methods of Property Valuation in Use in Sampled Cities in India

City		Valuation Method
1	Shillong, Delhi, Hyderabad, Lucknow, Visakhapatnam, Patna, Rajkot, Bhopal, Indore, Jabalpur, Varanasi, Agra, Allahabad, Meerut, Vijaywada, Dhanbad, Coimbatore, Chennai	UAV for estimating the ARV
2	Bengaluru	CVM based ARV system
3	Greater Mumbai, Faridabad, Durgapur, Nashik, Amritsar, Ludhiana, Jamshedpur	Annual Rateable Value (rent as the basis for estimating the ARV)
4	Kolkata	Annual Rateable Value/CVM for estimating ARV
5	Ahmedabad, Jaipur, Vadodara, Kochi, Surat	UAV per sq.m. as a basis for taxation
6	Pune	Annual Rateable Value (rent as the basis for estimating the ARV) & UAV for new properties
7	Nagpur	Annual Letting Value (rent as the basis for estimating the ARV)
8	Kanpur & Madurai	UAV for estimating the ARV for residential properties. CVM for estimating ARV for commercial properties.
9	Asansol	ARV/CVM for estimating ARV

Source: NIPFP (2009).
Notes: ARV= Annual rental value; UAV= Unit area value.

land and buildings, the assessment of the property is the sum of an assessment rate per square metre multiplied by the size of the land and an assessment rate per square metre multiplied by the size of the building.

Under the value-based approach, either the market value or the rental value of the property is assessed. Municipal laws have generally adopted 'annual rental value' for assessing property tax. In this system, the problem lies in determining the rental value of the property. Lack of an objective basis for determining the base creates enormous administrative problems. The application of rent control laws and various interpretations by the courts of laws in pronouncing judgments determining the tax base have only complicated the existing property tax scenario further.

Keeping in view these problems, the need was felt for adopting a new approach to define the tax base. The Government of India issued guidelines for a simple, user-friendly, transparent, objective-based system of valuation after the successful experiment of adopting the unit area method (UAM) of valuation by the Patna Municipal Corporation (NIPFP 2009). In UAM, an assessment of the annual rateable value (ARV) is done by applying unit area values (UAV) to the area of the property. To determine UAV, the entire municipal area is divided into more or less homogenous zones based on various factors such as (1) the cost of construction, (2) occupancy, (3) type of construction, (4) location on type of road, (5) prevailing market rents, (6) rent control rates, (7) usage, (8) existing infrastructure facilities available, (9) economic condition of the area, and (10) accessibility to major centres in the city. Various coefficients for each factor are simulated in working out UAVs for each zone for different types of properties.

Determination of Rate

The property tax rate varies according to the use of the property. Generally, residential property is taxed at a lower rate as compared to industrial and commercial properties, and owner-occupied residential property is taxed at a lower rate than rented property. Local bodies decide their own rate schedule for residential and non-residential buildings. The rates, as given in Table 8.2, indicate considerable variations across local bodies. Generally, local bodies (following the ARV method) adopt *ad valorem* rates and therefore, there exist wide variations in the rates; the lowest rates are in Karnataka and the highest in Maharashtra. Local bodies adopting UAM have more or less similar rates.

Table 8.2 Statutory Property Tax Rates in Select Cities in India

City		Property Tax Rate (% of ARV)	
		Residential	Non-residential
1	Shillong	6–10% (with minimum level)	
2	Delhi	6–10%	10%
3	Bengaluru	0.5%	2%
4	Greater Mumbai	30%	
5	Chennai	13.24–24.8%	
6	Kolkata	13% (11% General tax + 2% Howrah Bridge Tax)	
7	Hyderabad	17% to 30%	
8	Ahmedabad	Rs 10 per sq. m.	Rs 22 per sq. m.
9	Surat	Rs 10 to Rs 40 per sq. m.	Rs 20 to Rs 80 per sq. m.
10	Pune	14% to 38%	
11	Nagpur	12% to 31%	
12	Jaipur	District Level Committee (DLC) Rate	
13	Lucknow	15% of ARV derived from circle rates for commercial properties.	
14	Kanpur	10% of ARV up to Rs 1,200 and 15% for more than Rs 1,200	
15	Visakhapatnam	25.88%	30%
16	Patna	7–9%	
17	Vadodara	Rs 10 per sq. m.	Rs 20 per sq. m.
18	Rajkot & Faridabad	2.5%	5%
20	Bhopal, Indore, Jabalpur	6–8–10%	6–8–10%
23	Nashik	45–55%	48–64%
24	Amritsar, Ludhiana	10%	15%
26	Varanasi	15%	
27	Agra	13%	
28	Allahabad	11%	11%
29	Meerut	12.5%	12.5%
30	Vijaywada	22%	29%
31	Jamshedpur	6–8%	
32	Dhanbad	36–39%	
33	Kochi	Rs 12/sq. m.	Flat Rs 54 per sq. m.
34	Madurai	27%	
35	Coimbatore	7.5% to 18%	
36	Durgapur	10–30%	

Source: NIPFP Report (2009).
Note: ARV= Annual rental value.

Rate Administration

There is no fixed model for the administration of property tax by the local bodies—municipal corporations, municipalities, etc. While the structure of administrative organization as well as procedures vary considerably among states, in general, the organizational framework of property tax is a five-fold functional hierarchy which includes authorities at the levels of: (1) assessment (or valuation), (2) validation, (3) appeal for valuation, (4) amendment, and (5) appeal against revision. In most of the states, the involvement of elected representatives is noticeable at one or more stages of the property tax administration. For instance, in Haryana, Uttar Pradesh, West Bengal, Assam, and Rajasthan, municipal Acts assign the role to elected representatives either directly (that is, councils) or indirectly (that is, appointment of the authority by the council) at the level of property valuation. A similar kind of involvement at the stage of the validation process is observed in Haryana, Uttar Pradesh, West Bengal, Assam, Rajasthan, Gujarat, Madhya Pradesh, and Bihar. Except Bihar, the role of an elected council is also evident in the task of amending of valuation. However, in states like Andhra Pradesh, Odisha, and Kerala, municipal acts do not prescribe any involvement of an elected body in the administration of property tax. In essence, the property tax administration is characterized by the fusion of elected body members and appointed personnel at various stages of the tax administration.

To illustrate the organization for property tax administration, we give an example of the administration of the Municipal Corporation of Delhi (MCD). MCD's property tax department has two major departmental set-ups—one at the headquarters and the other at the field level (divided into zones and a few specialized centres for industrial and big properties). The head of the department is the assessor and collector (A&C in the rank of accountant general) assisted by an additional A&C and joint A&C, deputy A&C, and also assistant A&C. At the zonal level, joint A&C, deputy A&C, assistant A&C, zonal inspectors and assistant zonal inspectors manage the zonal offices. The number of joint A&Cs, deputy A&Cs, and assistant A&Cs at the headquarters and in zonal offices depends on the size and work load. The department performs the duty of collecting, scrutiny, verification, tax-related settlements, data management, and the upgrading of property tax records.

The tax can be paid online or at collection offices, which are located zone wise. Generally, the payment is made by the owner of the property by self-assessment. However, there is a penalty for making a willfully false declaration. Also, penalty is levied on non-payment of tax.

Assessment of the Existing System

The property tax base in India is narrow and restricted, with only about 50 to 55 per cent of the 71.5 crore urban properties paying property tax. The assessed value of properties for the purposes of taxation uniformly lags behind market values; in some places, assessed values are reported to be about 8 to 10 per cent of market values.

Recommended Reforms

One of the reforms required for property tax relates to collecting information in the open market on rentals and sale transactions. It is suggested that the department of property tax should involve professionally trained valuers; interact with the office of the stamp duty and registration fee, and with the School of Architecture and Planning for valuing properties.

Efforts should be made to pay due attention to four critical aspects for effective administration of property tax. These are identifying properties, record keeping, assessment, and collection. Improving the efficiency in collection alone will increase the revenue in the short run but will not provide the broader base necessary for long-run growth.

Finally, it is important to monitor and quantify the potential of the property tax in each corporation in order to plan for effective reforms in property tax administration.

Octroi

It is a tax on entry of goods into a local area for consumption, use, or sale. It is collected at the time of entry of goods into a local area at the check-posts surrounding the local area. The collection of tax is on the basis of the value of goods carried as declared by the goods-carrier at the check-post. It is not an accounts based levy. It is a traditional local commodity tax which provides liquidity to local governments. In the past, octroi was one of the important taxes levied by local bodies.

Constitutional Provisions

While there is no specific mention of octroi in the Indian Constitution, it is felt that octroi is covered by Entries 49 and 52 of the state list (list-II) and Entry 89 of the central list (list-I) of the Seventh Schedule of the Constitution.

Entry 52 of list-II covers 'Taxes on the entry of goods into a local area for consumption, use or sale therein'; Entry 89 of list-I covers 'Terminal taxes on goods or passengers, carried by railway, sea or air; taxes on railway fares and freights'. Entry 49 covers 'Cesses on the entry of goods into a local area for consumption, use or sale'.

While there is a minute difference between a terminal tax and octroi, the Supreme Court has considered these levies in a number of cases and pointed out that terminal tax and octroi, though different, are similar to each other in that they are leviable on goods brought into a local area. Terminal taxes are leviable on goods imported or exported from municipal limits denoting that they were connected with the traffic of goods.

As can be seen from this discussion, octroi is assigned to the states which have, in turn, assigned it to local bodies. However, as of now, this duty is more historical and only of academic interest.

Revenue Significance of Octroi

Octroi's share in the total yield of local bodies during the 1990s in major octroi levying states was in the range of 35 to 90 per cent. Octroi's share in the own revenue of local bodies during the 1970s and 1980s, on an average, for the high income states of Maharashtra and West Bengal varied between 31 to 44 per cent and for low-income states of Uttar Pradesh, Karnataka, and Rajasthan, the average contribution of octroi to the own revenue of local bodies was more than 70 per cent.

Present Status of Octroi

Octroi has been in existence in states across India since independence. However, it is now no longer regarded as a useful levy; in reality, octroi is a wasteful local levy causing enormous production losses due to the hindrance it causes to smooth traffic and trade flows. Also, it is the main cause of rampant corruption as the levy is check post–based and not an accounts-based tax. The tax also causes efficiency losses due to taxation and consequent revenue generation from inputs and capital goods.

Many commissions and committees appointed by the Government of India as well as by the state governments have examined the issue of its abolition and searched for some suitable alternatives.[1] However, due to its significant share in the own revenue of local governments, the levy has continued.

It was during the mid-1990s, when the Indian economy had undergone major reforms in many sectors, particularly in finance (including trade and commerce), that many states announced the abolition of octroi. Madhya Pradesh abolished it in 1975, Karnataka in 1979, Uttar Pradesh in 1990, and Rajasthan in 1998.

Presently, it is levied only in Maharashtra; that too, only in 16 large municipal corporations.

Recommended Reforms

To strengthen the finances of local bodies, the need of the hour is to abolish octroi in all the local bodies and provide them with some suitable alternative to strengthen their fiscal autonomy. It is recommended that a piggy back ride on State VAT (or GST, when implemented) and assigning entertainment tax to local bodies will extend their fiscal domain at the level of the third of the government.

---

[1] In 1950, the Motor Vehicles Taxation Enquiry Committee referred to the harmful effects of octroi on trade and commerce, and observed: 'that in some areas, the ill-effects on trade of local octroi, terminal tolls and similar taxes on goods-in-transit are today perhaps even greater than they were when the 1924–5 committee commented so adversely on this form of taxation.' In 1959, the M.R. Masani Committee on Road Transport Reorganisation considered the levy of octroi as a national waste and suggested its immediate abolition. The Planning Commission had this to say in 1966, 'There has been general agreement on the vexatious and inhibitory nature of Octroi duties and the abuses to which they are prone. From the point of view of intra state movement, the first recommendation we would reiterate concerns the need to do away with Octroi duties'. The Kelkar Committee condemned the 'canker of octroi' which had spread through the body politic of local administration, and called it a grave danger to the civic life of the community. The Lok Sabha Estimates Committee was more specific in 1975: 'One of the main obstacles in the way of quick and rapid movement of road transport in the country is the multiplicity of check-posts and payment of octroi duties at these check-posts'.

Other Local Taxes

The major portion of tax revenue collected by both the urban and rural local governments comes from the levy the above two taxes, which are property tax and Octroi. In addition, the urban municipalities and rural local bodies of the states levy a number of other local taxes, which are not fiscally significant but serve some useful purposes.

In some states, a form of shared taxation is practiced where surcharges are placed by local bodies on national or state taxes. By this a portion of local revenues gets linked to the more buoyant tax sources. In some States there are tax instruments for which the power of levy and collection of taxes are assigned to the states while the proceeds are fully or partly assigned to the municipalities. This may be on a differential basis in relation to three tiers of municipalities, namely, Municipal Corporations, Municipal Councils, and *Nagar Panchayat*s and to the Panchayats covered under the Seventy-fourth Constitution Amendment Act.

While the scope for tax charges by local governments remains limited, many local bodies pursue a form of cost recovery by way of levying property-tax-linked benefit taxes such as water benefit tax, education cess, conservancy surcharge, etc., as levied on the property tax base.

Some taxes are imposed by municipalities. These are land-based taxes such as Duty on Transfer of Property (Tamil Nadu, Hyderabad, Karnataka), Street Tax (Mumbai), local taxes on services such as Water Tax (Mumbai, provincial municipal corporations and municipalities in Maharashtra, Tamil Nadu, Karnataka, Hyderabad and Madhya Pradesh), Water Benefit Tax (Mumbai), Sewerage Tax (Mumbai, Tamil Nadu and Hyderabad), Drainage Tax (Madhya Pradesh), Sewerage Benefit Tax (Mumbai), Conservancy Tax (Mumbai Provincial Municipal Corporations), Cavenging Tax (Punjab), Latrine or Conservancy Tax (Hyderabad and Madhya Pradesh), Education Tax/Cess (Mumbai, Tamil Nadu and Maharashtra Municipalities), Fire Tax (Punjab and Madhya Pradesh), Lighting Tax (Hyderabad and Madhya Pradesh). Besides there are some local taxes on Business, Professions and Entertainments levied by various state municipalities such as Advertisement Tax (Kolkata, Tamil Nadu, Punjab, Karnataka, Hyderabad, and Madhya Pradesh), Theatre Tax (Mumbai, Mumbai Municipal Corporations, Maharashtra Municipalities), Show Tax (Punjab), Tax on Entertainment (Hyderabad and Madhya Pradesh Municipal Corporations). Some local taxes levied by urban municipalities include the taxes on entry or exit of passengers, goods, and services such as Pilgrim Tax (Maharashtra Municipalities and

Madhya Pradesh Municipal Corporations). There are some other local level taxes as well such as Taxes on Vehicles and Animals (Mumbai, Mumbai Provincial Municipal Corporations and Maharashtra Municipalities, West Bengal Municipalities, Punjab, Hyderabad, Andhra Pradesh Municipalities and Madhya Pradesh), Taxes on Carts and Carriages (Kolkata), a Tax on dogs (Mumbai, Hyderabad and Madhya Pradesh).

Some taxes are levied by rural local bodies of the states. There are some obligatory taxes as well as some optional taxes imposed by *Gram Sabha*. These are Taxes on Private Latrines payable by occupier or owner of the buildings to which such latrines are attached when cleaned by Gram Sabha Agency; taxes such as a light tax, if light arrangement have been made by Gram Sabha; a tax on a person for exercising any profession or carrying any trade or calling within the limits of Gram Sabha area. The optional taxes, fees, etc., imposed by the Gram Sabha of various States include Tax on animals used for riding, driving or burden; Tax on dogs or pigs payable by the owners thereof; a Temporary Tax for Special Works of Public utility; Tax for construction or maintenance of public latrines and a General Scavenging Tax for removal and disposal of refuse.

CHAPTER 9

NEED FOR FURTHER REFORMS

Since the beginning of the 1990s India has adopted the structural adjustment programme with reforms in major sectors of the economy. Reforms were attempted in public expenditure, followed by the disinvestment of public sector undertakings (PSUs). The objective was to increase operational efficiency through transfer of ownership to the private sector and improving management practices.

The structural adjustment programme has also been backed by reforms in the overall tax system since the 1990s. Efforts were made to attain a higher tax–GDP ratio by lowering tax rates, broadening the tax base, and rationalizing tax exemptions and incentives. Reforms were attempted, though at a later stage, at the states' level too.

FISCAL SIGNIFICANCE

In terms of revenue the existing tax system yields approximately 16.4 per cent of GDP. In developed countries, however, this proportion is more than 30 per cent. This is due to the fact that a major proportion of the population in India is dependent on agriculture and this sector is practically un-taxed. Also, the services sector which has a significant contribution in GDP is not fully taxed.

Due to the tax reforms initiated in the 1990s, growth in the union government's revenue from indirect taxes (such as customs duty and union excise duty) slowed down while revenue from direct taxes (like personal income tax and corporation tax) showed an accelerated growth.

Consequently, the centre's direct tax to GDP ratio recorded an upward trend (increased from 1.94 in 1990–1 to 5.73 in 2008–9) while the indirect tax–GDP ratio fell over time (declined from 8.17 in 1990–1 to 5.11 in 2008–9). At the same time, states' tax-GDP ratio showed a marginal increase.

In the late 1990s and the period following 2000, revenue from the states' indirect taxes relative to GDP recorded an upward trend. Taxes on commodities and services contributed 56.6 per cent to the total tax revenue of the centre and the states in 2009–10. Revenue from direct taxes showed a moderately high growth rate (18.4 per cent) during 1991–2 to 2009–10.

At the central level, higher service tax and customs duty collections neutralized the lower collections from income tax and excise duties resulting in the overall growth of gross tax revenue.

Sales tax has been the main source of revenue for state governments. It contributed more than 60 per cent of the states' own tax revenue. A major achievement at the states' level is the replacing of sales tax by State VAT to have a transparent and efficient tax system. However, direct taxes such as land revenue, agricultural income tax, and profession tax have remained insignificant sources of revenue for the states due to both political and structural reasons.

Taxes of the Union Government

The union government levies buoyant and broad-based taxes that have an all-India coverage on income and property as also on commodities and services. In addition, the union government levies taxes on imports and exports of commodities.

Taxes on International Trade

The union list authorizes the central government to levy tax on international trade which takes the form of 'customs duty'. Customs duty comprises export and import duties.

With the increasing volume of imports and exports during the period 1991–2 to 2009–10, customs duty occupies an important place in the overall tax revenue, with an annual growth rate of 8.40 per cent. However, with the opening up of the economy and the reduction of the effective rate of customs duty, its share has declined over time.

Export duty is levied on exports of specified commodities to mop up windfall export profits. The rate of duty and the possibility of levying this tax depend on the elasticity of demand for India's products in the international market. It is levied on free on board (FOB) value. In addition to export duty, export cess is leviable on the export of specified articles under various enactments passed by the government.

Import duty is levied as a wedge between domestic prices and prices of imported goods to guard against cheap imports and to provide a level playing field for domestic producers. It is imposed on almost all commodities imported into the country. The statutory rates of import duties, called tariff rates, are fixed by Parliament. However, the union government has the power, under law, to provide full or partial duty exemptions.

Basic customs duty is levied on almost all commodities. The standard rate of basic customs duty is *ad valorem* and applicable to all goods. Prior to 1991–2, the maximum rate of duty was 300 per cent which was reduced to 110 per cent in 1992–3, 50 per cent in 1995–6, 10 per cent in 2008–9, and remains unchanged at 10 per cent in 2012.

Current peak rate of duty is 10 per cent on non-agricultural items (except natural rubber sheets, fish, and cars). The average industrial tariff is about 9.4 per cent. Reduction in duty rates has been accompanied by reduction in dispersal of duty rates. The tax base for customs duty is primarily c.i.f. (cost, insurance, and freight) value of the goods imported. Rates in general are higher for consumer goods, finished goods, and industrial products as compared to capital goods, inputs, and agriculture goods. Changes in custom duty's rate structure were introduced after the opening up of the economy.

Besides basic customs duty, there are other forms of duties that are levied along with this basic duty. These are additional duty of custom or countervailing duty; special countervailing duty; national calamity contingent duty on mobile phones, two-wheelers, motor cars, and multi-utility vehicles; education cess; secondary and higher education cess; anti-dumping duty; and safeguard duty.

Apart from the general principles of commodity classification, rates are also determined on the basis of a number of Regional Trade Agreements that India has signed with various countries. Preferential duty rates and duty concessions are extended via these agreements to participating countries. With the adoption of the policy of liberalization and an open economy, customs duty rates are now comparable to the structures prevailing in other countries.

The Central Board of Excise and Customs (CBEC) is the apex organization for forming policy and its administration with regard to customs duty.

Central Taxes on Income and Property

Important taxes on income and property levied by the union government include corporation tax and personal income tax. The other taxes in this category include wealth tax, gift tax, and estate duty.

Corporation Tax

Corporation tax is a tax on corporate profits. It is the most important source of revenue for the central government and is also the most buoyant tax among the direct taxes assigned to the centre with an annual growth rate of 21 per cent.

Prior to 1994–5, distinction was made between widely held and closely held companies and between domestic and foreign companies. From 1994–5, this tax is levied only on the basis of the origin of a company, that is, whether a company is domestic or foreign.

In 1993–4, the tax rate varied from 45 per cent to 50 per cent for domestic companies and 65 per cent for foreign companies. Over the years, the range of rates has come down. Presently, the rate of corporation tax is 30 per cent for domestic companies and 40 per cent for foreign companies.

In addition to the tax on corporate income, there is a surcharge on corporation tax. Currently, the rate of surcharge is 5 per cent and 2.5 per cent on domestic and foreign companies respectively.

Since 2007–8 an additional cess of 1 per cent is levied on the amount of corporation tax and surcharge termed as 'secondary and higher education cess'.

Notwithstanding these statutory rates, the effective rates of corporation tax are much lower than the nominal (statutory) rates due to exemptions, concessions, and incentives given for depreciation and investment allowance, etc. In fact, certain tax incentives have been incorporated in the income tax structure to promote investment and capital formation in the economy. These include incentive for industrial development, for promoting investment in infrastructure, for environmental protection, and for developing social sectors.

Given all these concessions and incentives, some companies have been able to reduce their tax-liability to zero by working in backward areas, in infrastructure or power sectors, and in export processing zones or as export-oriented units (EOUs).

However, to mobilize some resources from such zero-tax companies, a minimum alternate tax (MAT) was introduced on their book profits in 1996-7. MAT's effective rate at the time of its introduction (in 1996-7) was 12.9 per cent of the book profit. It was gradually reduced to 7.5 per cent in 2001-2 and had been gradually increased to 15 per cent by 2009-10. MAT rate was further increased to 18.5 per cent through union budget 2011-12. The rate of MAT continued to be the same in 2012-13.

Dividend incomes from company shares were taxed in the hands of the recipient until 1997. However, through the Finance Act, 1997, this was replaced by a dividend distribution tax (DDT), levied on domestic companies on the profits distributed as dividend. It was levied at a rate of 10 per cent on distributed profits of companies. It was abolished in 2002, but was reintroduced in 2003 at a higher rate of 12.5 per cent. The current rate of DDT is 15 per cent.

Personal Income Tax

Personal income tax is a composite tax on an individual's aggregate income from all sources such as salary, income from property, interest income, business income, and income from shares. However, agriculture income being a state subject it is exempt from this tax.

With the overall growth of the economy and the consequent increase in per capita incomes yields from this tax steadily increased over the years with an annual growth rate of 17 per cent and a buoyancy value of 1.3 during 1991-2 to 2009-10.

In the early 1970s personal income tax had a marginal rate of 85 per cent with a large number of tax slabs. In addition, there was 15 per cent surcharge resulting in the effective marginal tax rate being 97.75 per cent. This was gradually reduced and brought down to 50 per cent by 1985-6. On the recommendation of the Tax Reforms Committee the marginal tax rate was further brought down to 30 per cent by 1997-8.

Currently, the general category of individual taxpayers are subjected to a rate schedule comprising of three slabs: 10, 20, and 30 per cent with an initial exemption limit of Rs 2 lakh.

To encourage investments in the desired sectors of the economy, the Income Tax Act offers a variety of exemptions and concessions under various clauses of section 10 of the Income Tax Act, 1961. In addition, some provisions have been incorporated in the income tax structure to promote savings and make investments more attractive. These include exemptions from specified financial assets subject to certain monetary limits; deductions from income, on a netting principle, of the whole of the funds invested in the national saving scheme, certain schemes of the Life Insurance Corporation of India and equity-linked saving scheme of mutual funds; and rebate in tax payable as a percentage of the funds invested in specified financial assets or construction of house property.

Capital Gains Tax

Capital gains tax is levied on profits made while selling/transferring a capital asset, that is, a house, an apartment, office space, factory, godown, or a plot of land or investments such as shares and bonds. The tax is levied on the difference between the purchase and sale price of financial and tangible assets.

Since capital gains are not annual accruals from a given source but represent appreciation in the market value of assets over a period of time, they are treated on a different footing and categorized as short-term and long-term capital gains, depending on the time period for which the investment has been under possession. Short-term capital gains are taxed at normal income tax rates. But, capital gains arising on the transfer of equity shares or mutual fund units are taxed at a flat rate of 15 per cent. In the case of long-term capital gains, assets other than equity shares or equity mutual funds, the rate of tax is 20 per cent. It is 10 per cent in the case of debt mutual funds, if the cost of acquisition is not indexed and 20 per cent if the cost of acquisition is indexed. Long-term capital gains from sale of equity shares or mutual fund units are exempt from tax. Also long-term capital gains are fully exempt if the proceeds are invested in specified savings plans/schemes. Capital gains tax is fully exempted on sale of a residential property, if the sale consideration is used for subscription in equity of a manufacturing SME company for purchase of a new plant and machinery.

Wealth Tax and Gift Tax

Other union taxes on income and property such as wealth tax and gift tax do not contribute significant revenue to the central kitty.

Wealth tax is levied on net wealth. Currently it is levied at a flat rate of 1 per cent with a basic exemption of Rs 30 lakh. No cess and surcharge are levied on wealth tax.

Gift tax is levied on gifts received by individuals and Hindu Undivided Families (HUFs). Prior to 1987–8, the rate structure for gift tax was highly progressive, ranging from 5 per cent on the value of taxable gifts not exceeding Rs 20,000 to 75 per cent on the value of taxable gifts in excess of Rs 20 lakh. The basic exemption limit was Rs 5,000. However, from assessment year 1987–8, a flat rate of 30 per cent is applicable on gifts over and above the exemption limits. From 1 October 2009, individuals and HUFs receiving shares or jewellery, valuable artifacts, valuable drawings, paintings or sculptures or even property valued over Rs 50,000 as gifts from non-relatives, have to pay this tax.

Administration of Taxes on Income and Property

The administration of taxes on income and property is entrusted to the Central Board of Direct Taxes (CBDT) which provides essential inputs for policy and planning of direct taxes in India and deals with the administration of direct tax laws through the income tax department.

Central Domestic Trade Taxes

In addition to taxes on international trade, the union government has the authority to levy taxes on manufacture and services. These are known as union excise duty and service tax respectively.

Union Excise Duty (CenVAT)

Union excise duty (UED) is levied on all goods manufactured or produced. Set-off is given for the tax paid on inputs used in the manufacturing of final products. UED is called central Value Added Tax (CenVAT) since 2001. In addition to CenVAT, some variants of it have been levied to fulfil different objectives. These include additional duties of excise (ADE), additional duty on tea and tea waste, additional duty on motor spirit, high speed diesel oil, additional duty of excise on pan masala and certain tobacco products and on textile and textile articles, and cesses and surcharges.

UED is one of the significant revenue providers. It contributed 16.49 per cent to the central government's total tax revenue in 2009–10 recording an annual growth rate of 9.05 per cent and a buoyancy of 0.71 during 1991–2 to 2009–10.

Revenue collected from cesses, surcharges, and some specified levies are earmarked for certain pre-determined purposes—education or upliftment of the workers engaged in a particular industry, etc. Cesses and surcharges do not form part of the CenVAT chain and therefore, no credit can be availed on these.

Prior to the reforms in the tax system, the UED structure was complex and highly distortionary. The tax structure was a mix of specific and *ad valorem* rates and varied from 2 per cent to 100 per cent. In effect the then prevailing UED was a manufacturer's sales tax administered at the factory gate. This was a cascading type tax as it was levied on inputs, capital goods, and final goods.

Various committees including the Indirect Tax Enquiry Committee (Jha Committee) suggested incorporating the VAT procedures in UED. Based on the recommendations of all such committees, VAT procedures were first introduced in 1986 in the form of ModVAT. Later, as recommended by the Tax Reforms Committee, rates were gradually unified. In 1999–2000 almost 11 tax rates were merged into one rate of 16 per cent and ModVAT was converted to CenVAT. For few goods special additional excises were levied with 8, 16, and 24 per cent rates. Under CenVAT input credit was provided for all inputs—capital as well non-capital goods. In 2008–9, the standard rate of excise duty was reduced from 16 to 14 per cent. Currently, while there are a large number of CenVAT rates, the standard rate is 12 per cent.

While the standard rate is 12 per cent, several commodities are charged excise duty at lower rates of 2 per cent, 6 per cent, and 8 per cent which creates distortions. Similarly, the existence of a number of exemptions and lack of effective monitoring mechanism leads to confusion and disputes. In this context to make the system more effective, a meaningful review of the existing tax system is required without affecting the growth momentum of the economy and moving forward on the road to a goods and service tax.

The excise duty structure is replete with exemptions of different kinds. The most important ones relate to small-scale industries (exemption is applicable to units whose clearances of excisable goods for home consumption were below Rs 4.5 crore in the preceding financial year) and to some specific areas like the North-Eastern states, Jammu and Kashmir, Uttarakhand, Himachal Pradesh, and Sikkim. Exemptions were provided to specified goods manufactured by an eligible unit in a specified state and/or located in a specified industrial growth centre, industrial infrastructure development centre or export promotion industrial park or industrial estate. The Union Budget 2012–13 provided full exemption to hand-made matches, new and retreaded aircraft tyres, and branded silver jewellery.

Service Tax

Apart from the UED levy on manufactured commodities, the central government also levies a tax on services. Except a few specified services which were assigned to states (entertainment tax, passengers and goods tax, and electricity duty) services were left in the concurrent list.

Drawing powers from the concurrent list, the union government initially levied service tax on three services—general insurance, telephone services, and services provided by stock brokers from July 1994 at the rate of 5 per cent. Since then the scope has been considerably enhanced and, until last year, 116 services were taxed at the rate of 10 per cent. The union budget 2012–13 has expanded the tax base by bringing all services into the tax net except for the 38 services mentioned in the Negative List. The rate of tax on services has also been increased to 12 per cent.

Among all the indirect taxes collected by the union, service tax has proved to be the most buoyant source of revenue contributing 9.35 per cent to the total tax revenue of the centre in 2009–10.

Input tax credit (ITC) is available for taxes paid on goods and services used as inputs in providing services.

Administration of Union Taxes on Commodities and Services

Taxes on commodities and services levied by the union government are administered by the Central Board of Excise and Customs (CBEC) under the Ministry of Finance, Government of India. CBEC is the supreme authority dealing with the tasks of forming policy concerning levy and collection of central excise duties and service tax and resolves administrative matters relating to it. The taxes are administered by CBEC through the Commissionerate of Central Excise and the Commissionerate of Service Tax.

STATE GOVERNMENTS' TAXES

The state governments levy taxes on income and property as also on commodities and services which generally have regional coverage. That is, the states are assigned those taxes that could be better administered at the state level allowing for regional variations.

State Taxes on Income and Property

The important taxes on income and property levied by state governments include land revenue, agricultural income tax, stamp duty and registration fee, and profession tax.

Land Revenue

Land revenue is the oldest source of tax revenue collected by the states. Yields from land revenue, however, have been declining over the years. Some states like Punjab, Haryana, and Arunachal Pradesh have abolished this tax. The contribution of this tax to the states' exchequers is negligible.

The structure of land revenue is heterogeneous. No uniformity exists either in the rate or in the base of the tax. In general, the rate is levied according to whether the land is irrigated or un-irrigated; or the crop sown on the land is commercial or non-commercial.

Rich states like Punjab and Haryana, which have witnessed a huge increase in agricultural productivity, do not levy this tax. Some states levy a cess/tax on commercial crops while other states do not have such provisions and as a result there is a certain degree of heterogeneity in the taxation of commercial crops.

Despite an increase in land productivity due to newer technologies (due to the Green Revolution, White Revolution, etc.) resulting in an increase in agricultural yields, there has been no commensurate increase in the land revenue rates.

To have sectoral equity taxation, it is useful to replace land revenue by a progressive tax such an agricultural holding tax, which could be levied on the basis of an operational holding.

Agricultural Income Tax

Agricultural income tax (AIT) is a levy on receipts of agricultural income. Presently it is levied in only five states—Assam, Karnataka, Kerala, West Bengal, and Tripura, and collected mainly from plantation crops. In comparison to other direct taxes the share of revenue realized from this tax has remained insignificant.

The share of agricultural income tax in states' own tax revenue has shown a declining trend over the years. It diminished at a steady rate from 0.6 per cent in 1991–2, 0.05 per cent in 2001–2, and further to 0.03 per cent in 2009–10.

The rate of tax varies from state to state. In case of individual taxpayers, the tax rate varies between 5 and 60 per cent while for companies it varies between 30 and 50 per cent. A progressive tax system exists for corporate taxpayers in the states except in West Bengal and Tripura. In addition, in Karnataka and Kerala, besides taxes on individuals and companies, a different tax rate is levied on firms at the rate of 40 per cent and 35 per cent of the total agricultural income, respectively, in the two states.

In general, agricultural income tax is characterized by a low tax rate, a narrow base, high exemption limits, and a large number of exemptions and exclusions. Also, non-imposition of this tax in most states and lack of its integration with personal income tax creates a loophole for evading this on non-agricultural income since part of one's non-agricultural income can be passed off as agricultural income. From the point of view of inter-sectoral equity, the system of AIT should be reformed in such a way that the states are able to mobilize much needed resources for development.

Stamp Duty and Registration Fee

Stamp duty and registration fee (SD and RF) are two components of a tax on property related to regulation of transactions of instruments. It is one of the important state taxes. Its share in states' own tax revenue increased from 7.42 per cent in 1991–2 to 10.90 per cent in 2009–10 with an annual growth rate of 16.59 per cent.

Stamp duty (SD) is levied on all documents related to a transaction. It is judicial as well as non-judicial. Registration fee (RF) is paid to the government when the documents or instrument are presented for registration in return for the safe custody of the registered documents. It is a payment made for the service rendered by the government in recording contracts and deeds, for maintaining a permanent database of registered instruments, and for providing information relating to such transactions to the public. Registration is compulsory for certain instrments (mainly immovable property) and optional for other financial instruments.

The rates of SD and RF as well as base are characterized by huge variations among the states. Some of the states levy additional duties or surcharges on basic SD. However, effective SD and RF rates are determined after taking into account exemptions and concessions.

Variations in SD and RF rates on many documents among the states has led to a diversion of economic activity and also loss of legitimate revenue of the states concerned. Moreover, with no scientific method of valuation in place, determining the market price of a property results in a proliferation of corrupt practices and the generation of 'black money'.

Reforms in SD's structure and administration are the need of the hour. Firstly, SD rates and slabs should be reduced. Secondly, the system of e-stamping has proved to be superior to the normal system of paying SD and could be usefully adopted by the states. Finally, setting up valuation committees will be a great improvement in the administration of the tax.

Profession Tax

Profession tax is a potential source of revenue for states. It is a tax on professions, trades, callings, and employment. Currently, this tax is levied by 17 states. It is levied on wage/salary earners and self-employed persons (like small traders, professionals, and owners of video libraries/theatres), including legal persons.

The share of profession tax in states' own tax revenue declined from 1.24 per cent in 1991–2 to 1.03 per cent in 2009–10, indicating its insignificance in states' own tax revenue.

The tax rate varies considerably among the states. It is generally specific and ranges between Rs 720 to Rs 2,500 per annum.

With a view to bringing in potential professional taxpayers into the tax net, the need of the hour is for states to undertake periodic surveys of different occupational groups. Also, the tax structure needs to be simplified, its tax base be broadened, and the constitutional ceiling of Rs 2,500 to be enhanced to Rs 25,000.

State Taxes on Commodities and Services

Important taxes on commodities and services levied by state governments include sales tax (State VAT), motor vehicles, and passengers and goods tax, state excise duty, electricity duty, and entertainment tax.

Sales Tax/State VAT

Sales tax is one of the most important sources of revenue for states. It yields approximately 61 per cent of states' own tax revenue which had a high annual growth rate of 13.85 per cent during 1991–2 to 2009–10.

Of late, sales has been replaced by state VAT, which has a three rate structure. Zero-rated items, that is, exempt items include natural and unprocessed products, goods which are legally barred from taxation, and goods which have social implications. Another category consists of basic necessities such as medicines and drugs, declared goods (such as iron, steel, and hides and skins), agricultural products, and food items. These are taxed at 4 per cent. The standard rate of State VAT is 12.5 per cent. In addition, there is a special rate of 1 per cent on bullion and silver and 20 per cent and above on petroleum products and liquor. Although the lists of goods have been specified to be taxed under the three rate categories for the states, there exist some variations in the list of items from state to state. Efforts are being made by the empowered committee of state finance ministers to ensure that there is complete uniformity in the rates.

While State VAT is a state subject, taxation of inter-state sales is included in the union list. To ensure equal treatment for commodities entering into inter-state trade and on those locally produced, the Parliament levies central sales tax (CST) on inter-state transactions. The current CST rate is 2 per cent on inter-state sales to registered dealers. In spite of the low CST rate on registered dealers, CST levy on the basis of 'origin' goes against the principle of a unified market. CST levied on inputs cascades and results in higher prices. Due to these reasons CST is being phased out and will be brought down to 'zero' per cent by the time GST is introduced in India.

Since VAT has replaced the prevailing sales tax in states, the organization for tax administration prevalent under sales tax has been adapted for VAT, with necessary changes to suit the VAT system. It is suggested that to implement VAT successfully the states should attempt re-engineering of the tax departments. Also, efforts are afoot to introduce a goods and services tax (GST) to replace the existing State VAT.

Motor Vehicles Tax and Passengers and Goods Tax

Motor vehicles tax (MVT) is levied on acquisition of vehicles and includes a one-off payment at the time of registering a vehicle. Passengers and goods tax (P&GT) is levied on passengers and goods carried by road or by inland waterways. Both these taxes are similar in nature and fall on the same base and are ultimately paid by the same group of people. Some of the states levy both these taxes but many of them have merged these two into one tax.

Although the revenue from both these taxes has increased in the recent years, MVT's share in the states' own tax revenue has remained around 6 per cent over the years, while P&GT has contributed in the range of 2 per cent to 3 per cent to states' own tax revenue.

The existing MVT tax structure shows wide variations in tax rates. There are different bases for computation and different rates, leading to differing incidence of taxes per vehicle in different states. Some states levy this tax on the basis of engine capacity defined in terms of cubic capacity (c.c.); in other states it is on the basis of unladen weight (ULW) and cost of the vehicle. The pattern of levy of the tax also shows variations among states. With regard to goods tax different methods of levy are followed. In some states the tax is levied at the rate of some percentage of the freight charged; other states follow the system of compounded levy.

It is, therefore, important that efforts are made to bring uniformity in the structure of motor vehicles tax and passengers and goods tax. Also, the two taxes, that is, MVT and PG&T, being similar in nature and also being administered by the same department primarily with the same objectives, be merged to have one rate for the combined tax which could be known as vehicle tax for personal vehicles and road tax for commercial vehicles. The reformed structure should have an *ad valorem* tax rate, resort to a tax system based on cost of purchase of vehicles with additional factors of: (i) occupancy, and (ii) length of routes or goods carried. Finally, some built in fiscal incentives could be adopted to provide an initiative for using non-polluting instruments in each of the vehicles.

State Excise Duty

State excise duty (SED) is levied to regulate and control overall activities in relation to intoxicants. Although the tax could be a potential source of revenue, its share in terms of states' own revenue went down from 15.2 per cent in 1991–2 to 13.3 per cent in 2009–10 with an annual growth rate of 12.12 per cent. However, in states such as Andhra Pradesh, Chhattisgarh, Karnataka, Madhya Pradesh, Rajasthan, Tamil Nadu, and Uttar Pradesh, SED's share in states' own tax revenue was much higher in comparison to the all-state average.

The *modus operandi* of administering SED is to issue permits or licences for manufacturing, trading, and consumption. The tax is collected in two components—excise duty and licence fee. SED rates and method of levy vary considerably among states. In general, the present SED system is heavily biased towards licence fee.

The point of levy being manufacture, the base of excise duty is narrow. The effort should be to levy the tax in relation to MRP linking this to the manufacturing cost of a product. Also, the current practice of monopoly licensing needs to be replaced by competitive licensing to ensure control on import, production, and sale of liquor in a state, and also for checking misuse of liquor and evasion of tax.

Electricity Duty

Electricity duty is a tax on the sale or consumption of energy. The share of electricity duty in states' own tax revenue declined at a steady rate from 4.46 per cent in 1991–2 to 3.37 per cent in 2009–10, indicating lack of buoyancy.

The rates and bases of levy vary widely among states. While in most of the states the duty is charged over and above the electricity tariff rate, in Manipur the cost of the tax is in-built in the tariff. Within a state too the rates vary according to the type of use, for example, domestic consumption, mines, commercial, or industrial use. In some states a lower rate of duty is charged for agricultural use. In some other states there is a different rate structure for metered and unmetered connections.

In most of the states the tax base is affected by a large number of exemptions. For example, exemption is granted for electricity sold for consumption to the central government; electricity used for construction, maintenance, or operations of railways; sale of electricity for agricultural purposes; and for SEZs.

The need of the hour is to make the tax structure progressive which is based on units consumed. Further, there is no reason for exempting agriculture from the payment of electricity duty. However, the duty in this case, can be charged at a lower rate. Duty should also be levied on captive generation of electricity for self use or for sale.

Entertainment Tax

Entertainment tax is a tax levied on the price charged for admission to any place of entertainment. The contribution of this tax to the states' exchequer is negligible. The share of this tax to the states' own tax revenue declined from 1.03 per cent in 1991–2 to 0.31 per cent in 2009–10. In the case of individual states, all states have exhibited a negative trend in the share of entertainment tax in the state's own tax revenue.

This is due to the fact that there has been a qualitative change in people's entertainment preferences during the recent period; and film shows, which are the principal contributors to entertainment tax revenue, have now been substituted by other forms of entertainment, within and outside homes. This has made it increasingly difficult for the government to revise the tax rates upwards.

While most of the states use the tax for general purposes, Tamil Nadu assigns 90 per cent of the collections from this tax to local bodies.

The base and rates of entertainment tax vary from state to state. In addition to taxes on cinemas and shows, in some states entertainment tax is also levied on horse racing and betting. Some of the states also levy additional duties or surcharges on the basic entertainment duty. Except for the levy assigned to local bodies, this tax will be subsumed under the goods and services tax (GST), when it is introduced.

Taxes Levied by Local Bodies

Normally, state governments assign some taxes from the state list, wholly or partially, to local bodies. In general, the local bodies have used property tax (house tax) and octroi as two important sources of revenue.

Property Tax

Property tax is an *ad valorem* tax levied by local bodies on owners of real property within their jurisdiction based on the value of such property. Municipal laws have generally adopted 'annual rental value' for assessing property tax. Rates for property tax rate vary according to the use of the property. Generally, residential property is taxed at a lower rate than industrial and commercial property, and owner-occupied residential properties are taxed at a lower rate than rented properties. There is no fixed model for the administration of property tax by local bodies. The base of property tax in India is narrow and restricted.

Octroi

Octroi is a traditional local commodity tax. In the past, octroi was one of the important taxes levied by local bodies. However, due to its adverse effects on trade and the economy, over time the tax has been abolished in all the states except in 16 municipal bodies in Maharashtra. Even there, the tax is likely to be abolished in the time to come.

Further Reforms

This analysis of the Indian tax system at the centre, states, and local governments indicates that reforms have been introduced in almost all the taxes during the last two decades. Introduction of VAT in place of complex, cascade type commodity taxes both at the centre and in the states, has been the most remarkable achievement. It was in fact a paradigm shift in the overall tax system.

While the report of the Taxation Enquiry Commission of 1953–4 (Matthai Commission) was a major study of the overall tax system highlighting a plethora of problems and suggesting solutions for them, the Indirect Taxes Enquiry Committee of 1978 (Jha Committee) highlighted the urgent need to reform the indirect tax system both at the central and state levels. The Tax Reforms Committee of 1991–3 (Chelliah Committee) came up with an important study recommending path-breaking reforms in both direct and indirect taxes at the central level. Its recommendations were also directed towards bringing the Indian tax system in tune with the structural adjustments to have an open economy and to have the Indian tax system at par with tax systems in the other countries in the world.

A path-breaking reform in the indirect tax system, supported by the recommendations of the Jha Committee and Chelliah Committee, was moving towards the introduction of a value added tax to replace the excise (at the centre) and sales tax (at the states) systems in the country.

However, due to a dichotomy in distributing tax powers between the centre and the states not only was the switch over to the VAT regime rather slow but this also made India adopt a system of dual VAT: Central VAT (CenVAT) at the central level and State VAT at the state level.

Keeping in step with the technological revolution, path-breaking recommendations for a modern tax administration, and for the introduction of a goods and services tax (GST) were given by Reports of the Task Forces on Direct (Government of India 2002), and Indirect Taxes (2002) (Government of India 2002).

It was felt that while the new VAT system was a definite improvement over the earlier system of excises and sales tax, it was fraught with certain weaknesses. First, because of separate taxation of goods and services the value of transactions needed to be split into the value of goods and the value of services for the purpose of taxation. This leads to greater complexities, and higher administrative and compliance costs. Second, due to further globalization of the Indian economy, a number of Free Trade Agreements have been signed in recent years. These allow 'duty free' or 'low duty imports' into India. Hence, there is a need to have a nation-wide simple and transparent system of taxation to enable the Indian industry to compete not only internationally but also in the domestic market. Third, CenVAT is levied up to the manufacturing level only. This causes cascading beyond the manufacturing level and also creates lack of transparency in the tax burden. It is, therefore, imperative to introduce GST to remove all these weaknesses. The GST system[1] will, therefore, be a step forward in reforms at the national as well as sub-national levels.

To pave the way for the introduction of GST, the Empowered Committee (EC) appointed a Joint Working Group (JWGgst) on GST. Based on its recommendations the EC brought out its First Discussion Paper on Goods and Services Tax in India in November 2009. The EC recommended that GST should subsume all indirect taxes on supply of goods and services:

1. Central VAT;
2. Central excise duties and additional excise duties levied on pan masala, petroleum and tobacco products, and those levied under Additional Duties of Excise (Goods of Special Importance) Act, 1957;
3. Additional customs duty in the nature of countervailing duties;
4. CVD and other domestic taxes imposed on imports to achieve a level-playing field between domestic and imported goods (which are currently classified as customs duty);
5. Cesses levied by the union—cess on manufactured bidis; rubber; tea; coffee; and cess on unmanufactured tobacco;
6. Surcharges levied by the union—national calamity contingent duty, education cess, and special additional duty of excise on motor spirits and high speed diesel (HSD); and
7. Service tax.

With regard to state GST, the EC suggested that the following taxes would be subsumed at the state level: state VAT/sales tax, entertainment tax, luxury tax, taxes on lottery, betting and gambling, entry tax not in lieu of octroi, and cesses and surcharges. According to the EC, alcoholic beverages should be kept out of GST.

With these central and state taxes being subsumed under GST, the proposed GST, as explained in greater details in Annexure A9.1, will have two

---

[1] GST is a multi-point sales tax with set-off for both goods and services. It is a tax on consumption. Its final and total burden is fully and exclusively borne by a domestic consumer of goods and services; no GST is charged on goods or services exported.

components—central GST (levied by the centre) and state GST (levied by the states). In the proposed GST scheme the base of the two GST components (central GST [CGST] and state GST [SGST]) will be the same. That is, the base of current CenVAT will be extended from the manufacturing to retail level. Also, with the introduction of GST, the current system of central sales tax (CST) will be replaced by an integrated GST (IGST), which will be destination based.

Like reforms in indirect taxes, reforms have also been introduced in direct taxes. Since the passage of the Income Act in 1961, amendments have been made almost every year through Finance Acts. In 1997, dividend distribution tax was introduced and the fringe benefit tax was also being levied with effect from 1 April 2006.

Owing to a plethora of changes in the original taxes on income and property, their structure has become very complex. Consequently, the cost of compliance as well as administration has increased. While efforts have been made to lower the marginal rate and rationalize the structure, it is felt that the strategy for broadening the base essentially comprises three elements. The first is minimizing exemptions. The removal of these exemptions will have three consequences: (i) it will result in a higher tax–GDP ratio; (ii) it will enhance GDP growth, since tax exemptions and deductions distort allocative efficiency; and (iii) it will improve equity (both horizontal and vertical), reduce compliance costs, lower administrative burdens, and discourage corruption. The second problem is related to ambiguity in the law, which facilitates tax avoidance. With a view to taking note of all these features, efforts have been made to redraft the overall Income Tax Act. The revised enactment will be known as Direct Taxes Code (DTC). The proposed DTC, as explained in detail in Annexure A9.2, will consolidate laws relating to all direct taxes, that is, income tax, dividend distribution tax, fringe benefit tax, and wealth tax so as to establish an economically efficient, effective, and equitable direct tax system which will facilitate voluntary compliance and reduce the scope for disputes and minimize litigation. Briefly, DTC will be a new law replacing the existing Income Tax Act for all the direct taxes; it will be expressed in a simple language; avoid ambiguity in provisions that invariably give rise to rival interpretations; will be capable of accommodating changes in the structure of a growing economy without resorting to frequent amendments; and will consolidate provisions relating to definitions, incentives, and procedure. It will be based on well-accepted principles of taxation and best international practices. The new direct tax code is expected to bring a sharp reduction in effective tax rates, engineered through both reductions in nominal rates and the redefinition of tax brackets.

The introduction of GST in the indirect tax system of the union and state governments and DTC in the direct taxes of the union government will establish an economically efficient, cost effective, and transparent tax system. It will make Indian taxpayers competitive at home as well as in the international market. However, the other taxes at the state level need to be further reformed. Special care needs to be taken to reform state taxes—SED, MVT, P&GT, and SD&RF on the lines recommended in this study. This will make the Indian tax system suitable for taking the country to new horizons of growth and prosperity.

Annexure A9.1

Goods and Services Tax (GST)

India's indirect tax system is unique. While the union government has the authority to impose a broad spectrum of union excise duties (UEDs) on the production or manufacture of goods, state governments are assigned the power to levy taxes on sale of goods.

Initially the authority to levy taxes on services was not specifically assigned to either of the governments; it was enshrined in the Residuary Entry in the union list. However, under certain specific provisions of the Constitution, the states are empowered to levy tax on some services—entertainment tax, electricity duty, motor vehicles tax, passengers and goods tax, and entry tax.

Due to this dichotomy of authority under the Constitution, India has not adopted a European-style VAT. It has gone in for a dual VAT, that is, VAT at the federal level (CenVAT) and VAT at the state level (State VAT).

Central VAT

Central VAT or CenVAT is levied by the union government at the manufacturing level on almost all manufactured goods except petro-products and tobacco.

Evolution of Central VAT

The Indian Constitution, under its union list empowers the central government to levy UED. Accordingly, the central government initially levied this duty on about a dozen articles at a very low rate. However, with the passage of time, the rates were revised and the tax base was enlarged to bring more items into its net. It was levied mainly on finished goods but also covered raw materials, intermediate goods, and capital goods.

The first reform in the UED regime was undertaken in 1986 through the introduction of modified value added tax (ModVAT) which was based on the report of the Jha Committee (Government of India 1978). This provided a set-off for the taxes paid on inputs used in about a dozen articles. In 1987, the scheme was extended to cover some additional commodities.

The process of reforms in indirect taxes got strengthened in the post-1991 reforms in the Indian economy. To begin with, based on the recommendations of the report of the Tax Reforms Committee (TRC), ModVAT was further extended to encompass a large number of commodities (Government of India 1991–3). ModVAT procedures have since been overhauled converting the then existing UEDs into Central VAT or CenVAT, which covers almost all items except high-speed diesel (HSD), motor spirit (gasoline), and matchboxes. Union budget 2006–7 converted CenVAT into a two-rate duty structure of 16 and 8 per cent. However, now the upper rate for CenVAT has further been reduced to 10 per cent.

CenVAT allows instant credit for all the taxes paid on inputs in the form of UEDs (ModVAT/CenVAT) or additional duties of excise (ADE). Input credit is also given for additional duty of customs which is known as countervailing duty (CVD)[2] and is collected at the time of imports. For capital goods, however, only 50 per cent of the duty can be claimed as input credit in a financial year; the remaining credit can be claimed in the next financial year, provided the goods are still in use (except for spares and components). A manufacturer producing only tax-exempt final products is not allowed to claim this credit. However, it is allowed to a

---

[2] This is levied as per the provisions of the Customs Act wherein this is referred to as Additional Duty of Customs. However, this is popularly known as countervailing duty (CVD). The rate of CVD tax on imported goods is equal to the tax rate of CenVAT levied on indigenously manufactured goods.

manufacturer roducing both dutiable and exempted final products in the same factory.[3]

Along with CenVAT, the central government also levies additional excise duty in lieu of sales tax;[4] additional duty of excise on textiles and textile articles; and cess on specified commodities.

Service Tax

The authority to levy tax on services was not specifically assigned to either of the governments in the Constitution. The union government, using the powers given in the Residuary Entry in the union list, started the levy of this tax with effect from 1 July 1994. Later the central government amended the Constitution to include service tax in the union list by inserting item 92(C) into the Seventh Schedule. This enables the centre to assign this tax to the states, solely or concurrently, whenever it so desires.

Initially, only three services were taxed—general insurance, stock broking, and telephones. The coverage of the tax was gradually expanded and presently service tax is levied on 116 services. At present the standard tax rate is 10 per cent. Service tax is now integrated with CenVAT.

State VAT

In addition to CenVAT on all manufactured goods as well as service tax (integrated with CenVAT) at the central level, all the states levy State VAT on goods sold within a state.

---

[3] This is subject to certain conditions—maintaining separate records with respect to inputs used to manufacture exempted products or payment of 8 per cent of the total price (excluding taxes) of the exempted final products or in the case of a few specified items, on reversal of the credit availed.

[4] Additional excise duty in lieu of sales tax has been levied since 1956 on tobacco, textiles, and sugar under a tax rental arrangement between the union and the states. According to this arrangement, the union government levied additional excise duty on these items and the states refrained from levying sales tax on them. The net proceeds of this duty were distributed among the states on the basis of consumption. With the efforts of the country to move towards VAT, the proceeds of this tax are now included in the shareable pool and the states have also been allowed to levy VAT on these items.

Evolution of State VAT

Multi-point sales tax is not new in India. Some of the states had adopted this form of tax even in the pre-independent era. Tamil Nadu[5] first levied a very low (one-fourth per cent, or 0.25 per cent) multi-point turnover tax in 1939. In the 1940s, this tax was adopted by many other states to mobilize additional resources.

Different models of single-point, double-point, and multi-point turnover tax were adopted in different states. However, the models adopted initially were replaced by a first-point sales tax and gradually almost all the states switched over to this system.

In addition to the first-point sales tax, the states also levied some other levies related to sales tax. These were in the form of additional sales tax, turnover tax, or surcharge on sales tax. Considerable variations existed among the states in these levies.

The first-point sales tax, as well as the other supplementary taxes, suffered from many weaknesses such as cascading and uncontrolled incidences, multiplicity of rates, vertical integration of firms, non-neutrality, and lack of efficiency in the tax system (Purohit 2001a). Given these deficiencies in the prevailing sales tax structure, efforts were made to replace it with a system of sub-national VAT.

The Government of India took the initiative to design an acceptable structure for VAT. This was accomplished by a study report titled 'Reform of Domestic Trade Taxes in India' in 1994 (NIPFP 1994). The Government of India sought comments on this study report from all the states and subsequently, a conference of chief ministers and finance ministers was convened on 24 May 1994 to discuss the report. The conference took the view that as VAT was a new tax, the report should be first reviewed by a small committee of finance ministers. Hence, a committee of eight finance ministers of states was constituted. This committee gave its report in August 1995 (see NIPFP 1995). The committee made some crucial recommendations (see Box A9.1.1). The report was discussed in the conference of finance ministers held on 4 July 1997. The conference recommended that all the states should shift to VAT at the same time after being given sufficient preparation time for implementing this tax and it was also suggested that a model VAT legislation should be prepared for guiding the states. Accordingly a model VAT law was prepared in 1998 and circulated among all the states.

---

[5] Formerly known as Madras state.

As the conference resolved that to prepare the states for the introduction of VAT, it was useful to have some guidelines, it decided to constitute another committee of state finance ministers to chart a time path for the introduction of VAT in all the states. The report of the State Finance Ministers Committee was submitted in August 1998 (see NIPFP 1998). Its recommendations are given in Box A9.1.2.

Under the sales tax regime, all the states have given huge concessions and sales tax incentives to attract new industries. To review all such

Box A9.1.1 Recommendations of the First State Finance Ministers Committee of 1995

The committee made the following recommendations:

'It would be desirable to adopt the VAT principle and give set off for tax paid on inputs including capital goods, but important and careful preparatory steps would be needed before full fledged State level VAT could be introduced. Such steps would include, *inter alia* the following points:

- Preparation of educational material which could be disseminated among the tax officers, trade, industry and the general public.
- Conducting workshops in different centers for tax officials and for trade and industry (separately).
- Developing a design for computerization of sales tax administration.
- Preparing model VAT legislation.
- Designing of a *Return Form* and other *Forms* needed together with the nature of documents to be maintained by the VAT taxpayers.'

Box A9.1.2 Recommendations of the Second State Finance Ministers Committee of 1998

The Committee recommended the following sequence of steps for the introduction of VAT at the state level:

1. Reducing the number of rates to four (including zero); the rates should not be below the agreed floor rates as per commodities.
2. Reducing the number of exemptions to the minimum in accordance with the recommendations of the first state finance ministers' committee.
3. To begin with reducing the effective rate of tax on inputs by allowing a partial set off.
4. Introducing computerization.

incentives, a small committee of chief ministers was set up under the chairmanship of Mr Jyoti Basu, the then Chief Minister of West Bengal which submitted its Report in 1999 (see NIPFP 1999).

The recommendations of the committees of chief ministers and finance ministers were:

- The number of rates prevailing under sales tax be reduced to a four-rate structure;
- The number of exemptions under sales tax be curtailed considerably;
- No new tax exemptions (known as incentives) be given to industries and the existing incentives be converted into deferment; and
- VAT should replace the existing sales tax system.

The resolutions of this conference were a landmark in the history of tax reforms at the sub-national level as it was decided that all the states and union territories should implement uniform floor rates with effect from 1 January 2000 and VAT from 1 April 2001.

To oversee the implementation of these decisions, the conference constituted a Standing Committee of State Finance Ministers. It was also decided that the interim period would be used for preparing, training, computerization, and publicity. However, the committee faced twin problems in implementing these recommendations. First, there were states that did not have sales tax (Arunachal Pradesh and Mizoram). The committee, therefore, recommended that these two states must introduce VAT by enacting suitable legislations so as to fall in line with the rest of the country and should issue notifications fixing the date on which they would introduce sales tax similar to that prevailing in other states.

The second problem related to states/union territories, which had not complied with the decision to have a uniform pattern of floor rates. The standing committee recommended that 25 per cent of Government of India's financial assistance to them be withheld with immediate effect. Also, it was suggested that a team of the empowered committee should visit these states/union territories[6] to convince them to implement this.

Thus, it was felt that prior to the introduction of VAT, some preparations were essential. The states had attempted to rationalize their existing sales tax system by adopting two major reforms.

---

[6] While the withholding of the grant was never implemented, the committee did visit the union territory of Puducherry to convince it of the need to fall in line for the sake of uniformity in the new tax system.

The first reform related to the adoption of a four-rate structure (zero, 4, 8, and 12.5 per cent) in the existing sales tax. These rates were in addition to two special rates of 1 and 20 per cent for a few specified items. The recommended rates were floor rates—the states had the freedom to adopt a higher rate on any of the commodities from the list. This checked the rate war and diversion of trade among the states. However, when the states started implementing the four-rate categories, many of them found it difficult to impose it on some commodities. Either there were problems with the classification of goods or there were administrative difficulties in implementing the floor rates. Hence, a few changes were made in the items falling under the exemption list and in other categories. This was necessitated due to the fact that the report of the Finance Ministers Committee (1995) had suggested that 'fine tuning of this classification would have to be done by a special group'. As this was not done prior to the adoption of floor rates, the commodity list had to be revised. However, under the VAT regime, states will have the three-rate categories of 0, 4, and 12.5 per cent.

The second reform pertains to the abolition of incentives related to sales tax as all the states have granted various incentives to new industries in the form of exemptions from tax on the purchase of inputs/sale of finished goods as well as sales tax loans and/or tax deferral. Various studies and committee reports (NIPFP 1998, 1999) have already argued against such incentives and pointed out that these incentives take the form of tax competition (war) or *harmful tax practices in a federation*.[7] In terms of loss of revenue, all the states collectively sacrificed about 25 per cent of the sales tax base.

In this context, it is important to note that initially all the sub-national governments stopped giving sales tax related incentives to new industrial units. However, there still exist concessions already granted to existing units. After the introduction of VAT, these incentives have been converted into a system of tax deferral or remission. This provided for the smooth functioning of the chain of VAT transactions.

To extend the tax reforms at the state level, VAT was to be made effective from 1 April 2001 by replacing the existing sales tax but due to some delays

---

[7] Empirical studies attempted for the NCR region indicate that the concessions of sales tax do not affect the location of industry. The concession could be relevant, if at all, when given by only one state. Similar results are seen from the other studies as well. When all the states give such concessions, it results in a zero sum game; no state benefits from such concessions. See for details, Purohit et al. (1992).

in preparations, it was postponed twice and was finally introduced in most of the states from 1 April 2005. Haryana was the first state to introduce VAT on 1 April 2003. Eventually, the rest of the states also implemented it (Box A9.1.3).

As of now, all the states have a system of VAT, known as State VAT. The coverage of tax includes the sale of all goods except diesel oil, petrol (gasoline), aviation turbine fuel (ATF), natural gas, and liquor. It has two basic rate categories of 4 and 12.5 per cent (standard rate) with some tax-exempt items and two special categories: 1 per cent on gold, silver, and ornaments, and 20 per cent on petroleum products.

Harmonization of Inter-state Tax under State VAT

Under the Indian Constitution, as stated earlier, taxation of inter-state transactions is a central subject. Entry 92A of the union list in the Seventh Schedule of the Constitution authorizes the levy of 'taxes on the sale or purchase of goods other than newspapers, where such sale or purchase takes place in the course of interstate trade or commerce.' However, while the authority to levy the tax remains under the jurisdiction of the union government, Section 9 of the CST Act entrusts the task of administering

Box A9.1.3   Introduction of State VAT in Indian States

States	No. of States	Date of Implementation
1	2	3
Haryana	1	1 April 2003
Andhra Pradesh, West Bengal, Kerala, Karnataka, Odisha, NCT Delhi, Tripura, Bihar, Arunachal Pradesh, Sikkim, Punjab, Goa, Mizoram, Nagaland, Jammu and Kashmir, Manipur, Maharashtra, Himachal Pradesh	18	1 April 2005
Assam, Meghalaya	2	1 May 2005
Uttarakhand	1	1 October 2005
Jharkhand	1	1 January 2006
Chhattisgarh, Gujarat, Madhya Pradesh, Rajasthan	4	1 April 2006
Tamil Nadu	1	1 January 2007
Uttar Pradesh	1	1 January 2008

the tax to the states. The states are also allowed to retain this revenue. In effect, the tax has been assigned to the states. Thus, the tax is administered, collected, and retained by the exporting state, on the basis of 'origin'.

Although CST serves the purpose of regulating the flow of inter-state movement of goods, it is not compatible with the concept of a unified market in a federal country like India. It is contrary to inter-jurisdictional equity, causes cascading, discriminates against consuming states, hinders the formation of a common Indian market, and causes the levy of tax on exports to other states. Also, its procedural requirement of a C Form causes corruption in the tax administration.

Phasing out of CST

Keeping in view these stated weaknesses and the demands of an open and liberalized economy, it was felt that an 'origin base' tax hampers inter-state trade and puts Indian industry and business at a considerable disadvantage in comparison to producers abroad, whose products are now being imported on an increasing scale. In addition, India has made a commitment in the summit meetings with heads of states of the SAARC region that all the SAARC countries should move towards free trade. In this context, it will not be possible to have any barriers to inter-state trade within India.

The realization that CST is distortionary and breaks the chain of transactions in the Indian common market made it imperative to abolish CST.

It was decided to phase out CST over time.[8] In doing so, the union government announced some compensatory measures for the states:

1. Withdrawal of the benefit of concessional CST rates on inter-state sales to government departments, against submission of Form D.
2. Enabling states to levy VAT on tobacco at the rate of 12.5 per cent.
3. Transferring to the states revenue from 33 services currently subject to service tax and assigning 44 new services to them (as and when taxed).
4. Filling any gap through budgetary support during 2007–8, 2008–9, and 2009–10, in case the measures indicated in (1), (2), and (3) do not fully cover the revenue loss.

---

[8] It was initially decided to reduce CST by 1 per cent point every year to reduce it to zero by 31 March 2010. Accordingly, it was reduced to 2 per cent by 1 April 2008.

Notwithstanding the resolve to reduce CST every year by one percentage point, owing to declining revenue of the states, a further reduction in the CST rate has not been done. However, the decision to reduce CST to zero per cent with the introduction of GST is firm.

Along with reducing CST, a regulatory framework in terms of a tax information exchange system (TINXSYS) for effective tracking of inter-state transactions has also been put in place (for details see Purohit 2012). The process of setting up TINXSYS is complete and the required data is uploaded by the states from time to time.

Introducing Integrated GST

With the introduction of GST, inter-state supplies of goods and services will be taxed under a new tax known as the integrated goods and services tax (IGST). Whenever a dealer enters an inter-state transaction, he will not pay state GST or central GST on that transaction. Instead he will pay IGST on value addition after adjusting available credit of IGST, CGST, and SGST on his purchases. The IGST rate will be equal to the rate of CGST plus SGST. It will be collected by the central government. The exporting state will transfer to the centre the credit of SGST used in the payment of IGST. The importing dealer will claim IGST credit while discharging his output tax liability in his own state. The centre will transfer to the importing state the IGST credit used in the payment of SGST. The relevant information will also be submitted to the central agency which will act as a clearing house mechanism, verify the claims, and inform the respective governments to transfer the funds.

This system will be superior to the existing CST model or any other model prevalent in the other federations in the world. In brief, the IGST model will have the following advantages:

1. It will maintain an uninterrupted input tax credit (ITC) chain on inter-state transactions;
2. No upfront payment of tax or substantial blockage of funds for the inter-state seller or buyer;
3. No refund claim in the exporting state, as ITC is used up while paying the tax; and
4. It will be a self-monitoring model.

Weaknesses in the Existing Dual VAT

The description of the existing system of dual VAT, as given earlier, indicates that it is characterized by some weaknesses.

First, CenVAT continues to be levied on goods manufactured or produced in India, which gives rise to definitional and valuation issues. In addition, manufacturing forms a narrow base and creates several impediments in an efficient and neutral tax system.

Second, the centre taxes services but that has been attempted independent of commodity taxes levied by the centre or the states. While it has broadened the tax base, its structure remains complex. The tax is levied on specified services, classified in different categories. This approach has spawned many disputes about the scope of each category. Also, there is no standardized nomenclature for services such as HSN for goods. The states are precluded from taxing services. This arrangement has posed difficulties in the taxation of goods supplied as a part of a composite works contract involving a supply of both goods and services, and under leasing contracts, which entail a transfer of the right to use goods without any transfer of their ownership. While these problems have been addressed by amending the Constitution to bring such transactions within the ambit of state taxation (by deeming a tax on them to be a tax on the sale or purchase of goods), services per se remain outside the scope of state taxation powers. This limitation is unsatisfactory.

Third, tax cascading occurs under both central and state taxes. The most significant contributing factor to tax cascading is the partial coverage of central and state taxes. For example, oil and gas production, mining, agriculture, wholesale and retail trade, real estate construction, and a range of services remain outside the ambit of CenVAT and the service tax levied by the centre. The exempt sectors are not allowed to claim any credit for CenVAT or the service tax paid on their inputs. Similarly, under State VAT, no credits are allowed for inputs in the exempt sectors, which include the entire services sector, the real estate sector, agriculture, oil and gas production, and mining. Another major contributing factor to tax cascading is CST on inter-state sales, collected by the state of origin, and for which no credit is allowed by any level of government. Thus, tax cascading remains the most serious flaw in the current system. It increases the cost of production and puts Indian suppliers at a competitive disadvantage in the international market. It creates a bias in favour of imports, which do not bear the hidden burden of taxes on production inputs. It also detracts from a neutral application of tax to competing products. Even if the statutory rate is uniform, the effective tax rate (which consists of the statutory rate on finished products and the implicit or hidden tax on production inputs) can vary from product to product depending on the magnitude of the hidden tax on inputs used in their production and distribution.

The intended impact of government policy towards sectors or households may be negated by indirect or hidden taxation in a cascading system of taxes.

Fourth, in spite of improvements in the tax design and administration over the past few years, the systems at both the central and state levels remain complex. Their administration leaves a lot to be desired. The complexities under State VAT relate primarily to classification of goods to different tax rate schedules. Theoretically, one might expect that lower tax rates will be applied to basic necessities that are consumed largely by the poor. This is not the case under State VAT. The lowest rate of 1 per cent applies to precious metals and jewellery, and related products—hardly likely to be ranked highly from the distributional perspective. The middle rate of 4 per cent applies to selected basic necessities and also a range of industrial inputs and IT products. In fact, basic necessities fall into three categories—exempt from tax, taxable at 4 per cent, and taxable at the standard rate of 12.5 per cent. The classification appears to be arbitrary, with no well-accepted theoretical underpinning. Whatever the political merits of this approach, it is not conducive to lower compliance costs. Most retailers find it difficult to determine the tax rate applicable to a given item without referring to legislative schedules. Consumers are even less aware of the tax rates applicable to various items. This gives rise to leakages and rent seeking.

Introducing GST

Recognizing the weaknesses of the existing dual VAT, efforts were made to have further reforms involving the introduction of a goods and services tax (GST). It is planned that GST will be introduced with effect from the 1 April 2012.

Like VAT, GST is also a tax on consumption. Its final and total burden is fully and exclusively borne by domestic consumers of goods and services. Since it is a tax on domestic consumption, no GST is charged on goods or services exported. It is an alternative mechanism of collecting tax. In many respects it is equivalent to a last point retail sales tax.

GST is a multi-point sales tax levied as a proportion of value added (that is, sales minus purchases, which is equivalent to wages plus profits). To illustrate, let us assume dealer A to be a raw material producer, B to be a manufacturer, C to be a wholesaler, and D to be a retailer. Dealer A sells his produce at Rs 100 and pays tax at the rate of 10 per cent. As dealer A is a producer of primary products his inputs can be assumed to be zero.[9] The sale price of Rs 100 will be the purchase price for dealer B, who is a manufacturer. This dealer will incur wages, salaries, and other manufacturing expenses and to all this he will add interest and his own profit. Assume that after adding all these costs, his sale price is Rs 200. On this sale price the gross tax (at the rate of 10 per cent) will be Rs 20. As dealer A has already paid tax on Rs 100 dealer B will get credit for this tax. Therefore, his net GST liability will be Rs 20 minus Rs 10 (tax paid on goods and services). That is, dealer B will pay only Rs 10 to the government. Similarly, the sale price of Rs 300 by dealer C will have a net GST liability of Rs 10 (Rs 30 – Rs 20 = Rs 10), and the sale price of Rs 400 by dealer D will also have net a GST liability of Rs 10 (Rs 40 – Rs 30 = Rs 10). This indicates that GST is a tax on each stage of the production and distribution process. The burden of paying GST falls on final consumers only. Thus, it is a broad-based tax covering the value added by each commodity and service in a firm during all stages of production and distribution. The difference between VAT (as levied so far in India) and GST (as now being proposed to be levied in India), is that under the former input credit is given only for the use of goods as input but under the latter, all goods and services used claim input credit.

The basic objective of a transition to GST is to have an efficient, effective, and taxpayer-friendly system of taxation of goods and services in line with best international practices. Also, there is a need for preserving the sovereign powers of the central and state governments in taxation matters.

In doing so, the proposed structure for GST (unlike the current system of VAT which encompasses goods only) will cover both goods and services. Both the goods and services will be part of the input credit claimed by the dealer of goods or supplier of services. For example, a manufacturer using raw material as inputs will claim input credit for the raw material and will also claim credit for the tax paid on the telephone service or the transport service that he uses for the manufacturing activity.

The Empowered Committee of State Finance Ministers (EC) constituted a JWG to give recommendations regarding a detailed framework to be adopted for GST. The JWG recommended a dual GST as it felt that a single harmonized GST is not possible given the prevailing centre–state relationship as well as the federal character of the economy.

---

[9] In practice the producers of primary products might use inputs. For example, a farmer uses seeds, feeds, fertilizer, pesticides, etc., for which he will have to be given credit.

Coverage, Base, and the Rate of GST

The proposed GST, as recommended by the EC and ratified by the central government, will replace the existing CenVAT[10] and service tax levied by the central government and State VAT and some other taxes levied by state governments.

The JWGgst recommended that GST should subsume all the indirect taxes on supply of goods or services: Central excise duties and additional excise duties levied on pan masala, petroleum, and tobacco products, and those levied under Additional Duties of Excise (Goods of Special Importance) Act, 1957; additional customs duty in the nature of countervailing duties; CVD and other domestic taxes imposed on imports to achieve a level playing field between domestic and imported goods (which are currently classified as customs duty); cesses levied by the union—cess on manufactured bidis, rubber, tea, coffee, and cess on unmanufactured tobacco; and surcharges levied by the union—national calamity contingent duty, education cess, and special additional duty of excise on motor spirit and high speed diesel (HSD).

It is to be noted that some of these levies are earmarked for predetermined purposes—education or upliftment of workers engaged in a particular industry, development of technology, etc. These do not currently form part of the CenVAT chain and are levied under independent Acts, legislated by different ministries. These levies, therefore, should be out of the purview of GST.

The JWGgst further recommended that the state GST should include in its purview State VAT, purchase tax, state excise duty, entertainment tax, luxury tax, octroi, entry tax in lieu of octroi, taxes on lottery, betting and gambling, and tax on consumption or sale of electricity.

The JWGgst report rightly pointed out that taxes on petroleum crude and its products contribute about 40 per cent of the revenue from central excise duty. Similarly, it contributes significantly to states' exchequers. Given the current scenario, these products are out of VAT. The JWGgst

---

[10] Central excise duties in this context include additional excise duties levied on pan masala, petroleum, and tobacco products, and those levied under Additional Duties of Excise (Goods of Special Importance) Act, 1957; additional customs duties in the nature of countervailing duties; CVD and other domestic taxes imposed on imports to achieve a level playing field between domestic and imported goods (which are currently classified as customs duty); cesses levied by the union (cess on manufactured bidis, rubber, tea, coffee, and cess on unmanufactured tobacco); and surcharges levied by the union (national calamity contingent duty, education cess, and special additional duty of excise on motor spirit and high speed diesel).

also recommended that petroleum crude, motor spirit (including Aviation turbine fuer [ATF]), and HSD should be put outside GST reflecting administrative considerations as is the prevailing practice in India. Taxation of the remaining products could be under GST.

With these central and state taxes being subsumed under GST, the proposed GST will have two components—Central GST (levied by the centre) and State GST (levied by the states). The rates of these two components will be prescribed separately keeping in view revenue considerations, total tax burden, and the acceptability of the tax. The effective rate of State VAT is currently 12.5 per cent, while the CenVAT rate is 10 per cent. Hence, the combined tax rate is 22.5 per cent. This has to be reduced to approximately 15 per cent, given the rate structure around the world.

In the immediate run, therefore, it is important that many of the central and state taxes that do not affect the GST system be excluded from GST. These taxes can be considered in the long run while designing a comprehensive state GST, wherein the centre withdraws from domestic trade taxes.

Finally, the overall tax rate at the last stage of transactions will be transparent. As of today, the given rate of State VAT causes considerable evasion of tax; a combined tax rate, of say 20 per cent, will only further accelerate evasion. Therefore, some remedial administrative measures are essential.

Although the GST rate structure is yet not crystal clear, over time, it has been given some perceptible shape. Various rates have been suggested by different government bodies at different time.

Initially, the EC suggested that the rate should be in the vicinity of the revenue neutral rate. Given the present rate of 10 per cent on goods (with some rates lower and some more than the 8 per cent rate) and 10 per cent on services under CenVAT and 12.5 per cent (with some other rate categories of 4 per cent, etc.) under State VAT, the revenue neutral rate will work out to be around 20 per cent—with the centre levying 12 per cent and the states levying 8 per cent.

It was, however, felt that a high GST rate of this level at the retail level will pose problems in the administration of the tax. With the noted exception of Scandinavian countries, where the standard rate is 25 per cent, only a few countries have been successful in levying a high GST rate. Successful models of GST suggest a tax rate in the region of 10 per cent or less.

It is suggested that the proposed GST rate should preferably be in the vicinity of 15 per cent of which a 7 per cent rate to be levied by Central GST and 8 per cent by State GST. This could be accomplished by readjusting the bases of both the components of GST, given the fact that approximately 40 per cent of CenVAT and State VAT (accruing from petroleum products), is not under VAT.

In addition, the Thirteenth Finance Commission (ThFC) suggested a rate structure of 5 per cent for CGST and 7 per cent for SGST. However, the fact that the design given by ThFC proposed radical changes in the fiscal space of both the centre and states which have not been accepted by the states, who are key partners in tax reform.

In addition to this, the EC suggested that the GST structure could afford to have two rate categories, that is 4 per cent on a select group of necessities and a 8 per cent standard rate on all items except for a special rate of 1 per cent on silver and bullion. Also, there will be a small list of exempt items.

The central government has come out with a proposal to have a single rate structure from 2014–15 onwards. However, in 2011–12 there were three-tier rate categories—6 per cent on essentials, 8 per cent on services, and 10 per cent as the standard rate. The standard rate will come down to 9 per cent in 2012–13 and will be 8 per cent in subsequent years. Similarly, the 6 per cent rate on essentials will increase to 8 per cent in 2014–15.

In both the scenarios petroleum products (which will be out of GST coverage) will be taxed at a higher rate of 20 per cent or more. While tobacco will be part of the GST base, the centre will levy a special excise to yield larger resources. It is, therefore, assumed that the tax rate for tobacco will almost be the same as at present.

Inter-state transactions will be governed by an 'integrated GST' (IGST) and, therefore, there will be no 'tax-exporting' to importing states. All inputs including capital goods will be given a set-off. Also, exports will be zero-rated. The proposed GST will thus be a consumption variant of VAT.

The proposed GST rate should be levied on all goods and services with a few exceptions. As of now, the notable exemptions under CenGST include those granted to small-scale industries and units under the backward area schemes. Exemptions from service tax should also be unified and the tax be made a general tax rather than a selective tax. On the same lines, under State VAT also all exempted goods need to be brought under the tax net. In doing so, there is a politico-economic argument to leave out essential commodities like food, medicines, and clothing from the tax base. However, empirical exercises indicate that the benefit of an exemption to a necessity is proportional to the amount spent on tax-exempted items. Hence, such exemptions benefit upper income families more because of their larger spending power. Hence, all these items must be brought under the tax net and the government should provide direct subsidy to poor consumers.

The next step involves making the Central GST and State GST bases similar. This will entail giving all the services to the states, except a few services to be placed under the negative list.

There should be sumptuary excises imposed on a few (not more than a dozen) select commodities. This will ensure the additional mobilization required to have a revenue neutral rate for Central GST.

A low rate will ensure an effective GST. The EC and central government should consider having GST rates in the vicinity of 15 per cent. Over a period of time the states and the centre are reaching to a consensus of having a 16 per cent rate; 8 per cent for each tier of the government.

Constitutional Amendments

Since the implementation of GST requires constitutional amendments to empower both the centre and the states to levy the proposed tax, the finance minister tabled the Constitution Amendment Bill in the Parliament[11] on 20 March 2011. The Bill has been cleared by the union cabinet and will now be referred to the Parliamentary Standing Committee for scrutiny.

The Constitutional Amendment Bill is essential to enable the centre to levy tax beyond manufacture and the states to levy a service tax. This bill will help in introducing GST and thus having a landmark reform in the indirect tax system in the country. This will be a single levy tax and will aim at creating an integrated national market for goods and services by replacing the plethora of indirect taxes levied by the centre and the states.

While scrutinizing this Bill it is hoped that the Standing Committee will be able to make the necessary changes to bring about a consensus between the centre and the states regarding important issues.

The centre has already proposed three drafts of the Bill in the recent past. In the first draft, circulated in July 2010, the central government introduced changes in the Constitution for levy of GST in place of excise by the centre and sales tax by the states. Necessary changes were proposed in the union and state lists and their related clauses.

---

[11] Bill No. 22 of 2011.

For the administration of the tax, the Bill suggested creating a GST Council of India and a Dispute Settlement Authority by a Presidential order.

While consensus has emerged on clauses regarding sharing of taxing powers, special powers, and devolution of tax, disagreements arose with issues relating to the proposed GST Council and the Dispute Settlement Authority. This was primarily due to the fact that in this draft, the centre had proposed that the union finance minister will have veto powers in the GST Council. It also proposed that the changes in GST could only be carried out with the consent of the union finance minister and a two-third majority of the states in the council.

After the states strongly opposed these proposals, the finance ministry came out with a somewhat watered down version in a second draft which stated that every decision of the council would only be taken after members present at a meeting reached a consensus. As this draft did not find favour with the states, in its attempt to break the deadlock, the centre sent the EC a third draft of the Bill, which proposed the creation of a GST Council through an act of Parliament instead of a Presidential order. Also, it is proposed that the decisions of the GST Council will be recommendatory and not binding on the states. However, issues regarding the composition and functioning of the GST Council have not been clearly spelt out.

Out of 26 states present at the EC meeting held on 11 February 2011, ten states opposed the third draft. Some states felt that the second draft was better than the third one because it clearly laid down the functioning and composition of the GST Council. While the Madhya Pradesh finance minister said that this will destroy the fiscal autonomy of the state, the Gujarat finance minister was of the view that the new draft amendment was retrograde in nature and completely against the principles of fiscal federalism.

The bone of contention preventing a consensus on the bill is the issue of fiscal autonomy of the states. As is evident, the existing division of tax powers between the centre and the states is such that the former collects 66 per cent of the resources leaving a meagre 34 per cent for the states. Hence, the states do not want to surrender their tax powers any further.

In this context, the states feel that the structure of the GST Council, as proposed in the second amendment to the Bill, is biased towards the centre. Also, the third amendment leaves the structure of the Council undefined, and this is all the more dangerous. The states, therefore, want to have a council which defines the structure before the bill is passed and it should also provide equal authority to them.

On the other hand, the centre seems to have the view that if the states are given more powers then this might harm the interest of the centre in due course and the centre will not be able to do anything to restrict this.

To remove this deadlock and to get the GST ball rolling, it is suggested that the GST Council should be constituted on the pattern of the present EC which has had an excellent track record of reforming the tax system over the last decade.

Accordingly, the proposed council should consist of the union finance minister and all finance ministers of states and union territories as its members. However, unlike the present EC, which is a 'Society' registered under the Societies Registration Act, the council should be a constitutional body and should have a defined regulatory authority with strict punitive powers.

In this composition of the GST Council, the centre would not be in a dominating position but its revenue interest will automatically be taken care of due to the fact that any change being effected will affect the centre and the states in a similar fashion. Hence, the council will not be able to take any decision against the centre's interests.

One of the issues that the standing committee should seriously consider relates to GST coverage which relates to the exclusion of some specific items that are presently within the ambit of sales tax or excise duty. The Constitution Amendment Bill limits GST coverage by excluding petroleum products which are taxable under sales tax levied by the states and the union excise duty levied by the centre. Though this has been done with the full consent of the states and concurrence of the centre, it needs reconsideration from the point of view of a rational tax policy.

It is proposed that the scope and definition of GST should not exclude petroleum products even if GST is not presently levied on these items. Excluding these items from the definition and coverage of GST in the Constitutional Amendment Bill will not provide any flexibility to levy GST on these items in the future if the states and the centre desire to do so. This will then require another constitutional amendment to enable them to levy GST on these items.

For a futuristic approach, it will be prudent not to confine the scope of the tax under the bindings of the Constitution. What is to be taxed or not taxed or what should be GST's coverage should be left to the EC or to the proposed GST Council. The Constitution should demarcate the broad areas of taxing powers as has been the case with sales tax and union excise duty in the past.

Here it is important to note that the economic rationale of excluding these commodities from the purview of GST is solely based on revenue considerations. No other considerations of tax policy or tax administration have gone into excluding petroleum products from the purview of GST.

The long-term perspective of a rational tax policy for GST, however, shows that at present these taxes constitute more than half of the retail price of motor fuel. In a scenario where motor fuel prices are deregulated, the taxation policy will have to be flexible and linked to global crude oil prices to ensure that prices are held stable and the pressure exerted on the economy during increasing price trends can be absorbed.

Further, the trend of taxation of motor fuel all over the world suggests that these items should not be used merely for raising resources. These items must be taxed according to the principle of 'green taxes'. Therefore, the trend all over the world is to bring these items first under GST and then levy additional taxes on them according to the quantum of pollution emitted by vehicles.

It is, therefore, important that the policy decision on whether petroleum products should be taxed under GST or subjected to supplementary taxes along with GST or kept completely out of GST (to be taxed under sales tax or union excise duties) should not be confined to the constraints of the Constitution. States and the centre should be free to levy GST as and when the need arises. Failing this, if the states later want to go in for a levy of GST on these items they will have to wait for a constitutional amendment. It will be prudent to leave the authority to exclude or include these items entirely to the Empowered Committee or the GST Council. Also, taxes on these items must be based on the principles of 'road user taxes' or 'fuel-taxes'.

Issues in Administration of GST

The road map for administering GST has become a perplexing issue. The main concern is about the authority to govern the tax, which will determine the cost of compliance by taxpayers.

The JWG on GST (JWGgst) appointed by the Empowered Committee (EC) suggested that taxpayers below a defined threshold limit would be accountable for the day-to-day administrative matters (including registration, collection, and ITC issues for both CGST and SGST) to the state authorities and the taxpayers above the prescribed turnover will be accountable to both central and state authorities.

The EC further considered these recommendations and put forth its view in 'A Model and Road Map for GST in India' (April 2008). Accordingly, the assignment of administrative tasks will be based on the threshold limits for gross turnover of goods or services of dealers. These have been categorized as:

1. Gross turnover of goods up to Rs 1.5 crore should be assigned exclusively to the states;
2. Gross turnover of services up to Rs 1.5 crore should be assigned exclusively to the centre; and
3. Gross turnover of above Rs 1.5 crore should be assigned to both the governments: for the administration of CGST to the centre and for the administration of SGST to the states.

This design for the administration of GST will not only involve both the tiers of government but will also require interaction between dealers and the officers of tax administration at the centre as well as in the states.

However, keeping in view the tenets of taxpayer convenience and least compliance cost, it is suggested that instead of involving both the governments in all the administrative procedures it will be rational to assign specific tasks to the centre and the states.

Therefore, the following roadmap is proposed for a rational administration of GST in India.

First, there should be a thorough re-engineering of the department of GST (that is, the SGST and CGST departments) at both the levels. This must be done in such a way that the responsibility, accountability, and authority of each tax department at the central and state levels can be established.

Second, given the limited number of officials at the central level, it is proposed that these officers be assigned special tasks to monitor the operations of a large number of dealers under CGST and SGST. Day-to-day operations relating to registration, payment of tax, and submission of returns for all the dealers (irrespective of their size) should be assigned to the states. That is the dealers will register and submit their returns to the state department where the dealer is located. In general, the dealers will interact with one tax authority only.

Third, payment of tax by a registered dealer will be made in the bank accounts of the concerned government. That is, tax receipts from SGST will be paid in the account of the state government and the tax receipts from CGST in the bank account of the central government.

Fourth, cross-verification of documents must be strengthened under the new regime. In the absence of proper cross-verification, dealers paying tax and claim undue credit for taxable sales. Tax evasion can be prevented by setting up departments similar to centralized, as well as the regional, anti-evasion organization in France. The central organization called the National Directorate of Verification, looks into cases of verification involving transactions above 300 million francs. Its authority encompasses both national and international tax cases. The Regional Directorate of Verification examines cases up to 300 million francs and covers districts or divisions. Drawing on the experiences of countries like France, it is proposed that this role be bifurcated between SGST and CGST officials. The former should look into the issues of cross-verification within state boundaries and the latter should deal with tax cases having inter-state and inter-country ramifications.

Fifth, auditing is essential to minimize the gap between reported tax and the actual statutory tax liability of a taxpayer. Therefore, there is need for a proper audit plan to cover different economic activities and a large variety of taxpayers, classified according to the level of turnover of goods and services. Also, it should include different procedures to identify and appropriately deal with non-compliance. Since a GST audit (whether for SGST or for CGST) involves local factors as well as inter-state issues, the role has to be assigned to both SGST as well as CGST officials. In general, cases involving inter-state boundaries should be taken up by CGST officials. This will entail proper coordination between top-level SGST as well as CGST officials in the selection of cases.

Finally, MIS has to be an integrated activity of SGST and CGST offices. The integration of information for SGST, CGST, customs, and income tax through a PAN number and the tax information exchange system (TINXSYS) will be an essential component of GST administration. While these aspects will remain with the concerned authorities, officials from other tax departments will also have access to such information whenever required.

This roadmap for the two tiers of governments will facilitate a functional allocation of tax responsibilities according to accountability, responsibility, and authority.

It is also extremely important that the business process model of GST is so developed that there is no need for taxpayers to interact with the tax department, unless called to do so. This will narrow down corruption. With this in view, it is suggested that a feasibility is attempted to study the structure and the possible administrative system to have a slab-based 'compound tax' for taxpayers. This will be a welcome reform to free taxpayers from needless harassment and end corruption in tax collection. This will involve the setting up of a business process model through the introduction of information and communication technology (ICT) that will help small as well as large dealers.

Conclusion

Commencing from a small turnover tax in the 1930s, India has come a long way in reforming its complex commodity tax system by introducing a dual VAT. It is now proposed to have a dual GST. However, this comes with a zero-rate CST, which should in the ultimate analysis be scrapped completely. Also, the dual GST model will be implemented in such a way that it is collected by one agency and paid to respective governments. More importantly, it is required that the interaction of taxpayers with the tax department is reduced considerably in order to end corruption. This is a must for the reforms to be implemented rationally.

ANNEXURE A9.2

Direct Tax Code (DTC)

Taxes on income and property assigned to the union government have become extremely complex over time. The plethora of exemptions and tax preferences to fulfil a variety of objectives has not only eroded the base, but has also complicated the tax system. The situation has led not only to high administrative and compliance costs but also significant distortions in resource allocation. In this context, to improve the efficiency and equity of our tax system by introducing moderate levels of taxation and expanding the tax base, the cabinet approved a new tax code, DTC, in August 2010 that is proposed to be effective from 1 April 2012, which when enacted will replace the existing archaic income and wealth tax laws in the country.

The purpose of the new code is to simplify the enormous complexities in direct taxes since the enactment of the Income Tax Act, 1961. This is a key reform initiative that is aimed at widening the tax net and increasing federal revenues.

The general provisions of DTC are:

1. It uses a new concept of 'financial year' in place of 'previous year' and assessment year.
2. Levy of surcharges and education cess is done away with.
3. Only two categories of taxpayers is proposed—'residents and non-residents'. The category of 'not ordinary residents' is to be abolished.
4. Income is proposed to be classified into two broad groups: income from ordinary sources and income from special sources. Income from ordinary sources refers to income from employment, house property, business, capital gains, and residuary sources. Income from the other category includes specified income of non-residents and winnings from lotteries and horse races.

The key proposals of the proposed DTC are now discussed.

Personal Income Tax

DTC attempts to broaden the base by doing away with several exemptions and preferences. In doing so, it seeks to widen the base of individual income tax in a number of ways. Benefits provided by employers such as the value of rent free or concessional accommodation; value of any leave travel concession; medical reimbursement; and the value of free or concessional medical treatment paid for, or provided by, is included in taxable income. Similarly, limited deductions will be allowed in medical expenses, interest on loans taken for higher education, rent paid, and donations to specified causes. This rationalizes and reduces the scope of deductions to a considerable extent when compared to the present regime.

Further, the code increases tax exemptions on income up to Rs 2.5 lakh for resident senior citizens and Rs 2 lakh for all individuals including women residents. Under the new regime 'gender distinction', in terms of a higher exemption limit for women taxpayers is removed.

Removing Housing Loan Exemptions

An important area where a substantial change is sought to be made to limit deductions is with respect to housing loans. Currently, interest paid on a housing loan is deductible from total income irrespective of whether the house is earning a rental income or not. In addition to this, repayment of the principal can also be utilized as part of investment under Section 80c. However, under the proposed code loans repaid will no longer be deductible. Also, interest paid on the loan will be deductible only when the house earns rental income and will be limited to the extent of rent received.

Taxation of Income from Employment, Retirement Benefits, and Perquisites

The new code proposes that certain items like income from an approved provident fund, superannuation fund, and new pension schemes will be deductible within the prescribed limit for calculating the gross salary of an individual. Exemptions such as house rent allowance, leave encashment, and medical reimbursement are retained. Exemption for medical reimbursement is increased to Rs 50,000. Also allowances to meet personal expenses have been introduced. Retirement benefits received by employees are proposed to be exempt up to a specified limit for all employees. Retirement benefits will include gratuity, voluntary retirement, commuted pension linked to gratuity received, and leave encashment salary at the time of superannuation.

Leave travel concessions and non-monetary prerequisites have been removed. Withholding tax on salaries is proposed to be part of the overall withholding tax provisions on all payments.

Taxation of Income from House Property

Regarding taxation of income from house property, DTC proposes:

1. In case of a let-out house property, gross rent will be the amount of rent received or receivable for the financial year and 20 per cent of the gross rent is deductible for maintenance and repairs.
2. Gross rent to be computed on the basis of actual rent received and not on a presumptive basis.
3. For a self-occupied property an individual or HUF will be eligible for deduction on account of interest on the housing loan for acquisition or construction of such house property (subject to a ceiling of Rs 1.5 lakh) from the gross total income.

Exempt-Exempt-Exempt Regime for Savings

DTC proposes to have all long-term retrial savings schemes in the prevailing Exempt-Exempt-Exempt (EEE) scheme. Under this method, contributions towards certain savings are deductible from income, the accumulation/accretions are also exempt from any tax incidence till such time as they remain invested and all withdrawals at any time are subject to tax at the applicable marginal tax rate.

Capital Gains Tax

A major rationalization proposed in DTC is in the treatment of capital gains. According to the new code, income from transactions in all 'investment assets' will be computed under the head 'capital gains'. It provides that gains (losses) arising from the transfer of investment assets will be treated as capital gains (losses). These gains (losses) will be included in the total income of the financial year in which the investment asset is transferred. Income under the head 'capital gains' will be considered as income from ordinary sources in case of all taxpayers including non-residents. It will be taxed at the rate applicable to that taxpayer.

In general, capital gains will be equal to the full consideration from the transfer of an investment asset minus the cost of acquisition of the asset, cost of improvements thereof, and transfer-related incidental expenses. However, in the case of a capital asset which is transferred anytime after one year from the end of the financial year in which it is acquired, the cost of acquisition and cost of improvements will be indexed to compute capital gains.

Additional deductions over and above the actual/indexed cost of acquisition/improvements have been provided in computing capital gains for various investment assets depending on their nature and holding period:

1. On transfer of equity shares or equity oriented mutual funds which have been held for more than one year and where STT has been paid on the transfer, a deduction equal to 100 per cent of the capital gains.
2. On transfer of equity shares or equity oriented mutual funds which have been held for less than one year and where STT has been paid on the transfer, a deduction equal to 50 per cent on the capital gains.

The proposed scheme is therefore especially beneficial for the low and middle income categories of taxpayers as they are to be taxed at their applicable marginal rate of 10 per cent or 20 per cent after the specified deduction for computing adjusted capital gains. The specific rate of deduction for computing adjusted capital gains will be finalized in the context of overall tax rates.

As there will be a shift from nil rate of tax on listed equity shares and units equity oriented funds held for more than one year, an appropriate transition regime will be provided, if required.

For taxation of capital gains arising from transfer of investment assets held for more than one year (other than listed equity shares or units of equity oriented funds), the base date for determining the cost of acquisition will be shifted from 1 April 1981 to 1 April 2000. Capital gains will be computed after allowing indexation on this raised base. Capital gains on such assets will be included in the total income of a taxpayer and will be taxed at the applicable rate. However, in case of capital gains arising from transfer of any investment asset held for less than one year from the end of the financial year in which it is acquired will be computed without any specified deduction or indexation. It will be included in the total income and will be charged to tax at the rate applicable to the taxpayer.

Income of Foreign Institutional Investors

Under DTC, a major area of dispute is whether income from transactions in the capital market should be characterized as business income or as capital gains. A foreign company is not allowed to invest in securities in India except under a special regime provided for foreign institutional investors (FIIs). This regime is regulated by the Securities Exchange Board of India (SEBI) under SEBI regulations for FIIs. The regulations provide that a FII can make investments in specified securities in India. A majority of the FIIs are reporting their income from such investments as capital gains. However, some of them are characterizing such income as 'business income' and consequently claiming total exemption from taxation in the absence of a permanent establishment in India. This leads to avoidable litigation. It is, therefore, proposed that income arising from purchase and sale of securities by a FII will be deemed to be income chargeable under the head 'capital gains'. This will simplify the system of taxation, bring certainty, eliminate litigation, and be easier to administer.

Further, capital gains arising to FIIs will not be subjected to TDS and they will be required to pay tax by way of advance tax on such gains as is the existing practice.

Corporation Tax

The new code proposes to make some significant changes in the treatment of the corporate sector.

In computing the taxable profits of an enterprise, its assets are segregated into business and investment assets. While value realized from the sale of the former will be included in the computation of the profits of the enterprise, in case of the latter, there is a separate regime for treating capital gains.

Reduction in the Corporate Tax Rate

DTC has proposed a corporate tax rate of 30 per cent (with or without surcharge and cess) for a domestic company which is less than the existing rate of 33.22 per cent including both surcharge and cess. It has also been proposed that the tax rate for foreign companies will now be the same as that for domestic companies instead of 40 per cent as per Income Tax Act. Dividend distribution tax (DDT) will continue at the rate of 15 per cent. Income distributed by mutual funds to unit holders of equity-oriented funds will pay a tax of 5 per cent of the income distributed. Similar will be the case for life insurance companies when they distribute income to policy holders of equity-oriented life insurance schemes. Deductions will be provided for DDT paid by subsidiary available against the DDT liability of the holding company.

For FIIs, if they have earned an income from such investments, majority of FIIs classify this as capital gains but some FIIs classify it as business income claiming total exemptions for taxation. It is therefore proposed by DTC that income on transactions from securities by FIIs will be chargeable under capital gains. FIIs will be required to pay such tax as advanced tax.

Further, a reduction in the tax rate is combined with a reduction in the number of exemptions available within the statutes. While exemptions relating to the development of infrastructure units remain, most of the other exemptions in the existing tax regime do not find place in the new code. Specifically, exemptions for investments in specified geographical areas, those related to the information technology and BPO sector, as well as those related to exports from special economic zones (SEZs) are excluded from the code.

Minimum Alternate Tax

Although, DTC earlier proposed to levy a minimum alternate tax (MAT) on the value of assets, it has now been revised and MAT will continue to be levied as in the present regime, that is, on the basis of book profits. It is proposed under DTC that the MAT rate will be increased to 20 per cent. However, no specification is made for credit of MAT.

MAT will be applicable to SEZ developers and SEZ units, contrary to the existing provision. The tax holiday under DTC will only be made available for units which are set up prior to the coming into force of DTC. Units in SEZs are entitled to get 100 per cent income tax exemption on export income for the first five years and 50 per cent for the next five years. They also get exemption on 50 per cent of the ploughed back export profits for the next five years after the first 10 years. SEZ developers will be subject to DDT similar to SEZ units.

Taxation of Non-profit Organizations

Presently, non-profit organizations (NPOs) enjoy exemption on their donations as well as any surplus that they create under Sections 80G or 35(1)(3) of the Income Tax Act. However, DTC proposes a tax exemption threshold limit beyond which NPO incomes will be taxed.

According to the code, NPOs will be able to carry forward 15 per cent of their surplus income, or 10 per cent of their gross receipts, to the next year as exempt from tax. The carried forward amount will have to be used within three years from the end of the relevant financial year.

Under DTC, incomes of public religious institutions will be exempt from tax subject to their fulfilling the following conditions:

1. It is to be registered under the code.
2. The trust/institution will apply its income wholly for public religious purposes.
3. It will be registered under the state law, if any.
4. It is established for the benefit of the general public.
5. The trust/ institution will file the return of tax bases before the due date.
6. It will maintain books of account and obtain an audit report from a qualified accountant in case its gross receipts exceed a prescribed limit.
7. The funds or assets of the trust/institution will be invested or held, at any time during the financial year, in specified permitted forms or modes.

8. The funds or assets of the trust/institution will not be used or applied or deemed to have been used or applied, directly or indirectly, for the benefit of interested persons.

Further, the code proposes to withdraw mandatory re-registration provisions for existing NPOs and provides that such organizations will only need to submit additional information or documents to facilitate administration under the new regime.

Partly religious and partly charitable institutions will also be treated as NPOs if they are registered under the code and income from charitable activities will also be liable to tax like other registered NPOs. The revised draft code also proposes to empower the central government to notify any NPO of public importance as an exempt entity.

Further, DTC proposes that tax exemption will be available to religious trusts and religious-cum-charitable trusts subject to laid down conditions.

Wealth Tax

DTC proposes certain changes in the levy of wealth tax. It is provided that every person, except non-profit organizations, will be liable to pay wealth tax on his/her net wealth. For the purpose of computing net wealth, any equity or preference shares held by a resident in a controlled foreign company will be considered taxable. Further, it has suggested that wealth tax will be levied on the same lines as provided in the Wealth Tax Act, 1957, that is, on specified unproductive assets.

Controlled Foreign Corporation

As an anti-avoidance measure, DTC proposes to introduce controlled foreign corporation (CFC) provisions. These will aim to tax the passive income of a foreign company which is controlled directly or indirectly by an Indian resident, where such income is not distributed resulting in tax deferral. In such a scenario, the proposed provisions will deem that the dividend has been distributed and thus, will be taxable in the hands of the resident shareholder.

General Anti-Avoidance Rule

A statutory general anti-avoidance rule (GAAR) can act as an effective deterrent and compliance tool against tax avoidance in an environment of moderate tax rates. In this context, DTC proposes to introduce GAAR to treat a transaction as a tax avoidance transaction, if it is undertaken with the main purpose of obtaining a 'tax benefit' and is entered into or carried on in a manner not normally employed for bonafide business purposes or is not at arm's length or abuses DTC's provisions or lacks economic substance.

According to the code, the power to invoke GAAR is bestowed with the commissioner of income tax. He is required to follow the principles of natural justice before declaring an arrangement as an impermissible avoidance arrangement. He will determine the tax consequences of such an impermissible avoidance arrangement and issue necessary directions to the assessing officer for making appropriate adjustments. The directions issued by him will be binding on the assessing officer.

Further, the code also proposes to follow certain safeguarding measures:

1. CBDT will issue guidelines on the circumstances under which GAAR may be invoked.
2. A threshold limit (possibly a monetary limit) will be prescribed for invoking GAAR.
3. The forum of dispute resolution panel (DRP) will be available where GAAR provisions are invoked.

Double Taxation Avoidance Agreement

The double taxation avoidance agreement (DTAA) provides for certainty on how and when income of a particular kind will be taxed and by which country to avoid double taxation of the same income. However, if two countries tax the same income, one based on the principle of residence and the other based on the principle of source, it could lead to double taxation of the same income. Hence, countries have agreed on certain principles to avoid double taxation and accordingly, entered into DTAAs.

According to the existing provisions in the Income Tax Act, between domestic law and the relevant DTAA, the one which is more beneficial to the taxpayer will apply. However, one of the exemptions to this is taxing foreign companies at a rate higher than that for domestic companies.

DTC proposes to retain the existing provisions of the Income Tax Act. However, DTAA will not have preferential status over domestic law in the following circumstances:

1. when GAAR is invoked, or
2. when controlled foreign corporation provisions are invoked or
3. when branch profit tax is levied.

Concept of Residence in Case of a Company Incorporated Outside India

DTC provides that a company incorporated in India will always be treated as a resident in India. However, a company incorporated abroad (foreign company) can either be resident or non-resident in India. It has been proposed in DTC that a foreign company will be treated as a resident in India if, at any time in the financial year, the control and management of its affairs is situated 'wholly or partly' in India (it need not be wholly situated in India, as at present).

It is therefore proposed that a company incorporated outside India will be treated as a resident in India if its 'place of effective management' is situated in India. The term will have the same meaning as currently laid down in the Tenth Schedule to the code:

'Place of effective management of the company' means:

(i) the place where the board of directors of the company or its executive directors, as the case may be, make their decisions; or
(ii) in a case where the board of directors routinely approve the commercial and strategic decisions made by the executive directors or officers of the company, the place where such executive directors or officers of the company perform their functions.

As an anti-avoidance measure, in line with internationally accepted practices, it is also proposed to introduce controlled foreign corporation provisions so as to provide that passive income earned by a foreign company which is controlled directly or indirectly by a resident in India, and where such income is not distributed to shareholders resulting in deferral of taxes, is deemed to have been distributed. Consequently, it will be taxable in India in the hands of resident shareholders as dividend received from the foreign company.

Conclusion

The proposed DTC is part of the government's tax reforms initiative to bring about wide-ranging and broad-based structural changes to the Indian direct tax system. It proposes to expand the tax base by doing away with various existing exemptions and preferences. In particular, the proposal to expand the tax base by rationalizing saving incentives, deductions for housing, and partial allowance for education and medical expenses will help expand the tax base and simplify the tax system.

References

Acharya, Sankar (2002), 'Managing India's External Economic Challenges in the 1990s', in M.S. Ahluwalia, Y.V. Reddy, and S.S. Tarapore (eds), *Macroeconomics and Monetary Policy*, pp. 215–44. New Delhi: Oxford University Press.

———— (2003), *India's Economy: Some Issues and Answers*, New Delhi: Academic Foundation.

———— (2005), 'Thirty Years of Tax Reforms in India', *Economic and Political Weekly*, 14–20 May, XL(20): 2061–70.

Aggarwal, P.K. (1995), 'India: A Review of Its Tax System and Recent Tax Reform Proposals', Paper presented at a symposium on Fiscal Reform and Economic Development, organized by the Faculty of Economics, Institute for Economic and Social Research, University of Indonesia, in cooperation with the EDAP–UNDP, 5–6 September.

Agha, Ali and Jonathan Haughton (1996), 'Designing VAT Systems: Some Efficiency Considerations', *Review of Economics and Statistics*, 78: 303–8.

Ahluwalia, Isher and I.M.D. Little (1998), *India's Economic Reforms and Development*. New Delhi: Oxford University Press.

Ahluwalia, Montek (2000), 'Economic Performance of States in Post-reform Period', *Economic and Political Weekly*, 6 May, XXXV(19): 1637–48.

Ahmad, Ehtisham and Nicholas Stern (1991), *The Theory and Practice of Tax Reform in Developing Countries*. Cambridge: Cambridge University Press.

Ahuja, G. and R. Gupta (2006), *Income Tax Mini Ready Reckoner including Wealth Tax*. New Delhi: Bharat Law House Pvt. Ltd.

Alm James, Patricia Annez, and Arbind Modi (2004), 'Stamp Duties in Indian States: A Case for Reform', Policy Research Working Paper 3413. Washington, DC: The World Bank.

Anand, Mukesh, Amaresh Bagchi, and Tapas Sen (2001), 'Fiscal Discipline at the State Level: Perverse Incentives and Paths to Reform', Paper presented at NIPFP–World Bank Conference, New Delhi, May.

Angrish, A.C. (1972), *Direct Taxation of Agriculture in India with Special Reference to Land Revenue & Agricultural Income Tax*. Mumbai: Somaiya Publications Pvt. Ltd.

Anwar, Muhammad Sarfraj, S. Davies, and R.K. Sampath (1996), 'Causality Between Government Expenditures and Economic Growth: An Estimation Using Cointegration Techniques', *Public Finance*, 5(12): 166–84.

Asher, Mukul G. (2002), 'Globalization and Fiscal Policy', in Mukul G. Asher, David Newman, and Thomas P. Snyder (eds), *Public Policy in Asia*. London: Quorum Books.

Bagchi, Amaresh (1994), 'India's Tax Reforms: A Progress Report', *Economic and Political Weekly*, 22 October, XXIX(43): 2809–15.

——— (1997), 'Fiscal Management—The Federal Dimension', in Parthasarathi Shome (ed.), *Fiscal Policy, Public Policy and Governance*, pp. 273–97. New Delhi: Centax Publications Pvt. Ltd.

——— (1998), 'India's Fiscal Reform: Some Signposts', *Vikalp*, 23: 9–22.

——— (2001), 'Perspectives on Correcting Fiscal Imbalance in the Indian Economy: Some Comments', *ICRA Bulletin: Money and Finance*, 2(4–5): 76–89.

——— (2002), 'Vision of the Kelkar Papers: A Critique', *Economic and Political Weekly*, 21–27 December, 37(51): 5125–34.

Bagchi, Amaresh and Pulin B. Nayak (1994), 'A Survey of Public Finance and the Planning Process: The Indian Experience', in A. Bagchi and Nicholas Stern (eds), *Tax Policy and Planning in Developing Countries*. New Delhi: Oxford University Press.

Bajpai, N. and J. Sachs (1999), 'The State of State Government Finances in India', Discussion Paper No. 719. Cambridge: Harvard Institute for International Development.

Bakshi, P.M. (2003), *The Constitution of India*. Delhi: Universal Law Publishing Co. Pvt. Ltd.

Balakrishnan, P. and B. Ramaswami (2000), 'Vision and Illusion in Fiscal Correction', *Economic and Political Weekly*, 1 April, XXXV(14): 1137–9.

Bardhan, Pranab (2004), 'Disjunctures in the Indian Reform Process', in Kaushik Basu (ed.), *India's Emerging Economy*, pp. 49–58. New Delhi: Oxford University Press.

Basu, Kaushik (1993), 'Structural Reforms in India, 1991–93: Experience and Agenda', *Economic and Political Weekly*, 27 November, XXVIII(48): 2599–605.

——— (2004), *India's Emerging Economy*. New Delhi: Oxford University Press.

Bedi, Rajni (2007), *Personal Income taxation: Performance, Reforms, Incentives*. New Delhi: Regal Publications.

Bhagwati, Jagdish (1994), *India in Transition: Freeing the Economy*. New Delhi: Oxford University Press.

——— (2004), *In Defense of Globalization*. New Delhi: Oxford University Press.

Bhagwati, Jagdish and T.N. Srinivasan (1993), *India's Economic Reforms*, New Delhi: Ministry of Finance.

Bird, R.M. (1993), 'Review of "Mahesh C. Purohit, Principles and Practices of Value Added Taxation: Lessons for Developing Countries" (Delhi: Gayatri Publications)', *Canadian Tax Journal*, 41(6): 1222–5.

Bird, R.M. (2000), 'CVAT, VIVAT and Dual VAT: Vertical "Sharing" and Interstate Trade', *International Tax and Public Finance*, 7(6): 753–61.

Bird, R.M. and Pierre Pascal Gendron (1998), 'Dual VATs and Cross-Border Trade: Two Problems, One Solution?', *International Trade and Public Finance*, 5(3): 429–42.

Burgess R.S.L. and N.H. Stern (1992), 'Taxation and Development', *Journal of Economic Literature*, XXXI(2): 762.

Burgess R., S. Howes, and N. Stern (1993), *The Reform of Indirect Taxes in India*. London: STICERD, London School of Economics.

—————— (1995), 'The Reform of Indirect Taxes in India', in Mahesh C. Purohit and Vishnu Kanta Purohit (eds), *Commodity Taxes in India: Directions for Reform*, pp. 34–89. Delhi: Gayatri Publications.

Buiter, W.H. and U.R. Patel (1992), 'Debt, Deficits, and Inflation: An Application to the Public Finances of India', *Journal of Public Economics*, 47(2): 171–205.

Byres, Terence J. (1998), *The Indian Economy: Major Debates Since Independence*. New Delhi: Oxford University Press.

Chaudhuri, Saumitra (2000), 'Fiscal Management: An Alternative View of the Circumstances'. *ICRA Bulletin: Money and Finance*, 2(2): 59–83.

Chelliah, R.J. (1989), 'Reorientation of India's Fiscal Policy', Gokhale Memorial Lecture.

—————— (1991), *Interim Report of The Tax Reform Committee*. New Delhi: Department of Revenue, Ministry of Finance, Government of India.

—————— (1992), 'Growth of Indian Public Debt', in Bimal Jalan (ed.), *Indian Economy: Problems and Prospects*. New Delhi: Viking-Penguin Books.

—————— (1993a), 'An Essay on Fiscal Deficit', R.R. Kale Memorial Lecture, Pune: Gokhale Institute of Politics and Economics.

—————— (1993b), 'Financial and Fiscal Sector Reforms in Asian Countries', *Asian Development Review*, 11(2): 47–71.

—————— (1994), 'An Agenda for Comprehensive Tax Reform', Professor C.N. Vakil Memorial Lecture delivered at the Conference of the Indian Economic Association, February.

—————— (1996), *Towards Sustainable Growth: Essays in Fiscal and Financial Sector Reforms in India*. New Delhi: Oxford University Press.

—————— (1999), 'Economic Reform Strategy for the Next Decade', *Economic and Political Weekly*, 4–10 September, XXXIV(36): 2582–7.

—————— (2002), 'Task Force Recommendations on Direct Taxes', *Economic and Political Weekly*, 14–20 December, 37(50): 4977–80.

—————— (2003), 'Reducing Poverty Through State Level Reforms', in Stephen Howes, Ashok K. Lahiri, and Nicholas Stern (eds), *State-level Reforms in India*. New Delhi: Macmillan.

Chelliah, R.J., Mahesh C. Purohit, Shyam Nath, and Shushma N. Shinde (1978), *A Survey of the Tax System in Assam*. New Delhi: NIPFP.

Chelliah, R.J., K.K. Atri, and T.S. Rangamannar (1996), *A Framework for Restructuring Public Expenditure (1995–96 to 2002–03)*. New Delhi: National Institute of Public Finance and Policy.

Cnossen, Sijbren (1989), 'What Rate Structure for a Goods and Services Tax? The European Experience', *Canadian Tax Journal*, September–October: 1167–81.

Dasgupta, Arindam (2002), *The Stamps and Registration Department in Karnataka: A Review of Institutions and Administration*. Mumbai: IGIDR.

Dholakia, Ravindra (2004), *Fiscal Sustainability of Debt of States*. Ahmedabad: Indian Institute of Management.

Dreze, Jean and Amartya Sen (1997), *India: Economic Development and Social Opportunity*. New Delhi: Oxford India Paperback.

Due, John F. (1990), 'Some Unresolved Issues in Design and Implementation of Value Added Taxes', *National, Tax Journal*, 48(4): 383–95.

Dutta Choudhury, M. (1990), 'Market Failure and Government Failure', *Journal of Economic Perspectives*, 4(3) 25–39.

Empowered Committee of State Finance Ministers (2007), *Report of the Joint Working Group on Goods and Services Tax*. New Delhi.

——— (2008), *A Model and Road Map for GST in India*. New Delhi.

——— (2009), *First Discussion Paper on Goods and Services Tax in India*. New Delhi.

European Communities (1985), 'Harmonization of VAT', *European Taxation*, International Bureau of Fiscal Documentation, 25: 140–3.

Favaro, Edgardo M. and Ashok K. Lahiri (2004), *Fiscal Policies and Sustainable Growth in India*. New Delhi: Oxford University Press.

Gandhi, Ved P. (1970), *Some Aspects of India's Tax Structure An Economic Analysis*. Mumbai: Vora & Co. Publishers Private Ltd.

Gillis, Malcolm, Carl S. Shoup, and Gerardo P. Sicat (1990), *Value Added Taxation in Developing Countries*. Washington, DC: The World Bank.

Government of India (1953), *The First Five Year Plan*. New Delhi: Planning Commission.

——— (1953–4), *Report of the Taxation Enquiry Commission*, (Vol. III). New Delhi: Ministry of Finance, Department of Economic Affairs.

——— (1971), *Report of the Direct Taxes Enquiry Committee*. New Delhi: Ministry of Finance.

——— (1972), *Report of the Committee on Taxation of Agricultural Wealth and Income*. New Delhi: Ministry of Finance.

——— (1978), *Report of the Indirect Taxation Enquiry Committee*. New Delhi: Ministry of Finance, Department of Revenue.

——— (1990), *Report of the Working Group for Review of the MODVAT Scheme*. New Delhi: Ministry of Finance.

——— (1991), *Tax Reforms Committee, Interim Report*. New Delhi: Ministry of Finance, Department of Revenue.

——— (1991–3): *Tax Reforms Committee, Interim and Final Reports*. New Delhi: Ministry of Finance.

——— (1992), *Tax Reforms Committee Final Report Part-I*. New Delhi: Ministry of Finance, Department of Revenue.

Government of India (1997), *Report of the Expert Group to Review Existing Fiscal Incentives for Savings*. New Delhi: Ministry of Finance.

——— (1997a), *Report of the Working Group on Expenditure Policy of the Steering Group on Financial Resources for the Ninth Plan*. New Delhi: Planning Commission.

——— (1999), *Report of the Expert Group on Service Tax*. New Delhi: Ministry of Finance.

——— (2000), *Report of the Expenditure Reforms Commission*. New Delhi: Ministry of Finance.

——— (2001), *Economic Reforms: A Medium Term Perspective*, Recommendations of Prime Minister's Economic Advisory Council, New Delhi.

——— (2001a), *Report of the Expert Group on Taxation of Services*. New Delhi: Ministry of Finance.

——— (2001b), *Report of the Advisory Group on Tax Policy and Tax Administration for the Tenth Plan*. New Delhi: Planning Commission.

——— (2002), *Report of the Task Force on Direct Taxes*. New Delhi: Ministry of Finance and Company Affairs.

——— (2002a), *Report of the Task Force on Indirect Taxes*. New Delhi: Ministry of Finance and Company Affairs.

——— (2004), *Report of the Task Force on Implementation of the Fiscal Responsibility and Budget Management Act, 2003*. New Delhi: Ministry of Finance.

——— (2004a), *Fiscal Responsibility and Budget Management Act*. New Delhi: Ministry of Finance.

——— (2004b), *Report of the Twelfth Finance Commission, 2005–10*. New Delhi: Government Printing Press.

——— (2004c), *Central Government Subsidies in India*. New Delhi: Ministry of Finance.

——— (2010), *Receipt Budget 2010–11*. New Delhi: Ministry of Finance.

——— (2011), *Indian Public Finance Statistics*, Ministry of Finance, New Delhi.

——— (2012), *Receipt Budget 2012–13*. New Delhi: Ministry of Finance.

Government of Karnataka (2001), *Final Report of the Tax Reforms Commission*. Bengaluru: Finance Department.

Government of Uttar Pradesh (1985), *UP Taxation Review Committee Report*. Department of Finance: Uttar Pradesh.

Guhan, S. (1995), 'Centre and States in the Reform Process', in *Future of Economic Reform*. New Delhi: Oxford University Press.

Gulati, I.S. (1993), 'Tackling the Growing Burden of Public Debt', *Economic and Political Weekly*, 1 May, XXVIII(18): 883–6.

Gupta, S.P. (1993), 'Planning and Liberalisation', *Economic and Political Weekly*, 23 October, XXVIII(43): 2349–55.

Howes, Stephen, Ashok K. Lahiri, and Nicholas Stern (2003), *State-level Reforms in India*. New Delhi: Macmillan.

International Monetary Fund (2003), 'Public Debt in Emerging Markets: Is it Too High?', *World Economic Outlook*, Chapter 3 (September).

International Monetary Fund (2010), *Statistical Year Book*, Washington DC.

Islam, M. Anisul (2001), 'Wagner's Law Revisited: Cointegration and Exogeneity Tests for The USA', *Applied Economics Letters*, 8: 509–15.

Iyer, S.V. (1993), *Simplification of Customs and Central Excise Procedures*. New Delhi: Economic and Scientific Research Foundation.

Jalan, B. (ed.) (1992), *The Indian Economy*. New Delhi: Viking-Penguin Books.

Jalan, B. (1996), *India's Economic Policy-Preparing for the Twentieth Century*. New Delhi: Viking-Penguin Books.

Japan Bank for International Cooperation (2001), 'India: Fiscal Reforms and Public Expenditure Management', JBIC Research Paper No. 11. Tokyo: Japan Bank for International Cooperation.

Jha, Ganganand (1987), *Agricultural Taxation in India (A Case Study of Bihar)*. Delhi: Capital Publishing House.

Joshi, Vijay and I.M.D. Little (1993), 'Macro-Economic Stabilisation in India, 1991–93 and Beyond', *Economic and Political Weekly*, 4 December, XXVIII(49): 2659–65.

—————— (1994), *India: Macroeconomics and Political Economy, 1964–91*. New Delhi: Oxford University Press.

—————— (1996), *India's Economic Reforms*. New Delhi: Oxford University Press.

Kangle, R.P. (1965), *The Kautilya Arthasastra—A Study*, Mumbai: University of Mumbai.

Keen, Michael (1998), 'Vertical Tax Externalities in the Theory of Fiscal Federalism', *IMF Staff Papers*, 45(3): 454–85.

—————— (2000), 'CVAT, VIVAT and all That: New Forms of VAT for Federal Systems', *Canadian Tax Journal*, 48(2): 409–24.

Keen, Michael and Stephen Smith (2000), 'Viva VIVAT!', *International Tax and Public Finance*, 7(6): 741–51.

Koptis, George (2001), 'Fiscal Policy Rules for India', *Economic and Political Weekly*, 3 March, XXXVI(9): 749–56.

Krishnamurthy, K. (2007), *The Indian Stamp Act—An Exhaustive Commentary with State Amendments, Rules and Notifications*, Tenth edition, volume 23(1). Nagpur: Wadhwa.

Krishna, Raj (1988), 'Ideology and Economic Planning', *The Indian Economic Review*, 1–26.

Krueger, Anne O. (2002), *Economic Policy Reforms and the Indian Economy*. New Delhi: Oxford University Press.

Kurian, N.J. (1999), 'State Government Finances: Survey and Recent Trends', *Economic and Political Weekly*, 34(19): 1115–25.

—————— (2000), 'Widening Regional Disparities in India: Some Indicators', *Economic and Political Weekly*, 35(7): 538–50.

Lindauer, L. David and Ann D. Velenchik (1992), 'Government Spending In Developing Countries—Trends, Causes, and Consequences', *The World Bank Research Observer*, 7(1): 59–78.

McCluskey, William J. and Riël C.D. Franzsen (2005), *Land Value Taxation: An Applied Analysis*. England: Ashgate Publishing Limited.

McLure, Charles E. Jr. (2000), 'Implementing Sub-National Value-Added Taxes on Internal Trade: The Compensating VAT (CVAT)', *International Tax and Public Finance*, 7(6): 723–40.

Mittal, V.S. (2004), *Indian Stamp Act*. Bhopal: Suvidha Law House Pvt. Ltd.

Mohan, Rakesh (2000), 'Fiscal Correction for Economic Growth: Data Analysis and Suggestion', *Economic and Political Weekly*, 10 June, XXXV(24): 227–2036.

Mundle, Sudipto and M. Govinda Rao (1992), 'The Volume and Composition of Government Subsidies in India: 1987–88', *Economic and Political Weekly*, 4 May, 26(18): 1157–72.

NCAER (2001), *Economic and Policy Reforms in India*. New Delhi: National Council of Applied Economic Research.

NIPFP (1989), *The Operations of Modvat*. New Delhi: NIPFP.

——— (1993), *Report on the Service Tax*. New Delhi: NIPFP.

——— (1994), *Reform of Domestic Trade Taxes in India—Issues and Options*. New Delhi: NIPFP.

——— (1995a), *Economic Reforms and the Stamp Act*. New Delhi: NIPFP.

——— (1995b), *Report of the Committee of State Finance Ministers on Sales Tax Reforms*, August. New Delhi: NIPFP.

——— (1996a), *Report of the Committee of Stamp Duty Reform*. New Delhi: NIPFP.

——— (1996b), *Report of the Group of Officials and Experts on Taxation of Inter-State Sales*. New Delhi: NIPFP.

——— (1998), *Report of the Committee of State Finance Ministers for Charting a Time Path for Introduction of VAT*, August. New Delhi: NIPFP.

——— (1999a), *Report of the Committee of Finance Secretaries for Identification of Backward Areas* (November). New Delhi: NIPFP.

——— (1999b), *Report of the Committee of Chief Ministers on Value Added Tax and Incentives to Backward Areas*. New Delhi: NIPFP.

——— (2009), 'Property Tax Potential in India's Cities and Town', A study Submitted to the Thirteenth Finance Commission. New Delhi: NIPFP.

OECD (Organisation for Economic Co-operation and Development) (2004), *Consumption Tax Trends*. Paris: OECD.

Owens, Jeffrey and Edward Whitehons (1996), 'Tax Reform for the 21st Century', *Bulletin for International Fiscal Documentation*, November/December: 538–47.

Ouanes, A. and Subhash Thakur (1997), *Macroeconomic Accounting and Analysis in Transition Economies*. Washington, DC: IMF.

Panagariya, Arvind (2004), 'India's Trade Reform', in S. Bery, B. Bosworth, and A. Panagariya (eds), *India Policy Forum 2004*. New Delhi and Washington, DC: NCAER and Brookings Institution.

Pandey, T.N. (2000), "The Evolution of Income Tax", *Business Line*, 14 February.

Pandit, V. (1995), 'Macroeconomic Character of the Indian Economy: Theories, Facts and Fancies', in P. Patnaik (ed.), *Macroeconomics*, pp. 187–216. New Delhi: Oxford University Press.

Pandit, V., K. Krishnamurty, and G. Mahanty (2000), *India: Economic Outlook, 2000–03*. New Delhi: Centre for Development Economics, Delhi School of Economics.

Patel, I.G. (1998), *Economic Reform and Global Change*. Delhi: Macmillan.

Premchand, A. (2000), *Control of Public Money: The Fiscal Machinery in Developing Countries*. New Delhi: Oxford University Press.

Purohit, Mahesh C. (1975), *Sales Taxation in India: An Economic Analysis of Its Structure and Operations with Special Reference to the Northern Zone*, pp. 12–18. New Delhi: S. Chand & Co.

——— (1988), 'Designing Value Added Tax—Lessons From Theory and Practice', *International Journal of Development Banking*, 9(1): 55–62.

——— (1990a), *Exemptions Under Additional Excise Duties in Lieu of Sales Tax: An Empirical Analysis of Loss of Revenue to the States*. New Delhi: NIPFP.

——— (1990b), 'Tax Reform in an Unconventional Economy', *Bulletin for International Fiscal Documentation*, April, 44(4): 185–93.

——— (1991), *Sales Tax and Value Added Tax in India*. New Delhi: Gayatri Publications.

——— (1993a), 'Adoption of Value Added Tax in India: Problems and Prospects', *Economic and Political Weekly*, 6 March, XXVIII(10): 393–404.

——— (1993b), 'Management of VAT in France', *International VAT Monitor*, August–September: 19–29.

——— (1993c), 'Indian Sales Taxes: An Approach towards State-VAT', *PTRIC Bulletin*, August: 297–309.

——— (1995a), 'Reform of Union Excise Duties', *Economic and Political Weekly*, 27 May, XXX(21): 1255–9.

——— (1995b), 'An Analysis of Recent Tax Reforms in India', *Asia Pacific Tax Bulletin*, July: 196–203.

——— (1997), 'Central Excise Duty and MODVAT', *Tax Notes International*, 26 May: 1709–13.

——— (1997a), 'Value Added Tax in a Federal Structure: A Case Study of Brazil', *Economic and Political Weekly*, 32(7): 357–62.

——— (1997b), 'Taxation of Services: Some Policy Imperatives for India', *Bulletin for International Fiscal Documentation*, 51(1): 35–46.

——— (1998), 'Transfer Pricing Regulations in India—Challenges Ahead', *Bulletin for International Fiscal Documentation*, October: 438–46.

——— (1999), 'Road User Taxation in India—A Comparative Perspective', *Bulletin for International Fiscal Documentation*, 53(5): 208–28.

——— (2000), 'Assignment of Taxing Power for Fiscal Balance', in D.K. Srivastava (ed.), *Fiscal Federalism in India: Contemporary Challenges—Issues Before the Eleventh Finance Commission*, pp. 312–19. New Delhi: NIPFP.

Purohit, Mahesh C. (2001a), *Sales Tax and Value Added Tax in India*. New Delhi: Gayatri Publications.

———— (2001b), 'Structure and Administration of VAT in Canada: Lessons for India', *International VAT Monitor*, November–December: 311–23.

———— (2001c), 'National and Sub-National VATs: A Road Map for India, *Economic and Political Weekly*', 3 March, XXXVI(9): 757–72.

———— (2002), 'Harmonizing Taxation of Interstate Trade Under A Sub-National VAT—Lessons from International Experience', *International VAT Monitor*, 13(3): 169–79.

———— (2003), 'Taxes on Commodities and Services in India: Estimating Revenue Potential of Harmonized Central and State Taxes', Study Report submitted to the Twelfth Finance Commission of India. New Delhi: Foundation for Public Economics and Policy Research.

———— (2005), *Structure and Administration of Sales Taxation in India: An Economic Analysis*, Second Edition. Delhi: Gayatri Publications.

———— (2006a), *State Value Added Tax in India: An Analysis of Revenue Implications*. New Delhi: Gayatri Publications.

———— (2006b), 'Tax Efforts and Taxable Capacity of Centre and State Governments in India', *Economic and Political Weekly*, 25 February, XLI(8): 747–55.

———— (2007), *Value Added Tax: Experiences of India and Other Countries*. Delhi: Gayatri Publications.

———— (2010), *Goods and Services Tax in India: Estimating Revenue Implications of the Proposed GST,* Study Report submitted to the Twelfth Finance Commission of India, New Delhi: Foundation for Public Economics and Policy Research. Available at http://fincomindia.nic.in/ShowContentOne.aspx?id=27&Section=1, last accessed on 12 September 2012.

———— (2012), *VAT and GST: Experiences of India and Other Countries*. New Delhi: Gayatri Publications.

Purohit, Mahesh C. and Vishnu Kanta Purohit (eds) (1995), *Commodity Taxes in India: Directions for Reform*. New Delhi: Gayatri Publications.

———— (2012), 'Road User Taxes in India: Issues in Tax Policy and Governance', A Study submitted to the SER Division, Planning Commission, Government of India, New Delhi by the Foundation for Public Economics and Policy Research, New Delhi. Available at http://planningcommission.nic.in/reports/sereport/ser/ser_ruti.pdf, last accessed on 22 April 2014.

Purohit, Mahesh C., C. Sai Kumar, Gopinath Pradhan, and O.P. Bohra (1992), *Fiscal Policy for the National Capital Region*. New Delhi: Vikas Publishing House.

Purohit, Mahesh C. and D.N. Rao (1994), 'Fiscal Intervention for Environmental Protection: A Cross-Sectional Analysis for Fiscal Prescriptions', Paper presented at the 50th Congress of the International Institute of Public Finance, Harvard University, Cambridge, USA, 22–25 August.

Rajaraman, Indra and Abhiroop Mukhopadhyay (2000), *Sustainability of Public Debt in India*, Issues Before the Eleventh Finance Commission. New Delhi: Eleventh Finance Commission.

Rajaraman, Indra, Hiranya Mukhopadhyay, and H.K. Amarnath (1998), *State Fiscal Studies: Punjab*. New Delhi: National Institute of Public Finance and Policy.

Rajaraman, Indra and M.J. Bhende (1998), *A Land-Based Agricultural Presumptive Tax Designed for Levy by Panchayats*. New Delhi: NIPFP.

Rakshit, Mihir (2002), 'On correcting Fiscal Imbalances in the Indian Economy', *ICRA Bulletin: Money and Finance*, July–September, 2(2): 19–58.

Ram, Rati (1998), 'Testing Wagner's Hypothesis from Multicountry Cross-Sections: A Panel Data Approach', *Public Finance*, 53(2): 145–58.

Rangarajan, C. and D.K. Srivastava (2003), 'Dynamics of Debt Accumulation in India: Impact of Primary Deficit, Growth and Interest Rate', *Economic and Political Weekly*, 38(46): 4851–5.

————— (2005), 'Fiscal Deficits and Government Debt Implications for Growth and Stabilization', *Economic and Political Weekly*, 40(27): 2919–34.

Rao, M. Govinda and Sudipto Mundle (1992), 'An Analysis of Changes in State Government Subsidies: 1977–87', in A. Bagchi., J.L. Bajaj, and W.A. Byrd (eds), *State Finances in India*, pp. 107–43. New Delhi: NIPFP.

Rao, M. Govind (2001), 'Taxing Services: Issues and Strategy', *Economic and Political Weekly*, 20 October, XXXVI(42): 3999–4006.

Research Institute for Development and Finance (2001), 'India: Fiscal Reforms and Public Expenditure Management', JBIC Research Paper No. 11, Japan Bank for International Cooperation.

Reserve Bank of India (2000), *Annual Report 1999–2000*, Mumbai: RBI.

Reddy, Y.V. (2000), *Monetary and Financial Sector Reforms in India*. New Delhi: UBS Publishers' Distributors Limited.

————— (2002), *Lectures on Economic and Financial Sector Reforms in India*. New Delhi: Oxford University Press.

Roy, Rathin (1998), 'Debates on Indian Fiscal Policy', in J. Byres Terence (ed.), *The Indian Economy-Major Debates Since Independence*, pp. 335–82. New Delhi: Oxford University Press.

Rustagi, T.R. (2006), 'Reforms in CenVAT and Service tax in India: A road map towards comprehensive GST', Paper presented at an International Seminar on Reforms in Fiscal and Monetary Policies: The Road Ahead. New Delhi: Foundation for Public Economics and Policy Research.

Schenk, Alan and Oliver Oldman (2001), *Value Added Tax: A Comparative Approach, With Materials and Cases*. New York: Transnational Publishers.

Schenone, Osvaldo Horacio (1987), *The Argentinean Experience with the Value-Added Tax*, DRD 235. Washington, DC: The World Bank.

Shalizi, Zmarak and Squire Lyn (1986), *Consumption Taxes in Sub-Sahara Africa: Building On Existing Instruments*. Washington, DC: The World Bank.

Shirazi, Javed Khalilzadeh and Anwar Shah (1998), *Tax Policy in Developing Countries*. Washington, DC: The World Bank.
Sen, Tapas K. (1992), 'Overview of Tax Systems In Indian States' (mimeo). New Delhi: National Institute of Public Finance and Policy.
────── (1997), 'Tax Administration at the State Level: Profession Tax' (mimeo). New Delhi: National Institute of Public Finance and Policy.
Sen, Tapas K. and R. Kavita Rao (1998), *State Fiscal Studies: Haryana*. New Delhi: National Institute of Public Finance and Policy.
Shah, C.H. (1986), *Taxation and Agricultural Development in India*. Mumbai: Himalaya Publishing House.
Shome, Parthasarathi (1996), 'Fiscal Policy in the 1990s—Needed Reforms and Ramifications for the Financial Sector', Sir Purshottamdas Thakurdas Memorial Lecture. Mumbai: Indian Institute of Bankers, December.
────── (1997a), 'Fiscal Performance and Tax Reform in the 1990s: Indian Experience and Cross-Country Comparisons', in Sudipto Mundle (ed.), *Fiscal Policy in India*. New Delhi: Oxford University Press.
────── (1997b), *India Tax Policy for the Ninth Five Year Plan*. New Delhi: Centax Publications Private Ltd.
────── (2000), 'India: Recent Development in Tax Policy and Agenda for Future Reform', in Surjit Bhalla (ed.), *New Economic Policies for a New India*, pp. 57–75. New Delhi: Indian Council of Social Science Research (ICSSR).
────── (2002), *India's Fiscal Matters*. New Delhi: Oxford University Press.
Shome, Parthasarathi (ed.) (1995), 'Comprehensive Tax Reform: The Colombian Experience', Occasional Paper No. 123. Washington DC: International Monetary Fund.
────── (ed.) (1997), *Fiscal Policy, Public Policy and Governance*. New Delhi: Centax Publications Private Ltd.
Shome, Parthasarathi and Hiranya Mukhopadhyay (1998), 'India: Economic Liberalisation of the 1990s—Stabilisation and Structural Aspects, and Sustainability of Results', *Economic and Political Weekly*, 33(29, 30): 1925–34.
Shome, Parthasarathi, Paul Bernd Spahn, T.K. Sen, and S. Gopalakrishnan (1996), 'Public Expenditure Policy and Management in India: A Consideration of the Issues', Working Paper No. 8. New Delhi: National Institute of Public Finance and Policy.
Srinivasan, T.N. (1993), 'Savings in the Development Process', *International Journal of Development Banking*, 11: 13–33.
Srivastava, D.K. (2005), *Issues in Indian Public Finance*. Delhi: New Century Publications.
Srivastava, D.K, C.B. Rao, Pinaki Chakraborty, and T.S. Rangamannar (2003) [2001], *Budgetary Subsidies in India: Subsidising Social and Economic Services*, available on the website of Planning Commission http://planningcommission.nic.in/reports/sereport/ser/stdy_bgdsubs.pdf, last accessed on 15 March 2014.

Srivastava, D.K., Saumen Chattopadhyay, and Pratap Ranjan Jena (1999), *State Fiscal Studies: Kerala*. New Delhi: National Institute of Public Finance and Policy.

Srivastava, D.K., Saumen Chattopadhyay, and T.S. Rangamannar (1998), *State Fiscal Studies: Assam*. New Delhi: National Institute of Public Finance and Policy.

Srivastava, D.K and Tapas Sen (1997), *Government Subsidies in India*. New Delhi: National Institute of Public Finance and Policy.

Srivastava, G.K. (1975), *Commercial Taxes in India*. Jaipur: Pitaliya Pustak Bhandar.

Stern, Nicholas (2002), 'Public Finance and Policy for Development: Challenges for India', Silver Jubilee Lecture, NIPFP, January.

Sury, M.M. (1997), *The Indian Tax System*. Delhi: Indian Tax Institute.

────── (2000), *Fiscal Policy Developments in India 1950–2000*. Delhi: Indian Tax Institute.

Tait, Alan A. (1988), *Value Added Tax: International Practice and Problems*. Washington, DC: International Monetary Fund.

Thornbury, Thomas G. (1991), 'A Better Way to Include General Insurance in VAT Systems', *International VAT Monitor*, May: 2–11.

Turnier, William J. (1984), 'Designing an Efficient Value Added Tax', *Tax Law Review*, 32: 435–72.

Tridimas, George (1992), 'A Note on The Effects of Government Expenditures on Private Consumption', *Public Finance*, 47(1): 153–61.

Vithal, B.P.R. (1992), 'Reducing Government Revenue Expenditure: Some Issues', in B. Amaresh, J.L. Bajaj, and William A. Byrd (eds), *State Finances In India*, pp. 513–19, New Delhi: Vikas Publishing House Pvt. Ltd., NIPFP.

Whalley, John and Deborah Fretz (1990), 'The Economics of the Goods and Services Tax', *Canadian Tax Foundation*, September, Paper No. 88.

Index

(Note: *b*, n, and *t* denote box, notes, and tables respectively.)

Accredited Client Programme 64
ad valorem rates 46, 50, 55, 106, 109–10, 112, 116, 248, 253–4, 256, 258, *see also under* motor vehicles tax (MVT); passengers and goods tax (P&GT)
Additional Commissioners of Commercial Taxes 236
additional duties of excise (ADE) 53, 114, 335, 349; on HSD 113; on motor spirit 113; pan masala and tobacco products 114
Additional Duties of Excise (Goods of Special Importance) Act 1957 53, 113, 233, 346, 361
Additional Duties of Excise (Textile and Textile Articles) Act, 1975 53
agricultural development: precondition for economic growth 168n6
agricultural holding tax (AHT) 159, 338
agricultural income tax (AIT) 41, 44, 92, 149, 159–62, 166–8, 191–2, 330, 338–9; administration of 166–7; in Bihar 161; evolution of 161; exemptions on 91, 164–6; fiscal significance of 161–2; rates for companies in states 165*t*; rates for individuals in states 164*t*; reforms for 167–8; state-wise revenue from 163*t*; tax structure of 162–4; weaknesses in system of 167
All-India Income Tax Committee 82
anti-avoidance measure 377, 379
anti-dumping duty 54–5, 331
Arthashastra of Kautilya 81, 224
Asia-Pacific Trade Agreement (APTA) 53n5
Assistant Commissioner of Commercial Taxes (ACCT) 237

Bangladesh-India-Myanmar-Sri Lanka and Thailand Technical and Economic Cooperation (BIMSTEC) 53
Bengal Agricultural Income Tax Act, 1944 167
Book profits 74–6, 80, 333, 376
brand name 117n21

capital gains tax 83, 88–91, 93, 178, 181, 334, 373–5; long-term 90; short-term 88–90
Central Board of Direct Taxes (CBDT) 66, 101–2, 104, 335, 378

INDEX

Central Board of Excise and Customs (CBEC) 55, 61–2, 64, 118, 124, 129, 135, 332, 337
Central Board of Revenue Act, 1963 101
Central Domestic Trade Taxes: Union Excise Duty (CenVAT) 335–7; administration of commodities and services 337
Central Excise Act, 1944 110n5, 112n11, 120
central excise duties 53, 105, 118–19, 337, 346, 361; filing of monthly return 120
Central Excise Tariff Act 1985 53, 112n12, 115
central sales tax (CST) 225, 232, 236, 341, 347, 356–8
Central Sales Tax Act, 1956 225, 236
CenVAT (Central Value Added Tax) 21, 105, 110–15, 121–2, 130–1, 133–7, 345–50, 358, 361–3, *see also* union excise duties (UEDs); evolution of 349–50; rates of 110–13, 115, 121, 336, 362; full credit allowed despite exemption 117–18; two-rate duty structure 349
CenVAT credit 111, 114, 117, 130–1, 134; for plastic material 118n23; Rules, 2004 127–8, 133–4; scheme 111, 127
cesses 50, 53–4, 56, 83, 85, 114, 157–8, 334–6, 346, 361, 375
Chelliah Committee 85, 109, 126, 345
Chelliah, R.J. 18, 80, 83
client services 64, 125, 135, 281
Commercial Tax Officer (CTO) 237
Commission for Disinvestment 11
Commissioner of Commercial Taxes (CCT) 190, 236–7, 240
commodities and services, state taxes 226–7*t*; taxes on 22, 28, 33, 35, 37, 45–6, 48–9, 224, 296–7, 337, 340

companies, tax rate profile of 74*t*
competitive licensing system 281
compound tax 370
Comprehensive Economic Cooperation Agreements (CECAs) 53
computerization 101, 181, 183, 279, 353; of Department of Excise 280
Concessions to Women in Madhya Pradesh, Revenue implications of 177*b*
controlled foreign corporation (CFC) 377
corporate: income tax rate 69, 71*t*, 79; investments 18, 81; taxpayers 76, 162, 339
corporation tax 28, 36–7, 66–7, 70, 77, 79–80, 103, 332, 375; fiscal significance of 67–9; minimum alternate tax, *see* minimum alternate tax; rate structure of 69–74, 375; reduction in rate of 375; revenue from 67; step system 69n4; surcharge on 70; zero-tax companies 67
countervailing duty (CVD) 53–4, 61, 122, 346, 349, 361
customs duty 28, 38, 48–53, 55–6, 61, 65, 106, 113, 330–2, 346, 361; administration of 61–4; change in peak rate of 56*t*; rates of 59–60*t*; revenue significance of 49–50, 51*t*; structure of 50–2, 56–60; tariff rates of 57–8*t*
Customs Tariff Act, 1975 50–5

daily stock register 120
differential tax rates 70; abolition of 79
Direct Tax Code (DTC) 347–8, 370–80
direct taxes 28–9, 33, 36–7, 41, 45, 67, 69, 103–4, 161, 329–30, 347–8; reforms in 92; of states 31

Direct Taxes Administration Enquiry Committee 82
Director General Export Promotion 62
Director General of Revenue Intelligence (DGRI) 62
Director General Safeguard 62
Directorate of Preventive Operations 62
Dispute Settlement Authority 365
dividend distribution tax (DDT) 67, 76, 80, 103, 333, 347, 375–6; rate structure of 76–7
domestic companies 67, 69–70, 73, 76, 79–80, 103, 332–3, 375, 378; paying DDT 80; rate categories for 69
double taxation avoidance agreement (DTAAs) 378–9
dual VAT 136, 345, 348, 357, 359, 370

Education tax/cess 54, 73, 85, 114, 127, 327, 331, 346, 361
electricity duty 45, 47, 224, 281–2, 286, 289, 296–7, 340, 343, 348; exemptions on 286–9; fiscal significance of 282; rates of 287–8*t*; reforms of 289; revenue from 283–5*t*; structure of 282–6
Empowered committee (EC) 191, 234–5, 341, 346, 353, 360, 367
entertainment tax 45, 47, 224, 289–90, 294–7, 340, 343, 346, 348, 361; administration of 295–6; assessing system of 296; concessions and exemptions 295; fiscal significance of 290–3; rates in states 310–18*t*; reforms for 296; revenue from 291–3*t*; structure of 294
equity-oriented funds 76, 89, 375
e-stamping 183, 192, 340
estate duty 36, 66, 98, 100–1, 103–4, 332

excisable goods 114, 116, 120, 128, 133–4, 336
excise duty 53–4, 105–6, 109–17, 119–22, 265, 271, 274, 278–9, 281, 330, 342; area-based exemptions 117, 122–3; exemption 112, 116; on alcoholic liquors 46, 105, 265; on motor spirit 113; structure 109–11, 116, 336; under miscellaneous Acts 53
exemptions 118; list of services for 129; schemes of 116, 122
Expenditure Reforms Commission (ERC) 10
expenditure, reforms in 10–15
export duties 49n1, 50, 65, 331, *see also* import duties

Finance (No. 2) Act, 2004 114
Finance Act: of 1987 74; of 1994 127, 133; of 1997 76, 333, 347; of 2001 113; of 2002 103, 113; of 2003 54, 113; of 2004 98; of 2007 114; of 2008 113
fiscal deficit 3–5, 9–10, 15; indicators of 6–8*t*; revenue and 3–9
fiscal policy, objectives of 1–2
fiscal reforms 3–18; at state level 20–1
Fiscal Responsibility and Budget Management (FRBM) Act 4–5, 9–10, 15
fixing accountability 124–5
foreign companies 67, 69–70, 73, 79–80, 103, 164, 332, 374–5, 377–9
foreign institutional investors (FIIs) 374–5
Free Trade Agreements (FTAs) 53, 345

General Anti-Avoidance Rule (GAAR) 92, 378–9
gift tax 36, 66, 69, 97–100, 103–4, 332, 334–5; assessment of 100;

exemption on 99–100; objective of 97; rate structure of 98–9; revenue significance of 98
Global System of Tariff Preferences (GSTP) 53n5
Goods and Services Tax (GST) 22, 111, 124, 236, 297, 326, 341, 344–8, 357, 359–68, 370, *see also* Integrated Goods and Services Tax (IGST), Joint Working Group on GST (JWGgst); administration of 367–70; Constitutional amendments on 364–7; of State 346–7, 357, 361; of Union 347, 357, 362, 364
Goods and Services Tax (GST) Council of India 365–7
goods tax 45–7, 257, 263–4, 337, 340–2, 348
Green Revolution 3, 158–9, 338
gross domestic product (GDP) 4–5, 10, 15, 17, 28–9, 31, 33, 36, 39, 47–8, 329–30
gross state domestic product (GSDP) 156, 168, 174, 187, 232
gross tax revenue 36, 38–9, 44, 48, 67, 84, 126, 330; share of personal income tax in 37

Harmonized System of Nomenclature (HSN) 51, 115, 358
health sector, exemptions to 117
high net-worth individuals (HNIs) 97
Hindu undivided families (HUFs) 82, 94, 96–9, 102n18, 335, 372

import duties 38, 50, 52–5, 61, 65, 330–1; statutory rates as tariff rates 50
incentives and exemptions 77, 80, 103
income and property taxes 22, 28, 33, 36, 39, 41, 101, 103–4, 332, 334–5, 337–8; administration of 101–2; revenue from 150–1*t;* revenue from Union Taxes on 68–9*t*
Income Tax 74, 77, 81–5, 88, 90, 93–4, 98, 101–2, 106, 161, 330; assessment of 90–1, 103; laws of 91, (*see also* Indian Income Tax Act, 1961); personal 28–9, 36–7, 66, 77, 79, 82–5, 88, 90–3, 95, 103, 332–3; rates of 84; reforms for 92–3
Income-tax Act: 1886 161; 1961 70, 73–5, 77–9, 81–3, 88–9, 98, 161, 167, 334, 376, 378–9; 1961 and Direct Taxes Code (DTC) 347; 1961, exemptions under 333–4; 1961, for foreign companies 375; 1961, returns filed 123; 1961, tax exemptions/rebates/incentives in 85, 87
India–Afghanistan Preferential Trade Agreement 53n6
India–Bhutan Trade Agreement 53n6
India–Chile Preferential Trade Agreement 53n6
Indian Court Fee Act 1870 169
Indian Income Tax Act, 1961 83, 161
Indian Made Foreign Liquor (IMFL), excise duty on 271, 274, 276
Indian Motor Vehicles Act 1914 248n12; of 1939 248, 253
Indian Stamp Act 1899 169, 174–5, *see also* stamp duty (SD)
India–Nepal Trade Treaty 53n6
India–Singapore Comprehensive Economic Cooperation Agreement 53n6
India–Sri Lanka Free Trade Agreement (ISFTA) 53n6
indirect tax system 20, 28–9, 31, 36–8, 48–9, 329–30, 337, 345–9, 361, 364
Indirect Taxes Enquiry Committee (Jha Committee) 108, 336, 345, 349

indirect tax–GDP ratio 31, 330
inflation 9, 93, 97
infrastructure investment, tax incentives for 78
input service distributor 130
Input tax credit (ITC) 234, 337, 357
Integrated Goods and Services Tax (IGST) 347, 357–9, 363, *see also* Goods and Services Tax (GST)
interest payments 4, 10–11, 17
International Monetary Fund (IMF) 5
international trade 49, 65, 169, 335; customs duty on 65; taxes on 330–2
inter-state tax 355–7
investment-linked tax incentives 73, 78

Jha Committee. *See* Indirect Taxes Enquiry Committee
Joint Working Group on GST (JWGgst) 346, 361, 367

Kaldor, Nicholas 82, 94, 97
Kelkar Committee Report (Task Force on Indirect Taxes Report) 22, 111, 326
Kelkar Task Force on Direct and Indirect Taxes 20
Kelkar, Vijay 83

land customs stations (LCSs) 64
land revenue 41, 149–50, 152, 156–9, 185, 191, 330, 338; administration of 158; cess on 157; exemptions on 157–8; fiscal significance 150–6; Large taxpayer units (LTUs) 119; liberal deductions 72; licence fee in states 277*t*; reforms for 159–60; in state 152*t*, 153–5*t*, 193–200*t*; structure of 156; surcharge on 157; tax structure of 156–7; weaknesses in system of 158–9

Local Finance Enquiry Committee, 1953 97
local taxes 327–8
long-term capital gains 72, 75, 90, 334
luxury tax (hotel tax) 234, 346, 361

M.R. Masani Committee on Road Transport Reorganisation 326
management information system (MIS) 123, 133, 181, 237, 279–80, 369
Manusmriti 81
minimum alternate tax (MAT) 74–6, 77*t*, 80, 103, 333, 375–6
modified value added tax (ModVAT) 110, 336, 349
motor vehicles tax (MVT) 46–7, 224, 240–1, 248, 253–5, 257, 263–4, 296–7, 341–2, 348; ad valorem rates 256; administration of 253–4; assessment of 254–5; fiscal significance of 240–1; growth rate of revenue from 241; incentives on 256; one-time tax 255; pollution-abatement incentives 256; rates of 249–52*t*; reforms for 255–7; in states 242–5*t*; structure of 248–53
Motor Vehicles Taxation Enquiry Committee 326n1
multi-point sales tax 224, 232, 346n1, 351, 359
Municipal: laws 344; taxes 327

National calamity contingent duty (NCCD) 54, 61, 113, 331, 346, 361
New Exploration Licensing Policy 72
non-agricultural income 91, 160–1, 167, 191, 339, *see also* agricultural income tax (AIT)
non-profit organizations (NPOs), taxation of 376–7

Octroi 319, 324–7, 344, 346, 361; Constitutional provisions 325; reforms for 326; revenue significance of 325; status of 325–6

pan masala 112n12, 114, 116, 121, 335, 346, 361; evasion of excise duty 116n19; special levy on 121

passengers and goods tax (P&GT) 46–7, 224, 241–8, 254–5, 257–8, 263–4, 296–7, 340–2, 348; ad valorem rates 256; administration of 263; combined tax 264; fiscal significance of 257–8; one-time tax 255; pollution-abatement incentives 256; rates of 262*t*; reforms of 264; in states 259–61*t*; structure of 258–63; tax incentives 256; weaknesses in system of 263–4

Permanent Account Number (PAN) 103, 369

personal income tax 66, 82–3; fiscal significance of 83–4; rate structure of 84–7

Preferential Trade Agreements (PTAs) 53

profession tax 41, 44, 93, 149, 185–7, 190–2, 330, 338, 340; administration of 190, 323–4; assessing system of 324; and capital gains tax 373–4; evolution of 81–2; and exempt-exempt-exempt regime for savings 372–3; fiscal significance 186–7; and housing loan exemptions 371–2; and income from employment, retirement benefits, and perquisites 372; income from house property 372; and income of foreign institutional investors 374; rate of 321–2; rate of cesses and surcharges 86*t*; rate structure in states 218–23*t*; reforms for 190–1, 324; states' share of 186, 187*t*, 188–9*t*; structure of 187–90, 319–21

property tax 41, 178, 181, 185, 319, 323–4, 327, 344; rebates on 319; unit area method (UAM) in 321; value-based approach to 321

property valuation methods 320*t*; area-based approach 320; unit area method (UAM) 321; value-based approach 320–1

public debt 15–18

public sector undertakings (PSUs) 9, 11, 329

reforms 18–22, 28–9, 36, 55, 61, 67, 80, 103, 329, 344–8, 353–4, *see also under* Tax Reforms Committee (TRC): in capital gains tax 334; in corporation tax 332–3; fiscal significance of 329–30; in personal income tax 333–4; for simplification of tariff system 61; in wealth and gift taxes 334–5

Regional Trading Agreements (RTAs) 52–3, 65, 331; and trade liberalization 53

registered dealers, submission of returns 238

Registration fee (RF) 21, 41, 44–5, 93, 97, 149, 168–70, 171–3*t*, 174, 175*t*, 177–85, 192, 338–9, 348; administration of 179–80; assessing structure of 178–9; citizen's charter for 184; constitutional provisions 169–70; on conveyance 176*b*; fiscal significance 170–4; reforms for 181–5; in states 201–13*t*, 214–17*t*; structure of 174–8; Torrens

system 184–5; weaknesses in 180–1
Reserve Bank of India, for market-oriented government borrowings 14
residence: concept of 379; in company incorporated outside India 379
revenue and capital expenditure 3, 10, 12–13t, 14, 17
revenue deficit 3–5, 9;
revenue receipts 4, 10, 41
rural local bodies taxes 328

safeguard duty 55, 62, 331
sales tax, see State VAT
savings: incentives for 87–8; and investment gap 18; Investment as percentage of GDP 19t
Secondary and higher education cess 54, 114, 127, 331–2
Securities Exchange Board of India (SEBI) 374
securities transaction tax (STT) 89, 91, 373
Service Tax Rules, 1994 130
services (import), taxation on 128, see also import duty
services, taxation of 105, 119, 125–36, 281, 330–3, 335–7, 346, 350, 358, 363–4; administration of 129–33; Advance Ruling on 133; appeals and remedies for 133; banks' payment 131; fiscal significance of 126; mode of payment 131; negative list of 39, 126, 128–9, 141–8, 337, 364; reforms for 134–5; structure of 127–9; weaknesses in system of 133–4
'Sevottam' through Aayakar Seva Kendras: administration of tax through 102
short-term capital gains, taxation on 88–9, 334

show tax 294, see also entertainment tax
simplified assessment procedure (SAP) 109
small-scale industries (SSI) 72, 116, 336, 363; exemptions for 116–17, 122, 124; land use for 157
social sector development, incentives for 79
Societies Registration Act 366
South Asia Free Trade Area (SAFTA) 53n5
special additional duty (SAD) 21, 54, 113; on motor spirit and HSD 113
Special Additional duty of Customs (Special CVD) 54
special duty of excise 113–14
Special Economic Zones (SEZs) 72, 76, 78, 286, 289, 343, 375–6
stamp duty (SD) 41, 44–5, 93, 97, 149, 168–70, 171–3t, 174–5, 177–84, 192, 338–9, 348; administration of 179–80; assessing structure of 178–9; citizen's charter for 184; constitutional provisions 169–70; on conveyance 176b; fiscal significance 170–4; rates of 169, 175–7, 181, 192, 340; reforms for 181–5; reforms in 340; in states 201–13t; structure of 174–8; surcharges on 176; Torrens system 184–5; weaknesses in 180–1
stamp duty and registration fee (SD&RF): Department of 180–1, 185; Computerization of 183
standard rates 52, 112, 121, 232, 331, 336, 341, 359, 362–3
State Electricity Boards (SEBs) 20
State Excise Acts 280
state excise duty (SED) 45–6, 224, 265–6, 271, 274, 276, 278–81, 296–7, 340, 342, 348; administration of 276–9; fiscal significance of 266; methods of

levying 272–3*t;* rate structure of 274–6; reforms for 280–1; revenue from 267–70*t;* in states, rates of 275*t;* structure of 266–74; weaknesses in system 279–80

State Finance Ministers Committee 1995, recommendations of 352*b;* of 1998 352*b*

State governments taxes 337; agricultural income tax 41–4, 338–9; on commodities and services 45–8; electricity duty 343; entertainment tax 343–4; excise duty 342; income and property taxes of 39–45; on land revenue 41; motor vehicles tax and passengers and goods tax 341–2; on income and property 338; profession tax 44, 340; stamp duty and registration fee 44–5, 339–40

States of India, list of 23–4

State VAT 45–6, 224–5, 232–6, 296–7, 330, 340–1, 350–1, 353–5, 358–9, 361–4, 366–7; administration of 236–40; adoption of 352*b;* appeals and revision of 239–40; assessment of 239; commodities exempted from 297–9; commodities taxable at 1% Rate 299; commodities taxable at 5% Rate 299–302; commodities taxable at 20% or more 302–4; electricity duty 47; entertainment tax 47–8; evolution of 351–5; fiscal significance 225–32; incentives for industrial development 234–5; of inter-state trade 235–6; motor vehicles tax and passengers and goods tax 46–7; non-taxation of 21; payment of 238; replacing sales tax by 21; state excise duty 46; structure of 232–4

structural tax reforms 83

subsidies 3, 10–11, 14–15; to food and fertilizers 15

surcharges 21, 69–70, 73–4, 85, 113–14, 176, 191–2, 235, 294, 332–6, 346, 375

tariff system, simplification of 61

tax: assignment of 2*b*, 136; on cinema 294; deferral 234, 354, 377; evasion of 82, 90–1, 97, 101, 167, 191, 264, 280–1, 342, 362, 369; exemptions on 72, 234, 347, 377; as loan 235; rate structure 84–7; waiver of 234

tax deduction at source (TDS) 103, 374

tax effort 152, 156, 170, 174, 186–7, 227, 232; in MVT and P&GT 241–8

tax incentives 18, 20, 70, 72, 77, 80–1, 91, 103, 256, 332; under VAT 305–9*t;* for Industrial Development 77–9; reforms on 79–81

tax information exchange system (TINXSYS) 357, 369

Tax Reforms Committee (TRC) 18, 55, 83, 85, 95, 109, 126, 333, 336, 345, 349

tax revenue 38–9, 41, 44–8, 149–51, 162, 169–70, 191–2, 224–5, 266, 290, 338–43; AIT share in 162; growth rate of 170; from states 170; of Central Government 40t; in states 42–3*t*

tax system 82–3; administration of 102–3, *see also* 'Sevottam' through Aayakar Seva Kendras; benefits of 72, 378; collection system of 103; and deductions 78–9, 87; powers between union and states 24–7;

Taxation Enquiry Commission of 1953–4 (Matthai Commission) 345

tax–GDP ratio 20, 29–31, 32*t,* 33, 329–30, 347; in select countries 30–1*t*
taxes levied by local bodies: Property Tax 344; Octroi 344;
Taxpayer Identification Number (TIN) 109, 238–9, 369; formats of 239*b*
textile sector 111, 122; CenVAT abolished for 112
Torrens system of Registration 184–5
total tax revenue 31–6, 38–9, 49–50, 95, 106, 330, 335, 337
trade name, *see* brand name

Union budget 76, 111–12; of 2006–7 349; of 2010–11 76, 88, 102–3, 112; of 2011–12 88, 333; of 2012–13 84–5, 88, 92, 112, 116–18, 336–7
union excise duties (UEDs) 20–1, 28, 31, 38–9, 105–6, 111–12, 135, 335–6, 348–9, 366–7, *see also* CenVAT (Central Value Added Tax); administration of 118–21; fiscal significance of 106–8; items attracting 136–41; rate structure 108–12; reforms for 123–5; and Service Tax revenue from 107–8*t;* structure of 115–18; types of 112–14; weaknesses in system of 121–3
union government taxes 330, 348; on commodities and services 37–8; corporation tax 36–7; customs duty 38; excise duty 38–9; on income and property 36, 332; on international trade 330–2; personal income tax 37; service tax 39
Union Territories: list of 24; levy of motor vehicle tax 248; implementation of uniform floor rates 353

Valuation of goods 120
value added tax (VAT) 5, 54, 134–6, 225, 232, 234–6, 238–9; replacing sales tax by 21, dual VAT 345, 348

wealth tax 36, 66, 68, 93–8, 103–4, 332, 334, 347, 377; assets exemptions of 96; on companies 94n15; cost of collecting 96; evolution of 94; exemptions under 95–6; rate structure 95; reforms for 97; revenue significance of 95; weaknesses in system of 96
Wealth Tax Act, 1957 94–5, 377
Wilson, James 81
World Trade Organization (WTO) 62; Agreement on Customs Valuation 62

zamindari, abolition of 157
zero-rate CST 109, 232, 370
zero-tax companies 67, 74, 333

About the Authors

Mahesh C. Purohit is Director, Foundation for Public Economics and Policy Research, New Delhi.

Prior to this, he has worked as Professor at the National Institute of Public Finance and Policy, New Delhi; a faculty member at the Gokhale Institute of Politics and Economics, Pune; a Senior Research Fellow at the Centre for Advanced Studies in Industrial Economics and Public Finance, University of Bombay, and as a Post-Doctoral Fellow at the Department of Economics, University of California, USA. He has also been a visiting Professor at the Institute of Fiscal and Monetary Policy, Tokyo, and at the International Tax Programme, Harvard Law School, Cambridge, Massachusetts.

He has been Member-Secretary of the Empowered Committee of State Finance Ministers to Monitor Sales Tax Reforms and Secretary to the Committee of Chief Ministers on VAT and Incentives to Backward Areas.

He has also worked as International VAT Expert at the National Board of Revenue, Ministry of Finance, Government of Bangladesh, and as Chief Technical Advisor of the Department of Technical Cooperation and Development, UNDP, Mogadishu, Somalia.

Some of his recent publications include *Non-tax Sources in India: Issues in Pricing and Delivery of Services* (co-authored) (2010) and *Value Added Tax: Experiences of India and Other Countries* (2007).

Vishnu Kanta Purohit is currently a Professor at the Foundation for Public Economics and Policy Research (FPEPR), New Delhi. Prior to joining this, she was an Associate Professor in Economics at the Indraprastha College for Women, University of Delhi.

Earlier, she has worked as Assistant Professor at the Department of Economics, Ahmedu Bello University, Zaria (Nigeria); Senior Research Fellow at the Department of Economics, University of California, Berkeley

(USA); and at the Gokhale Institute of Politics and Economics, Pune. She has also been a visiting Professor at the *Maison des Sciences De L'Homme,* Paris (France).

Some of her publications include *Commodity Taxes in India: Direction for Reform; Profitability in Indian Industries* and *Firm Size and Profitability.* Her latest book, *Non-tax Sources in India: Issues in Pricing and Delivery of Services* (co-authored) was published in 2010.